Theatre to Cinema

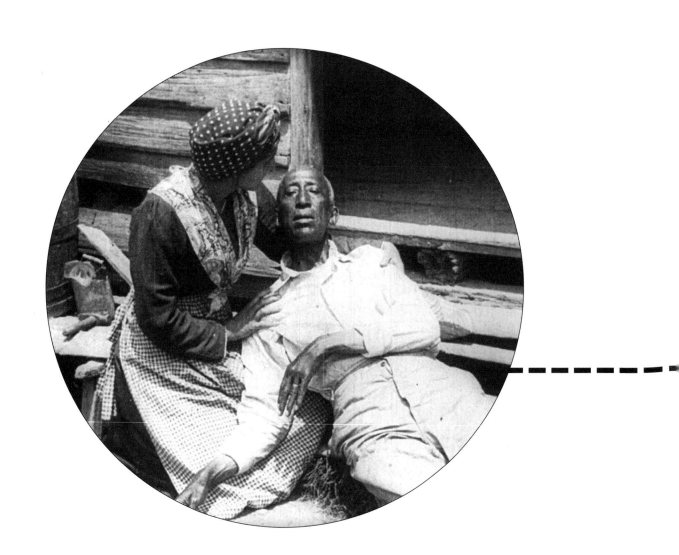

BEN BREWSTER
LEA JACOBS

Theatre *to* Cinema

Stage Pictorialism and the
Early Feature Film

OXFORD UNIVERSITY PRESS
1997

Oxford University Press, Great Clarendon Street, Oxford OX2 6DP

Oxford New York
Athens Auckland Bangkok Bogota Bombay Buenos Aires
Calcutta Cape Town Dar es Salaam Delhi Florence Hong Kong Istanbul
Karachi Kuala Lumpur Madras Madrid Melbourne Mexico City
Nairobi Paris Singapore Taipei Tokyo Toronto Warsaw

and associated companies in
Berlin Ibadan

Oxford is a trade mark of Oxford University Press

Published in the United States
by Oxford University Press Inc., New York

© Oxford University Press, 1997

British Library Cataloguing in Publication Data
Data available

Library of Congress Cataloging in Publication Data
Data applied for

ISBN 0–19–818267–8
ISBN 0–19–815950–1 (pbk)

1 3 5 7 9 10 8 6 4 2

Printed in Great Britain
on acid-free paper by
Bookcraft Ltd.,
Midsomer Norton, Somerset

Molly's Book

Preface

IN 1993, the major focus of Le Giornate del Cinema Muto, the silent film festival in Pordenone, was the year 1913. Seeing a programme of films made in a particular year rather than a selection from a national cinema or the work of a particular director confirmed a more general intuition that we had from viewing many films of the 1910s over the years. There was a qualitative change in filmmaking in Europe and America in that year. One Pordenone regular commented that she found films before 1913 good in context—an impressive achievement for 1910, an advanced film for 1911—but that starting in 1913 she found films that were just good.

We would account for the changes which occur in this period as a function of a complex set of conditions, involving both the mode of production of films during the transition to features, and the available models for the structure and style of the new, longer film. First, the transition from a variety programme of one-reel films to features which could be individually advertised encouraged the production of culturally ambitious and potentially prestigious projects, and led to a corresponding increase in film budgets. This occurred first in Europe, where exhibitors could negotiate for films individually, allowing them to programme a mix of films of varying lengths, and only later in the USA, where many exhibitors were locked into accepting the weekly or twice-weekly programme of one- and two-reel films distributed as a block by a national distributor.

Filmmakers appealed to a variety of cultural forms in constructing the early feature, including the novel, the magazine serial, and the stage. The theatre, in particular, had already influenced even ambitious one-reel films like those of Film d'Art, acted by members of the Comédie Française, or the many theatrical adaptations of the Vitagraph Company. But as films became longer, the relatively more complex plots found in plays and novels made them even more important as models. According to still unpublished research by Michael Quinn, theatrical adaptations accounted for between 50 and 60 per cent of Paramount's output of features between 1913 and 1915, and the company estimated that later in the decade they still accounted for about 25 per cent of the total yearly output.

Of course in this period the theatre itself encompassed a wide variety of narrative modes, acting styles, and uses of *mise-en-scène*. None the less, critics as diverse as A. Nicholas Vardac, Peter Brooks, Martin Meisel, and Michael Booth have suggested that the popular nineteenth-century stage was intimately concerned with the metaphor of the stage picture, to the point of conceiving of plays as a series of pictorially representable moments. Meisel has suggested that this way of thinking extended well beyond the theatre, and had important ramifications both for painting and for the tradition of novel illustration. From the other direction, Michael Fried has used a notion of the theatrical to illuminate the history of painting in the same years. We focus upon the theatrical tradition discussed by Vardac, Meisel, and others to explain the development of film style in the 1910s not just because stage influence can be traced in certain films which are adaptations of stage plays, but also, as we will try to indicate, because the theatre served as one of the nodal points for conceptualizing 'the pictorial' and hence provided a more general guide for cinematic *mise-en-scène*.

In exploring the notion of pictorial effect we hope to redress what we take to be an over-emphasis on the development of editing technique in the history of early film, an emphasis that has worked to focus attention on filmmaking in the USA at the expense of Europe and, in the American context, on particular directors and studios, e.g. Griffith at Biograph, at the expense of others, e.g. Vitagraph, where developments in staging and acting played a more important part.

We would also like to distinguish this study from work which aims to use early film as a means of documenting theatre history. Stephen Johnson neatly sums up the questions that historians looking at early films as evidence of theatrical performances must pose: 'To what extent was the original theatrical production altered for film recording? To what extent did the limitations of the camera alter or distort the theatrical performance?' We do not seek to clear away these 'alterations and distortions' in order to recover a theatrical performance in a more or less pristine state. The technical requirements of the cinema necessarily transformed staging and acting techniques. As film historians, we are interested in tracing out what the process of transformation entailed and how it gave rise to something new.

Finally, it should be noted that while we do aim to make a contribution to the history of filmmaking in the 1910s, and while we do address issues of national context in terms of our comparisons of European and American filmmaking traditions, we are not here concerned with the immediate and proximate conditions of theatrical performance in the sense that, for example, Jim Davis is in his studies of the Britannia, Hoxton, or David Mayer is when he writes on Irving's productions of *The Bells*. We are interested in a more abstract conception of the theatrical and the pictorial, and how it impinged on filmmaking. Moreover, one of our working assumptions is that this taste for the pictorial largely crossed most social boundaries (with some protestations from the critics), and thus we do not deal directly with the differences between working-class and upper-class theatre, nor with how class, gender, and ethnic divisions affected the audience for the early feature. There are larger implications for these important questions in our work, particularly where the emergence of modern conceptions of 'high' and 'low' culture are concerned, but we hope to demonstrate that a close attention to questions of technique will reveal much that an immediate concentration on social context would overlook.

This book has been many years in the making, so our list of acknowledgements is correspondingly long.

First, for providing research funding, time (including leave), and facilities, we have to thank the University of Kent at Canterbury, England, and the University of Wisconsin, Madison, Wisconsin. We were also beneficiaries of grants from the Rockefeller Foundation and the Institute for Research in the Humanities at the University of Wisconsin-Madison.

The films which form our most important source material were nearly all preserved by archives which are members of the Fédération Internationale des Archives de Film, to whose activity all film scholars are incalculably indebted. Although the films we discuss have been preserved by a much broader range of these archives, here we would like especially to thank those we visited in the course of our research: the Cinémathèque Française, Paris and Fort de Saint-Cyr, and especially Dominique Païni and Claudine Kaufmann; the Cinémathèque Royale, Brussels, and especially Gabrielle Claes and Sabine Lenk; George Eastman House, Rochester, New York, and especially Paolo Cherchi Usai and Jan-Christopher Horak; the Motion Pictures, Broadcasting and Recorded Sound Division of the Library of Congress, Washington, and especially David Francis, Patrick Loughney, and Paul Spehr; the National Film and Television Archive, London, and especially Elaine Bowers; the Nederlands Filmmuseum, Amsterdam and Overveen, and especially Frank van der Maden; and the Wisconsin Center for Film and Theater Research, Madison, Wisconsin, and especially Maxine Fleckner-Ducey.

As well as archival viewings we have also seen some of the same films, and many others, in film theatres and at film festivals. Details of *mise-en-scène* and gesture are often only visible on a large screen, and books like ours would be immeasurably the poorer if programmers abandoned screening the often little known films from the period we are concerned with. Special thanks are owed to the annual Giornate del Cinema Muto at Pordenone, Italy, and Livio Jacob and Lorenzo Codelli; to the Mary Pickford Theatre at the Library of Congress, Washington; to the Museum of Modern Art, New York; and to the National Film Theatre, London, and especially the late John Gillet.

For paper materials, we are particularly indebted to the library of the University of Kent at Canterbury, and especially R. Stephen Holland (who helped us not only as curator of special collections but also as an expert in our field); the Memorial Library of the University of Wisconsin, Madison, especially the Inter-Library Loan department, the Kohler Art Library (special thanks to William Bunce), the Microform Library (special thanks to Ed Duesterhof), the Mills Music Library (special thanks to Gerry Laudati), and the department of Special Collections; the library and archives of the State Historical Society of Wisconsin; the library of the Information

Division of the British Film Institute, London (special thanks to Gillian Hartnoll); the Theatre Museum, London; the British Library, London and Colindale; the Billy Rose Theatre Collection, Performing Arts Center, New York Public Library; the Museum of the City of New York (special thanks to Marty Jacobs); Special Collections of the library of the University of California, Los Angeles; and the library of the Academy of Motion Picture Arts and Sciences, Los Angeles.

For the illustrations to this book we have to thank the photographic department of the library of the University of Kent at Canterbury, and especially Jim Styles; the University of Wisconsin Extension Photographic Media Center, and especially Jerry Erdmann; the Wisconsin Cartographic Laboratory and Onno Brouwer; and the University of Wisconsin-Madison Department of Information Technology Media Laboratory. Permission to reproduce Figure 2.5 was kindly granted by the Museum of the City of New York. Figure 3.1, from the Iveagh bequest, is reproduced by kind permission of English Heritage. Figure 4.25 is reproduced by permission of the Victoria & Albert Museum, and Figures 4.71, and 4.72 by permission of The Theatre Museum, Covent Garden and the Victoria & Albert Museum. Figure 4.77 is from the Billy Rose Theatre Collection, and is reproduced with the permission of the New York Public Library for the Performing Arts, Astor, Lenox, and Tilden Foundations.

Finally we have been given encouragement and assistance by many individuals in addition to those already named: our colleagues at the University of Kent, especially Elizabeth Cowie, Michael Grant, Louis James, Alan Millen, Stephen Neale, and the late Jan Shepherd; faculty and students at the University of Wisconsin-Madison, especially Tino Balio, Chris Becker, Donald Crafton, Julie D'Acci, Mary Ann Fitzpatrick, Scott Higgins, Michele Hilmes, J. J. Murphy, Michael Quinn, Sally Ross, and Kristin Thompson; and the members of Domitor, the International Association for the Study of Early Cinema, especially Richard Abel, Stephen Bottomore, Carlos Bustamante, Roland Cosandey, André Gaudreault, Natasha Nusinova, and Yuri Tsivian. Thanks are also due to Eileen Bowser, Noël Burch, Susan Dalton, the late Donie Durieu, Nataša Ďurovičová, Murray Glass, Christine Gledhill, Stephen Johnson, Nicola Mazzanti, Charles Musser, Dana Polan, Barry Salt, David Shepard, Ben Singer, and Marc Vernet. We are grateful to Tom Gunning for generously taking time to work his way through an initial draft, to David Mayer for his comments on this draft and for all his help with the stage versions of *The Whip*, and especially to David Bordwell, an enthusiastic reader and 'silent' partner in our seminar on the early feature.

Contents

Technical Note

THERE are many examples in this book of detailed description of films, and the reader may need some guide to the conventions we have used in these descriptions. This will be especially necessary if the reader is more familiar with writing on theatre than on film, but some of our conventions may also be unfamiliar to film historians. This is because much film description is adapted to films made later than most of the ones we consider, and in a tradition that accepts the shot as the natural unit for the analysis of films. As we explain in the first part of this book, we are sceptical of the validity of this assumption for films of the period we are primarily concerned with, the 1910s. This is not to say that we do not divide our descriptions up into shots (defined as units of film which purport to have been filmed continuously from one camera position or a continuously moving camera position and are divided from their predecessors and successors by a cut, dissolve, or fade), but that we do not take the shot as a syntagmatic unit to which can be attributed a set of paradigmatic values—shot scale, length, presence or absence of camera movement, etc. Hence, with few exceptions, we have not isolated such paradigmatic information, but, if it is mentioned at all, embedded it in the body of the description. For example, to call a shot a 'long shot', a term whose reference is the framing of a human body, it has to be clear which character visible it is a shot of; but many of the long scenes in films of the 1910s have several significant characters in them at different depths and hence difference scales, and the characters often move during the shot from one such scale to another.

It is in an attempt to capture a different register of the visual properties of a film than the shot, what we will be calling their 'pictorial' register, that we have devoted so much space and effort to descriptions. Some of our descriptions concern sections of the action which are only part of the shot. Others describe the action over a number of shots without specifying how many of them there are and their precise sequence. When we do lay out a sequence of shots in detail, we number them in sequence (including any titles in that sequence). When we have been able to prepare a complete shot breakdown of the film, the first number in our description will be the number of the shot in the film, or more rarely we will start with the number of the shot in some smaller subunit, which we will define. Otherwise we will simply start the described sequence with shot 1. The one important exception is the 1914 film version of *Uncle Tom's Cabin*, where we have used the numbering in the script deposited at the Copyright Office, for reasons explained in Chapter 4 (which means that, in this case, titles are numbered in a separate sequence from shots).

In describing a shot, we divide the space laterally into left, centre, and right, axially into front or foreground, midground, and rear or background. We have followed film conventions and used left and right from the point of view of the spectator, not that of the actor facing the audience; i.e. our convention is the opposite of that of most theatrical play scripts. We have maintained this convention in our descriptions of stage settings, but have left citations from play scripts as we found them. On the rare occasions when we have needed to use stage conventions, we say 'stage left' and 'stage right', to make the distinction clear. We have avoided other lateral terms like 'prompt' and 'opposite to prompt' and '*côté cour*' and '*côté jardin*'. Note, however, that 'Borelli's left hand' means her anatomical left hand, so, if she is facing camera, it is to the right of her from the viewpoint of the audience. Finally, if a series of items of furniture or characters are listed without directional indications, the earlier named will be to the left of the later.

As already mentioned, shot-scale terms are relative to a human body, and are always linked explicitly or implicitly to the relation to the frame of a character. Obviously, such terms are points on a continuous grade, and are more important in relation to the scale of other characters or the same character in other shots than they are absolutely. Our terms are as follows: 'very long shot' means that the character is dwarfed in his or her surroundings; 'long shot' that the character is framed from head to toe; 'medium long shot' that he or she is framed from the knees up; 'medium shot', from the waist up; 'medium close-up', the head and shoulders alone; 'close-up', the face alone; 'big close-up', less than the whole face. Inserts are close shots of other parts of the body (hands or feet) or objects such that the relevant object occupies most of the frame.

Camera movements are described as 'pans', where the camera rotates on a vertical axis (i.e. from left to right, or vice versa), 'tilts', where the axis of rotation is horizontal (up or down), and 'tracks', where the camera moves bodily. 'Reframe' is used to mean any small movement (usually a pan) that maintains a significant character or moving object in a favourable position in the frame.

In the plans of the set that accompany some of our descriptions, the camera position is at the bottom of the plan, unless otherwise indicated by arrows.

INTRODUCTORY

I claim that every object, taken from a given viewpoint and shown on the screen to spectators, is a dead object, even though it has moved before the camera. The proper movement of an object before the camera is yet no movement on the screen, it is no more than raw material for the future building-up, by editing, of the movement that is conveyed by the assemblage of the various strips of film. Only if the object be placed together among a number of separate objects, only if it be presented as part of a synthesis of different separate visual images, is it endowed with filmic life.... Editing is the basic creative force, by power of which the soulless photographs (the separate shots) are engineered into living, cinematographic form.[1]

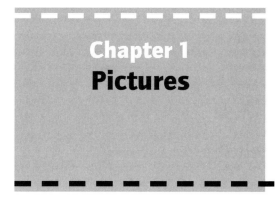

Chapter 1
Pictures

FIRST published in 1928 in the introduction to the German edition of his book on film technique, this proclamation of the Soviet film director Vsevolod Pudovkin expresses an outlook on the nature of the cinema that still underlies most critical, historical, and theoretical considerations of cinema and films, despite the relative loss of prestige of the particular school of filmmaking, Soviet montage cinema, that Pudovkin wished to promote. Most discussion of films that goes beyond mere plot summary to describe and analyse the ways a film produces its effects starts from shots in their relations to other shots. Stylistic history of cinema discusses the origins of the close-up, of alternating editing, of shot-reverse-shot, of the point-of-view shot; stylistic analysis discusses average shot length, variation in shot scale, rhythms in the alternation of shots, or more broadly, schools of filmmaking based on differences in editing—American 'invisible editing' versus Soviet montage cinema, for example; theory discusses the Kuleshov effect, the possible syntagmatic organization of shots in films, and 'suture', the relation between the film spectator and the kind of coherence he or she can find in a series of shots.

One reason for the success of this programme is convenience. Shots are (or appear to be) relatively unequivocal objects of investigation, found in almost all kinds of films (even animated ones), usually in a sufficiently large number in any one film to allow for all sorts of variation and hence subtle and detailed analysis. When they become more equivocal, as in montage sequences in American films, where multiple superimposition often makes it hard to say where one shot begins and another ends, those sequences can usually be isolated from the rest of a film so as to leave shot-by-shot analysis unimpeded, and those films that lack shots (such as some abstract films) or where the number of shots are so few as to tend to make such analysis banal, are rare enough or sufficiently off the beaten track of the film scholar to be ignored. On the other hand, the content of individual shots—staging, lighting, composition, blocking, acting—is much harder to analyse (except unsystematically, by an immediate correlation with plot, as when chiaroscuro lighting is described as 'sinister'). Hence a concentration on editing and the shot in Pudovkin's sense.

So self-evident has this centrality of the shot become, it is worth emphasizing that, before the

3

Russian montage theorists, it had no such importance— indeed, it is arguable that the 'shot' in Pudovkin's sense did not exist. In America, film scriptwriters div-ided their scripts into 'scenes', and commentators discussed films in terms of scenes. 'Shot' was used only when what was at issue was how the length of footage was made—thus some scenes are 'glass shots' (part of what seems to be a landscape or large building is in fact a picture on a glass sheet in front of the camera lens). 'Editing' was originally taken over from publishing terminology to mean the tightening up and smoothing process which intervened between the rough assembly of the film and the finally released version; the assembly of the negative was called 'cutting' and was performed by the cameraman with the assistance of lowly 'cutters'. 'Photoplays'—the term was preferred by the film trade to the vulgar 'movies'—were thought of as a sequence of 'scenes' on the model of the stage play. Such 'scenes' might materially correspond to 'shots', i.e. they might be lengths of film footage demarcated by cuts or dissolves (which is why it is possible for film history to conceive the early history of cinema in terms of shots and editing in the later sense), but this corres-pondence is deceptive. In a script, a scene was numbered and described, and then, usually inset, would follow one or more separately listed and numbered 'inserts'. Some of these inserts would be titles (usually by the mid-1910s dialogue titles), some close-ups, memory flashes, vision shots, cutaways. Conventionally (though this would not always be notated), the inserts were each followed by a 'return to scene'. Thus, what for Pudovkin might be a relatively large number of 'shots' could constitute a single 'scene'.

At the beginning of the 1910s, scenes were in general long and inserts few, so scenes and shots largely coincide, but as the number of cuts in a scene began to grow, the response was not a shift of emphasis to the lengths of footage between cuts, but to the scene considered as a multiple entity. Thus, in their manual *How to Write Photoplays*, John Emerson and Anita Loos advise screenwriters they need not specify the cuts: 'Of course, a director will change his camera many times during a scene to get long shots, close-ups, etc.; but these changes of camera need not bother the scenario writer to any extent, as any good director understands this technique and may be trusted to take the scenes in a manner that will get over the meaning of the author. If there is some special point which the author wishes emphasized by a close-up, there is no harm in noting it in the script.'[2] By the end of the 1920s, this sense of a scene was embodied in the 'master shot' method of filmmaking (consolidated by the fact that in the early sound cinema there were usually far fewer cuts in the sound than in the image track— i.e. a whole scene often consisted of a single continuous recording of dialogue, with the different pieces of the image track made up of material shot simultaneously with another camera or 'wild' shots containing no synchronized dialogue).[3]

Despite modern commentators' emphasis on the shot, the scene in this sense remained crucial to classical narrative filmmaking. Pudovkin was well aware of this way of conceiving film construction; his account is not a universal theory of cinema so much as a polemic against this method of constructing the scene: 'Terms such as "interpolation" and "cut-in" are absurd expressions, the remnants of an old misunderstanding of the technical methods of the film. The details organically belonging to scenes . . . must not be interpolated into the scene, but the latter must be built out of them.'[4]

The success of the shot- and editing-based understanding of film is not simply a matter of descriptive convenience. Pudovkin and his colleagues were eager to locate a peculiar aesthetics of the film medium, a field of devices which were specific to that medium, not borrowed from any of the other arts. Editing seemed to provide such a field. Moreover, an emphasis on the importance and centrality of film editing, that is, on the combination of lengths of moving photographs of objects, people, events, and actions, rather than on those moving photographs themselves, seemed to conjure the suspicion that the moving-picture camera was no more than a sophisticated copying device, that any art there was in the cinema resided in the objects, people, events, and actions that had once been in front of the passive camera. As Hans Richter put it:

On the roof of a tenement block one day, sets were put up and—so Henny Porten says, discussing the early days of the cinema—Messter began to film her in a (much abridged) *Das Käthchen von Heilbronn*. Smoke from the chimney pots cast a magical veil over the sets. The sun shone, Henny Porten entered stage left on cue (as was customary in the theatre), acted her scene, Messter cranked, and she exited. The whole business lasted some three to five minutes, then they were finished—as was the film. The film was the actress.[5]

The contaminating art in Richter's example is the theatre, and early film aestheticians' predominant demarcation dispute was with the aesthetics of theatre, or with 'theatricality' in films and film-making traditions. This brings us to the relations between theatre and cinema which are the central concern of this book.

According to Pudovkin and Richter, although the earliest films were actualities, as soon as the cinema turned to fiction, it took the theatre as its model, and the true history of the medium since then has been one of its emancipation from the tutelage of the theatre, the discovery of an autonomous cinematic aesthetic:

The first films consisted of primitive attempts to fix upon celluloid, as a novelty, the movements of a train, a landscape seen from a railway-carriage window, and so forth. Thus, in the beginning, the film was, from its nature, only 'living photography'. The first attempts to relate cinematography to the world of art were naturally bound up with the Theatre. Similarly only as a novelty, like the shots of the railway-engine and the moving sea, primitive scenes of comic or dramatic character, played by actors, began to be recorded. . . . The first experiments in recording serious and significant material appeared. The relationship with the Theatre could not, however, yet be dissolved, and it is easy to understand how, once again, the first steps of the film producer consisted in attempts to carry plays over on to celluloid. . . . The film remained, as before, but living photography. Art did not enter into the work of him who made it. He only photographed the 'art of the actor'. Of a peculiar method for the film actor, of peculiar and special properties of the film or of technique in shooting the picture for the director, there could as yet be no suspicion.[6]

This view dominated film history for many years. Georges Sadoul says of Méliès, 'theatrical imperatives continue to weigh on the productions of Star Film',[7] and Jean Mitry of Griffith, 'with his short films, America discovered a new art, quite different from the theatre, the decalcomania of which was all that could initially be achieved'.[8] The same view is expressed today by a writer who is not a film historian: 'Many early movies were stagy. Vaudeville turns and other theatrical material were presented as if seen inside a stage frame, not a picture frame. . . . But the more the medium advanced, the closer it came to its dramatic pictorial ancestors and the further from the stage.'[9]

Professional film historians today, however, have largely ceased to speak of a theatrically dominated early cinema. This is probably one of the many transformations in our understanding of early film history that was brought about by the Conference of the International Federation of Film Archives (FIAF) held in Brighton in 1978. At that conference, as many as possible of the films held by member archives thought to have been made before 1905 were viewed together, by archivists and invited film historians. It immediately became clear that early filmmakers borrowed from whole series of sources unlinked to the theatre (short stories, novels, strip cartoons, political caricatures, lantern slides, wax museums, pyrotechnic displays), and that the kinds of theatre they drew on when those sources were theatrical were so diverse (from vaudeville dog act to Shakespeare via conjuring trick, féerie, and Grand Guignol) as to make 'theatrical' a vitiatingly vague term.[10] Attention among scholars has shifted to a reconsideration of the notion of the 'primitivity' of the cinema before about 1907, no longer considered negatively as an absence, a vacuum filled by inappropriate theatrical devices, but as a differentia specifica of early films which demands positive characterization.[11] As for the cinema after 1907, the predominance of accounts of classical cinema centring on devices of narration has directed attention to the importance of literary narratives, particularly short stories, as influences on its formation.[12] Theatre is probably less considered, whether as a positive or as a negative influence on the cinema, by film historians today than at any other time.[13]

The strongest arguments for a continuity between theatre and early cinema have in fact been made not by film historians but by theatre historians. Historians of nineteenth-century popular theatre, who are particularly interested in the mise-en-scène rather than the texts of the plays of the period, have the problem that staging and acting have to be reconstructed from a variety of not very trustworthy sources: reviews, memoirs, descriptions of performances, playbills, specially posed publicity photographs or woodcut illustrations, even ceramics. Early cinema seems to offer a direct view of acting and staging at the beginning of the twentieth century. And indeed, by the turn of the century some significant theatrical stars had appeared before the camera to perform fragments of their stage successes, and many early fiction films drew their plots from well-known plays. However, writers such as David Mayer and Stephen Johnson, while stressing the significance of these moving photographic records of theatrical practice, are also well aware of the differences between moving photographs and theatrical performance, the most obvious of which are the lack of spoken dialogue[14] and the brevity of films before about 1910 (we will discuss other important differences below).[15]

A much broader claim about the relationship was made nearly fifty years ago by A. Nicholas Vardac in *Stage to Screen: Theatrical Origins of Early Film. From Garrick to Griffith.*[16] Basing his argument on promptbooks, set designs, theatrical cuts, photographs, and clippings files, mostly in the Harvard Theatre Collection, Vardac argued that a large part of nineteenth-century theatre was cinema *manqué*. Indeed, as his subtitle indicates, he traces this proto-cinematic tendency in the theatre back to the eighteenth century. He does this via the notion of a very general cultural project, a kind of *Kunstwollen*, which the theatre participated in, and whose origins he finds in the Enlightenment. This project demanded 'realism' in the arts, but this realism can be understood in two ways, which Vardac does not always clearly distinguish. On the one hand, there is the demand that works of art should deal with the important social and psychological issues of the day; on the other, a demand that, whatever is being represented, the representation be 'lifelike'. This second demand is a demand for illusion, and by no means necessarily implies the first. Having posited the first demand, Vardac generally ignores it, on the grounds that, as he says, for the practical stage designer, it makes no difference whether you need to represent a drawing-room or fairyland; realism and escapism both require the same illusory techniques.[17]

Vardac examines the staging practices (mostly in England and America) in a number of kinds of theatre—the popular sensational drama usually known as 'melodrama', his principal example being Dion Boucicault,[18] the 'archaeological' costume drama of Charles Kean, the pantomime or *féerie*, and the more respectable spectacle drama of Irving and Belasco. All of these tendencies were, he argues,

essentially cinematic and were eventually more appropriately realized in the cinema. Melodrama was particularly constrained by the stage, because its audience's craving for sensation demanded rapid changes of place, time, and situation, but the illusory representation of such sensational incidents as volcanic eruptions, burning buildings, railway accidents, shipwrecks, and so on, demanded very elaborate mechanical sets, which were hard to change rapidly even in big, well-staffed metropolitan theatres; this problem was exacerbated by the fact that, as a popular form, melodrama had to be able to tour, and the smaller, less well-equipped and staffed provincial theatres in the USA could not accommodate elaborate three-dimensional sets, but tended to retain the older system of backdrops, borders, and wings. As a result, the contrast between the desire for complete illusion and what was actually seen on the stage became acute. Film solved these problems. Real eruptions, fires, train wrecks, and so on could be photographed with the moving picture camera, and editing meant that such sensational scenes could be changed as often as desired. The same film could also be projected in a moving picture theatre anywhere in the country and not have to compromise to accommodate local deficiencies. Hence popular melodrama rapidly disappeared from the live stage once moving pictures took over its subject-matter and adapted its techniques. The other genres lasted longer, but Vardac cites reviews complaining about the difficulty of sustaining the illusion even in the most lavish stage spectacles, notes the disappearance of the pantomime from the American stage in the twentieth century, and claims that Belasco was fighting a rearguard action in attempting to maintain his staging methods until the 1920s. However, and here Vardac returns to the first definition of realism, the cinema notably failed in its attempts to assimilate the naturalistic drama of Ibsen. The kinds of stage play that seem to Vardac the most direct forebears of contemporary drama were those that lay outside the proto-cinematic project.

Some of the difficulties with this account have already been referred to—these theatrical genres were certainly not the only sources that the cinema drew on, especially in its first twenty years. But even when dealing with the period after this, when theatrical models became more obviously pertinent to the much longer films being made, Vardac's account is unhelpful to the film historian. Partly this is because, beyond the realism supposedly guaranteed by moving photography, and the flexibility granted by editing, cinematic techniques and their development are not specified, and nineteenth-century staging is described metaphorically using cinematic terms like 'alternation' or 'cutting'. Thus it is impossible to analyse how early filmmakers actually responded to the theatre, either in assimilating it or in rejecting it—it is as if an entirely naïve filmmaker would automatically reproduce and perfect the work of an Irving as a result of the nature of his medium.

However, there are more serious objections to Vardac's thesis. In particular, he finds it unproblematic to claim that the illusionism desired by the nineteenth-century theatre audience was better satisfied by moving photographs of sensational or spectacular scenes than it was by stagings of such scenes. In the era of *Cats* and *Les Misérables*, it seems hard to believe the claim that competition with the cinema has driven spectacle from the theatre. Despite the care with which he describes nineteenth-century popular theatre (his thoroughness in this respect is surely the reason the book has gone unchallenged for so long), he shares a common mid-twentieth-century prejudice against it, and against all popular theatre, and so remains blind to the fact that spectacle did not disappear from the stage when the plays of Eugene O'Neill began to be performed on it. On the other hand, he feels no need to argue his claim that cinema is naturally spectacular, but this is by no means self-evident. David Mayer notes how unimpressive is the scene of the chariot race in the 1907 Kalem version of *Ben Hur*, despite the fact that real chariots, horses, and riders have been photographed engaging in a real race, and argues that such films were fairly unsuccessful attempts to emulate stage spectacle rather than the other way about.[19] Some of Vardac's own quotations suggest the same. When Ashton Stevens reviewed the San Francisco presentation of Nance O'Neill's production of Thomas Bailey Aldrich's *Judith of Bethulia* in 1906, he condemned it as no better than moving pictures: 'The whole thing might be read at a ladies' club to the accompaniment of moving pictures. It is vivid only in a moving picture way; even the tent scene.'[20] When Belasco signed a moving-picture contract with Lasky in 1914, interviews he gave suggest he felt he could give the younger art a helping hand rather than that he was deserting a sinking ship.[21]

We are also dubious about Vardac's citations of contemporary reviews to demonstrate audiences' dissatisfaction with stage illusion. He is particularly fond of taking quotations from reviews of the first production of a play which praise its realism, and then ones from reviews of revivals that denounce the failure, often of the same sets and stage machines.[22] But this is simply the nature of illusionistic effects in any medium—they wear out quite rapidly. The cinema has not solved this problem; special effects a decade old no longer convince us today.

More fundamentally, the aspiration to an integral reproduction of reality, an aim of art which certainly existed in the nineteenth century, and one which the development of moving photographic pictures was expected to advance, if not realize, was itself contradictory. First, the technology could not actually reproduce the effect of being in the presence of the reality represented. In the period with which we (and Vardac) are concerned, film lacked three dimensions, and usually natural colour and dialogue, all of which the theatre could provide. However, the sense of being present at the simplest of events is highly synaesthetic—all the senses participate in the global impact of the event, constituting what Michel Chion calls a perceptual 'lump' (*boule*). No cinema can actually replicate this 'lump'; instead it renders it with a whole battery of devices which are not simulations, devices of editing, scale, contrast. The most visceral moments of presence in the cinema are what Chion calls 'renderings', not replications, of reality.[23] Noël Burch argues, however, that the rendering process is not so much a matter of supplying the deficiencies of the recording apparatuses, as it were, adding to them, as of controlling, often literally reducing, their powers. He notes the example of Grimoin-Sanson's Cinéorama, devised for the Paris Exposition Universelle of 1900, in which film recorded by ten cameras facing out in all directions from the gondola of an ascending balloon was projected on to a circular screen by ten projectors mounted under a mock-up of the gondola. The audience in the gondola then saw a 360-degree moving panorama of what it looked like to rise up in a balloon.[24] However 'realistic' the effect achieved, the banality of this is clear; it would have been just as easy, and presumably more 'realistic', to have flown the audiences who witnessed the show in a real balloon. To fulfil the aim of producing a fully 'lifelike' rendering of reality, it was necessary to make that reality intelligible, by framing it, composing it, orchestrating it in time. For Burch, the history of the 'primitive' cinema is a history of the discovery and installation of means of cinematic representation to control the dispersal, the haemorrhage of significance characteristic of simple replication.[25]

Although realistic detail was an important constituent of what a nineteenth-century audience experienced as an overwhelming spectacle, photographic realism alone does not constitute spectacle. Photographs can be intimate as easily as they can be spectacular, and the same is true of film. Sheer scale is an important factor, but for much of the first twenty years of cinema, screens were relatively small as compared with the proscenium openings of metropolitan theatres. It was possible, as it was not (except by use of miniatures) in the theatre, to present mass scenes in very long shot, but, as we shall see in Part 4 below, early film audiences, and especially those familiar with the live stage, were not willing to adopt the scalar relativism required to be impressed by small pictures of large things. Felix Salten, a German theatre critic who was already writing scripts for films, complained about the diminutive size of the figures in the spectacle scenes in the 1912 film version of *Quo Vadis?* and the grotesque contrast between them and the giants in closer shots, demanding a screen big enough to give the same sense of spectacle as in a theatre: 'It should be possible to project any scenery that requires size and breadth in that size and breadth. For this one would need a screen that has more or less the area of our theatrical proscenium openings. In the cinema as in the theatre, the natural size of the human body should be the unchanging unit of measurement. And, as required, the whole projection surface or only a section of it should be used.'[26]

Finally, a spectacular effect depends on the audience's perception of the disproportion between the reality represented and the means used to represent it—it is the very impossibility of having a train crash on stage that makes even a very tacky simulation of it in the theatre impressive. Photography suffers from a modified form of what might be called the 'Par-

meno's pig effect'.[27] Its products are not 'real things' like the pig to which Parmeno's mimicked pig was preferred, but they rapidly came to be seen as mere mechanical copies of such things. The earliest viewers experienced the movement in moving pictures as the result of a technical marvel, but once they were familiar with the moving picture camera as a recording device, the effect was lost. Special trick effects remained wonderful for longer, though audiences eventually became disenchanted with them, too, as noted above. Simply photographing something hard to stage with a moving-picture camera was not sufficient to produce the spectacle demanded. Such moving photographs had to be spectacular independently of the reality of what they represented.

It seems important to insist on the demand for spectacle as such, not on a demand for 'realism', and particularly not on a demand for the kind of realism offered by photographs (or, more precisely, 'photographic' has to be seen to be a particular connotation endowing certain images with a 'real effect', not as a kind of equivalent of the 'real thing'). 'Spectacle' described a kind of staging that appealed primarily to the eye, and what appealed to the eye was conceived in terms of painting rather than photography, and if photography was appealed to, it was as a genre of picture, not as a token of reality. Thus, when the Lasky company made a film adaptation of Charles A. Kenyon's play *The Kindling* in 1915, Wilfred Buckland built sets imitating Jacob Riis photographs of tenements to create an appropriate mood for the film. Vardac notes the demand for pictorialism in nineteenth-century theatre, but for him such pictorialism was a constant feature—it could be traced back to the Renaissance stage, and in the nineteenth century it characterized the 'old' staging method of flats, drops, and wings as much as the 'new' staging with three-dimensional furnishings and box sets. The dynamic factor was the attempt to make these pictures more and more 'realistic', eventually outrunning the possibilities, first of the old staging, then of the new, and only achievable by the cinema. As always for Vardac, 'realistic' can only mean 'photographic', and 'photographic' only 'indistinguishable from reality'. However, the effects achieved by the acknowledged masters of pictorial theatre, Henry Irving and David Belasco, while extremely picturesque, are only like photographs in so far as certain schools of late nineteenth-century photography attempted to reproduce the effect of paintings, or photographs came to define a recognizable style or styles for pictures, as Jacob Riis's photographs did. The illustrations of Irving's *Faust* published in the contemporary press draw on romantic, Gothic graphic traditions, and descriptions of the production show that Irving was seeking just such a pictorial effect.[28] Belasco did occasionally resort to an accumulation of realistic detail that was hailed as photographic by contemporary commentators, most famously in the scene in a Child's Restaurant in his 1912 production of *The Governor's Lady*, but the emphasis is always on how that detail creates atmosphere, which a photograph as such may well lack.[29] It is noteworthy that most of his settings were more picturesquely exotic than a New York restaurant—the Western fort in *The Girl I Left behind Me* (1893), the port of Nagasaki in *Madame Butterfly* (1900), the Japanese bamboo forest in *The Darling of the Gods* (1902), the Californian Sierra in *The Girl of the Golden West* (1905), to name only a few. All of these settings provided the occasions for the extended gradual changes in lighting that were a Belasco trademark, and which the cinema has never attempted to emulate.[30]

It is by an examination of the notion of the pictorial and pictorial effect in theatre that we shall attempt in this book to recast Vardac's account, specifying what filmmakers might have looked for from the theatre to help them make the new, longer films that began to be required of them after 1910. This is not to say that these filmmakers simply took over the pictorial techniques of the stage. On the contrary, they started from an already sophisticated battery of filmmaking techniques which were relatively independent of the theatre, and they were perfectly aware of the technical differences between the two media. Rather they shared the widespread conception of the theatre as a matter of pictures, and sought ways to find equivalents of these pictures for a new kind of cinema. To grasp this process it is necessary both to understand what was meant by pictorialism in general and in the theatre in particular, and also how such a pictorialism was modified in its transfer to a new medium.

The importance of the spectacular and the pictorial in nineteenth-century theatre has received much attention in recent years, most notably in Michael Booth's studies, especially *Victorian Spectacular Theatre*,

and in chapter 3 of Martin Meisel's *Realizations*. Despite the numerous instances they can cite where scenes from plays are praised for being 'just like a picture', and the variety of ways they describe that theatrical technicians appealed to and exploited features of painting (ways which we will examine again and again in this book) it is important to realize that 'spectacle' was a term as likely to be used pejoratively, especially by the cultural élite. Aristotle had argued that spectacle (*opsis*), the part of drama that appealed merely to the eye, was subordinate to the words of drama, indeed 'has nothing to do with poetry', by which he seems to mean the composition of a play.[31] Aristotle's prestige and the obvious appeal of this opinion to writers have meant that throughout the period when spectacular theatre flourished, most published comment subordinated the visual aspects of production to the texts and deplored the theatrical impresario's emphasis on the former. Many of the new theatrical movements of the late nineteenth and early twentieth century, from naturalism to symbolism and expressionism, and the new methods of staging the classics that accompanied them, can be seen as attempts to re-establish the centrality of the text to the theatre.

The prejudice against a theatre of pictures which pervades twentieth-century commentary is not limited to a defence of the text, however. It is also found in much art history and art criticism, in the form of a prejudice against the kind of pictures that this theatre appealed to, pictures that can be called 'theatrical'. If cinematic modernists like Pudovkin or Richter saw theatre as stifling the development of an authentically cinematic art, some modernist art critics have attempted to free the notion of the picture from theatricalism. Although the cinema plays almost no part in the writings of the principal critics we wish to discuss, Michael Fried and Svetlana Alpers,[32] their position has recently been extended to the cinema by Anne Hollander. Before discussing how theatrical pictorialism helps to explain the ways in which theatre was appropriated as a model by filmmakers, it seems important to clarify what a theatrical pictorialism is in relation to these arguments. Although these authors are by no means unanimous in their formulations of the question, a key place in the arguments is taken by the issue of address—the degree to which a painting acknowledges the spectator or not. This distinction, expounded by Fried in relation to painting, is central to an understanding of the conception of pictorialism we wish to propose in relation to cinema.

Hollander's book is a little like Vardac's, in so far as she wants to claim that a series of characteristics of post-Renaissance painting are like the cinema, anticipate moving pictures. However, it is only some schools of painting that exhibit these characteristics, precisely those that are anti-theatrical. She posits a connection between such paintings and cinema in the claim that 'films are essentially dramatic and not theatrical.'[33] On the face of it, such an opposition seems paradoxical, but it has a considerable history, documented by Jonas Barish in his survey of the seemingly universal suspicion of the theatre, *The Anti-theatrical Prejudice.*[34] Often invoked by proponents of the text, in particular those who would rather read plays than see them staged, it is also appealed to by promoters of theatrical reform. Hollander's use of it can be traced to such a reformism, that of Denis Diderot, though her more immediate source is Michael Fried's study of Diderot's place in eighteenth-century French art criticism, *Absorption and Theatricality.*

Fried's book is concerned with two related phenomena: first, the beginnings of a new sense of the picture or '*tableau*' in France in the early eighteenth century (anticipated to a degree, as he notes, by Shaftesbury in England); and an emphasis in art criticism and in painting itself on 'absorption'. '*Tableau*' ceased to designate the portability of paintings on wood or canvas as opposed to murals and came to indicate a relationship between the viewer and the painting, the way the viewer was captivated by the self-contained unity of what he saw on the canvas (hence the term quickly came to be used metaphorically to denote particular kinds of viewing experience independently of whether what was seen was in fact a painted flat surface). 'Absorption' denoted both a purely contemplative relation between the viewer and the painting, and the nature of the kinds of painting which allowed such disinterested contemplation—in particular, paintings such as those of Chardin showing children absorbed in play, oblivious to any spectators in the painted world, and *a fortiori* to the viewer of the painting. 'Absorptive' paintings of this type are opposed to those that solicit attention,

where the subjects are on display, either apparently engaging the viewers (addressing them by look or gesture), or revealing the self-consciousness that suggests an awareness of the regard of an unacknowledged viewer. This second kind of painting is, in this discourse (and clearly in Fried's own assessment), inferior, and another way to describe it is, of course, to say that it is 'theatrical'.

Diderot was a strong proponent of this anti-theatrical programme in his writings on the visual arts, but he also extended it to the theatre itself. In discussing his own plays, and especially *Le Fils naturel*, seen as models for a reformed theatre, he appealed to the analogy with the picture to free the stage from those quintessentially theatrical moments known as *coups de théâtre* where a sudden change in the dramatic situation achieves a maximal effect on the audience: 'An unforeseen incident that turns into action and suddenly changes the positions of the characters is a *coup de théâtre*. An arrangement of those characters on the stage, so natural and so true that, if faithfully rendered by a painter, it would please me on the canvas, is a picture.'[35] These prescriptions are made in relation to the play Diderot pretended he had witnessed secretly, unbeknownst to most of the actors, who were themselves the characters of the play, repeating the actions as a family ritual—as the father is made to say to his son in proposing this ritual: 'It is not a matter of setting up a stage here, but of preserving the memory of an event that concerns us, and performing it as it occurred.'[36] But Diderot managed to be there, not addressed, but witnessing the action. This idea of a work witnessed by but not addressed to its spectator is one definition of the absorptive picture. In contrast, the *coup de théâtre* is defined by both an acknowledgement of the spectator's presence—in the organization of plot to produce striking effects for an audience—and a strong emphasis on narrative action.

Thus, Diderot's drama both does and does not partake of the theatre. The dialogue form of his commentaries on his play, the *Entretiens sur Le Fils naturel*, precisely allows him to advance (via his character Dorval) a kind of drama which at the same time he (as himself) can admit to be theatrically impossible. It sometimes almost seems that his notion of the tableau derives not just from the painting but also from the table, as in Quesnay's *Tableau économique*, which sets up the elements of a social situation side by side upon the page, and formulates their inter-action as a continuing process, not a sequence of cause and effect with a beginning, a middle, and an end, i.e. not as an action in the Aristotelian sense.[37]

Fried does not go so far as Diderot here in advocat-ing the elimination of action. He notes that the mid-eighteenth-century shift in taste usually thought of as a 'neo-classical' reaction against the rococo in-sisted on the supremacy of history painting, and hence precisely the representation of significant action, among the genres. He links this to the absorp-tive programme by arguing that this renewed inter-est involved a greater emphasis on a momentary representation, with the characters' involvement in the sequence of events implied in that single moment guaranteeing their absorption, and hence the ab-sence of theatricality. Svetlana Alpers, however, in a paper cited approvingly by Fried, and at greater length in her book *The Art of Describing*, links theatri-cality to a broader tradition which, from the Renais-sance on, privileged the history painting, and insisted on the representation of significant action as the true task of painting: 'In referring to the notion of art in the Italian Renaissance, I have in mind the Albertian definition of the picture: a framed surface or pane sit-uated at a certain distance from a viewer who looks through it at a second or substitute world. In the Re-naissance this world was a stage on which human fig-ures performed significant actions based on the texts of the poets.'[38] The reference to the stage here derives not from Alberti so much as from the claim, most re-cently reiterated by Ernst Gombrich on a number of occasions, that the renewed interest in the represen-tation of space in the Renaissance was connected with the rise of religious drama.[39] Alpers counter-poses to this narrative conception of the picture one she calls descriptive characteristic of Dutch genre painting, but also found in Northern landscapes and in non-Dutch painters such as Caravaggio and Ve-lasquez, where the visual appearance of the world as such is at stake. In so far as seeing is central to such paintings, they exert an immediate fascination on the viewer. This fascination is one of the properties Fried attributes to absorptive paintings, and Alpers aligns her opposition with his. Thus, in citing Roger de Piles's preference for Rembrandt over Raphael be-cause a friend who had walked past Raphael's Vatican frescoes without noticing them was captivated by a

Rembrandt self-portrait, she suggests that his attribu-tion of this superiority to Rembrandt's use of colour really stands in for the absorption Fried counterposes to theatricality.[40]

Despite Alpers, and despite Diderot, the term *tableau* in the eighteenth century usually carries strong implications that pictures should represent actions. Thus de Caylus, in a discussion of literature appealing to painterly models, wrote of Camoëns, 'however, his poem presents images rather than pic-tures [*tableaux*], that is, descriptions rather than inter-esting actions,' with a note that 'a picture, to speak precisely, is the representation of the moment of an action'.[41] Caylus is concerned with the problem that received its most famous formulation later in the cen-tury in Lessing's *Laocoön*, how different arts could rep-resent different subjects, and, in particular, how static visual arts like painting and sculpture, as op-posed to verbal arts such as epic, could represent events unfolding in time. The answer was found in the selection of what Lessing called 'the most fruitful moment'[42] to depict, a moment of harmonious re-pose which nevertheless revealed the traces of the causal process that brought it about and carried the implications of the consequences that were to follow. In eminently Aristotelian fashion, painting was res-cued from the charge of being mere *opsis* in so far as it was able, like drama, to imitate action, understood as a causal process with a beginning, middle, and end.

This problem might seem irrelevant to drama (con-ceived of as drama staged rather than in a book), since drama can represent action in time directly, but a shift was under way in the conception of drama at this time from a rhetorical one focused on the speeches of the actors to a spectacular one emphasiz-ing what could be seen on the stage.[43] The new con-ception of the picture was rapidly adapted to this new conception of drama. By the middle of the eighteenth century, and markedly in the writings of Voltaire, the notion that a play and the actors' performances in it could be metaphorically described as a series of 'pic-tures' was well established. For Voltaire, the presen-tation of such 'pictures' on stage was closely tied to the notions of action and theatrical effect—precisely the *coups de théâtre* deplored by Diderot: 'Plays used to have to be made up of long speeches: they were beau-tiful conversations rather than an action. . . . This form, which excluded any theatrical action, also excluded those grand expressions of the passions, those striking pictures [*tableaux*] of human misfortunes, those terrible and piercing characteristics that tear out the heart; the latter was touched, where it should have been lacerated.'[44]

However, the application of an Aristotelian conception of painting as imitative of action to drama paradoxically produced an anti-Aristotelian tendency in drama. Action as movement was arrested into action as simultaneously rendered causal sequence. The temporal foreshortening this demanded is well illustrated by an example of Edward Mayhew's cited by Meisel, the cuts that became customary at Othello's second entrance in Act II, scene 3 of Shakespeare's play in the late eighteenth century and persisted as stage tradition throughout the nineteenth (the Boito-Verdi opera has the same compression). The initial exchange between Othello and Montano and part of Iago's admonishing speech were cut, so that

Othello appears, and standing with his sword drawn immediately under the archway, brings all to a climax by shouting at the top of his voice, 'Hold for your lives!' at which instant Montano receives his hurt and staggers into one corner. Cassio, conscience stricken by the sound of his General's voice, occupies the other. The rest of the performers put themselves into attitudes—the stage is grouped—and a picture formed, of which the Moor is the centre figure. After this there is a pause; when Othello, having looked around him, walks forward, and the half exclamation of *Why, how now, ho! whence ariseth this?* becomes an inquiry.[45]

While such pictorialism guaranteed the intelligibility and significance of the action, it threatened the overall causal unity of the drama as the causal connections were, so to speak, retracted into the series of pictures. Commentators often condemned the kind of drama that resulted in Aristotelian fashion as episodic. More commonly, it was thought of as 'situational'. This situational dramaturgy is the subject of the next chapter of this book. What needs to be emphasized here is that the pictures to which this dramaturgy appealed were not of Fried's absorptive type, and that nineteenth- and early twentieth-century theatre did not in general attempt to follow Diderot in trying to place on the stage a world that 'is no more concerned with the spectator than if he did not exist'.[46] Indeed, in so far as commentators could grasp this notion, they found it untheatrical, indeed, unaesthetic.

Thus, in an essay published in 1800 which praises the pictorial (*malerisch*) character of French tragic acting (with reservations, which will be discussed in Part 3 below), Wilhelm von Humboldt condemns Diderot's notion of a 'peep-show' theatre:

Diderot claims to have witnessed his *Natural Son* acted by its own protagonists as the repetition of a real occurrence. He clearly implied that this was to see genuine nature and truth, so that both poet and actor had much to learn from it. It may be an instructive lesson to repeat an interesting scene from life as it were theatrically, but how something that was not intended for a spectator could be any kind of a work of art I cannot conceive, nor what Diderot, sitting concealed in a corner, could have learnt from it as an artist; what he saw was certainly neither nature nor art, and I know not what else it might have been besides.[47]

If Humboldt found Diderot hard to understand, only a few years later his central arguments seem to have been forgotten. In 1824, a commentator, far from contrasting *tableau* and *coup de théâtre*, entirely identifies them, defining the former as 'the marked wordless scene, general pantomime, *coup de théâtre*, obligatory at the end of each act of a melodrama'. The commentary was intended to be malicious, but could be cited quite seriously in Arthur Pougin's *Dictionnaire historique et pittoresque du théâtre* in 1885.[48] The term 'picture' was used in a variety of specialized ways in the nineteenth-century theatre, many of which we will be discussing in this book, but all of them appeal to the 'anti-absorptive' sense that emerged in the eighteenth century.

However, something very close to the absorptive picture has often been taken to be characteristic of the cinema. Christian Metz has argued that the theatre is exhibitionist—the actors on the stage know they are being watched by the audience, and the audience know that the actors know. In the cinema, on the contrary, the actor is absent; only his image is present, and the spectator is correspondingly in the position of a voyeur:

It is enough, it is even essential . . . that the actor should behave as though he were not seen (and therefore as though he did not see his voyeur), that he should go about his ordinary business and pursue his existence as foreseen by the fiction of the film, that he should carry on with his antics in a closed room, taking the utmost care not to notice that a glass rectangle has been set into one of the walls, and that he lives in a kind of aquarium, one which is simply a little less generous with its 'apertures' than real aquariums (this withholding of things being itself part of the scopic mechanism).[49]

This is, of course, Diderot's notion of the spectator in his ideal theatre. Metz notes that theatre and cinema share 'the distance instituted by the look—which transforms the object into a *picture* (a "*tableau vivant*")', but insists that the presence of the actors implies their consent and hence an acknowledgement of the spectator that the cinema lacks.[50]

Metz's argument is concerned with the technology of the cinema, but he notes that these effects are those of that technology in the institutions of the fiction cinema with which we are currently familiar. Tom Gunning gives this a more historical basis, and explicitly links it to Fried's terms, when he contrasts the early cinema with that exemplified by the films D. W. Griffith directed for the Biograph Company in the 1910s by asserting that in the former 'theatrical display dominates over narrative absorption',[51] whereas the latter creates a diegetic world and 'like ink into a blotter, we become absorbed into this diegetic world through our act of voyeurism'.[52]

We might note here that narrative, which was played down by Fried as a characteristic of the absorptive picture, and counterposed to it by Alpers, appears for Gunning as aligned with it. The notion of the picture that dominated nineteenth-century pictorial theatre was in no way anti-narrative, and in emphasizing the importance of this notion to the cinema of the 1910s, we implicitly reject historical distinctions based on the presence and absence, or dominance and subordination, of narrative. However, we would note a more profound opposition between pictorial in our sense and that basically shared by Fried, Metz, and Gunning, in the link between their various senses of the absorptive picture and the shot-based approach to cinema described at the beginning of this introduction.

Accounts such as those of Metz and Gunning are not traditional editing-based histories of cinema, of course. Rather than considering the relations between shots along the length of the film, they concentrate on the relation between the spectator and the world depicted in the film, analysed into that between spectator and film and that between camera and filmed event. This does, however, tie them to the shot and relations between shots, in so far as the shot is, precisely, the unit of film defined by a relation between the camera and a recorded event.

However, the dynamics of address and spectatorial response appear differently if the scene, rather than the shot, is taken to be the basic unit. The organization of components of *mise-en-scène* in ways designed to underscore particular dramatic effects, along the lines of Diderot's *coup de théâtre*, become evident once one attempts to deal with changes within the shot, and with units larger than the shot conceived to have a dramatic unity equivalent to that of the theatrical scene. At its broadest, a picture designated everything that became visible when the curtain rose or the lights went up after a change of décor. More locally, a scene could be punctuated by what are often called 'tableaux' even in English, moments when the actors formed (and held for a longer or shorter time) a grouping, each adopting a posture or making a gesture suited to the dramatic situation. Such pictures underlined the significance of the situation, and also, by interrupting the flow of the action, modulated the rhythm of the performance as a whole. Finally, on the most local level, each actor was enjoined to consider his or her part as a sequence of pictures, each posture or gesture being studied as an attitude of its own. These three levels are considered in this book in Parts 4, 2, and 3, on staging, the tableau, and acting, respectively.

Crucial here is the ability of the picture to articulate and thus make intelligible the relatively large space beyond the proscenium 'window', and the relatively long temporal unit constituted by a theatrical scene. Pictorial effects convey to the audience which of the many objects and people visible to them are significant for the development of the action, while changes in the stage picture overall, and in the attitudes of the actors, indicate new centres of attention and changes in the situation. Shot-based accounts of the cinema assign these functions largely to framings that isolate the significant element—hence the importance in such accounts of the emergence of the close-up—and to the shot changes that shift the attention from component to component of a scene. The problem with this approach is that editing developed by no means evenly. In particular, cutting rates remained much slower in European films until the 1920s. Barry Salt presents histograms comparing the average shot lengths (ASLs) of European and American films: 'There are no American films in the sample with ASLs longer than 10 seconds in the 1918–1923 period, and hence the mean value of the Average Shot Length for this period is 6.5 seconds, whereas for the previous six years 1912–1917, the mean value of the ASL for American features was 9.6 seconds. On the other hand, for European features, the 1912–1917 mean value of the ASL was 15 seconds, which only decreased to 8.6 seconds for the next 6 year period.'[53] Nevertheless, the emergence of the longer film, which presented new problems of plot complexity and the articulation of much longer spans of time, was initiated in Europe, despite the fact that many early European features have what is sometimes described as 'primitive' or 'backward' editing.

To take a perhaps extreme example, the Italian film *Ma l'amor mio non muore!* (But my love does not die!)[54] of 1913 has a long scene—really, an act—representing a dinner party at the home of Colonel Holbein in the Grand Duchy of Wallenstein, where the adventurer Moïse Sthar, invited because he is supposedly courting the Colonel's daughter Elsa, steals the secret plans to the Duchy's defences. The scene is restricted entirely to a single setting, the Holbeins' salon, photographed along its diagonal so that a dining-room and a study are visible through large wall-openings rear left and right, respectively. The scene lasts 13 minutes 5 seconds (at 16 frames per second) in current prints, which probably lack many of the intertitles there would have been in the original, and there are only four changes in camera set-up in the scene: closer shots with the camera more or less at the same angle showing the study, first when Holbein and a fellow officer examine the plans, then when Sthar steals them, and the area around the piano in the salon when Sthar, supposedly listening to Elsa's playing, watches the officers off right in the study. The only other changes are entrances and exits and regroupings of characters in different parts of the set. Editing is used here to help establish the crucial event for the plot— the detection and theft of the plans—but this effect seems like a stronger version of articulations achieved elsewhere in the scene by pictorial changes.

The overall slowness of editing and the tendency to use depth in many European films of this period once led one of us to propose that complex staging was the European alternative to the American development of editing,[55] but here we would like to suggest rather that pictorialism was part of both European and American filmmaking traditions, and that its relation to changes in editing is complex. Sometimes film editing came to interfere with the methods of stage pictorialism; this is particularly true of the way the timing of changing attitudes by actors was disrupted by rapid shot change. At others, editing could be adopted as a new kind of pictorialism, as in the example from *Ma l'amor mio non muore!*, or in the use of flurries of shots from extreme angles to underline spectacular moments in the 1914 World version of *Uncle Tom's Cabin*, discussed in Part 2, below.

As this last remark indicates, our conception of 'pictorialism' goes well beyond the use of frame compositions that a painter or an art historian would recognize as typical of painting in any period. Although the model for the idea of a picture in theatre and cinema derives from history painting, and paintings have been reproduced as tableaux vivants on the stage, both as an autonomous genre, and as part of plays (e.g. Greuze's 'L'Accordée de village' in *Les Noces d'Arlequin* in Paris in 1761, and David Wilkie's 'Distraining for Rent' in *The Rent Day* in London in 1832), and in films (e.g. *Hell Bent*, Universal 1918, which begins with actors holding poses reproducing Frederick Remington's 'The Misdeal'), most stage pictures were directly invented for the production in which they occurred, and even when a freezing of the action was involved, this was not long enough to allow the kind of teasing out of the narrative role of all the details typical of painting, especially nineteenth-century narrative painting. Pictures in theatre and cinema were not autonomous narratives; they were part of the narrative structure of the play as a whole, and a way of articulating the relation of the play's story in time. We have referred to this interplay between temporal unfolding and punctual picture as a 'situational' approach to narrative. It is to the notion of the dramatic 'situation' that we turn in the next chapter.

1. *Film Technique and Film Acting: The Cinematic Writings of V. I. Pudovkin*, trans. Ivor Montagu, Introd. Lewis Jacobs (New York: Lear Publishers, 1949), pp. xiv–xv.

2. John Emerson and Anita Loos, *How to Write Photoplays* (New York: James A. McCann Co., 1920), 54. Film scripts have generally followed these prescriptions of Loos and Emerson ever since.

3. See David Bordwell, 'The Introduction of Sound', in David Bordwell, Janet Staiger, and Kristin Thompson, *The Classical Hollywood Cinema: Film Style and Mode of Production to 1960* (London: Routledge, 1985), 298–308, esp. 308.

4. Pudovkin, *Film Technique*, 23.

5. *The Struggle for the Film*, trans. Ben Brewster (Aldershot: Scolar Press, 1986), 65. Richter's second book on the cinema was written in the later 1930s, but not published until the German edition appeared in 1976. Henny Porten is not currently credited with appearing in an adaptation of *Das Käthchen von Heilbronn*; see Corinna Müller, 'Filmografie', in Helga Belach, *Henny Porten: der erste deutsche Filmstar, 1890–1960* (Berlin: Haude and Spener, 1986), 171–232.

6. Pudovkin, *Film Technique*, 51–2.

7. *Histoire générale du cinéma* (Paris: Denoël, 1948; repr. 1973), ii: *Les Pionniers du cinéma (de Méliès à Pathé), 1897–1909*, 402.

8. *Histoire du cinéma: Art et industrie* (Paris: Éditions Universitaires, 1967), i: *1895–1914*, 408. Mitry's account is critically discussed by Tom Gunning in *D. W. Griffith and the Origins of American Narrative Film: The Early Years at Biograph* (Urbana, Ill.: University of Illinois Press, 1991), 34.

9. Anne Hollander, *Moving Pictures* (Cambridge, Mass.: Harvard University Press, 1991), 50.

10. This point was made before 1978 by John Fell in his book *Film and the Narrative Tradition* (Norman, Okla.: University of Oklahoma Press, 1975).

11. See Noël Burch, *Life to Those Shadows*, trans. Ben Brewster (London: British Film Institute, 1990), 186 ff.; Tom Gunning, 'The Cinema of Attractions: Early Film, Its Spectators, and the Avant-Garde', *Wide Angle* 8, no. 3/4 (Fall 1986), 63–70, repr. in Thomas Elsaesser and Adam Barker (ed.), *Early Cinema: Space, Frame, Narrative* (London: British Film Institute, 1990), 56–62.

12. Although Kristin Thompson is careful to discuss the relations between drama and the transition to the classical American narrative cinema in part 3 of Bordwell *et al.*, *Classical Hollywood Cinema*, she argues there (pp. 163–73) that it became standard practice to develop film scripts from story outlines, whether deriving from plays or from narrative sources, and hence a short narrative form underlies even the most direct theatrical adaptations in the cinema. Moreover, the general account of classical cinema given by David Bordwell in part 1 of the same work draws so heavily on literary narratology as to make the literary influences more salient.

13. An important exception is Barry Salt, who has always insisted on the influence of Reinhardt's theatrical productions and the German operetta on Lubitsch's films, for example (in a paper at the conference Silent Cinema, 1916–26: Space, Frame, Narrative held at the University of East Anglia, Norwich, in 1983, and in 'From German Stage to German Screen', in Paolo Cherchi Usai and Lorenzo Codelli (eds.), *Prima di Caligari: Cinema tedesco, 1895–1920* (Pordenone: Edizioni Biblioteca dell'Immagine, 1990), 402–22, and emphasized the adoption of theatrical prescriptions by filmmakers in America (in ch. 10 of the second edition of his *Film Style and Technology: History and Analysis* (London: Starword, 1992), 111–13). Rick Altman, too, has deplored the neglect by film historians of the stage adaptations that usually intervene between nineteenth-century novels and twentieth-century film adaptations; see 'Dickens, Griffith, and Film Theory Today', *South Atlantic Quarterly*, 88, no. 2 (Spring 1989), 321–59.

14. The early synchronized sound films made with the Gaumont Chronophone, Messter Tonbild, and other processes were mostly of songs or operatic arias, and relate to variety theatre performance more than they do to straight drama, though at least one of the surviving films made for the Edison Kinetophone in 1913 was a comic playlet, *The Politician*. However, very few of these films have yet been recombined with their soundtracks (which were recorded separately on phonograph cylinders or discs, so surviving films often lack their discs and vice versa), so they do not yet constitute a source which would supply this difficulty.

15. See David Mayer, 'The Victorian Stage on Film: A Description and a Selective List of Holdings in the Library of Congress Paper Print Collection', *Nineteenth Century Theatre*, 16, no. 2 (Winter 1988), 111–22; and Stephen Johnson, 'Evaluating Early Film as a Document of Theatre History: The 1896 Footage of Joseph Jefferson's *Rip Van Winkle*', *Nineteenth Century Theatre*, 20, no. 2 (Winter 1992), 101–22.

16. A. Nicholas Vardac, *Stage to Screen* (Cambridge, Mass.: Harvard University Press, 1949). Hassan El Nouty has made a similar case for French nineteenth-century theatre in *Théâtre et pré-cinéma: Essai sur la problématique du spectacle au XIXᵉ siècle* (Paris: A.-G. Nizet, 1978). Although his is in many ways a more subtle and interesting account of the nature of nineteenth-century French drama than Vardac's is of English and American, his sources are principally the texts of the plays themselves rather than direct evidence of their staging, and he is even less specific about the early cinema and how it borrowed from or realized nineteenth-century theatrical aims than Vardac is. His discussion of the nature of theatrical and cinematic space will be examined in Part 4, but here we have restricted our argument about the overall connections between theatre and cinema to the example of Vardac.

17. 'Romantic conceptions of the playwrights might become more and more exaggerated in their never-ending quest for escape, but it would never do for the scene-builder to follow a similar pattern. His job was to render believable upon the stage the increasingly glamorous, unreal, and spectacular ideas of the romantic playwrights. The more romantic the subject-matter the more realistic must be its presentation upon the boards, else the entire effect would be lost' (*Stage to Screen*, p. xx).

18. Martin Meisel similarly refers in passing to 'Dion Boucicault, the most cinematic of English melodramatists' (*Realizations: Narrative, Pictorial and Theatrical Arts in Nineteenth-Century England* (Princeton: Princeton University Press, 1983), 51).

19. David Mayer (ed.), *Playing out the Empire: Ben-Hur and Other Toga Plays and Films, 1883–1908: A Critical Anthology* (Oxford: Clarendon Press, 1994), p. xi. The fact that Klaw and Erlanger, the owners of the theatrical rights to Lew Wallace's book, sued Kalem for copyright infringement over this film, thereby establishing the important precedent that a film screening was the equivalent for copyright purposes of the performance of a stage adaptation, might suggest that they feared competition from the cinema. However, rights holders sue infringers they do not take seriously as competitors, and, as Mayer notes, another motive claimed in this case was a concern that the very weakness of the cinematic

adaptation might damage the reputation of their play.

20. *San Francisco Examiner* (7 Jan. 1906), cit. Vardac, *Stage to Screen*, 84.

21. 'Why I Stayed out and Why I Went into the Movies', *New York Times* (31 May 1914), section VII: 8, col. 3.

22. e.g. Vardac, *Stage to Screen*, 29–30 (*Arrah-na-Pogue*), 33 (*Little Emily*), 37 (*Oliver Twist*).

23. See Michel Chion, 'Quiet Revolution . . . and Rigid Stagnation', *October*, 58 (Fall 1991), 69–80, esp. 71.

24. Although cameras and projectors were built, films taken, and demonstration shows successfully mounted, fire inspectors refused to allow the Cinéorama to open at the Exposition. See Jacques Deslandes and Jacques Richard, *Histoire comparée du cinéma*, ii: *Du cinématographe au cinéma, 1896–1906* (Paris: Casterman, 1968), 39–55.

25. See *Life to Those Shadows*, 6–42, and esp. 39–40. For a general account of the relation between the recording technologies of the cinema and realism, see Ben Brewster, 'Film', in Michael Irwin and Daniel Cohn-Sherbok (eds.), *Exploring Reality* (London: Allen & Unwin, 1987), 145–67.

26. 'Zu einem Kinodramen, Anmerkungen', *Dresdner Neueste Nachrichten*, 112 (27 Apr. 1913, 1st edn.), 1; repr. in Jörg Schweinitz (ed.), *Prolog vor dem Film: Nachdenken über ein neues Medium 1909–1914* (Leipzig: Reclam, 1992), 365.

27. According to Plutarch, an actor's attempt to imitate the squealing of a pig was condemned as 'not as good as Parmeno's pig'. When he revealed that the sound was coming from a real piglet concealed under his cloak, his critics remained unimpressed—they still preferred Parmeno's pig. For Plutarch, 'this plainly demonstrates that the very same sensation will not produce a corresponding effect a second time in people's minds unless they believe that intelligence or conscious striving is involved in the performance' (*Table-Talk*, part 5, 1, 674, trans. Herbert B. Hoffleit, *Plutarch's Moralia*, Loeb's Classical Library (London: Heinemann, 1969), viii. 383). Traditional commentators disagree as to whether Parmeno was an actor esteemed for his vocal mimicry or a painter who had painted a pig so lifelike that viewers thought they heard it squeal.

28. See Michael Booth, *Victorian Spectacular Theatre, 1850–1910* (London: Routledge, 1981), ch. 4 and plates 15, 16, 19, and 20.

29. 'The restaurant is done in the usual white tiling. The egg boiler, steaming coffee urn, steaming hot water heater, wheat cake griddle, egg-frying apparatus, etc. are all in evidence. In fact, the place is exactly reproduced in every detail. The piles of oranges, apples, grapefruit, etc., are all arranged in the window. The pastry counter is well stacked, not forgetting the bowl of doughnuts. Baked apples and prunes are set out. Thick crockery dishes, cups, saucers, pitchers, small individual platters, etc. are in evidence. A lamp hangs over the Cashier's desk. Hooks are placed at intervals on the wall for the hats and coats of customers and signs are tacked up notifying the guests to "Look out for your overcoat." Some of the tables have the card "Reserved". Other tables are roped off and stacked with chairs, showing that business is virtually over and that although the place will be open until midnight (this being Saturday) only a few stray guests are expected owing to the weather. Some of the lights are turned off' (Belasco's promptbook, cit. Lise-Lone Marker, *David Belasco: Naturalism in the American Theatre* (Princeton: Princeton University Press, 1975), 62. See also ills. 3). A souvenir programme for the play in its file in the Museum of the City of New York (*The Story of the*

Governor's Lady Told in Pictures) proclaims: 'Someone has said of *The Governor's Lady* that "its fidelity to life is photographic".'

30. The actinic properties of motion picture film do not accommodate the latitude of lighting levels which would allow a fourteen-minute dawn (as in *Madame Butterfly*) or an eclipse of the sun over most of an act (*The Wife*, 1887). See Lea Jacobs, 'Belasco, DeMille and the Development of Lasky Lighting', *Film History*, 5, no. 4 (1993), 405–18.

31. Aristotle, *The Poetics*, 6, 28 in Aristotle, *The Poetics*, Longinus, *On the Sublime* and Demetrius, *On Style*, trans. W. Hamilton Fyfe and W. Rhys Roberts, Loeb Classical Library (Cambridge, Mass.: Harvard University Press, 1927), 29.

32. Fried mentions the cinema in passing, via a reference to Stanley Cavell's *The World Viewed: Reflections on the Ontology of Film* (New York: Viking Press, 1971); see *Absorption and Theatricality, Painting and the Beholder in the Age of Diderot* (Berkeley: University of California Press, 1980), 182, n. 13.

33. Hollander, *Moving Pictures*, 25.

34. Jonas Barish, *The Anti-theatrical Prejudice* (Berkeley: University of California Press, 1981), esp. 324 ff.

35. *Entretiens sur Le Fils naturel* in *Œuvres complètes de Diderot*, x: *Le Drame bourgeois*, ed. Jacques Chouillet and Anne-Marie Chouillet (Paris: Hermann, 1980), 92; cit. Fried, *Absorption and Theatricality*, 95.

36. *Le Fils naturel*, in *Œuvres complètes de Diderot*, x: *Le Drame bourgeois*, ed. Jacques Chouillet and Anne-Marie Chouillet (Paris: Hermann, 1980), 16.

37. François Quesnay, *Tableau économique, avec ses explications*, separately paginated part 8 of Victor Riqueti, marquis de Mirabeau, *L'Ami des hommes, ou traité de la population*, rev. edn. (Avignon, 1758–61). The same tabular impulse seems to be behind Dorval's demand for the representation of conditions or estates rather than characters: '[*Dorval*]: Up to now, character has, in comedy, been the main object, and condition only accessory. Character was the source of the whole plot. The general circumstances that would bring it out were sought for, and then linked end to end. It is condition, its duties, advantages, awkwardnesses, which ought to provide the basis for the work. . . . [*Me*]: So you want to see acted the man of letters, the philosopher, the trader, the judge, the lawyer, the politician, the citizen, the magistrate, the financier, the great lord, the steward. [*Dorval*]: Add to the list all the relationships: the father, the husband, the sister, the brothers' (*Entretiens sur Le Fils naturel*, 144–5).

38. *The Art of Describing: Dutch Painting in the Seventeenth Century* (Chicago: University of Chicago Press, 1983), p. xix. The paper is 'Describe or Narrate? A Problem in Realistic Representation', *New Literary History*, 8 (1976–7), 15–41; for Fried's reference, see *Absorption and Theatricality*, 194, n. 88.

39. 'I agree with those who connect this decisive change with the new role of the popular preacher in the thirteenth century. It was the friars who took the Gospel story to the people and spared no effort to make the faithful re-live and re-enact it in their minds. It is well known that St Francis celebrated Christmas at Greccio in this way, actually bringing an ox and ass into the church, and maybe also a live baby. It was in the Franciscan tradition also that there grew up that important technique of devotion which involves this kind of imaginative identification. That great historian of Christian iconography, Émile Mâle, stressed the critical importance in this context of the *Meditations on the Life of Christ* by the Pseudo-Bonaventura, and of the miracle plays. He has been accused of

overstatement, and no doubt there were other factors, but I still think he had the right intuition, and that the change of attitude to the sacred narrative engendered by the new conception of teaching and preaching cannot be left out of the history of art.' (E. H. Gombrich, *Means and Ends: Reflections on the History of Fresco Painting* (London: Thames and Hudson, 1976), 33–4.) Gombrich has also linked the rise of perspective in the ancient world to a theatrical influence: 'It is surely no accident that the tricks of illusionist art, perspective and modelling in light and shade, wereconnected in classical antiquity with the design of theatrical scenery. It is here, in the context of plays based on the ancient mythical tales, that the re-enactment of events   according to the poet's vision and insight comes to its climax and is increasingly assisted by the illusions of art' (Ernst Gombrich, *Art and Illusion: A Study in the Psychology of Pictorial Representation*, rev. edn. (New York: Bollingen Foundation/Pantheon Books, 1961), 131).

40. 'Color is used here as a term referring to their [Rembrandt's and Caravaggio's] absorption in the act of representation or imitation' ('Describe or Narrate?', 26–8). The work by de Piles referred to is *Cours de peinture par principes* (Paris: J. Estienne, 1708; repr. Geneva: Slatkine Reprints, 1969), 14–17, also discussed by Fried, *Absorption and Theatricality*, 92.

41. Anne-Claude-Philippe de Turbières, comte de Caylus, *Tableaux tirés de l'Iliade, de l'Odyssée d'Homère et de l'Énéide de Virgile, avec des observations générales sur le costume* (Paris: Tilliard, 1757), p. xiii, cit. Fried, *Absorption and Theatricality*, 215, n. 90.

42. Gotthold Ephraim Lessing, *Laocoön: An Essay on the Limits of Painting and Poetry* (first published 1766), trans. Edward Allen McCormick (Baltimore: Johns Hopkins University Press, 1962), 19.

43. Kirsten Gram Holmström, *Monodrama, Attitudes, Tableaux Vivants: Studies on some Trends of Theatrical Fashion, 1770–1815* (Uppsala: Almqvist & Wiksells Boktryckeri, 1967), 11–39, esp. 21–3.

44. *Appel à toutes les nations de l'Europe, des jugemens d'un écrivain anglais; ou, manifeste au sujet des honneurs du pavillon entre les théâtres de Londres et de Paris* (1761), in *Œuvres complètes de Voltaire*, vol. xxiv: *Mélanges*, part 3 (Paris: Garnier Frères, 1879), 219; cit. Holmström, *Monodrama*, 22.

45. Edward Mayhew, *Stage Effect; or, the Principles which Command Dramatic Success in the Theatre* (London: Mitchell, 1840), 52, cit. Meisel, *Realizations*, 39–40. The citations from *Othello* follow Mayhew rather than standard modern editions.

46. *Entretiens sur Le Fils naturel*, 103.

47. 'Ueber die gegenwärtige Französische tragische Bühne. Aus Briefen', first published in *Propyläen*, 3, no. 1 (1800), cited from *Wilhelm von Humboldts Gesammelte Schriften*, ed. Königlich Preussischen Akademie der Wissenschaften, *Werke* (ed. Albert Leitzmann), vol. ii, part 1, section 2: *1796–1799* (Berlin: B. Behr's Verlag, 1904), 399. The characterization of Diderot's conception of the theatre as a 'peep-show' is from Holmström, *Monodrama*, 39; her use of the term derives from the twentieth-century German theatrical reformers' critique of the naturalistic theatre as a '*Guckkästchentheater*'.

48. Philadelphe Maurice Alhoy, François Antoine Harel, and Auguste Jal, *Dictionnaire théâtral* (Paris: J.-N. Barba, 1824); cit. Arthur Pougin, *Dictionnaire historique et pittoresque du théâtre* (Paris: Librarie de Firmin-Didot et Cie., 1885), art. 'tableau'.

49. Christian Metz, 'Story/Discourse (A Note on Two Kinds of Voyeurism)', in *Psychoanalysis and Cinema: The Imaginary Signifier*, trans. Celia Britton, Annwyl Williams, Ben Brewster, and Alfred Guzzetti (London: Macmillan, 1982), 96.

50. 'The Imaginary Signifier', in *Psychoanalysis and Cinema: The Imaginary Signifier*, trans. Celia Britton, Annwyl Williams, Ben Brewster, and Alfred Guzzetti (London: Macmillan, 1982), 62–3.

51. 'The Cinema of Attractions', in Elsaesser and Barker, *Early Cinema*, 59. The paragraph containing this passage is absent from the first publication of the article.

52. *D. W. Griffith*, 264. Fried's book is cited as a reference to this passage.

53. Barry Salt, *Film Style and Technology*, 146–7. The contrast may be even greater than these figures imply, because he counts intertitles as separate shots, so a single take with two dialogue intertitles inserted will be counted as five shots. European films often hold a scene in this way, shooting it from a single set-up and then inserting intertitles *ad libitum*; American films, on the contrary, tend to use a characteristic 'dialogue' micro-sequence, with two shots of the character speaking the lines (usually the two ends of a single 'take', i.e. one and the same moving photograph) bracketing an inserted title, and to alternate such micro-sequences with equivalents for each conversational partner.

54. In this book, we refer to films by the title used at first release in the country of production. At the first mention of a non-English title, we give a translation in brackets. This is a translation of the original title, not necessarily (or even usually) the original English or American release title.

55. Ben Brewster, 'La Mise en scène en profondeur dans les films français de 1900 à 1914', in Pierre Guibbert (ed.), *Les Premiers ans du cinéma français* (Perpignan: Institut Jean Vigo, 1985), 209–11 (in English in Thomas Elsaesser and Adam Barker (eds.), *Early Cinema: Space, Frame, Narrative* (London: British Film Institute, 1990), 49–52).

WITHIN the nineteenth-century traditions of staging and painting with which we are concerned, pictorial effects were understood to underscore narratively significant elements. Conversely, the interest in creating pictorial effects had ramifications for narrative form. Indeed one can find examples, such as the 1839 Newgate novel *Jack Sheppard*, discussed by Martin Meisel, in which the pictures became so important that George Cruikshank the illustrator could claim creative priority over the writer William Ainsworth.[1] More generally, we would like to consider how the models of narrative employed by nineteenth and early twentieth-century critics and practitioners opened the way to an integration of pictorial effects.

It should be noted that this way of formulating questions about pictorial effect runs counter to present-day conceptions, which tend to oppose narrative and spectacle or at least to see them as distinct registers of the text. For example, Tom Gunning's distinction between the cinema of attractions and a later cinema of narrative integration opposes two modes of address, as already noted. The first is a mode which directly solicits the spectator's engagement with a visual display, which he calls 'theatrical', although it is exemplified by the realistic illusion of motion offered in the first *actualités* as well as the magical illusion offered by the trick film.[2] In the later narrative fiction film another mode of address predominates, one which subordinates theatrical display in the interests of narrative absorption, and makes overt visual display take second place to the linear chain of cause and effect motivated by psychologically coherent and compelling characters. Gunning conceives of cinema after the early period as a dialectic between these two modes of address. Moments of display—a slapstick gag or a bit of spectacular staging such as the chariot race in *Ben-Hur* (1925)—are embedded within a narrative like plums in a pudding, remaining discrete entities due to their distinctive way of engaging the spectator's attention.

The term 'cinema of attractions' seems to us compelling in relation to film before 1907, particularly in so far as it captures the commonality of the actualities of the Lumières and the trick films of Méliès. But to counterpose it to narrative does not take account of the way that the idea of the stage picture functioned within the nineteenth-century theatrical tradition, which we will argue conceived of narrative as a series of pictorially representable moments, nor with the way this tradition was taken up and transformed in the feature film of the 1910s.

Kristin Thompson has proposed another way of understanding the development of various uses of *mise-en-scène* as well as cinematic devices in the films of the 1910s.[3] She argues that prior to about 1912–13, stylistic devices were introduced in order to ensure narrative clarity, for example the cut-in to reveal a vital detail of a scene, or eye-line matches to specify the direction of a character's glance. By the early 1910s, filmmakers had mastered devices for telling stories clearly, and began to experiment with the use of devices for their expressive qualities as opposed to what was strictly necessary for the comprehension of a story. For example, she argues that in two films of 1913, Paul von Woringen's *Die Landstrasse* (The Highroad) and Victor Sjöström's *Ingeborg Holm*, filmmakers withhold explicit depictions of emotion for expressive purposes. In *Die Landstrasse*, an escaped convict commits a murder, but a passing tramp is arrested and falsely convicted. As the trial scene ends and the courtroom empties, the convict speaks with the defendant's lawyer, his back remaining to camera. Similarly, the painful separation of the eponymous Ingeborg Holm from her young son is staged in a single take without cut-ins and with the actress's back to the camera for much of the scene. The boy is having trouble tearing himself away from her, and Ingeborg ducks inside a doorway when he is not looking to make him think she has gone, waits until he has exited, and then emerges from the doorway and faints. The withholding of a central character's facial expression is not essential for the conveyance of narrative information, indeed it might be thought to interfere with clear exposition, but Thompson argues that this kind of staging functions expressively, to create suspense in the first case, and, in the second, to increase the sense of Ingeborg's anguish.

We agree with Thompson that there are decisive changes in film style and structure around the years 1912–13. But her explanation of this periodization assumes much too rigid a distinction between the textual elements which convey information about narrative action and those elements which do something more or other than simply describe what happens. While the pair narrative clarity/expressivity

may not be the precise equivalent of denotation/connotation as used by Roland Barthes, his argument about the latter applies to the former as well, namely, denotation or the straightforward conveyance of information does not operate apart from, or prior to, connotation or expressivity.[4] One understands the denoted action of a scene, Ingeborg Holm ducking inside a doorway for example, through and because of its connotations, our typologies of maternal love and grief. And, in denoting certain events, even the earliest film narratives mobilize connotations in this way—indeed, given the early weakness of devices to convey spatio-temporal information, they had to rely even more on connotations to tell their stories. For example, *The Kleptomaniac* (Porter for Edison, 1905) has two separate lines of action, one centred on a rich woman, the other on a poor one, both of whom are arrested for shoplifting. But the use of a simple scene-by-scene construction with each story told separately means that there is not, until the final two scenes, any clear account of the spatio-temporal relations between these stories. Nevertheless, the film is perfectly clear, because the parallelism can be correlated with a familiar moral schema, which is confirmed by the final emblematic shot of a statue of justice, its blindfold awry and its scales unbalanced by money. The clear connotation sustains an unclear denotation, rather than the connotative structure being added to a clear denotation.

Moreover, it is not simply that new stylistic options for telling stories evolved in the period 1912–13. There was a change in the kinds of stories that could be told. Developments in staging and acting style as well as other aspects of film technique constituted part of a development of longer, more complex plots which was attendant upon the transition to features. Thus, it is necessary to examine the ways in which filmmakers handled stories in this period if one is to understand new uses of *mise-en-scène*. It is in this context that the techniques of play construction developed in the nineteenth-century theatre become particularly important for film.

For nineteenth-century writers on the theatre in England and America, the Crummles' troupe of actors in Charles Dickens's *Nicholas Nickleby* became a byword for a particular kind of dramaturgy:

The plot was most interesting. It belonged to no particular

age, people, or country, and was perhaps the more delightful on that account, as nobody's previous information could afford the remotest glimmering of what would ever come of it. An outlaw had been very successful in doing something somewhere, and came home in triumph, to the sound of shouts and fiddles, to greet his wife—a lady of masculine mind, who talked a good deal about her father's bones, which it seemed were unburied, though whether from a peculiar taste on the part of the old gentleman himself, or the reprehensible neglect of his relations, did not appear. This outlaw's wife was somehow or other mixed up with a patriarch, living in a castle a long way off, and this patriarch was the father of several of the characters, but he didn't exactly know which, and was uncertain whether he had brought up the right ones in his castle, or the wrong ones, but rather inclined to the latter opinion, and being uneasy, relieved his mind with a banquet, during which solemnity somebody in a cloak said 'Beware!' which somebody was known by nobody (except the audience) to be the outlaw himself, who had come there for reasons unexplained, but possibly with an eye to the spoons. . . . At last it came out that the patriarch was the man who had treated the bones of the outlaw's father-in-law with so much disrespect, for which cause and reason the outlaw's wife repaired to his castle to kill him, and so got into a dark room, where, after a great deal of groping in the dark, everybody got hold of everybody else, and took them for somebody besides, which occasioned a vast quantity of confusion, with some pistolling, loss of life, and torchlight; after which the patriarch came forward, and observing, with a knowing look, that he knew all about his children now, and would tell them when they got inside, said that there could not be a more appropriate occasion for marrying the young people, with the full consent of the indefatigable page, who (being the only other person surviving) pointed with his cap into the clouds, and his right hand to the ground; thereby invoking a blessing and giving the cue for the curtain to come down, which it did, amidst general applause.[5]

Considered with respect to the canons of classical narrative, the stage melodrama so described appears deficient or risible due to an overabundance of 'action', that is, an overly complex plot in which an accumulation of reversals and recognitions strains the limits of credibility, even comprehension. In the play put on by the Crummles troupe this complexity is partly the result of multiple lines of action whose interconnections only gradually become apparent. Thus, the connection between the outlaw's wife and the patriarch—his failure to bury her father's bones—is not immediately revealed, nor is the nature of

the outlaw's own crimes. The plot summarized in *Nicholas Nickleby* is also complicated by a large number of misrecognitions—the misplaced children of the patriarch, the patriarch's own occulted identity as persecutor of the dead father, the outlaw in disguise at the banquet, and the final darkness in which 'everybody got hold of everybody else and took them for somebody besides'. Although this is not emphasized in Dickens's parody, the melodramatic plot has also been characterized by frequent and startling reversals. The nineteenth-century drama critic William Archer makes this point in the context of an essay on Victor Hugo's plays. 'In which of these plays, again, are there any scenes of magniloquence and magnificence comparable with the third and fourth acts of "Hernani"? In which is the action so crisp, so rapid, so irresistible? It passes from suspense to surprise, from surprise to suspense, without an instant's pause. The tables are always being turned upon some one; and is not that the central secret of melodrama?'[6] To take a less contentious example than Hugo, in the conclusion to Pixérécourt's *Le Fanal de Messine* (1812), the villain Aymar arranges the wreck of the boat of the heroine, Phrosine. As she clings to a rock, he gives the signal for one of his soldiers to push her into the sea. The hero, Mélidore, betrays himself by his cries; he is captured, disarmed, and tied to a column. But then, Phrosine reappears to beg for his life, having been rescued by Mélidore's servant, Fidelio. The two lovers are about to be killed when the sailors of the fleet arrive, having been alerted by Fidelio, and effect their rescue.[7] Fidelio thus engineers two reversals off-stage in the course of but three scenes.

The kind of plot frequently stigmatized as 'melodramatic', then, is not simply one involving violence or spectacular incidents, but one with a characteristic structure, with the multiple recognitions and abrupt reversals which have been discussed (and frequently deplored) by dramatists and drama critics since the nineteenth century. This conception of the melodramatic plot survives well into the twentieth century, as in a 1919 photoplay-writing manual: 'Melodrama is of a less exacting quality of plot than the true drama. In its best aspects it is no less plausible than the drama, yet in movement and in vigor of action it strikes a much swifter pace.'[8]

Implicit in this usage is a negative definition of the

melodramatic plot. That is, it is understood as a failure to motivate a complex series of reversals and recognitions properly, hence, as a grotesque or inept variant of the classical model of tragic narrative. However, the melodramatic plot has also been conceived in terms which do not call so directly on the categories of Aristotle's *Poetics*. A model of plot as a series of discrete moments called 'situations' was quite prevalent in nineteenth-century dramaturgy and it survives, although in a modified form, until well into the twentieth. In present-day usage, 'situation' usually refers to a narrative premiss, as in this *New York Times* review of *Love Potion No. 9* : 'The situation is this: Paul (Tate Donovan), a shy biochemist, and Diane (Sandra Bullock), an animal psychologist who is also shy, find themselves in possession of a love potion that works on chimpanzees.'[9] The designation 'situation comedy' also employs the term in this sense. Although there are earlier examples of this usage, in the nineteenth century the term was usually used to refer to parts of a story rather than the premiss of the narrative as a whole. The *Oxford English Dictionary* defines it as 'a particular conjunction of circumstances (esp. one of a striking or exciting nature) under which the characters are presented in the course of a novel or play', citing the earliest usage in 1779 in Sheridan's *The Critic*, an example worth quoting at length. The playwright Puff demonstrates a scene from his latest work to the critic Sneer, in which two girls, rivals for the affections of Don Whiskerandos, both confront him at dagger point. Their respective uncles enter the scene:

PUFF. Now, gentlemen, this scene goes entirely for what we call SITUATION and STAGE EFFECT, by which the greatest applause may be obtained, without the assistance of language, sentiment or character: pray mark! . . .

(*The two Uncles at the instant with their two swords drawn, catch their two nieces' arms, and turn the points of their swords to* WHISKERANDOS, *who immediately draws two daggers, and holds them to the two nieces' bosoms.*)

PUFF. There's situation for you!—there's an heroic group!—You see the ladies can't stab Whiskerandos—he durst not strike them for fear of their uncles—the uncles durst not kill him, because of their nieces—I have them all at a dead lock!—for every one of them is afraid to let go first.

SNEER. Why, then they must stand there for ever.

PUFF. So they would, if I hadn't a very fine contrivance for't—Now mind—

(*Enter* BEEFEATER *with his Halberd.*)

BEEFEATER. In the Queen's name I charge you all to drop
Your swords and daggers!

(*They drop their swords and daggers.*)

SNEER. That is a contrivance indeed.

PUFF. Aye—in the Queen's name.[10]

The situation in Puff's play takes the form of a tableau, and as Martin Meisel has persuasively demonstrated, situations were frequently marked by such pictorial effects, to the extent that, at least during the early nineteenth century, situation and effect were used interchangeably to refer to stage pictures.[11] This point is underscored by a modern source: *An International Dictionary of Theatre Language* (1985) defines situation not only as 'the state of events in a play' but also, in British usage, 'the position of the performers on the stage at any particular moment'.[12] But apparently this equation of situation and picture was not limited to Britain, as the *Grand Larousse de la langue française* gives the following definition of 'personnage en situation': 'characters placed in the scene in a manner to produce an effect on the spectators.'[13] And the Littré *Dictionnaire de la langue française* (1875) illustrates its definition of the term with a citation of Louis de Cahusac: 'Every truly theatrical situation is nothing but a living picture (*tableau vivant*).'[14]

In fact, for eighteenth-century commentators, with the characteristic exception of Diderot, the terms '*tableau*' or 'picture' and '*coup de théâtre*' (the English equivalent of which seems to have been Puff's 'stage effect') form an associated group with the term 'situation'. Each writer distinguishes between these terms, but uses them in such a way that what is a situation for one will be a picture for another, and so on. Voltaire sees the defining characteristic of a stage picture as the fact that it is an effective part of the drama which is conveyed visually, not by words.[15] Similarly, François Riccoboni, discussing 'le jeu pantomime,' notes that because it cannot make recourse to language, pantomime is not effectual for the purposes of exposition, or detailing a character's thoughts; it can only show situations and thus express sentiments.[16] On the other hand, Joseph de la Porte and Sébastien-Roch-Nicholas Chamfort, in their *Dictionnaire dramatique* of 1776, define *tableau* as a descriptive speech—the kind of speech needed especially for *récits*, narrations by characters of crucial events which, for reasons of practicability or decorum, take place off-stage: 'Tableaux are particularly necessary in *récits*: as the action described cannot take place before the spectator's eyes, it must at least be painted to his mind with images so striking that they make the same impression on him as if he saw them with his bodily eyes.'[17] For them, as for Voltaire and Riccoboni, it is 'situation' which characterizes significant moments of drama which are not conveyed in characters' speeches, because the character does not know that there is a situation, or else because the situation so tears the character that he or she is left speechless or speech is superfluous to the spectator's appreciation of the position. Situations are distinguished from *coups de théâtre* because the latter are transitory surprises and relatively superficial (in anachronistic language, a matter of *syuzhet* rather than of *fabula*), whereas situations are lasting and 'much more closely bound up with the action'.[18] Puff does not use 'picture'—he refers to what would certainly be a stage picture to a nineteenth-century dramatist by the sculptural metaphor 'an heroic group'—but he vaunts the same moment of the play as 'what we call SITUATION and STAGE EFFECT, by which the greatest applause may be obtained, without the assistance of language'. Thus, when one of these terms appears explicitly in an eighteenth- or nineteenth-century source, one can generally assume that the others are implicit in the context.

Our concern here is to demonstrate the extent to which playwriting technique, and later script construction for films, made use of a conception of plot as a series of situations. In this context, 'situation' should not be assimilated to either narrative and spectacle as these concepts are currently invoked. Rather, the term crosses this divide. Situations were conceived of as static states of affairs, an atemporality which made them particularly amenable to pictorial representation. The way they mobilize the visual register can perhaps best be understood in comparison with the 'fruitful moments' defined by Lessing with respect to the visual arts and discussed in Chapter 1 above, moments that should be selected for representation because they anticipate or sum up a series of cause and effect relationships. In so far as film or theatre, unlike painting, depend upon a linear, temporal unfolding, the production of a stage picture that encapsulates a situation can require an interruption of narrative flow. None the less, the interruption only makes sense as part of what it interrupts. There may be a cessation of temporal continuity in the stage picture, but the system of cause and effect, and the diegetic world this system entails, does not 'fade', indeed, it is often made much more palpable.

It should be noted that despite its evident usefulness to playwrights and screenwriters, the situational model of plot construction has frequently been derided by critics, perhaps because it is potentially in conflict with the Aristotelian model, as will be discussed below. The example of *The Critic* suggests that the word was already current as part of a specialized technical vocabulary (parodied by Sheridan). This hypothesis seems to be confirmed by reviews of the play, referring to 'the trick of Stage Situation' or satire directed against 'stage-trick, situation and pantomime'.[19] Littré cites another use of the term, from Voltaire, which is also technical: 'It is almost always situation (*la situation*) which makes for success in the theatre.'[20] This usage can also be found in later English playwriting manuals. For example *How to Write a Good Play* (1892): 'A careful study of plays that have been successful in a marked degree, will show that each period has handed down to its successor many "situations" and incidents which, when skillfully developed by good acting, have been made acceptable;' and, in a manual of 1888: 'The would-be dramatist is urged to note "situations" which grip him; note how the playwright built up to the situation and what its "motive" was.'[21] Significantly, when the term is used by critics, it is frequently identified with hack work (indeed this is the whole thrust of Sheridan's parody). *The Oxford English Dictionary* cites two examples of this kind of usage, one explicitly referring to melodrama: 'It has some striking scenes, but I think the "situations" are produced by rather extravagant means'; and 'It [a book] is wildly melodramatic, and full of "situations" from beginning to end.'[22] Even one of the writing manuals evidences a similar distrust of the concept: 'The more literal phase of the Crummles system, writing up to certain "situations," scenes, and "effects," needs but the slightest allusion.'[23]

The dislike of situations arises from the sense that they are stereotyped or mechanical contrivances. But it is precisely their stereotypical nature that makes them useful as an aid in plot construction. Invention becomes a matter of combining pre-existing situations, of motivating them and, as Frank Archer notes, making them acceptable to contemporary audiences if they are likely to be found 'unacceptable', which may mean either 'morally repugnant' or 'overly familiar'. Both playwriting manuals, such as Archer's and, later, photoplay-writing manuals such as Palmer's *The Photoplay Plot Encyclopedia* and Wycliff A. Hill's *Ten Million Photoplay Plots*, provide extensive lists of situations.[24] In its most scholarly versions this way of thinking about plot construction gives rise to attempts to derive a narrative lexicon—a comprehensive list of the situations of which all known plots, and all the as yet unwritten plots, are comprised. The *locus classicus* for this view is a remark of Goethe's recorded in the *Conversations with Eckermann*: 'Gozzi believed that there were only thirty-six tragic situations; Schiller thought there must be more, but he was unable to find even so many as Gozzi.'[25] In 1895, writing what he hoped would be an impetus to the generation of more original plots, Georges Polti took Goethe at his word (but generalized from 'tragic' to 'dramatic') and tried to list the thirty-six dramatic situations, basing his study upon both classical and modern European works, as well as Indian and Chinese narratives.[26] Each situation is described with relevant examples and several variants, and takes the form of a condition specified in terms of the necessary agents or what he calls 'dynamic elements'. Thus, the first situation, Supplication, requires that the roles of Persecutor, Suppliant, and Power in Authority be distributed among one or more characters. Étienne Souriau's *Les Deux cent milles situations dramatiques* continues in this same tradition, although he obviously calculates the number of situations in the narrative lexicon somewhat differently than does Polti.[27]

While the attempt to catalogue all possible situations gives rise to some dubious categorical distinctions (as, for example, Polti's distinction between situation thirteen, enmity of kinsmen, and situation fourteen, rivalry of kinsmen),[28] much of this work is animated by a strong sense of what constitutes the structure, as opposed to the content, of a situation. Polti describes situations as the states which precede and follow a reversal:

Aristotle has taught us to distinguish between 'simple'

tragedy (in which the superiority remains upon the same side until the end, and in which, consequently, there is no sudden change of fortune, no surprise) and 'complex' tragedy (the tragedy of surprise, of vicissitude), wherein this superiority passes from one camp to the other. . . . What is any keen surprise if not the passing from a state of calm into a Dramatic Situation, or from one Situation into another, or again into a state of calm?[29]

Situations thus exist on the cusp of actions; they give rise to actions and are in turn altered by them. The photoplay-writing manuals make similar definitions of the situation as that which precedes or delays action. Wycliffe A. Hill explains: 'By suspense we mean the sustaining of a dramatic situation. Every climax in the story must be preceded by an element of suspense or uncertainty as to what the outcome of the situation will be, and the spectator must be "kept guessing" what the final result of the series of dramatic situations that he is witnessing will be.'[30] Palmer defines situation as 'when the characters are so brought together that their contrasts and conflicts are clear and dramatic, that the central character is placed in a dilemma in which he must make a choice, or in a predicament in which a change will be suffered, or is confronted with an obstacle to overcome.'[31]

Souriau gives what is perhaps the most carefully worked-out definition of the situation as an unstable constellation of forces precariously held in check but none the less liable to break out into action:

It is between these two [the initial situation and the denouement]—and to take us from the former to the latter—that the dramatic spring should be at work: most specifically in those moments of extreme tension when the microcosm, the group of essential characters, seem braced against each other as if held by lockjaw, constituting a kind of jam, a locking into place which would apparently bring everything to a halt, were there not precisely in the situation itself something that forces it to rebound: which obliges one or other character to act, to break the architecture in order for another one to arise later.[32]

Souriau argues that in the best plots the reasons for the modification of the situation arise logically from the forces in conflict and notes with scorn that some dramatists break up seemingly insoluble situations by an arbitrary intervention, without any preparation or internal motivation: 'Thus, the heroine is arbitrarily made to fall ill, or the inconvenient husband to die, or the dangerous lover to be called away.'[33] One is reminded of *The Critic*, in which Puff resolves the narrative impasse with the device of the guard who orders everyone to drop their weapons in the Queen's name.

The body of writing on the situation thus encompasses a variety of definitions of the term—as a deadlock, a temporary suspension of the action, a point of equilibrium among the forces that propel the narrative. Common to all of these is a sense that the linear progress of the narrative is arrested or blocked. Of course, most narratives employ devices for delaying the final resolution, and pose obstacles that the protagonist must overcome. But an obstacle is precisely understood in relation to the hero's goals and narrative trajectory and is therefore clearly bound to the sequential logic of the plot. To think of a story in terms of situations, as opposed to a series of obstacles, grants a certain autonomy to each discrete state of affairs. Situations can be thought of independently of the particular plots and characters which motivate them, as the lists of situations in plot encyclopedias attest. A weakening or even disregard of narrative continuity and logic is thus implicit in the concept.

The conception of plot as a series of situations would seem to invite the kind of criticism that Aristotle makes of the episodic plot, which he defines as a 'plot in which the episodes do not follow each other probably or inevitably', and condemns with the comment that 'Bad poets write such plays because they cannot help it, and good poets write them to please the actors.'[34] None the less, modern critics and practitioners have been at pains to reconcile an analysis of plot in terms of situation with the norms of narrative continuity and logic. Often the student of dramatic writing is advised, in the words of the Palmer encyclopedia, that situations are merely the 'backbone' of the drama but not its 'flesh and blood'. Close attention to the motivation and resolution of situations is frequently recommended. In a formulation that will be echoed by many subsequent critics, Dumas *fils* writes: 'But a situation is not an idea. An idea has a beginning, a middle and an end, an exposition, a development and a conclusion. Anyone can invent a dramatic situation, but it has to be prepared, made acceptable, made possible, above all it must be re-solved (*dénoué*).'[35] And, from Alfred Hennequin's *The Art of Playwriting*:

Do not use a striking situation as a climax just because it has elements of strength. A 'strong' situation is a fine thing; and, once found or imagined, it should be placed where it can be laid hold of at a moment's notice. But, as part of an actual play, it will be worse than wasted unless it is the natural outcome of all the action that has preceded. The grand climax must not be tacked on at the end of a row of incidents; it must appear to grow out of them as naturally and inevitably as a flower from its bud.[36]

The *Photoplay Plot Encyclopedia* stresses the importance of being able to combine situations in appropriate ways:

If a writer starts a play effectively, but then allows it to become dull and lifeless and undramatic (as many beginners do), it indicates that he has been unable to combine situations. The most practical use of a work of reference of this kind becomes apparent in such a case. Having begun a story on a plane of dramatic interest, let us say that the writer is unable to find a situation which will logically follow the first, that he is 'stumped' for further plot developments. By referring to the classified situations he will find all of the possible developments from that beginning, and will be able to make an intelligent and dramatic choice.[37]

One of the clearest attempts to graft the situational model of plot on to one more classically conceived may be found in the attempts in several handbooks to graph or chart a narrative. They divide plot into a beginning, middle, and end, structured around a crisis or climax which culminates at the close of the middle section. Graphically, this takes the form of a pyramid or rising curve which peaks at the climax and falls off rapidly thereafter.[38] However, both Hennequin's *Art of Playwriting* and the *Palmer Handbook of Scenario Construction* go on to subdivide the rising line or curve into a series of smaller peaks, each of which is conceived as a distinct situation (Figure 1.1).[39] Hennequin writes: 'If the story grows continually in interest, the introduction of the various characters, with their conflicting aims, will lead to a series of situations and climaxes, which themselves will be arranged in a climax.'[40] Although such graphs do unite the two ways of thinking about plot, it should be clear that if the individual peaks representing situations become too 'strong', or 'high', then they risk obliterating the shape of the rising curve representing the plot as a whole. Indeed, Hennequin notes:

The rage for strong situations, so prevalent at the present day, has led to the construction of plays in which there are two or more grand climaxes of apparently equal importance. Indeed, in not a few of our most successful plays, the growth and fall take up but a brief portion at the beginning and end; all the remainder consisting of a series of grand climaxes following one another as rapidly as the writer can manage to bring them about. Plays thus constructed must be regarded as inartistic, though here, as everywhere, success must inspire a certain degree of respect. It is this class of plays that appeals most strongly to the uncultured. The 'gallery' does not know very much about art, but it can tell a strong situation as unerringly as can the parquet. A good play, from the standpoint of the gallery, is one made up of a succession of knock-down effects; and so long as the gallery exists as a paying institution, so long will such plays be in demand.[41]

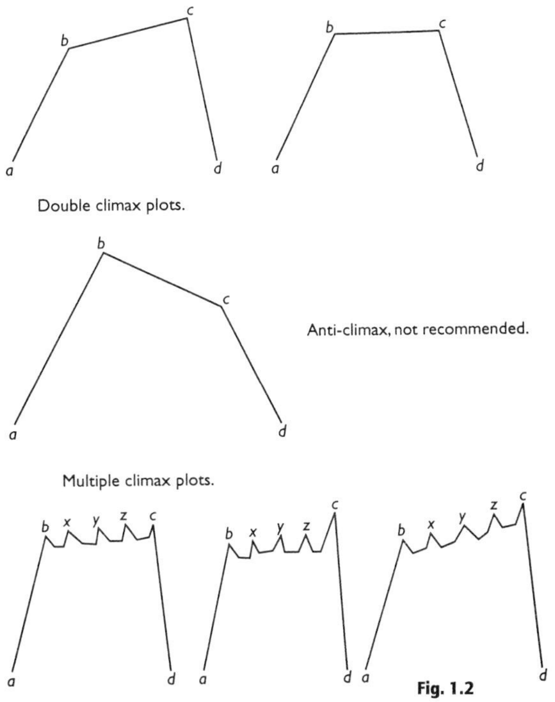

Being a practical man, Hennequin goes on to provide a series of models for the dramatist who wishes to construct multiple-climax plots, warning only against the anticlimax, in which the final situation is less powerful than those which have preceded it (Figure 1.2). The shape of these graphs indicates how the emphasis on each distinct state of affairs can ultimately break up the rising line of the plot, the emotional and logical continuity of the linear chain of cause and effect.

One of the frequent objections to popular, spectacular theatre was that it introduced powerful situations in arbitrary or mechanical ways simply to create 'effects', a term which was used to refer variously to moments of emotional intensity, of suspense, and of spectacular display. For critics such as William

Double climax plots.

Anti-climax, not recommended.

Multiple climax plots.

Fig. 1.2

Archer, and later Souriau, the problem was the sacrifice of narrative logic to the creation of such thrilling situations, or their resolution. For example, in the context of a discussion of the proper uses of coincidence in play construction, Archer writes:

Madame X. has had a child, of whom she has lost sight for more than twenty years, during which she has lived abroad. She returns to France, and immediately on landing at Bordeaux she kills a man who accompanies her. The court assigns her defence to a young advocate, and this young advocate happens to be her son. We have here a piling of chance upon chance, in which the long arm of coincidence is very apparent. The coincidence would have been less startling had she returned to the place where she left her son and where she believed him to be. But no! she left him in Paris, and it is only by a series of pure chances that he happens to be in Bordeaux, where she happens to land, and happens to shoot a man. For the sake of a certain order of emotional effect, a certain order of audience is willing to accept this piling up of chances; but it relegates the play to a low and childish plane of art.[42]

And, in another context, Archer stigmatizes as melodramatic plays which allowed what he considered much too wide a latitude in the motivation of situations.

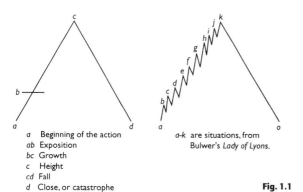

a   Beginning of the action
ab Exposition
bc Growth
c   Height
cd Fall
d   Close, or catastrophe

a–k are situations, from Bulwer's *Lady of Lyons*.

Fig. 1.1

Melodrama is illogical and sometimes irrational tragedy. It subordinates character to situation, consistency to impressiveness. It aims at startling, not at convincing, and is little concerned with causes so long as it attains effects. Developments of character are beyond its province, its personages being all ready-made, and subject at most to revolutions of feeling. Necessity and law it replaces by coincidence and fatality, exactitude by exaggeration, subtlety by emphasis.[43]

A similar attitude toward the melodramatic plot is evident in the passage in the photoplay manual already cited which defines melodrama as 'of a less exacting quality of plot than the true drama'. And, from a 1907 essay 'The Melodrama': 'To attempt to give an account of the plot would be useless. The more you examine it, the less there is. There is an abundance, an inordinate abundance, of situation; but there lies the distinction. The play is made up of a succession of exciting scenes, punctuated by comic episodes; but when you try to work out interrelations you are doomed to failure.... To feel the real spell of the play, you must slough off sophistication and let logic go, allowing yourself to be concerned exclusively in the situation of the moment.'[44]

The nature of melodramatic implausibility remains difficult to specify, however, in so far as an audience's sense of what is realistic or convincing is itself historically and generically bound.[45] Thus, Archer may find melodrama implausible because he disapproves of the genre, whereas its traditional audience, spectators whose expectations were formed by the genre, might well find it more convincing. But it does seem clear that, in relation to the ideals of plausibility and verisimilitude adopted by the critics of the respectable theatre, melodrama is 'less exacting'; that is, it frequently has recourse to external or arbitrary incidents as a means of creating and resolving situations. Providential recognitions, of the sort that Dickens mocks in the Crummles troupe's play from *Nicholas Nickleby*, are one such means of resolving situations. This is a device which Dickens himself employs at the end of this very novel, when the wicked patriarch Ralph Nickleby is driven to suicide by the discovery that the runaway boy Smike, whom he has hounded to death as a means of getting revenge on his nephew Nicholas, is in fact his own son.

It might be argued that the incidents which bring about a happy resolution at the end of plays are im-plicitly motivated by a notion of divine order or what Peter Brooks calls the moral occult.[46] But melodrama makes use of coincidence to set up situations as well as to resolve them, and these are not motivated as providential occurrences (unless one assumes a particularly malign deity). As James Smith notes: 'Each situation is more or less self-contained, and the dramatist sweeps us from one thrill to the next without bothering to explain the logical links between them. Often there are none, for when the persecution of innocence is at stake the conventions of melodrama allow plausibility and common sense to be violated with impunity. . . . To postpone a happy meeting, separated sisters suffer untimely fainting fits or sudden arrest, and both parents of *The Foundling of the Forest* regularly relapse into insensibility, delirium or stark madness whenever the plot threatens a premature family reunion.'[47] The example of *Les Deux Orphelines* to which Smith alludes is worth a closer examination as it provides a strikingly complex instance of a situation created by the multiplication of coincidences, both fortunate and unfortunate. The orphaned Henriette refuses to marry the hero, Roger de Vaudrey, because his guardians, the Count and Countess de Linières, object to their union. In ignorance of Henriette's refusal, Madame de Linières comes in disguise to Henriette's apartment to investigate her and, pleased with the girl, reveals her true identity and asks about Henriette's past. Henriette tells the story of her adopted sister Louise, from whom she has been separated (unbeknownst to Henriette, the blind Louise has been kidnapped and is forced by her captors to beg in the streets). Henriette describes a token found on the baby Louise which Madame de Linières recognizes as identifying the illegitimate daughter taken from her years before. As they talk, singing is heard in the street below, and Henriette recognizes Louise's voice. Just as she is about to rush outside, the police knock at the door and prevent Henriette from leaving. As Louise's voice fades into the distance, the Count de Linières has Henriette arrested on a false charge to prevent her marrying his ward. The tortuousness of the description necessary to explain this single scene is indicative of the complexity of the plotting. Three lines of action—Henriette's search for Louise, Madame de Linières's recognition of her daughter, and the obstacle which the Linières pose to the marriage of Roger and Henriette—are woven together through coincidence to form a single situation.

Thus, *pace* Archer[48] who claims that melodramas are badly plotted, the concatenation of arbitrary circumstances which create the situation just described in *Les Deux Orphelines* is quite skilfully contrived. But, in general, melodrama provides little or no motivation of the coincidences which create interesting or powerful impasses, apart from Agathon's justification, cited by Aristotle, that 'it is likely that many quite unlikely things should happen'.[49]

It is not only the wide latitude in the motivation and resolution of situations that makes stage melodrama the (negative) exemplar of situational dramaturgy, but also, famously, its reliance on strong or emphatic situations accompanied by highly spectacular staging. While tableaux are the most common (and the cheapest to stage), other forms of spectacular staging could also be brought to bear, usually at moments of suspenseful impasse, such as the approaching train which threatens Snorkey tied by the villain to the railroad tracks in *Under the Gaslight* (Augustin Daly, 1867) or, in *Uncle Tom's Cabin* (George Aiken, 1853), the raging snow storm that initially prevents Eliza and little Harry, pursued by slave-catchers, from crossing the Ohio river to safety. The 1850s are usually given as the period when this kind of staging escalates, at least in England and America, when the final act of melodramas come to be organized around a sensation scene, as in the burning building in Boucicault's *The Poor of New York* (1857), or the sea-cave with rising tide which threatens the life of the heroine in the penultimate act of his *The Colleen Bawn* (1860). In 1862, referring to this latter sensation scene in the opera by Julius Benedict from Boucicault's play, a music journal quotes the *London Athenaeum*'s rather huffy view of the libretto: 'The tale seems to us fitter for a play with ballads or songs, than for a work which is to be entirely conducted in music. The great situation is hardly to be treated, save in the most melo-dramatic form by carpentry and gymnastic work.'[50] Despite critical disapproval, however, by the last third of the century melodramas frequently included more than one sensation scene per play, giving rise to the multiple-climax structure to which Hennequin refers.[51] The Drury Lane autumn drama is the epitomy of this type of theatre. For example, Michael Booth describes the Augustus Harris

and Henry Pettitt spectacle *Pluck* (1882) as having 'wearied critics with seven long acts and interminable waits, despite a scene with two train wrecks, a snowstorm in Piccadilly Circus, a mob breaking real glass bank windows, and a burning building'.[52]

Writing in 1870, Percy Fitzgerald complained about the trend for sensation scenes: 'The taste of the town now requiring great scenic *tours de force*, and the theatres competing with each other in the attraction of objects from outside, which seemed to defy reproduction on the stage, it was necessary that the writer should, like Mr Crummles' dramatist, construct his piece in the interest of "the pump and washing-tubs", or kindred objects. Hence the panorama of fires, underground railways, music halls, steamboat piers, dry arches and such things.'[53] It should be noted that for Fitzgerald the problem is not that the spectacular sets somehow swamp or 'stop' the narrative, but rather that the play has been built around situations which themselves have been chosen to exploit some capacity of *mise-en-scène*. There is some evidence to support this account of the priority accorded to *mise-en-scène* in nineteenth-century play construction. David Mayer suggests that Henry Herman, credited with the story for Wilson Barrett's *Claudian* (1883), had devised machinery intended to simulate an earthquake prior to inventing this plot, and thus was provided with the play's climactic scene, and the end of the second act.[54] Clearly, the wide latitude allowed by melodrama in the motivation of situations helped to further this approach to play construction, so that it was relatively easy to work in a fire or train wreck or horse race, scenic elements which were the stock-in-trade of theatres like Drury Lane in this period. Similarly, stories could be chosen for adaptation, or old plays for revival, because they contained situations which gave scope for new developments in staging. For example, Stephen Holland suggests that one reason for the adaptation of *Uncle Tom's Cabin* that appeared at the Britannia Hoxton early in 1854 so soon after the publication of the novel in England lay in the development of techniques for staging the movement of ice floes on a river, and characters crushed or dragged under beneath them.[55] According to Holland, this technique was initially developed for a melodrama at the Ambigu-Comique in Paris which opened on 20 October 1853. The play was adapted in England with similar staging as *The Thirst of Gold, or*

The Lost Ship and the Wild Flower of Mexico (Ben Webster, Adelphi, 4 December 1853) and *A Struggle for Gold, or The Orphan of the Frozen Sea* (Edward Stirling, City of London Theatre, 23 January 1854 and Marylebone Theatre, 20 February 1854).[56] Percy Fitzgerald describes the staging used in the British productions as a combination of white canvas to represent moving ice, and black bombazine to represent the murky waters, and Holland's evidence suggests that traps were also used to give the illusion of the villains being 'engulfed' by the ice.[57] In the 1854 Britannia production of *Uncle Tom's Cabin*, the action of the pursuit across the ice was rewritten to show slave-catchers sinking between ice floes, an effect which does not occur in the novel, nor in the American theatrical versions, but which was probably dictated by the staging borrowed from the Ambigu-Comique.[58] Thus, in this instance, possibilities for staging seem to have played a large role in determining the selection of the novel for adaptation, and the specific choices made about how to adapt the story for the stage.

We would emphasize that the kind of spectacular staging associated with melodrama in the latter half of the nineteenth century was not simply a function of violent or impressive spectacle, but of introducing such devices within a particular narrative context. This is not to deny that there were moments of pure spectacle with little narrative import; such moments occur quite frequently in the 'discovery' scenes in which a curtain or flat is raised to reveal a spectacular full stage set, often at the beginning of an act.[59] None the less, in their most important structural role, as climaxes and scene or act ends, stage pictures derived from situations. Most of the playwriting manuals strongly recommend ending acts on situations,[60] and these in turn were usually given in the form of a tableau. The strength of this convention is indicated by William Archer's complaint about it in 1913 in a discussion of what he regarded as old-fashioned act-endings:

Some modern playwrights have fled in a sort of panic from the old 'picture-poster situation' to the other extreme of always dropping their curtain when the audience least expects it. This is not a practice to be commended. . . . I am far from pleading for the conventional tableau at the end of each act, with all the characters petrified, as it were, in penny-plain-twopence-coloured attitudes. But it is certainly

desirable that the fall of the curtain should not take an audience entirely by surprise.[61]

Similarly, sensation scenes, although they are and were typically discussed solely in terms of their staging, did have a powerful narrative rationale and function, at least when a situational model of plot is taken into account. For example, the tenement fire in *The Poor of New York* produces one of the strongest situations in the play.[62] Act 4 ends with Badger fainting and thus unable to reveal to Paul Fairweather the location of the receipt which would prove that the villain Bloodgood stole a fortune from Paul's father some twenty years earlier. The fifth and final act opens with Bloodgood having bought the tenement in which the receipt is stashed, and Badger, living elsewhere and now acting on behalf of Paul and his family, eager to re-enter the building to retrieve it. The fire in the penultimate scene is set by Bloodgood to destroy the receipt which he could not find. Like the fainting of Badger at the end of Act 4, then, the fire delays the moment in which he is able definitively to weigh in against the villain on Paul's behalf. Indeed, the play holds this moment in suspense until the final wedding scene: Dan rescues Badger's body from the flames in the penultimate scene but it is not clear whether or not the receipt has been retrieved, or if Badger even lives. The sensation scene thus encompasses the climactic situation of the play, with the Fairweathers' last recourse at risk, and seemingly beyond reach due to the ferocity of the blaze. Not only is it visually the most powerful moment in the act but also the moment of the most compelling impasse.

William Archer eloquently articulates the modern reaction to this kind of structure when he recommends that in the serious drama which 'depicts social phenomenon or environment' there should be no marked crisis, and 'just enough story to afford a plausible excuse for raising and lowering the curtain'.[63] More generally, by the turn of the century, the situational dramaturgy which Archer sought to moderate was often identified with melodrama (and less problematically with farce) and opposed to what should be done on the legitimate stage. But it would be a mistake to regard this way of thinking about the relationship between story and picture as exclusively or even primarily limited to the 'low' theatrical genres. We agree with Michael Booth that in the late nineteenth century the taste for the spectacular and the picturesque cut across all social classes, and was as likely to be found at the Lyceum as the Standard.[64] Moreover, the evidence of the playwriting manuals and plot encyclopedias suggests that the notion of the situation was found useful as an aid in plot construction in many theatrical genres. Indeed, one can see why this would be the case, given that the situation was central to the way writers and most critics conceived of the dramatic climax, and the structure of scene and act ends. The concept played a crucial role not only in inventing stories designed for any medium, but also in establishing the rhythm and pacing of the theatrical plot in particular. As Hennequin notes, each act required a climax, and each climax a picture, and this became the way stories were built up for the theatre, scene by scene and act by act. This way of thinking about play structure was even enshrined in the playbills for nineteenth-century dramas, which listed the big scenes and tableaux, and in some theatre programmes even the time at which they would occur.

The 'politer' drama might make use of less sensational spectacular effects—Belasco's or Irving's celebrated 'aesthetic' lighting as opposed to train crashes and exploding volcanoes, for example—none the less, the way of organizing the plot and introducing pictorial elements was not fundamentally different.[65] Thus, the much-praised fourteen-minute lighting transformation which represents the coming of dawn in *Madame Butterfly* (Belasco, 1900) fits precisely Georges Polti's definition of a situation as a state of suspense which precedes a dramatic reversal. After a three-year hiatus, and having seen her lover Pinkerton's ship sail into the distant harbour, Cho-Cho San eagerly awaits the dawn and his return; with it, we await her discovery of his betrayal. This may not be melodrama of the Drury Lane sort: the situation depends more on a sense of character psychology; it is, by the standards of the legitimate stage, 'better' motivated and prepared. But, considered as a means of orchestrating a climax through a particular congruence of suspense and pictorial effect it surely bears comparison to the scene of Snorkey tied to the railroad tracks, or of Badger and Dan faced with the burning tenement.[66]

In his essay on the cinema of attractions, Tom Gunning cites a review of the 1925 film version of *Ben-Hur* which listed the following 'tableaux vivants': '8:35 The Star of Bethlehem/ 8:40 Jerusalem Restored/ 8:59 Fall of the House of Hur/ 10:29 The Last Supper/ 10:50 Reunion.'[67] We see this, not as a survival of the cinema of attractions within the context of the Hollywood feature film, but rather as the continuation of a theatrical tradition in which stories are divided into big scenes or situations themselves pictorially conceived, staged, and even advertised.[68] The example is perhaps too easy, given the powerful stage tradition at work in this case, and the even older iconographic tradition around representations of the Last Supper and other incidents from the Passion. But we would argue that this model of dramatic narrative was more generally operative in early narrative filmmaking, becoming especially important in the 1910s during the transition to features.

What survives from the popular nineteenth-century theatre in the 1910s feature is not simply a conception of plot as a series of situations (a mode and model of plot construction which it might be argued remains operative even in Hollywood today) but more importantly, a set of staging practices linked with situational dramaturgy. In classical Hollywood cinema editing works against the construction of a scene around powerful, epitomizing pictures; rather, the scene is broken down into a series of shots which interact with one another in complex ways to create a sense of space, of the pacing of the scene and of its significance. But, as has already been noted, editing was by no means accorded this prominence in the cinema of the 1910s. Within this context pictorial effects developed along the lines of theatrical models were important because they provided ways of underscoring the dramatic action and punctuating the scene's duration. While spectacular staging of the sort discussed by Vardac and others as 'proto-cinematic' is perhaps the most obvious place to look for connections of this sort between theatre and cinema, it seems appropriate to begin instead with an investigation of the tableau. As we have suggested, 'situation' and 'tableau' were used as equivalent terms for much of the nineteenth century; and, as a device, the tableau is the literal embodiment of the idea that situations should take the form of pictures.

1. Meisel, *Realizations*,. 247–51 and 265–71.
2. Tom Gunning, 'The Cinema of Attractions', in Elsaesser and Barker, *Early Cinema*, 59.
3. Kristin Thompson, 'The International Exploration of Cinematic Expressivity', in Karel Dibbets and Bert Hogenkamp (eds.), *Film in the First World War* (Amsterdam: Amsterdam University Press, 1995), 65–85.
4. Roland Barthes, *S/Z* (Paris: Éditions du Seuil, 1970), 13–16.
5. Charles Dickens, *Nicholas Nickleby* (London: Penguin, 1978), 378–9.
6. 'The Plays of Victor Hugo', in *About the Theatre: Essays and Studies* (London: Fisher Unwin, 1886), 308.
7. This touches on just a portion of the plot summary which may be found in its entirety in Willie G. Hartog, *Guilbert de Pixerécourt: Sa vie, son mélodrame, sa technique et son influence* (Paris: Honoré Champion, 1913), 156–61.
8. A. Van Buren Powell, *The Photoplay Synopsis* (Springfield, Mass.: The Home Correspondence School, 1919), 40.
9. *New York Times* (13 Nov. 1992), B9.
10. *The Critic* in *The Dramatic Works of Richard Brinsley Sheridan*, ed. Cecil Price (Oxford: Oxford University Press, 1973), ii. 543 ff.
11. Meisel, *Realizations*, esp. 38–51.
12. Joel Trapido (ed.), *An International Dictionary of Theatre Language* (Westport, Conn.: Greenwood Press, 1985), 794.
13. *Grand Larousse de la langue française*, ed. Louis Guilbert, René Lagane, and Georges Niobey (Paris: Librairie Larousse, 1971–8), vi. 5547.
14. Émile Littré, *Dictionnaire de la langue française* (Paris: Hachette, 1875), art. 'Situation, Terme de Littérature', citing Louis de Cahusac, *La Danse ancienne et moderne ou Traité historique de la danse* (The Hague [in fact Paris]: Jean Neaulme, 1754), iii. 150; repr. in *Épitre sur les dangers de la poésie suivie de La Danse ancienne et moderne ou Traité historique de la danse* (Geneva: Slatkine Reprints, 1971), 174.
15. Voltaire, *Appel à toutes les nations*, 219–20; cit. Holmström, *Monodrama*, 22.
16. François Riccoboni, *L'Art du théâtre, suivi d'une lettre de M. Riccoboni fils à M*** au sujet de l'art du théâtre* (Paris: Simon et Giffart, 1750; repr. Geneva: Slatkine Reprints, 1971), 83.
17. *Dictionnaire dramatique* (Paris: Lacombe, 1776), i. 314. Dene Barnett points out in *The Art of Gesture: The Practices and Principles of 18th Century Acting* (Heidelberg: Carl Winter, 1987), 34: 'Both imitative and indicative gestures were used with vivid effect to depict, to bring before the eyes, indeed to recreate on stage the distant, past or imagined events—battles, warriors and dragons—which were the subjects of descriptive passages and narratives.' As his examples on pp. 215–20 indicate, the difference between a *récit* and a wordless picture was thus less than might be imagined.
18. *Dictionnaire dramatique*, iii. 152.
19. A review in *The Public Advertiser*, 1 Nov. 1779; 'Hah! to Mr Sheridan', *St James's Chronicle*, 11–13 Nov. 1779; both cited in *Dramatic Works of Sheridan*, ii. 478 and 481.
20. Littré, *Dictionnaire*, art. 'Situation', citing Voltaire, '[Remarques sur] *Ariane*, Tragédie [de Thomas Corneille]', in *Les Œuvres complètes de Voltaire/The Complete Works of Voltaire*, lv: *Commentaires sur Corneille*, critical edn. by David Williams, part III (Banbury: Voltaire Foundation, 1975), 988.
21. Frank Archer, *How to Write a Good Play* (London: Sampson Low, Marston & Co., 1892), 96; *Playwriting: A Handbook for Would-be Dramatic Authors by 'A Dramatist'* (London: Macrae, Curtice & Co., 1888), 12–13.
22. 'Situation', definition 9b: citing from 1830, W. Irving, *Life and Letters* (1864) ii. 446; and from 1864, G. A. Lawrence, *M. Dering* (i).
23. Archer, *How to write a Good Play*, 96.
24. Ibid.; Frederick Palmer, *Photoplay Plot Encyclopedia*, 2nd edn. (Los Angeles: Palmer Photoplay Corporation, 1922); Wycliffe A. Hill, *Ten Million Photoplay Plots* (Los Angeles: Feature Photodrama Company, 1919; repr. New York: Garland Publishing, 1978). All of these sources list both comic and tragic situations. To give just one example, Palmer's 'Twenty-eighth Situation—Obstacles to Love' is broken down into 'A (1)—Marriage Prevented by Inequality of Rank. (2)—Inequality of Fortune an Impediment to Marriage. B—Marriage Prevented by Enemies and Contingent Obstacles. C (1)—Marriage Forbidden on Account of the Young Woman's Previous Betrothal to Another. (2)—The Same Case, Complicated by an Imaginary Marriage of the Beloved Object. D (1)—A Free Union Impeded by the Opposition of Relatives. (2)—Family Affection Disturbed by the Parents-in-law. E—By the Incompatibility of Temper of the Lovers' (p. 43).
25. The conversation of 14 Feb. 1830, *Gespräche mit Eckermann*, Part 1, p. 394, in Johann Wolfgang Goethe, *Gedenkausgabe der Werke: Briefe und Gespräche*, ed. Ernst Beutler (Zurich: Artemis Verlag, 1949). Eckermann in fact borrowed the record of this conversation from Frédéric-Jacob Soret, *Conversations avec Goethe*. See *Goethes Gespräche*, vol. iii, part 2 (Zurich/Stuttgart: Artemis Verlag, 1971), 565, fragment no. 6506. There is a record of a very similar remark of Goethe's in an earlier conversation of 25 Sept. 1823, recorded by Friedrich Kanzler von Müller (*Goethes Gespräche*, vol. iii, part 1, p. 584, fragment no. 5266): 'Gozzi claimed there were only thirty-six motifs (*Motive*) for a tragedy.' No commentator on these passages seems to offer any source for the Gozzi attribution, though the context makes it clear it was Carlo Gozzi Goethe was thinking of.
26. Georges Polti, *Les Trente-six situations dramatiques* (Paris: Mercure de France, 1895). Subsequent citations refer to *The Thirty-Six Dramatic Situations*, trans. Lucile Ray (Franklin, Oh.: James Knapp Reeve, 1924).
27. Étienne Souriau, *Les Deux cent mille situations dramatiques* (Paris: Flammarion, 1950).
28. Polti, *Thirty-Six Dramatic Situations*, 44 and 48.
29. Ibid. 121.
30. Hill, *Ten Million Photoplay Plots*, 75. The most common definition of the situation in the photoplay manuals is in terms of suspense. See also Henry Albert Phillips, *The Photodrama* (New York: Stanhope-Dodge Publishing Co., 1914; repr. New York: Arno Press, 1970), 161 and 167; Victor Oscar Freeburg, *The Art of Photoplay Making* (New York: Macmillan, 1918), 240; Jeanie MacPherson, *Preparation and Motivation*, one of a series of lectures especially prepared for student-members of the Palmer Course and Service (Hollywood: Palmer Photoplay Corporation, 1923), 8–9.
31. Palmer, *Photoplay Plot Encyclopedia*, 12.
32. Souriau, *Les Deux cent mille situations dramatiques*, 45.
33. Ibid. 46.
34. *Poetics*, 39.
35. Alexandre Dumas fils, *Histoire du supplice d'une femme: Réponse à M. Émile de Girardin* (Paris: Michel Lévy Frères, 1865), 5.
36. Alfred Hennequin, *The Art of Playwriting: Being a Practical Treatise on the Elements of Dramatic Construction Intended for the Playwright, the Student and the Dramatic Critic* (Boston:

Houghton, Mifflin & Co., 1897), 119. Although he does not draw the same conclusions about Hennequin's references to situations, Barry Salt (*Film Style and Technology*, 111–13) discusses his text in relation to the development of the early feature.

37. Palmer, *Photoplay Plot Encyclopedia*, 13.

38. For an early example of this representation of narrative as a pyramid, see Gustav Freytag, *Technique of the Drama: An Exposition of Dramatic Composition and Art*, trans. Elias J. MacEwan (Chicago: Scott, Foresman & Co., 1894), 115 (original German publication 1863).

39. Hennequin, *Art of Playwriting*, 99 and 116; *Palmer Handbook of Scenario Construction* (Hollywood: Palmer Photoplay Corporation, n.d. [1922?]), ii. 160–2.

40. Hennequin, *Art of Playwriting*, 116.

41. Ibid. 121.

42. William Archer, *Play-Making: A Manual of Craftsmanship* (London: Chapman & Hall, 1913), 219.

43. *About the Theatre*, 320.

44. Harry James Smith, 'The Melodrama', *Atlantic Monthly*, 99 (Mar. 1907), 324. We are indebted to Ben Singer for this reference.

45. See Gérard Genette, 'Vraisemblance et motivation', in *Figures II* (Paris: Éditions du Seuil, 1969), 71–99.

46. Peter Brooks, *The Melodramatic Imagination* (New Haven: Yale University Press, 1976).

47. James Smith, *Melodrama* (London: Methuen, 1973), 24.

48. This is not just Archer's view, of course. For another example see Souriau, *Les Deux cent mille situations dramatiques*, 43–6, esp. the remarks on *La Muette de Portici*, 43.

49. *Poetics*, 71.

50. 'Mr. Benedict's "Lily of Killarney" ', *Dwight's Journal of Music* (29 Mar. 1862), 413.

51. See also Booth, *Victorian Spectacular Theatre*, 63: 'Thus well before the middle of the century processions, lavish display, large numbers of actors (and horses), and catastrophe and conflict by land and sea were already features of spectacle melodrama. Improving technology, increased resources, and a stress in melodramatic writing on the spectacular event led to spectacle scenes becoming the pivot of much staging, the centre or—when sensations and spectacles occurred in each act—centres around which the play was constructed, scenic pegs on which to hang a connecting narrative.'

52. Ibid. 70.

53. Percy Fitzgerald, *Principles of Comedy and Dramatic Effect* (London: Tinsley Brothers, 1870), 23–4.

54. Mayer, *Playing out the Empire*, 30.

55. Robert Stephen Holland (ed.), 'Introduction to the play by Colin Hazlewood, *The Christian Slave; or, The Life and Death of Uncle Tom, A Drama in two Acts*, A parallel diplomatic text based on unpublished manuscripts in the Lord Chamberlain's Collection in the British Library (BL Add 52958X) and the Frank Pettingell Collection in the University of Kent at Canterbury Library', MA Thesis (University of Kent at Canterbury, 1983), p. viii.

56. Ibid., p. viii.

57. Percy Fitzgerald, *The World behind the Scenes* (London: Chatto and Windus, 1881; repr. New York: Benjamin Blom, 1972), 68.

58. Holland, 'Introduction to Hazlewood', p. ix.

59. Michael Booth, *Victorian Spectacular Theatre*, 65–6, cites a compelling example, the opening of the Prologue of Wilson Barrett's production of *Claudian* (W. G. Wills and Henry Herman, 1883) at the Princess's, London, where the curtain rose to display an impressive set of a slave market in Byzantium prior to the action of the play. On the pulling back of the curtain to 'discover' a scenic picture see Meisel, *Realizations*, 46–7, and Part 4, below.

60. *Playwriting: A Handbook for Would-be Dramatic Authors by 'A Dramatist'*, 18: 'Pay great attention to your curtain. In melodrama it should certainly be upon a situation of some sort'; Frank Archer, *How to write a Good Play*, 92, comments approvingly that Acts 1 and 4 of The Favourite of Fortune (Westland Marston, 1866) end on strong situations; Hennequin, *Art of Playwriting*, 177–8, recommends that the conclusion of an act should be a 'climax', noting further that 'Since the action of the play is to be interrupted, in order to hold the attention of the audience over the intervening period, the conclusion of the act must be so arranged as to leave the spectator in a state of strong suspense.'

61. William Archer, *Play-Making*, 250–1.

62. Dion Boucicault, 'The Poor of New York', in Daniel C. Gerould (ed.), *American Melodrama* (New York : Performing Arts Journal Publications, 1983), 31–74.

63. William Archer, *Play-Making*, 38.

64. Booth, *Victorian Spectacular Theatre*, 3.

65. Booth, ibid. 124, discusses the prestige accorded Irving's lighting effects; see also Lise-Lone Marker, *David Belasco*, 78–98.

66. Similarly, for an analysis of the importance of situation and pictorial effect in the more culturally ambitious plays of Henry Arthur Jones see Joel H. Kaplan, 'Henry Arthur Jones and the Lime-lit Imagination', *Nineteenth Century Theatre*, 15, no. 2 (Winter 1987), 115–41.

67. Gunning, in Elsaesser and Barker, *Early Cinema*, 61, citing Vardac, *Stage to Screen*, 232.

68. Advertising based upon the big situations and tableaux of a play is most pronounced in early and mid-nineteenth-century playbills. For example, a playbill advertising a benefit for Frank Towers, Royal Victoria Theatre, 15 Mar. 1860, in the Pettingell Collection of the University of Kent at Canterbury Library, lists among other items on the programme a two-act drama, *Red Rover, or the Mutiny of the Dolphin*, which is divided into the following big scenes: 'Ancient Harbour of Newport, with the Rover's Vessel Floating Out to Sea. | The Sea Shore. The Females prepare to embark on board the Pirate Ship. | Wilder's Heroic Conduct. | Broadside View on the Red Rover! | The Unsuspecting Females led into the Lion's Den. | Preparations for Sailing. | The Tailor turned Sailor. | TABLEAU. Fore & Aft Deck of the Rover's Vessel.' An American example can be found in a playbill for *Uncle Tom's Cabin*, Grand Opera House, New York City, 27 Oct. 1877, held in the Museum of the City of New York, in which the list of major sets and songs is accompanied by a running plot summary, with the biggest scenes set off by capital letters: 'Sold in Bondage. Mr. Shelby's Plantation. A Winter Night's rejoicing of the Slaves. SONG AND CHORUS, "Is Massa gwine to sell us today?" By the Jubilee Singers | Tavern on the banks of the Ohio. Eliza followed by the bloodhounds. A hundred dollars for a boat. View of the Ohio River. | ESCAPE OF ELIZA ON THE FLOATING ICE. | AND THE BAFFLED PURSUERS. THRILLING TABLEAU | Chant and Chorus, "The Gospel Train, or git on board, children," By the Jubilee Singers | St. Clair's House and Grounds on Lake Pontchartrain. | A CORRECT REPRESENTATION OF A SOUTHERN HOME! | SONGS BY MISS GEORGIE ALLEN. Miss Ophelia's first appearance in the South. Babies under foot—how shiftless. Topsy's History. De Chile dat never was born. | SONG AND BREAKDOWN, "I'SE SO WICKED." | Tavern by the River. The Kentuckian. "That's my mind on it." Meeting of George and Eliza. Rocky Pass.

The Pursuers. Escape of George and Eliza. "Friend, Thee's not wanted here." Thrilling Tableau. Sunset on the lake. Eva and Uncle Tom. "I see a Band of Spirits Bright." Eva's Bed-Chamber—Love, Joy Peace! | DEATH OF EVA. | Solemn and Impressive Tableau. Hymn, "The Sweet Bye and Bye." Song "Tell me where my Eva's Gone?"—By the Jubilee Singers. Topsy and the Stockings. "I isn't half so wicked as I used to was." St. Clair to Eva in Heaven. Topsy and Aunt Ophelia. The death of St. Clair. | SLAVE MARKET IN NEW ORLEANS. | The Beautiful Plantation Slave Melody, "Massa's in the Cold, Cold ground," by the Jubilee Singers. Uncle Tom sold to Legree. Courtship of Aunt Ophelia and the Deacon. Legree's house. The Mississippi River by Moonlight. Parlors of Aunt Ophelia Vermont. | GREAT PLANTATION SCENE. | By the Georgia Jubilee Singers. The Jubilee Singers in their Chants and Shouts of "Old Sheep know de Road—de young lambs must learn de way," "The Old Home aint what it used to be," and "Dat sweet ham bone." Plantation Festival Scene by Jubilee Singers, and the | WONDERFUL BANJO SOLOS by the great HORACE WESTON and WARREN GRIFFIN. | Arrival of the flat boat with Congo Melodists. Street in New Orleans. Young Shelby searching for Uncle Tom. A Lawyer's information never gratis. Legree's house. Cassy and Legree. The Lock of Hair. The workings of a Guilty Conscience. "Do you know that I have made up my mind to kill you?" The last blow. Retribution. The old shed. | DEATH OF UNCLE TOM. | "I've got the Victory, the Lord has given it to me, Glory be to His Name." "Nearer, my God to Thee."—Jubilee Singers. Magnificent Allegorical Tableau, "Eva in Heaven."'

Introduce as many tableaus as possible into your story. For instance, you might have thought out a scene wherein a guilty wife, listening through a keyhole, overhears another woman denounce her to her husband. It would be a much finer picture were your husband and the slanderer to meet in a drawing room with a great flight of stairs leading up to a curtained door—the guilty wife suddenly throws aside the curtains and steps out to say 'It's all true'—the husband and the other woman look aghast as the wife stands motionless in this moment of confession.

John Emerson and Anita Loos, *How to Write Photoplays* (1920)

THE TABLEAU

EMERSON and Loos's own film of 1916, *The Social Secretary*, contains the following scene: Mayme, secretary to Mrs de Puyster and in love with her son Jimmie, is embroiled in an attempt to save her employer's family from scandal. A gossip columnist, the 'Buzzard', warns Mrs de Puyster that he has seen her daughter, Elsie, going into the apartment of a foreign count. The film establishes an alternation between Mrs de Puyster and Jimmie, who climb the front stairs to confront the Count in his sitting-room, and Mayme, who sneaks up a fire escape to the Count's back bedroom where Elsie is hiding. In the front room, as the Buzzard looks on, Jimmie argues with the Count and demands to be allowed to search the flat. Meanwhile, Mayme tries to persuade a reluctant Elsie to descend the fire escape. Mayme finally gets Elsie out of the window, but does not have time to escape herself before Jimmie breaks down the door. As Mayme hides her face with her coat, Jimmie drags her into the front room. Mayme's entrance, like that of the guilty wife described in *How to Write a Photoplay*, significantly alters the dramatic situation and provokes a strong reaction from all of the characters present. This revelation is not organized as a tableau, however, but rather, in the following series of shots:

1 Medium long shot. The Count's sitting-room. Mrs de Puyster looks off rear left towards the bedroom. The Buzzard, to her right, listens in the doorway. Mayme enters, rear left.

2 Close-up, same angle. Mayme. Mrs de Puyster's hand pulls the coat away revealing Mayme's face. Mayme raises her head and looks off right, then left.

3 Medium shot. The Count front left, and Jimmie midground centre. Both express amazement. Jimmie is horrified to see his girlfriend.

4 As 1. The Buzzard comes through the door, right, and closes it. Jimmie enters left, crosses, and addresses the Buzzard. Jimmie walks off left.

5 Medium shot. Mayme and Mrs de Puyster.

6 Medium close-up. The Buzzard. Amazed, he stares off left.

7 Medium close-up. Jimmie. He expresses despair.

8 As 3. The Count alone. He looks amazed.

9 As 5. Mayme looks down. Mrs de Puyster expresses disapproval.

10 Title: 'So she has been the Count's confederate all the time.'

The scene continues in the same vein, with Mayme unable to make any explanation in the presence of the Buzzard. Most of the shots are medium close-ups or medium long shots which isolate the reactions of one or two characters at a time. The space is thus highly fragmented, with closer views used to emphasize the facial expressions of the actors. There is no point in the scene in which all of the characters are shown together, in a single 'picture', which would summarize and typify their various reactions to the revelation of Mayme's presence, nor do any of the actors ever hold a pose. In *The Social Secretary*, Emerson and Loos ignore the prescription they made a few years later in *How to Write Photoplays*.[1]

This discrepancy between a prescription in a screenwriting manual and the same authors' practice in a film is not just an isolated aberration of Emerson and Loos. The various outlines that Giovanni Pastrone wrote for the 1914 film *Cabiria* use the words *quadro* and *scena*, Italian equivalents of 'tableau' or 'picture', introduced immediately after the description of a plot incident. For example, when Maciste (in the drafts named 'Ercole', i.e. Hercules), fleeing from the priests of Moloch with the rescued child Cabiria, bursts in on Sophonisbe's tryst with Massinissa, the final outline runs as follows: 'Inside garden—

Massinissa's meeting with Sophonisbe—Hercules and the little girl—Scene—Sophonisbe saves the child.' When, later, the hero Fulvius Axilla ('Plinio', i.e. Pliny, in the drafts) is told by Sophonisbe that Cabiria is dead, the final outline runs: ' "Dead! . . . Ah! Oh!, etc." Pliny's grief—Picture—.'[2]

However, in neither case in the finished film is there a tableau. The scenes are not broken up into closer shots, like those of *The Social Secretary*, but neither is there any freezing of the action; at least two of the four or five characters involved in the scene are always in movement. In the first incident (shot 190 in the continuity referred to above), Maciste breaks in as Massinissa is pleading with Sophonisbe, kneeling at her feet. Massinissa rises and stands so as to shield Sophonisbe, who veils her face (Figure 2.1). Maciste kneels and begs Sophonisbe to protect Cabiria, as Sophonisbe's attendant enters and listens. In the second (shots 462–4), Fulvius kneels at Sophonisbe's feet

2.1

2.2

while Massinissa and Maciste look on. She ignores his plea, so he rises and goes to join Maciste, but returns as Massinissa begins to question Sophonisbe on his behalf. Sophonisbe replies in a dialogue title: 'She is no more.' In the next shot, with an identical framing, Fulvius is ushered back to Maciste by Massinissa after a brief gesture of despair (Figure 2.2).

These two examples from very different film-making traditions suggest that an appeal to the idea of the tableau by filmmakers in the 1910s is not a simple anachronism. Rather, the appearance of the term signals a set of functions performed by the stage picture: to punctuate the action, to stress or prolong a dramatic situation, and to give a scene an abstract or quasi-allegorical significance. Filmmakers still felt that certain dramatic situations called for this constellation of functions, to the point that they still used the term 'tableau' as shorthand for what occurred at these points, even recommended 'tableaux' to others, but might not in fact resort to any direct reproduction on film of the stage tableau. Instead

other stylistic means were developed to this end. Tableaux became rarer as such, but their place continued to be felt.

The tableau thus provides an example of a theatrical device which, while not being adopted into film in any straightforward way, still affected how filmmakers conceived their practice. Examples like the ones above, where it is possible to bring together films and written texts by filmmakers using the term 'tableau', are rare. Nevertheless, the relationship can be approached in another way, by examining stage productions that can be shown to incorporate tableaux, and comparing them with their film adaptations. In this part we attempt to trace the cinematic vicissitudes of the theatrical tableau, primarily by a consideration of a series of adaptations, theatrical and cinematic, of Harriet Beecher Stowe's novel *Uncle Tom's Cabin*. However, before doing so, it is important to explicate the term 'tableau', in order to distinguish how we shall be using it from other usages.

1. We should point out that the print of *The Social Secretary* that we have seen, from the EmGee Film Library, calls the heroine's employer Mrs de Puyster, not Mrs von Puyster, as 1916 reviews and summaries of the film do. This strongly suggests that it derives from the reissue of 1924, which the *American Film Institute Catalog of Motion Pictures Produced in the United States*, vol. F 2: *Feature Films 1921–1930*, ed. Kenneth W. Munden (New York: R. R. Bowker Co., 1971), entry F2.5214, suggests was re-edited. It is therefore possible that 1916 prints did have a tableau shot (though it is hard to imagine how such a shot could have been staged, given the tight space of the set). Even if this is the case, its

removal is symptomatic of the problematic character of the tableau in the cinema.
2. Giovanni Pastrone, *Cabiria, visione storica del III secolo a.C.*, titles by Gabriele D'Annunzio, introduction by Maria Adriana Prolo, continuity described from an original tinted and toned print by Roberto Radicali and Ruggero Rossi (Turin: Museo Nazionale del Cinema, 1977), 200: 'Interno giardino—Incontro di Massinissa con Sofonisba—Ercole e piccina—Scena—Sofonisba salva la bimba' and p. 202: ' "Morta! . . . Ah! oh: ecc." Dolore di Plinio—Quadro—.'

Chapter 3
The Stage Tableau in *Uncle Tom's Cabin*

IN nineteenth-century French theatre, the word 'tableau' had a number of meanings, two of which are important for our purposes, both being transferred to early film. Arthur Pougin's *Dictionnaire historique et pittoresque du théâtre* of 1885 clarifies the contemporary usage. Explaining that the term referred to the board on which coming attractions were announced, Pougin continues:

The term 'tableau' is also applied to certain material divisions in works which are complicated in their staging. Any change in the setting during an act produces a new tableau. If, for example, a five-act play contains twenty parts with the action performed in twenty different settings, it is said to be in five acts and twenty tableaux. All *féeries* are like this, as are certain dramas. With very few exceptions, the curtain is only lowered at the end of each act; the other changes in setting take place in full view of the audience.

Lastly, the word 'tableau' is applied to the plastic and pictorial effect produced at the end of an act by the grouping of the principals and extras who have taken part in the action. A critic wrote in 1824: 'Tableau: the marked wordless scene, general pantomime, *coup de théâtre*, obligatory at the end of each act of a melodrama. Guilbert de Pixerécourt is a master of the art of the tableau—it is the least blameworthy of this writer's talents.'

Although Pougin does not say so explicitly, when actors reached the poses constituting the composition of a tableau in the second sense, they froze in position for a short but definite period. According to Jan Shepherd, the musical scores of early nineteenth-century English melodramas indicate that tableaux should be held for a number of measures of *Rule Britannia*, variously four or eight.[1]

In English usage, tableau in the first sense, i.e. as a segment of the play demarcated by a change of setting, was usually translated as 'scene' (the term rarely being used, unlike the French *scène*, for a division of an act marked by the entrance or exit of a speaking character without a change of setting). In the second sense, i.e. as a static grouping of characters or a pose, technical writings such as promptbooks use 'picture'. In less technical contexts the original French word was often adopted directly. The term 'picture' was also used to designate a setting. For example, this use is found in the stage directions for the beginning of the third act of Henry C. De Mille and David Belasco's 1890 play *Men and Women*: 'There is heard the distant sound of a bell striking twelve o'clock. . . . At the eighth stroke the curtain is raised, being timed so as to reveal the whole stage picture on the twelfth stroke.'[2]

Another well-known type of stage picture is the 'tableau vivant'. Pougin defines this separately from the other uses of 'tableau', as 'the precise reproduction by living but motionless people of celebrated and universally familiar pictures or sculptural groups'. One of the earliest famous tableaux vivants occurred in a stage play: the reproduction of Greuze's *L'Accordée de village* in the Comédie Italienne's production of *Les Noces d'Arlequin* in Paris in 1761.[3] The theatre occasionally resorted to such paintings later, e.g. David Wilkie's *Distraining for Rent* in Douglas Jerrold's 1832 melodrama *The Rent Day*, and (as a parody), the 'tableau as of Napoleon on the Bellerophon, after the celebrated picture by Orchardson', in the 1904 staging of *Peter Pan*.[4] Such tableaux vivants were usually both preceded and followed by a curtain, unlike the tableaux produced by actors stopping in a pose in the course of the action. They are also isolated special cases. Otherwise, the tableau vivant's career was largely extra-theatrical. Most commonly it appeared as a party piece for amateurs, as illustrated in the Vitagraph film *Coronets and Hearts* of 1912, where the hero first sees the heroine performing a tableau vivant at a ball in her house (Figure 2.3). It enjoyed a brief vogue as a commercial entertainment in the 1830s and 1840s, although the scantiness of the performers' attire led to its banning in New York.[5] It can even be found in the unlikely setting of the *Parteitäge* and trade union congresses of the German Social Democratic Party in the 1890s, where delegates were entertained with such tableaux vivants as Humanity Freed from the Shackles of Militarism by Labour.[6] As these examples indicate, the tableau vivant did not always reproduce an existing painting or sculpture, but could also constitute a picture in a more generalized sense—the portrayal of an emotion (an 'attitude'), or the allegorical representation of a virtue or other abstract quality. Such generalized tableaux vivants have more in common with some of the tableaux we will be discussing, but this part of our book will largely ignore the genre of the tableau vivant to concentrate on the dramatically integrated tableaux and their film equivalents.

Early French film catalogues mostly use 'tableau' in a sense corresponding more or less to the modern 'shot', and this is usually translated into English as

2.3

'scene', the contemporary term for a shot.[7] Thus the 1907 Pathé Catalogue describes *Le Chat botté* (Puss in Boots) as a 'Féerie cinématographique en sept tableaux', and prints have seven scenes each preceded by a title, the last scene containing a magical transformation of the décor (using a dissolve) for the apotheosis indicated in the title ('Fiançailles. Apothéose.').[8] The English Pathé Catalogue of 1905 calls these 'scenes'. 'Tableau' is used by American film catalogues in the theatrical sense of a static pose, particularly if this is an extra-diegetic allegory, e.g. the 'Tableau' of Justice in Edison's *The Kleptomaniac* of 1905, referred to in Chapter 2, above.[9]

Modern cinema historians use the term 'tableau' in a slightly different sense to describe a characteristic type of shot in early films, and a type of construction which relies on that type of shot. This is the centred axial long shot, looking at an interior as if at a box set on stage from the centre of the theatre stalls. Many early films consist largely of such shots, linked by intertitles; they lack scene dissection, or even alternation between simultaneous scenes. This has come to be called 'tableau construction', though the term is also, unfortunately, used more loosely to refer to any film with slow cutting.[10]

To avoid confusion, we will use 'picture' to refer generally to a stage setting or film image with a strong pictorial effect and a descriptive rather than narrative function. Unless otherwise stated, 'tableau' will be used narrowly to mean Pougin's 'plastic and pictorial effect' achieved through the freezing of the action, on stage or in film.

Having given these definitions of the term

'tableau', we can now proceed to examine how such tableaux were deployed in a production, or rather a long series of productions, a theatrical tradition. Play versions of *Uncle Tom's Cabin* followed immediately upon the publication of Harriet Beecher Stowe's popular novel in 1852.[11] By the 1870s touring companies performing nothing but *Uncle Tom's Cabin* travelled throughout rural areas of the USA, a practice which continued well into the 1920s. On the basis of the surviving promptbooks, it seems that most of these companies utilized George Aiken's 1852 adaptation of the novel, which also more or less influenced the film versions discussed here.[12] But by the late 1870s aspects of *mise-en-scène* which are not specified in Aiken's original version, such as the bloodhounds which pursue Eliza across the ice, had become canonized as part of the performance tradition.[13] Some tableaux are noted in the published Aiken play, some are noted in pencil in the surviving promptbooks, and still others are described in published versions of the play by other authors. Hence it is possible to reconstruct the most frequently used theatrical tableaux and compare them with the way filmmakers subsequently handled the same scenes.

Uncle Tom's Cabin was thus the centre of a vital and long-running performance tradition and, until a generation ago, the story was universally familiar. More recently, the representation of black characters in the play versions and the original novel came to epitomize white patronization of blacks, and the protests this aroused have driven the story so far from popular consciousness that we have felt it necessary to include a plot summary as an appendix to this book. Our interest in it lies not in its current ideological status, but in the fact that it is possible to document the range of tableaux employed, which is not the case for many other comparable stage melodramas.[14]

In order to encompass the major events of the novel, Aiken's version of *Uncle Tom's Cabin* was unusually long, divided into six acts and thirty scenes. It was one of the first melodramas in the USA to be performed by itself without an accompanying farce or other playlets. Versions of the play by Edward Fitzball, Mark Lemon and Tom Taylor, and Charles Hermann are shorter; they skip the section of the novel which deals with the St Clares to concentrate on the events on the Shelby and Legree plantations.[15] Another British version apparently eliminated the events on the Shelby plantation to focus on the stories of Tom and Eva. A handbill for the Theatre Royal, Bristol in the Pettingell Collection advertises 'The Second Part of *Uncle Tom's Cabin*,' a play beginning with Tom's trip down the Mississippi by steamboat, and his rescue of Eva.

There are other important variations in plot among the various published versions. Two plays unify the story by collapsing the characters of Haley the slave-trader and Legree into one—called Haley in the Fitzball version and Legree in the Lemon and Taylor—so that a single character personifies the evils of slavery. These authors unify the story still further by introducing Eliza and Harry at the Legree plantation, in place of the new character Emmeline who is threatened by Legree's sexual advances in the novel. In Lemon and Taylor, Eliza is recaptured after her escape across the Ohio, and George Harris, passing for white and accompanied by Topsy disguised as his boy servant, follows Eliza to Legree's plantation on the Red River. Some versions end happily. In Fitzball, Tom is saved by George Shelby and returned to his family. Tom dies at the end of the Lemon and Taylor play, but the last scene is of George, Eliza, Cassy, and Topsy making their escape, as Cassy kills Legree.

The tableaux in these versions of *Uncle Tom's Cabin* appear in similar scenes, even when there are marked variations in plot and in the overall organization of acts and scenes. For example, in many versions including the Aiken, the end of the second act is the scene on a high rocky pass, in which George Harris, with the help of the Quaker Phineas Fletcher, defends his family from the slave-catchers who pursue them. A tableau occurs at the end of this scene, after Phineas Fletcher has pushed Tom Loker off the cliff. In the Lemon and Taylor version, a similar tableau occurs but at the end of the last act; in this instance it is Cassy who pushes Legree off a high rocky pass, followed by a tableau. All of the versions of the play which deal with the Shelby plantation include a tableau of Eliza crossing the Ohio river on the ice. In most cases this occurs at the end of the first act, but in Lemon and Taylor it occurs in Act 2, scene 4, the penultimate scene of the act. In this case the crossing of the ice is not necessary for the plot, since Eliza is immediately recaptured by her pursuers and taken down south to the Legree plantation. Thus, what was originally a daring escape becomes a failed escape attempt; but the tableau is retained even when the plot is altered. There are other tableaux which appear in more than one version of the play: Tom surrounded by his family just before he is taken away by Haley (Hermann, Fitzball), the end of the slave market scene in which Tom and Emmeline are bought by Legree (Aiken, Hermann), Tom refusing to whip Emmeline (Aiken, Hermann), Tom's death (Aiken, Hermann), and a final tableau which varies widely given changes in the ending (to be discussed later).

In all of the versions, most of the tableaux occur at scene ends. In one of the promptbooks for the Aiken version, the prompter has noted that a relatively long scene in the typescript, Act 6, scene 5, should be broken down into three shorter scenes.[16] The first of these short scenes ends with Legree striking Tom, who falls unconscious and is carried off stage. The second scene, beginning with the entrance of Shelby, Marks, and Cute, ends with the death of Legree. The third scene, between young Shelby and Tom, ends with the latter's death. The prompter notes the addition of a tableau on Legree's line 'Well, his mouth is shut up at last—that's one comfort' at the point at which Legree strikes Tom down. A new tableau is thus introduced to mark the end of the first, short scene; the device helps to make the transition between Tom's exit and the entrance of Shelby, Marks, and Cute.

As the theatre historian Russell Jackson has noted, the tableau was also sometimes known as a 'strong curtain' and frequently prompted applause, sometimes giving rise to a second picture.[17] One version of *Uncle Tom's Cabin*, by Charles Morton, actually spells out the tableau to be used for the second curtain. Act 3 ends with Eva's death scene as follows:

ST. CLARE. *(sinking on his knees)* Farewell beloved child! *(Solemn music, slow curtain.) (Second curtain, same positions.)*
TOPSY. *(sobs)* Oh, missie Eva—darlin missie Eva. *(sobs) (If slaves are used, they sing hymn for second curtain)*

The use of tableaux as a cue for applause helps to explain their occurrence at the end of acts or big climactic scenes in all of the versions of *Uncle Tom's Cabin*. This placement was the commonest one for theatrical tableaux, to the point that some commentators assume it was the only one. There were others, however. Tableaux could be used within scenes, to punctuate a surprising revelation or reversal, as in the example from *How to Write Photoplays*, or even to mark the entrance of a leading character or actor, as with Henry Irving's first entrance as Mathias in Leopold Lewis's *The Bells*.[18]

This is borne out by the theatrical versions of *Uncle Tom's Cabin*. Although they are not as clearly marked in the playscripts, there are some instances in which we believe scenes began with strong pictorial effects, if not static tableaux, crowd scenes 'discovered' when the curtains were pulled back to reveal a vista of a busy open-air space. The written descriptions call for movement on the part of extras while none the less constituting a stage picture. Lemon and Taylor describe the beginning of the third act as follows: '*Legree's Plantation on the Red River. House stretches obliquely up the stage. Machine for weighing cotton stands in front. Slave quarters and fields in distance, with the swamp beyond. As the curtain rises, the slaves are discovered, some grouped with their cotton baskets and resting, others slowly bringing their loads in from the plantation.*' The fairhand copy of Hermann also has Act 3, scene 3 occur on Legree's plantation, the set including his mansion, the cotton weighing house in the distance, and slaves picking cotton. Sometimes the big set provided the backdrop for a large-scale musical number, a dance or choral piece, after which the action resumed. The handbill for 'The Second Part of *Uncle Tom's Cabin*' referred to above advertises Act 3, scene 3 as containing 'Legree's Cotton Plantation—Trio (New American Melody), "The old Folks at Home"—The Process of Picking, Weighing and Housing the Cotton.' In Aiken's published version, Act 6 opens quite simply, without any intimation of a picture: '*Dark landscape. An old, roofless shed. Tom is discovered in shed, lying on some old cotton bagging.*' However, in one of the promptbooks a notation has been made, indicating a more elaborate opening of the scene: '*Plantation. Dance breakdown. When all off W[ait]. Slow flats. Music. Lights. Lights full on scene 1 = Act VI. Cotton plantation. Niggers discovered end of dance. W[ait].*' It seems that in this production the act began with a view of the plantation, and that slaves danced a breakdown. The flats then moved in as the scene shifted to Tom and Cassy in the shed. Once the scene was over, the flats moved out again, to reveal the slaves on the plantation, their dance now finished. John C. Morrow also cites an unidentified promptbook from the Harvard Theatre Collection which suggests a similar scene, although placed at the opening of Act 5, scene 3, the first scene on the Legree plantation in the Aiken version: '*Plantation of Legree—Negroes picking cotton at back—full stage—Characteristic cotton field—Negroes sing, dance and introduce specialties. At end of which Legree enters on horseback and scatters Negroes R & L.*'[19]

Other spectacular settings for *Uncle Tom's Cabin* included the slave market set, which, like the plantation set, was often used as a back drop for musical numbers, and a vista of a steamboat on the Mississippi, conveyed by means of a panorama in one early production.[20] Harry Birdoff describes the use of a panorama showing a steamboat on the Mississippi in the Jarrett and Palmer production of *Uncle Tom's Cabin* in 1878. By the time of the Peck and Fursman production in 1888, this kind of spectacle had become more elaborate, involving a re-enactment of a historical regatta between the Robert E. Lee and the Natchez on the Mississippi.[21]

The true tableaux in *Uncle Tom's Cabin*, however, did not depend upon the sheer spectacle of the plantation, auction, or riverboat scenes, i.e. they did not have an essentially descriptive function. Rather, they served to sum up a specific narrative point in pictorial form. As Martin Meisel has argued, the tableau represents a moment of suspended action, a moment chosen so that the grouping of figures epitomizes the forces arrayed in conflict.[22] It arrests the flow of the narrative so as to produce a heightened sense of its significance.

A writer in *The Stage* (19 August 1881) described one strategy of tableau construction: 'To intensify a particular climax forming a picture in which each character takes a different attitude, though at the same time one exemplifying the dominant idea, or a portion of it, is a task to fulfil which successfully taxes the imagination, ingenuity and general perception of effect of the person responsible for it.'[23] A good tableau, then, brings a set of meaningful units—the conventional postures or attitudes assumed by the actors—into relation with one another.

The description of the tableaux in the Hermann version of *Uncle Tom's Cabin* provides a clear example of tableau construction through grouping together figures in incongruous 'attitudes' or emotional postures. The tableau at the end of Act 1 is described as follows:

Eliza rushes on to a high bank, exclaims 'Heaven protect me!' *then leaps from the bank to a raft of ice; and springing from one block to another, reaches, with her child, the opposite shore; here a stranger helps her up. (A girl, attired to represent Eliza in the distance, and a* CHILD *to personate the man who receives her, will add much to the effect of the scene.)* HALEY *and* SLAVES *rush on; in vain he urges them to follow.*

TABLEAU *of Vengeance and Disappointment on the one bank—Gratitude to Providence on the other.*

In the fairhand copy, a prompter has made a similar notation for the scene on a high rocky pass, following the death of Loker: '*Tableau of Horror L.H. Gratitude R.H.*'

Though without a description which specifies the various attitudes or postures to be assumed by the actors, many other tableaux in *Uncle Tom's Cabin* focus on a moment of conflict by grouping together characters in postures which represent seemingly irreconcilable emotional or moral states. For example, in both the Fitzball and Hermann versions the tableau of Uncle Tom taking leave of his family includes Haley. Fitzball describes the end of the scene as follows:

CHLOE. *(holding Tom)* No—oh murder! Oh fire! Childrens, childrens! Come and kiss your daddy—*(Shelby goes out C.)* Them going to take'm away. *(Children run down R.)* What'll we do! What'll we do!

TOM. *(kissing them)* Bless'm all—bless'm all!

HAL.. *(flourishing whip)* Come nigger, I can't spare no time for nonsense. *(Music. Tom tries to break away.)*

TOM. Chloe, now Chloe!

(Picture closed in.)

[In pencil] *(—Song—W[ait])*

This tableau depends upon a contrast between two attitudes: Haley flourishing his whip, and Chloe and the children hanging on to Tom. Indeed, in the Hermann version the tableau is prompted by Haley's entrance.[24] It is not simply Tom's farewell to his family which is emphasized, then, but the conflict between the slave trader and the loyal wife.

Another example of a tableau constructed through contrast is Tom's refusal to whip Emmeline (Act 5, scene 3 in Aiken; Act 3, scene 3 in the fairhand copy of Hermann).[25] Legree orders his overseers, Sambo and Quimbo, to take Tom away and whip him for his refusal to follow orders. But in the Aiken version, while the dialogue calls for Sambo and Quimbo to take Tom off stage, the tableau shows Legree himself about to administer the punishment:

Music. Sambo and Quimbo seize Tom and drag him up stage. Legree seizes Emmeline, and throws her round. She falls on her knees, with her hands lifted in supplication. Legree raises his whip, as if to strike Tom. Picture closed in.

The tableau has Legree rather than his overseers lift the whip, constituting a composite image at the expense of a linear presentation of the narrative events. This is motivated by its furnishing the most effective visual summary of the conflicts that have been played out in the scene. The composite character of the image is also what gives the tableau its punctuating force.

Another, perhaps more familiar, strategy for heightening the narrative significance of the picture was to utilize iconography that evoked relatively abstract or generalized meanings. The final apotheosis scene of *Uncle Tom's Cabin* offers the best example of this tendency, which is operative to some degree in many other instances.

As the play has been given many different endings over the years, it is necessary to summarize some of the more important variants. The version of the ending printed in Aiken has become the stereotype of the apotheosis scene:

Gorgeous clouds, tinted with sunlight. Eva, robed in white, is discovered on the back of a milk-white dove, with expanded wings, as if just soaring upward. Her hands are extended in benediction over St Clare and Uncle Tom who are kneeling and gazing up to her. Expressive music. Slow curtain.

I. Blaine Quarnstrom has suggested that the staging of this tableau could be quite extravagant, especially in large city productions, 'some of them flying winged angels during the Allegory as well as both Little Eva and Uncle Tom'.[26] But touring Uncle Tom troupes could not carry the equipment which permitted this kind of spectacle. The Harmount troupe, which toured the rural Midwest from 1903, evolved an alternative. Following Uncle Tom's death, the backdrop was lifted to show a painted drop of the 'Rock of Ages'—a young woman clings to a cross, her only support in a stormy sea. The Rock of Ages drop gave way to a view of clouds, created by layering scrim and solid cloud drops. The cloud drops were lifted one by one, finally revealing Eva seen through a circle of clouds painted on the final drop.[27] Thus, both the ending described in the printed Aiken text and the one actually employed by the Harmount troupe introduce elements of Christian allegory.

Other versions of the play ended with a historical tableau in celebration of the nation. Although invoking an ideology very different from that of the apotheosis, these tableaux functioned similarly to introduce an abstract interpretive framework at one remove from the immediate interests of the plot. In 1852–3, English productions of *Uncle Tom's Cabin* frequently ended on a patriotic note. In the Fitzball version, Uncle Tom is rescued by Mr Shelby and returns to Aunt Chloe in Kentucky. Mr Shelby then frees his slaves, and George Harris pronounces the final speech: 'And, oh, if it be possible there can be any human heart which advocates the cause of slavery! let it turn hither, and contemplate the real felicity of a good Christian! who has just set captivity free, and broken the chains of bondage!' The disposition of the characters at the final curtain is noted in the script: Topsy, Chloe, Tom, George, Eliza, Shelby, Mrs Shelby, Senator Bird, Mrs Bird. Three children stood downstage of this group. Upstage a banner unfurled which read: 'No Slavery!' *Hail Columbia* was played in the orchestra.

Whether or no the Hermann version of *Uncle Tom's Cabin* was produced in America, the ending of the published version could have been used on either side of the Atlantic in 1852: George Harris and little George Shelby appear on Legree's plantation in search of Uncle Tom and form a tableau beside the slave on his deathbed. However, the fairhand copy of Hermann adds a second picture, designed to appeal to the patriotism of British audiences. Following the death of Uncle Tom, there is a scene change. George and Eliza arrive in Canada at what is described as a 'British fort'. The script calls for flags, soldiers, and the orchestra to play 'Rule Britannia'.

Historical tableau endings for American audiences were introduced somewhat later in the century, presumably once the play's anti-slavery, and by implication pro-Union, stance had become less controversial. In 1897, for example, Barbour and Harkins added a tableau of Lincoln signing the Emancipation Proclamation.[28]

Whether they employ Christian or national iconography, the allegorical tenor of these final tableaux is

EVA DRESSING UNCLE TOM.

" There sat Tom, on a little mossy seat in the court, every one of his button
holes stuck full of cape jessamines, and Eva, gaily laughing, was hanging a wreath
of roses round his neck."—Page 152.

2.3

the reference to the sacrificial ox is not reproduced under the picture, presumably because this edition appeared too early in 1852 for the line to have achieved canonical status (Figure 2.4).[29] But the visual prominence traditionally accorded to this scene derives from Tom's quotation of the Bible. Both the theatrical realizations and the book illustrations opportunistically seized upon this moment in which the dialogue lends the picture of Tom wreathed in flowers a symbolic status.

The predilection for symbolic or quasi-allegorical tableaux apparent in the garden scene may well have influenced the creation of other tableaux within the performance tradition. Recall Hermann's instructions for the scene of Eliza crossing the Ohio which called for a *'Tableau of Vengeance and Disappointment on the one bank—Gratitude to Providence on the other.'* This stage direction invokes the kind of description of gesture frequently found in works such as the *Conférence de M. Le Brun sur l'expression générale et particulière* or Henry Siddons's *Practical Illustrations of Rhetorical Gesture*, an English adaptation of J. J. Engel's *Ideen zu einer Mimic.*[30] Forming the theoretical basis for important nineteenth-century acting manuals, these works illustrated the physical representation of abstract emotional states such as anger, astonishment, vengeance, and so on. Thus, Hermann's direction for a *'Tableau of Vengeance and Disappointment'* may well have been as much a way of signalling to the actors the postures they were to assume as an indication of how audiences were to interpret the scene. But even if we cannot assume that the audience immediately read the end of Act 1 as a picture of Gratitude to Providence and Vengeance, there is at least an indication that actors and playwrights conceived of tableaux in such terms. The tendency already discussed to construct tableaux out of opposed elements would have underscored a conception of the actor's pose in symbolic terms. For example, the tableau of Eliza praying on one bank and Haley cursing on the other presupposes some sort of moral contrast between them. Later stagings of the same tableau set up a different contrast, between mother and baby on the one hand, and the pack of hounds nipping at her heels on the other. But the point is that in either case the tableau arrests the narrative flow at a moment which produces a highly charged and schematic opposition between two terms. Hence the sense of 'stepping back'

unmistakable. It is more difficult to discern this kind of abstraction in the case of other stage tableaux, which did not usually depend to such an extent on extra-diegetic references. None the less, the performance tradition does seem to have favoured ones which entailed an abstract point or moral. In the Aiken version, the scene of Tom and Eva in the garden (Act 2, scene 2) begins: *'Tom discovered, seated on a bank, with Eva on his knee—his buttonholes are filled with flowers, and Eva is hanging a wreath around his neck.'* The entrance of St Clare and Ophelia prompts Tom's line: 'Look yer; I'm the ox, mentioned in the good book, dressed up for sacrifice,' dialogue which appears in both the novel and the Aiken play. Not only was the opening of this scene selected for a theatrical tableau, it was also illustrated in many editions of the novel, although in the Cruikshank illustration shown here

2.5

from the story to emphasize abstract or general qualities. The tableaux in *Uncle Tom's Cabin* can be summed up in the abstract captions employed by nineteenth-century illustrators as well as playwrights: 'Gratitude and Vengeance' or 'Maternal Fortitude'.

While the possibilities for schematization and abstraction were crucial in determining the selection of scenes and incidents for a tableau, it is important to note that, with the exception of the ending, most remained narratively integrated. By far the most common narrative motivation for tableaux was surprise or astonishment. This convention extends well beyond the performance tradition of *Uncle Tom's Cabin*. Evoking a story related in Shakespeare's *King John* in which a blacksmith is immobilized by the news of King Arthur's death, Siddons recommends that 'the man struck with sudden astonishment ought to remain fixed like a statue to his posture for

the time'.[31] In his 1775 performance as Hamlet, David Garrick held his pose of terror and astonishment at the sight of his father's ghost 'for so long that some spectators wondered if he needed prompting'.[32] So common was this way of motivating the close of an act that Rossini parodies it at the end of the first act of *The Barber of Seville*. The revelation of the Count's true identity to the officer of the guard produces a '*quadro di stupore*' in which all the characters on stage (except Almaviva and Figaro) are immobilized:

> Fredda ed immobile
> Come una statua,
> Fiato non restagli
> Da respirar.[33]

The convention extended to colloquial usage. One of the *Oxford English Dictionary*'s citations for 'tableau' is of such a usage: 'She overheard a gentleman ask another, pointing to two of the witnesses, "Which of those old cats is Mrs C.?" Mrs C. leaned over and said, "That particular tabby, sir, is behind you." Tableau!'[34]

Based upon the evidence of the promptbooks, a tableau of this type appears in the scene in a tavern, Act 1, scene 4 in the Aiken version (although as we shall see there is evidence of more than one way of motivating this particular tableau). Eliza and Harry are resting in a back room of the tavern, exhausted by their escape and frustrated to find that the ferry across the river is not operating due to ice. Haley arrives at the tavern and meets Marks and Loker. Phineas Fletcher, Eliza's ally, enters the scene at this point and joins the men in conversation. Several promptbooks have the notation '*story*'.[35] Phineas here tells Loker and Marks a story which is not in the Aiken text. The point of this story is partly to distract their attention as Eliza tiptoes across the rear to escape through the window, but in two promptbooks Phineas describes the escape of an imaginary or absent slave in such a way as to tell Eliza how she can escape.[36] The slave-catchers make a deal, which Eliza overhears, dividing up the profits to be made from the sale of the runaways. According to the printed version of the Aiken, Loker 'strikes his hand violently on the table' when the deal between the men is completed (all of the promptbooks indicate that the striking of the table was amplified by a 'crack' from the wings). Eliza, who is already outside the window, screams in response to the sound: 'They all start to their feet. Eliza disappears. Music, chord.' Although a tableau is not explicitly called for here, it seems likely that the men freeze at the point at which Eliza screams since arresting the action of the slave-catchers at this point would give her time to make a getaway. Certainly, the use of sound—the 'crack' from the wings, Eliza's scream—provides the conventional motivation of the tableau as a moment of surprise.

Surprise was not the only means of motivating the suspension of the action for the tableau, however. It was also possible to produce a situation in which the characters effectively immobilized each other, usually through the threat of violence, as is indicated by the example of Sheridan's *The Critic* already cited. This kind of tableau occurs in the Edison version of the scene in the tavern, in which Phineas pulls a gun on the slave-traders to prevent them from following Eliza out the window. It seems unlikely that this scene-end would have been entirely without theatrical precedent, and a photograph of this scene from the Brady stage production shows a similar disposition of these characters in a very similar tavern set (Figure 2.5). Another motivated tableau of this type occurs in Act 2, scene 3 of the Aiken version, in which Phineas Fletcher tricks Haley, Marks, and Loker into a cellar and prevents them from pursuing George Harris by holding a chair over their heads:

(The trap is forced open. Haley and Marks appear. Phineas seizes a chair and stands over trap—picture.)
PHINEAS. Down with you or I'll smash you into apple-fritters!
(Tableau—closed in).

A similar use of the tableau is found at the end of Act 1 in the Hazlewood version. Hazlewood introduces a new comic character, Jemima, who holds a gun on the slave-catchers, keeping them immobilized, so that Eliza may cross the Ohio.

A number of conclusions can be drawn from this examination of the theatrical adaptations of *Uncle Tom's Cabin* about the use of pictures and tableaux in these plays. First, there was a strong performance tradition for *Uncle Tom's Cabin* which, despite variations in the text and staging used, singled out a series of moments in the story as canonical—as necessary elements without which a production of *Uncle Tom's Cabin* would not be a proper production of *Uncle Tom's Cabin*; and the customary representation of most of these canonical moments involved one or more pictures or tableaux. Second, pictures and tableaux most frequently occur at the end of a scene, but are also found at the beginning and in the middle of scenes. Third, pictures and tableaux varied in their motivation, some constituting a composite summary of a complex plot situation, some an allegorical commentary on the action, some a moment of verisimilitudinous stasis. Although these moments clearly draw on the body of nineteenth-century practices involving the realization of abstract ideas analysed by Martin Meisel and others, it is important to stress also their contribution to the texture of the drama, the way they interrupt the continuity of the action and rhythmically articulate the performance of the play. It is these functional aspects of the tableau that become especially important when we turn to the fate of the tableau in the different medium of the cinema.

1. Personal communication.

2. Reprinted in Barrett H. Clark *et al.* (eds.), *America's Lost Plays*, vol. xvii (Princeton, NJ: Princeton University Press, 1940; repr. Indiana: Indiana University Press, 1963), 313. Very occasionally, 'picture' was also used in the sense of scene as segment, e.g. by Charles E. Blaney: 'The public that demanded a quick succession of pictures—that is, scenes—have gone over to the moving picture houses' ('Good and Bad Melodrama', *New York Dramatic Mirror*, 19, no. 1533 (9 May 1908), 2; cit. Roberta Pearson, *Eloquent Gesture: The Transformation of Performance Style in the Griffith Biograph Films* (Berkeley: University of California Press, 1992), 134).

3. See Holmström, *Monodrama*, 217–19. This book gives a clear account of the early history of the genre.

4. See the end of Act 1 of Douglas Jerrold's *The Rent Day*, playtext in the Pettingell Collection at the Library of the University of Kent at Canterbury; Roger Lancelyn Green, *Fifty Years of 'Peter Pan'* (London: Peter Davies, 1954), 53 and the illustrations between pp. 66 and 67.

5. See Richard D. Altick, *The Shows of London* (Cambridge, Mass.: The Belknap Press of Harvard University Press, 1978), 342–9; and Robert C. Allen, *Horrible Prettiness: Burlesque and American Culture* (Chapel Hill, NC: University of Carolina Press, 1991), 92–4.

6. See Friedrich Knilli and Ursula Münchow (eds.), *Frühes deutsches Arbeitertheater, 1847–1918* (Munich: Carl Hanser Verlag, 1970), 23, 286–302, and the illustrations on pp. 497–9.

7. But recall the remarks in Ch. 1 about the discrepancies between the film 'scene' before 1920 and the modern 'shot'.

8. The American *Star Film Catalog* seems to have a slightly different usage (unless Georges Méliès simply wanted his advertising to exaggerate the number of scenes in his films); each significant dramatic incident is called a scene, even when no change of décor or shot is involved, while 'tableau' refers to a spectacular décor; thus, *Blue Beard* (*Barbe bleue*) is described as 'A great fairy drama, with spectacular tableaux, in twelve scenes,' and three of these 'scenes' ('9. At the Place of Execution. 10. The Rescue of Fatima. 11. Death of Bluebeard.') occur within a single setting and in continuous time. The film catalogues referred to in this book can be conveniently consulted in two microfilm collections: British ones and the 1907 French Pathé Catalogue in *Early Rare British Film-Makers' Catalogues, 1896–1913* (London: World Microfilm Publications, 1983, eight reels), and American ones in *Motion Picture Catalogs by American Producers and Distributors, 1894–1908*, ed. Charles Musser (Ann Arbor: University Microfilms, 1984–5).

9. Edison Catalog Form no. 267, 10 May 1905, no. 6116. See also Howard Lamarr Walls, *Motion Pictures, 1894–1912 identified from the Records of the United States Copyright Office* (Washington: Copyright Office, Library of Congress, 1953): 'H56410. The Kleptomaniac. Tableau.'

10. For an example of the term 'tableau' for a kind of shot typical of early film, see Burch, *Life to those Shadows*, 164.

11. References to *Uncle Tom's Cabin; or, Life among the Lowly* (first published by John P. Jewett, Boston, 1852) in this book will be to the Penguin Classics edition, ed. and introd. Ann Douglas (London, 1986).

12. George Aiken, *Uncle Tom's Cabin; or, Life among the Lowly*, published in French's Standard Drama, the Acting Edition, no. 217 (New York, n.d.); repr. in Daniel C. Gerould (ed.), *American Melodrama* (New York: Performing Arts Journal Publications, 1983), 75–133. The Billy Rose Theatre Collection at the Performing Arts Research Center of the New York Public Library has three promptbooks based on this edition. According to John H. McDowell, 'Scenery and Staging of *Uncle Tom's Cabin*: Selected Scenes', *Ohio State University Theatre Collection Bulletin*, no. 10 (1963), 19, the OSU theatre collection has ten such promptbooks. William A. Brady's New York production of 1901, for which there is an annotated typescript in the Museum of the City of New York, is also an adaptation of the Aiken version.

13. Harry Birdoff, *The World's Greatest Hit: Uncle Tom's Cabin* (New York: S. F. Vanni, 1947): on the proliferation of Uncle Tom troupes see p. 257 and on bloodhounds p. 295.

14. For the modern attack on the novel see James Baldwin 'Everybody's Protest Novel', first published in *Partisan Review* in June 1949 and repr. in *Notes of a Native Son* (Boston: Beacon Press, 1955), 13–23. For a history of the reception of both the novel and the Aiken play, see Thomas F. Gossett, *Uncle Tom's Cabin and American Culture* (Dallas: Southern Methodist University Press, 1985). Gregory A. Waller describes conflicts surrounding the staging of *Uncle Tom's Cabin* in Lexington, Ky., in the 1900s, in *Main Street Amusements: Movies and Commercial Entertainment in a Southern City, 1896–1930* (Washington: Smithsonian Institution Press, 1995), esp. 44–6.

15. We consulted versions by Edward Fitzball, Mark Lemon and Tom Taylor, Charles Hermann, and Colin Hazlewood in the Pettingell Collection at the Library of the University of Kent. There were two copies of the version by Hermann, *Uncle Tom's Cabin: A Drama of Real Life*, one published by Samuel French (London, n.d.) and one handwritten (hereafter referred to as the fairhand copy). R. S. Holland ('Introduction to Hazlewood') has traced the history of the production of all these versions. Although they were first produced in England, there are promptscripts of the Lemon and Taylor, and the Hermann in the Billy Rose Theatre Collection, so it is possible that they were also performed in the United States. The Billy Rose Theatre Collection also contains a typescript of a version by Charles Morton prepared for copyright deposit in 1912.

16. This promptbook, signed J. S. MacNeill and not dated, is one of three promptbooks utilizing the Aiken text in the Samuel French edition in the Billy Rose Theatre Collection (another is unsigned, while the third is signed J. B. Wright and dated 1866).

17. Russell Jackson, *Victorian Theatre* (London: A. & C. Black, 1989), 160–2.

18. See Leopold Lewis, *Henry Irving and 'The Bells': Irving's Personal Script of the Play by Leopold Lewis*, ed. and introd. David Mayer (Manchester: Manchester University Press, 1980), 44 and 80 n. 6. It should be noted, however, that the descriptions of this tableau cited, by Edward Gordon Craig and Eric Jones-Evans, are based on performances dating from the turn of the century, when 'Irving in *The Bells*' had become an institution, and there had to be a pause for the applause greeting the star's entrance. Neither the script, nor the review of the first performance in the *Observer*, 26 Nov. 1871 (reprod. on 100–3 of Mayer's edition), which carefully describes the curtain calls for Irving, then still a little-known actor, suggest that there was a pause or such applause at this point then.

19. John C. Morrow, 'The Harmount Company: Aspects of an *Uncle Tom's Cabin* Company', *Ohio State University Theatre Collection Bulletin*, no. 10 (1963), 28.

20. Hermann describes the setting for the auction scene, placed at

the opening of Act 3 in his version: '*Splendid hall—figures of Justice, Liberty, and Mercy, in niches—a rostrum for selling Negroes—Negroes grouped about— Auctioneer smoking—Tom, Emmeline, Emmeline's Mother, etc., etc. grouped.*' The fairhand copy notes a tableau at this point. Aiken's description of the same scene notes simply '*An Auction Mart. Uncle Tom and Emmeline at back. Adolf, Skeggs, Marks, Mann, and various spectators discovered.*' But Morrow, 'Harmount Company', 29–30, suggests that the Harmount troupe's opening of the scene was quite elaborate, beginning with a painted backdrop showing river boats at a levee, and a crowd. He also cites one Harvard promptbook in which specialty numbers were introduced in front of this backdrop, after which the dancers carried out the platform and auction block for the scene to follow.

21. Birdoff, *World's Greatest Hit*, 233–4 and 320.

22. Meisel, *Realizations*, 38–51, the chapter entitled 'Speaking Pictures: The Drama'. The argument of our book as a whole owes a great deal to this chapter of Meisel's.

23. Cit. Jackson, *Victorian Theatre*, 160–2. See also Brooks, *Melodramatic Imagination*, 61–2, citing Abel Hugo, Armand Malitourne, and J.-J. Ader, *Traité du mélodrame* (Paris: Delaunay, 1817): 'At the end of each act, one must take care to bring all the characters together in a group, and to place each of them in the attitude that corresponds to the situation of his soul. For example: pain will place a hand on its forehead; despair will tear out its hair, and joy will kick a leg in the air. This general perspective is designated as Tableau. One can sense how agreeable it is for the spectator to take in at a glance the psychological and moral condition of each character.'

24. In the typescript version of Hermann the timing of the tableau is uncertain, but the fairhand copy clearly specifies that the tableau follows upon Haley's entrance.

25. A similar scene, played with Eliza and Harry rather than Tom and Emmeline, appears in Fitzball, Act 2, scene 3, and may have had a tableau.

26. 'Early Twentieth Century Staging of *Uncle Tom's Cabin*: Harmount's Tom Show–Selected Scenes', *Ohio State University Theatre Collection Bulletin*, no. 15 (1968), 40.

27. Ibid. 40–1.

28. Birdoff, *World's Greatest Hit*, 318.

29. The Cruikshank illustration appears in the edition of John Cassell, London, 1852; for other editions which also illustrate this moment see Clarke, London, 1852; John P. Jewett, Cleveland, 1852; Nathaniel Cook, London, 1853; Simpkin, Marshall, London, 1857; Houghton Mifflin, Boston, 1882; Cassell, London, 1896; Blackie, London, 1908.

30. Originally published in 1698, Le Brun's lecture was translated into English by John Williams as *A Method to Learn to Design the Passions Proposed in a Conference on Their General and Particular Expression* and published by the translator in London in 1734 (see the reprint by the Augustan Reprint Society, Publication number 200–1, William Andrews Clark Memorial Library, University of California, Los Angeles, 1980). For Henry Siddons, see *Practical Illustrations of Rhetorical Gesture and Action; adapted to the English Drama: From a Work on the Same Subject by M. Engel* (London: Richard Phillips, 1807). The influence of these works, and more generally the role of postures and attitudes in the development of pictorial acting styles is discussed in detail in Ch. 5 below.

31. Siddons, *Practical Illustrations*, 78–9.

32. Joseph R. Roach, *The Player's Passion: Studies in the Science of Acting* (Newark: University of Delaware Press, 1985), 87.

33. The chorus can be translated: 'Frigid and motionless, like a statue, unable to draw a breath.'

34. First edition, 'Tableau', definition 2c, citing the *Westminster Gazette* (18 Oct. 1894): 5, col. 2. Walter Benjamin noted that the French word was used in the same way in Berlin: 'a family row. The mother is just about to pick up a pillow to hurl at the daughter, the father is opening a window to call a policeman. At this moment a stranger appears at the door. "Tableau", as they used to say around 1900' ('What is Epic Theatre? [First Version]', in *Understanding Brecht*, trans. Anna Bostock (London: New Left Books, 1973), 5; and *Gesammelte Schriften* (Frankfurt-am-Main: Suhrkamp Verlag, 1977), ii. 522.

35. All three promptbooks based upon the Aiken text in the Samuel French edition in the Billy Rose Theatre Collection indicate that Phineas re-enters the scene at the point when Marks says 'these yer arrangements are my forte'. The unsigned version notes the word 'story' at this point, while the Wright version has the dialogue spoken by Phineas, telling a story about another runaway. The Brady typescript in the Museum of the City of New York has the story written out in full.

36. An anecdote attributed to Hobart Bosworth describes a production in which he appeared in 1887 which involved 'the scene where Fletcher holds the attention of Loker and the other slave-driver down stage while he describes to Eliza the way she is to escape through the window "at back" with her pickaninny'. See Ralph Eugene Lund, 'Trouping with Uncle Tom', *Century*, 115 (1928), 335.

Chapter 4
The Fate of the Tableau in the Cinema

Uncle Tom's Cabin was first adapted into film in 1903, and there were at least six other adaptations during the silent period. We have been able to examine three of these in detail: the adaptations by Edison in 1903; by Vitagraph in 1910; and by World in 1914.[1] Before proceeding to an analysis of the tableaux, or lack of them, in these adaptations, something should be said about the tableau in early cinema generally.

Although modern viewers and film historians often assume a direct continuity in acting practice from nineteenth-century theatre to early film, in fact the actors in the latter rarely hold a pose for a prolonged period. Unlike theatrical performances, films did not stop for scene or act changes, nor were they designed to solicit applause. Hence there was no need for the 'strong curtain', one of the primary functions of tableaux in the theatre. None the less, the other functions of the tableau adduced above—summary of a situation, allegorical commentary, punctuation of important narrative moments—did form part of film dramaturgy, especially in the period of the early feature, hence the presence of tableaux or their cinematic equivalents.

Tableau-like shots are most frequent in films with strong ties to the theatre or the graphic arts. They are pronounced in religious films such as the Pathé films of Christ's Passion, inheritors of a strong iconographic tradition. Indeed, as already remarked, there is a tableau of the 'Last Supper' in the 1925 film *Ben-Hur*. In *L'Assassinat du duc de Guise* (The Assassination of the Duc de Guise), which utilized actors from the Comédie Française, the *mise-en-scène* is predicated upon the assumption of poses by the acting ensemble.[2] Film adaptations of stage plays with an ongoing performance tradition, like *East Lynne* and *Uncle Tom's Cabin*, also observed the canonical tableaux in some form, as we shall see.[3]

In these instances the freezing of the actors is usually narratively motivated. It is as if the filmmakers needed a reason to bring the flow of the action to a halt. In the earlier of the National Film and Television Archive's two versions of the Pathé *La Vie et la Passion de Jésus-Christ* (The Life and Passion of Jesus Christ), when the soldiers come to arrest Jesus in the Garden of Gethsemane, a tableau is produced when Judas counts his money in the foreground while in the background the soldiers physically hold back the disciples

2.6

2.7

2.8

2.9

(Figure 2.6).[4] In the same scene in the later version, a pose is motivated when Jesus intervenes to prevent Peter from killing one of the guards (Figure 2.7). In *L'Assassinat du duc de Guise*, the king has the conspirators swear to commit the murder; their pose with swords lifted is thus explained as a vow (Figure 2.8). The final tableau of this film, in the last scene, 'Le Corps de Garde', is motivated as a moment of surprise and horror, when the Duke's mistress pulls off the king's mask, confirming that he is indeed behind the murder.[5]

Examples of motivated tableau of this sort can be found in American films as well. Eileen Bowser notes a review of *Gold Is Not All* in the *New York Dramatic Mirror* which complains that at the moment when the rich and poor women meet 'the two gaze at each other over-long'.[6] Bowser points out that the pause

criticized in *Gold Is Not All* served 'to emphasize the moment, the contrast that the two [women] represented'.[7] It is a kind of tableau, though brief and motivated by the poor woman's picking up and returning the handkerchief the rich woman has dropped. Similarly, in *The Country Doctor*, the doctor (Frank Powell) is called on an emergency visit to a farmhouse. He prepares to perform a surgical procedure to save a young girl in danger of dying from diphtheria. The nursemaid from his household arrives at the farmhouse and begs him to come home; his own daughter, also suffering from the disease, is in dire need of the procedure. There is a momentary pause, as Powell stands immobilized between the nursemaid and the mother of the dying girl, the tableau motivated by his being torn between his professional duty and his familial obligation.

2.10

2.11

2.12

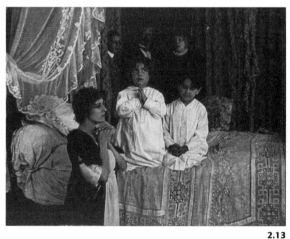

2.13

Strongly motivated tableaux continue to occur in feature films. Despite the fact that *Cabiria* eschews tableaux where the script seems to call for them, there is one tableau in the film. Fulvius Axilla announces to Cabiria's parents that, although he did find their lost daughter, he was later forced to abandon her in mortal peril; all three characters bow their heads and remain quiet in grief (Figure 2.9). The features we have seen by Albert Capellani—*Les Misérables, Quatre-vingt-treize* (Ninety-Three), *Notre Dame de Paris*—frequently make use of tableaux. Thus, in *Notre Dame de Paris*, when Frollo discovers Esmeralda sleeping in Quasimodo's cell and threatens her virtue, Quasimodo enters, frees Esmeralda from Frollo's clutches and starts to strangle him. Esmeralda seizes Quasimodo's arm from behind and orders him to stop, resulting in a first tableau, with Esmeralda on the left,

Quasimodo leaning over Frollo and Frollo cowering right (Figure 2.10). Quasimodo then crosses to front left, and Esmeralda pulls herself to her full height, stares at Frollo and points to the door midground left (Figure 2.11). Again all freeze, then relax as Frollo slinks to the door and exits left. Feuillade uses tableaux much more sparingly than does Capellani, but certain crucial situations are so represented in *Judex*. One example is the scene that follows the Comte de Trémeuse's suicide, in which the Comtesse's two sons vow to seek vengeance on the man that brought about their father's death (Figure 2.12). Another is the moment when the Comtesse is reconciled to Jacqueline, the daughter of her enemy, by seeing her with her small son and his friend the Licorice Kid, heads bowed in prayer (Figure 2.13); the film thus produces a tableau of goodness and inno-

2.14

2.15

2.16

2.17

cence to explain and help motivate the Comtesse's acceptance of Jacqueline. In a scene in *Alias Jimmy Valentine* Tourneur uses tableaux as the protagonists remember their previous life of crime; cutaways show incidents from the past, as they freeze in slightly varied attitudes four times (Figures 2.14 to 2.17).

But as we have noted, even in the very earliest films tableaux are not simply carried over wholesale from the theatre. One common variation on a definite freeze on the part of all of the actors within the shot is to incorporate limited forms of figure movement within the picture. The scourging of Christ in the earlier NFTVA Pathé Passion offers an example of repetitive movement. Midground centre there is a whipping-post against a backdrop representing an obliquely receding vault. As Christ is taken down from the whipping-post, a crowd of torturers and high priests' spies scorn and threaten him, forming a group reminiscent of paintings of the same subject (Figure 2.18). Rather than holding a stationary pose, they all cyclically repeat brief gestures preserving the overall picture without stasis.

Another strategy is to have one actor or group of actors move while the others maintain a pose. The scene of the crucifixion in the later NFTVA Pathé Passion evokes a composition also familiar from painting, showing Christ in the centre with the thieves left and right, all three crosses rising above a crowd of soldiers, disciples, and other onlookers (Figure 2.19). Most of the crowd remain still, but the leader of the high priests' spies (the figure in the striped cloak in the foreground of Figure 2.19) makes agitated gestures, apparently in remorse. Inversely, in the final scene of *Au pays noir* (In the Black Country),

2.18

2.19

2.20

2.21

when the miner hero discovers that his eldest son is among the dead after a mining accident, he, his wife, and their other children form a static group representing domestic grief; meanwhile, the gendarmes and other miners in the foreground continue the mine rescue work (Figure 2.20).

In some films a strong pictorial effect is created without a definite freeze by the use of big sets organized in perspective in which the movement of human figures is minimized by the scale and apparent depth of the shot. We have suggested that a similar emphasis on setting, as opposed to the actor's pose, existed in the scene-opening pictures in the stage productions of *Uncle Tom's Cabin*. In the theatre, such stage pictures were often combined with processions, an established part of the spectacle in theatrical pantomime and burlesque.[8] In film, long shots of

processions or massive assemblies could provide the outlines of a picture while accommodating the movement of individual actors. Such pictures are most evident in big-budget spectaculars which employed large sets and large numbers of extras. For example, at the end of part 2 of *Cabiria*, Croessa the nursemaid is captured by Carthaginians angered at the rescue of her charge. Outside the temple of Moloch, Croessa, held by the priests, appears on a raised platform (Figure 2.21). The crowd is arranged in the left foreground, below the platform, and on the right, all along the stairs which lead to the temple entrance in the background. While Croessa moves in response to the threatening gestures of the Carthaginians, the general effect is of a static picture, until the end of the shot with its procession towards the interior of the temple, where Croessa is to be sacrificed.[9]

2.22

2.23

2.24

2.25

The introduction of repetitive or limited forms of figure movement within the shot was not the only way to render the picture more dynamic; a variety of cinematic devices could also have this effect. Unlike the scene in which Croessa is menaced by the Carthaginians, many of the big sets in *Cabiria* are displayed with oblique tracking shots. While the set is the dominant feature of shot 112, in the interior of Moloch's temple, or shots 254 and 256, the banquet hall of Sophonisbe's father, dramatic changes in perspective and shot scale emphasize the mobility of viewpoint (Figures 2.22 and 2.23).

Before classical Hollywood editing conventions were fully in place, the possibility of a change in framing still affected the use of tableaux in cinema. In the earlier NFTVA Pathé *Passion*, for example, the scene in which Veronica displays the napkin with Christ's

features after she has wiped his face takes the form of a picture with limited movement (Veronica turns from side to side holding up the napkin for the crowd to see). But, in the later version, there is a cut from a long shot of Veronica displaying the napkin amidst the crowd to a medium shot of Veronica alone against a neutral background (Figures 2.24 and 2.25). The change of framing performs many of the same functions as the quasi-tableau in the earlier version: it provides dramatic emphasis, directs the spectator's attention, and slows down the pace of the action. This cut in to a closer view in the later version also bears resemblance to another device of early film, the emblematic close up.

From almost as early as films began to have more than one shot, it was customary to begin, or more frequently end a film with a shot epitomizing the subject, like the frontispiece of a book. These shots, called 'emblematic shots' by Noël Burch, echo stage tableaux in many ways.[10] They can be allegorical, like the 'Tableau' of corrupted justice at the end of *The Kleptomaniac*, or sensational, like the famous close shot of the bandit Barnes shooting at the audience which could be placed at the beginning or the end of *The Great Train Robbery*, or summarizing, like the matching opening and closing closer shots in *Bold Bank Robbery*, showing the villains in a drawing-room in expensive suits and in gaol in convict garb, respectively. Later, especially in Pathé films, the closing emblematic shot is a cut-in on the final scene, showing, for example, the main character's reactions—Max weeping at the end of *Les Débuts d'un patineur* (First Attempt at Skating), or Alphonse chewing the eponymous prop at the end of the Biograph film *The Curtain Pole*—or summing up the final resolution—the reunited families at the ends of *Rescued by Rover* and *A Drunkard's Reformation*. These last examples involve still poses, and so constitute true tableaux. Most of the others do not, but the cut-in is nevertheless functionally the equivalent of a tableau.

Finally, cutting not only provided the possibility of moving in for a closer view, it also obviated one of the theatrical motives for tableaux. Although scene transitions in early film were not necessarily direct cuts—dissolves, cuts to intertitles, and (later) fades out and in were also used—these transitions were always brief.[11] It was thus possible to terminate a scene-end tableau relatively quickly, that is, without the 'wait' routinely noted (usually as a 'W' in a circle) in many promptbooks for stage melodramas, and without pausing while the curtain was drawn, a process often noted '*picture closed in*'.

The cinematic tableau was thus rendered more dynamic than its theatrical equivalent. In part this resulted from the introduction of limited forms of figure movement within the shot. It was also achieved by the introduction of cinematic devices; the use of camera movement, the emblematic close-up, and rapid scene changes. The extent to which the cinema altered the traditional form of the theatrical tableaux is evident in the earliest version of *Uncle Tom's Cabin*.

The Edison film version of 1903, *Uncle Tom's Cabin; or Slavery Days*, remains the closest to the theatrical performance tradition.[12] The filmmakers' strategy for abbreviating the lengthy Aiken play within the short-film format seems to have been to string together the scenes and incidents consecrated within the performance tradition. Intertitles like 'Tom and Eva in the Garden' and 'Tableau: the Death of Uncle Tom' almost function as captions, identifying scenes in terms of the conventional tableau, even though the incident occasioning that tableau may occur long after the scene's opening. The film also retains a speciality act, the dance at the opening of the auction scene, which is mentioned in two of the Aiken promptbooks, and familiar bits of stage business, such as Topsy plaguing Aunt Ophelia. The scene of the race between the Natchez and the Robert E. Lee, filmed with model steamboats, may have derived from the sensation scene described by Birdoff, first staged in 1888.[13]

The film consisted of 14 single-shot scenes, two with superimpositions, each preceded by a title, as listed below.[14]

Scene 1. Eliza Pleads with Tom to Run Away.
Scene 2. Phineas Outwits the Slave Traders.
Scene 3. The Escape of Eliza.
Scene 4. Reunion of Eliza and George Harris.
Scene 5. Race between the Rob't E. Lee and Natchez.
Scene 6. Rescue of Eva.
Scene 7. The Welcome Home to St Clare, Eva, Ophelia, and Uncle Tom.
Scene 8. Eva and Tom in the Garden.
Scene 9. Death of Eva.
Scene 10. St Clare Defends Uncle Tom.
Scene 11. Auction Sale of St Clare's Slaves.
Scene 12. Tom Refuses to Flog Emaline.
Scene 13. Marks Avenges the Death of St Clare and Uncle Tom.
Scene 14. Tableau: Death of Uncle Tom.

Despite the evident theatrical influences, there are no prolonged freezes. Scene 2 concludes with a definite but brief freeze, the tableau already discussed which is motivated by Phineas drawing his guns (Figure 2.26). Most of the other canonical tableaux from the stage tradition of *Uncle Tom's Cabin* could be illustrated with frame stills from this version, but none of these 'tableaux' involves a static pose held for more than a fraction of a second.

The title of Scene 8 evokes one of the canonical tableaux: Tom and Eva in the garden. However, after a lengthy cake-walk by the slaves, the scene merely has

Tom accompany Eva out of the house and sit under a tree with her in his lap as he reads her the Bible and gestures to heaven (Figure 2.27); St Clare enters with Aunt Ophelia, expresses anxiety about Eva's health, and Tom carries Eva back into the house. There is no sign of the wreath, and no true stasis, though, of course, Tom and Eva are relatively static while she is in his lap.

In some cases, stasis is broken up by repetitive movement. Thus, Scene 3, Eliza crossing the Ohio, shows the river represented by a moving backcloth with painted lumps of ice. Eliza moves perpendicularly to the lens axis on a conveyor belt or truck obscured by some painted rocks in the foreground. Dogs and slavers run across the forestage from right to left. Tom Loker tries to pull the lawyer Marks out of the river into which he has fallen (Figure 2.28). The move-

ment is repetitive—Marks is pulled out by his umbrella, but only emerges part way and then falls back in. Similarly, Scene 4, corresponding to the scene on a rocky pass in Aiken, ends with a static composition, but one incorporating repetitive movement. To the right of a cabin (according to the Edison catalogue the home of the Quaker girl Ruth, Phineas's intended) are two painted flats representing a rocky cliff face. At the end of the scene, Phineas, George, and Eliza stand between the two flats, 'up on the rocks', looking down on Marks and the fallen Loker. Marks has turned away from them and faces the camera, his knees knock together as he tries to shield himself from the fugitives' bullets with his open umbrella, and the third slave-hunter shakes his fist at the fugitives (Figure 2.29).

In other cases, what was a tableau in the theatrical performance tradition is marked by a spectacular cin-

2.26

2.27

2.28

2.29

2.30

2.31

2.32

2.33

ematic device which does not entail immobilizing all the actors within the scene. Scene 9, the death of Eva, uses superimpositions to show an angel taking Eva to heaven. The actors round the bed are static, but the superimposed figures are in continuous motion (Figure 2.30). Scene 14, the death of Uncle Tom, shows George Shelby kneeling by Tom's bedside. Tom gestures in response to a painted angel which appears in the upper right-hand corner of the frame (Figure 2.31). As Tom dies, the angel disappears giving way to the apotheosis, a series of superimposed drawn images described by the Edison catalogue as 'visions': 'John Brown being led to execution [Figure 2.32], a battle scene from the Civil War, and a cross with a vision of emancipation, showing Abraham Lincoln with the negro slave kneeling at his feet with broken manacles.'[15] These visions are certainly reminiscent

of the allegorical tableaux used in the theatre. But the circularly vignetted images, clearly drawings rather than photographs, are substituted for one another within the same general scene in what looks like a lantern-slide show rather than the realization of pictures with immobile human figures.

Perhaps the most frequent alternative to a long-held pose is what we can call a 'truncated tableau'. Scene 10, the auction scene, ends with the actors in the postures described in the published version of the Aiken text: Tom and Emmeline kneeling, and Legree standing between them with raised whip (Figure 2.33); but this is only held for a few frames. Scene 12 takes place on a cotton field set. Tom refuses to whip Emmeline and is tied to a tree, right. Legree orders his overseer to whip Tom, but the overseer is stopped by Cassy, who pulls the whip from his hand. Emmeline pleads with Legree and Legree moves to attack her, but he is stopped by Cassy threatening him with the whip. Both the refusal (Figure 2.34) and Cassy's second intervention (Figure 2.35) result in groupings and poses like the stage tableaux, but there is no wait: in the first case, the pose is immediately broken and the scene resumes; in the second, there is an immediate cut to the intertitle introducing the next scene. *Uncle Tom's Cabin* is Porter's first film to use cuts to and from intertitles as scene transitions, rather than dissolves. The markedly truncated tableaux at these scene-ends might thus indicate experimental uncertainty rather than a regularized practice. Whichever is the case, it suggests that the filmmakers already felt that scene-ends had to be handled differently in the cinema.

The Edison version of *Uncle Tom's Cabin*, made in 1903, was sold only as a single subject, and was, as far as we know, intended to be projected as a whole. At any rate, the only divisions in it are the fourteen scenes, each with its introductory title. The Vitagraph version of 1910 and the World of 1914 were multiple-reel films. By 1910, most moving-picture houses in the USA were showing half-hour or hour-long programmes of short films based on the 1,000-foot reel unit, which took a little over a quarter of an hour to project. Most films were a full reel, and exchanges and theatres rented film from producers in reels, but a certain number of the reels contained two shorter subjects adding up to 1,000 feet, known as 'split-reel' subjects. The films were interspersed with music, songs, and sometimes live acts, and the programme was repeated continuously, in metropolitan houses from the early afternoon until the theatre closed late at night. Longer stories were occasionally screened serially, the different reels being issued at intervals, with the narrative in each reel partly self-contained, so as to be intelligible to the viewer who missed one or more of the parts. The Vitagraph *Uncle Tom's Cabin* was such a film. It was in three parts, which were issued on the Tuesday, Friday, and Saturday of the week ending Saturday, 30 July 1910. This meant that it was possible for exhibitors to wait until the Saturday and show all three reels together, and despite the competition among theatres to show only the newest films, some theatres seem to have done this. However, each of the three reels has a fairly autonomous narrative, with a partial resolution at the end, especially for all characters other than Uncle Tom himself, who is the

2.34

2.35

only one to appear more than briefly in all three parts. The alternation between the stories of George and Eliza on the one hand and Tom and the St Clares on the other found both in the book and in the Aiken play is rigorously avoided; George is eliminated and Eliza's adventures after crossing the Ohio are omitted, as is any reference to the fates of Topsy and Aunt Ophelia after St Clare's death. In many ways, the Vitagraph version is the furthest from the Aiken or any other play text of all the film versions we have seen.

Even if the reels were screened one after the other, few theatres in 1910 would have been equipped to show the film without pauses to load each new reel, and even in those with the two projectors necessary for continuous projection across a reel-end, it is probable that the projectionist would have left a short break, or used a device such as a dissolve or announcement slide used elsewhere in the programme to mark a division between 'numbers'.[16] This produced a situation at the reel-end very like that at a curtain in a stage play. And the reel-ends in the Vitagraph version of *Uncle Tom's Cabin* seem to have been typical moments for act-end tableaux.[17] Reel one ends as Tom bids farewell to the slaves on the Shelby plantation and is carried off by Haley. There is indeed a brief tableau, as two slaves kneel front centre, and Tom, standing above them in irons in Haley's wagon, blesses them, but the scene ends with the wagon exiting, and Mrs Shelby collapsing in tears in her husband's arms—i.e. the scene has a brief anticlimactic epilogue rather than closing with the tableau (Figures 2.36 and 2.37). Plot summaries indicate that the last scene of reel two was that of Eva's death.[18] Neither print that we have seen has any kind of ascent to heaven or vision of angels, but in neither case are we confident that the scene is complete. The National Film and Television Archive print ends before Eva's death. Murray Glass's print has more of the same final scene, including Eva's death, and a tableau with St Clare burying his face in Tom's shoulder and Tom gazing heavenward. Scratches on the print suggest that this is near a reel-end, but it is not clear that there may not once have been sufficient extra footage to include some kind of supernatural manifestation. The end of the third reel is the scene of Tom's death, with the winged figure of Eva appearing over his dying body. Certain narrative elements remain unresolved—the escape of Cassy and Emmeline is not assured, and Legree is still alive—but the contemporary descriptions referred to above tell us that this would have been the last scene, though the tableau might have been extended to include the carrying of Tom's soul to heaven.

Within each reel, however, there is no significant subdivision. There are 38 intertitles for 63 picture shots in the NFTVA print. The intertitles are descriptive titles, specifying time and space for the next sequence, and filling in non-visualized narrative information. Thus, the film consists of a series of short scenes, neither the integral 'sequence shots' of the Edison version, nor the complex sequences of feature filmmaking. Within each reel, there are no significant pauses in the action such as would be accompanied by a curtain or open-stage scene change in a theatrical presentation.

Correspondingly, few of the canonical tableaux appear in the form typical of the stage versions, or even truncated, as in the Edison version. The elimination of George Harris, Loker, and Marks takes with it the scene in the rocky pass and the arrival in Canada. Eliza does escape across the frozen Ohio River, and she is pursued by bloodhounds, following the stage tradition rather than the novel, but the incident is presented as follows:

27 The Ohio River. A painted backdrop represents the river filled with ice floes. A strip of real water across the middle ground contains moving papier mâché floes. Eliza runs in front left, carrying Harry, sees the river blocking her way, kneels, and prays. Artificial snow is blown on to the scene. She jumps on to one of the floes and exits left, jumping from floe to floe (Figure 2.38).

2.36

2.37

2.38

2.39

2.40

28 Title: 'The pursuers baffled by the Ohio River.'
29 As 27. A white man with dog standing right. Haley rides in front left and dismounts. Snow falls. His horse exits right as two slaves lead their horses on left. All scan the horizon rear left, searching for Eliza (Figure 2.39).
30 Title: 'Eliza saved by Phineas, the Quaker.'
31 Similar backdrop to 27, but a different foreground bank, with bushes. Eliza, carrying Harry, enters midground left jumping from floe to floe. As she staggers, about to fall into the water, a man in Quaker garb runs on front left, seizes her hand, and helps her off front left (Figure 2.40).[19]

Thus, all the elements of the tableau of *Vengeance and Disappointment on the one bank and Gratitude to Providence on the other* are present, but not in a single picture; rather they are dispersed across a series of shots and titles.

Tom's goodbye to Chloe and the children is a single shot, but the elements of the tableau are, again, presented in succession rather than simultaneously. The scene (33) opens with Tom saying goodbye to the children. One of them is in his lap, Chloe holds another in the cabin doorway to his right. Haley enters left, and calls roughly to Tom. Chloe and the children exit into the cabin, then Haley puts irons on Tom's wrists. Young George Shelby enters right, looks at the fetters in horror, swears to save Tom as soon as he is able, and exits right. Tom turns and says farewell to his cabin, then follows Haley off left.

Other tableaux are more conventionally presented. At the end of the slave market scene (69), Tom and Emmeline kneel front centre, with Legree standing over them threatening them with his whip (Figure 2.41). In the cotton field (76), after Sambo has caught Tom helping Lucy, Cassy steps between Sambo and Tom to prevent Tom from being beaten, leading to a true motivated tableau (Figure 2.42), but the scene then continues, as Sambo exits and Tom succours Lucy. In the weighing shed (78) there are two tableaux: when Tom kneels and returns the whip to Legree, refusing to beat Lucy (Figure 2.43); and at the end, after Sambo and Quimbo have dragged Tom away, when Cassy steps between Legree and Lucy to save her from a beating (Figure 2.44).

Thus the only frozen pictures in the film are motivated tableaux, and even they rarely constitute the end of a scene, with a direct cut to a title or the next scene.

2.41

2.42

2.43

2.44

Rather, the action continues to empty the frame, or close with an anticlimactic picture, what might be called a weak tableau, as at the end of the first reel. If the truncated tableaux in the Edison version are a response to a sense that cinema required a different kind of scene-ending from that of the stage, the surviving reel-ending in the Vitagraph version can be seen as a more developed response to the same requirement. Where incidents that provided the stage tradition with opportunities for tableaux fall within a reel, the Vitagraph version either disperses the elements of the tableau in time and across shots, or extends the action after the tableau. The World version carries the same tendencies much further.

We have studied four different prints of the version produced by World in 1914, one in the National Film Archive in London (hereafter NFTVA), two in the Li-

brary of Congress, Washington DC (LoC1 and LoC2), and a copy distributed as a videocassette by Grapevine Video (GV).[20] No print is complete, and the ordering and length of shots vary. However, we have also been able to consult the script deposited together with frames of the scenes of the film at the Copyright Office, in conformity with the 1912 Copyright Act. The celluloid frames themselves have decomposed, but a comparison of the script with the surviving prints suggests that it is a sequential description of those frames, and constitutes a virtually complete shot breakdown of the film. We are thus reasonably confident that we have been able to reconstruct the film as it was when copyrighted in the summer of 1914, and virtually every scene in the reconstruction survives in one or more of the surviving prints. The shot numbering of the examples in the following analysis follows the scene numbering of the copyright script, dividing the scenes as (*a*), (*b*), and so on, when there is more than one shot to a scene.[21]

The film was released in five reels, and would have been sold on a states rights basis, i.e. by a regional distributor booking a small number of prints into theatres, not all of them primarily moving-picture theatres, in the territory to which he was granted exclusive rights. By 1914, even such theatres would have been equipped with multiple projectors, at least in larger towns, so the film could have been screened continuously, as a modern feature film is, but many theatres continued to allow a short break at the ends of reels, and most films continued to be made, like the Vitagraph version, with partly self-contained reels. This seems to be the case with the World *Uncle Tom's Cabin*. The script indicates the reel-ends, and LoC1 is still divided at the same places: after Eliza's flight from the Shelby plantation; after the Harrises reach safety in Canada; after Eva's death; and as Emmeline escapes Legree's attentions and comes to talk to Tom on the doorstep of his cabin. Only this last break is not a major punctuation point in the narrative.

If most of the reels are thus analogous to acts, the reel-endings are where one might expect to find tableaux of the 'strong curtain' type exemplified in the staging tradition. However, as with the Vitagraph version, this does not seem to have been the only way to end a reel for the World filmmakers. Indeed, only one of the reels of the World version ends in a tableau.

This is the end of reel two, Scene 104, as the fugitives arrive in Canada. Phineas Fletcher, the Harrises, and Jim Vance (a runaway who accompanies George on his flight in this version) are shown backs to camera in a long shot on a hill overlooking a village with a church steeple. A rectangular soft-edged iris closes in. All but George fall on their knees and thank God, while George stands in the centre, arms raised to heaven, and the pose and the contraction of the iris are momentarily held (Figure 2.45). None of the surviving prints has more than a few frames after this. It is possible that it was once held for much longer, but it looks more likely that there was a truncated tableau of the type found in the Edison version.

The end of the whole film intercuts the death of Tom in the presence of the adult George Shelby, Junior, with the ambush and shooting of Legree by the slave whom Tom refused to whip (in this version a young man); there is also one shot (Scene 211) to show that Cassy and Emmeline escaped safely. There is a shot of Tom's vision of Eva, essentially similar to those in the Edison and Vitagraph versions. Tom is alone in his hut, lying on a mattress, Little Eva's spirit is superimposed, Tom reaches out to her joyfully, her image fades, and Tom falls back as if dead. However, according to the script, this scene, 191, occurs before the final alternation, well before Young Shelby arrives by the bedside in time for the dying Tom to recognize him. After the deaths of Tom and Legree, there is a single shot (Scene 213) of Young Shelby kneeling beside a grave marked 'In Memory of Uncle Tom,' and a final close-up (Scene 214) of the last two pages of the novel (echoing the opening of the whole film), with a final moral summation: 'Into the land of eternal love which knows no race or class.' This ending is surprisingly understated, and it is interesting that none of the surviving prints places the vision scene as early as the script. Two have it as a shot out of any narrative concatenation, immediately preceding the shot of Tom's grave, adding weight (and a traditional character) to the end. GV substitutes for the brief motto a title quoting the Emancipation Proclamation, superimposed over a still picture of Lincoln, again an appeal to tradition, reminiscent of the Edison version.

The end of reel one also uses an alternation: between Eliza and George Harris as each leaves their respective plantation at night, ending as George joins Jim Vance and the latter says goodbye to his mother. Reel two begins with Subtitle 17—'Haley learns of the escape of Eliza and her boy'—and after a short se-

2.45

2.46

2.47

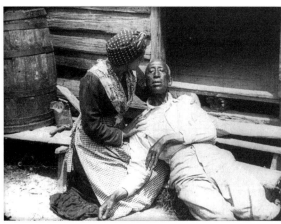

2.48

2.49

quence showing a furious Haley berating the Shelbys (Scene 44, Subtitle 18 and Scene 45), the alternation continues with shots of both George and Vance, and Eliza and Harry. The final embrace of Vance and his mother at the end of reel one (Scene 43), and the jump to the next morning at the beginning of reel two constitute a clear reel-end punctuation.

The end of reel four (Scene 171) presents no such breathing space. A few scenes earlier, there is what seems a more appropriate breaking-point: after Cassy's interruption of Legree's beating of Uncle Tom (Scene 163). Subtitle 54 announces Cassy's demotion to field slave and Emmeline's promotion to Legree's housekeeper, which sets in train the final episode of the two women's escape, itself leading directly to the death of Tom. It seems possible that this was planned to be the end of the reel, but the distribution of

footage between reels four and five was too uneven, so the break in the final cut was at an arbitrary point. If the reel-end were at the more motivated point, it would resemble that of the end of the first reel of the Vitagraph version. After he refuses to whip the young slave, Tom is dragged off by the overseers to the slave huts. Emmeline sees this in a cutaway, runs to the house, and appeals to Cassy. When Cassy reaches the huts (Scene 162), Legree is about to whip Tom. She seizes his arm from behind, they argue, then Legree turns back to Tom to whip him. Cassy places herself between them and Legree stops, giving a clear tableau pose (Figure 2.46, compare with the scene in the cotton field in the Edison version, Figure 2.35, and the Vitagraph version, Figure 2.42). But then Legree backs down, orders the overseers away, and follows them off. Cassy turns to Tom, lying on the threshold of the

2.50

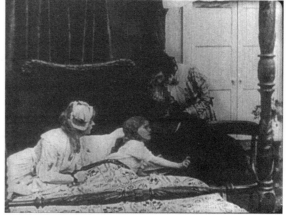

2.51

2.52

2.53

hut. As she kneels to tend him, there is a cut-in to medium long shot (Scene 163, Figures 2.47 and 2.48). This cut-in would provide the punctuation appropriate to a reel-end, but the narrative incident would be an anticlimactic epilogue.

The punctuating cut-in, and also a vignette, are found where one of the canonical tableau points occurs within a reel: the scene of Eva and Tom in the garden. After Subtitle 35—'Two Years Later. Uncle Tom tells Eva of the New Jerusalem'—Scene 121(*a*) is a long shot of the garlanded Tom sitting on a garden bench with Eva sitting in his lap holding an open Bible. A circular vignette closes round the couple, and then there is a cut-in on the same axis to Scene 121(*b*), a similarly vignetted medium shot of them (Figures 2.49 and 2.50). Tom's gesture to heaven is repeated in the cut-in.

A much more elaborately edited, and therefore linearized, treatment of a canonical tableau is found at the death of Eva.

Subtitle 38. Spring brings sadness into St Clare's home.

Scene 126. Slightly oblique long shot from the foot of Eva's bed, showing her supported by pillows rear centre and the door to the room rear right, with Marie and Augustine St Clare sitting left and right of the bed and Ophelia standing at the bedhead right. Eva speaks earnestly to her father (Figure 2.51).

Subtitle 39. 'Papa before I die, promise to free Uncle Tom.'

Scene 127. As 126. St Clare promises. Eva lies back on the pillow. The others are despondent (Figure 2.52).

Scene 128. Medium long shot of the other side of the door of 126. Tom on his knees right praying (Figure 2.53).

Scene 129(*a*). Medium shot of a louvre-shuttered window in an ivied wall right. Topsy looks off right into the window (Figure 2.54). She turns to face front and prays.

2.54

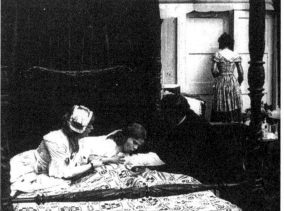

2.55

2.56

2.57

2.58

2.59

Scene 129(b). As 126. Ophelia goes to the door right and opens it (Figure 2.55).

Scene 130. As 128, but slightly tilted up. The door opens and Ophelia appears (Figure 2.56). Tom rises, they converse, Ophelia weeps. She exits back into the room, followed by Tom.

Subtitle 40. 'In Heaven above, where all is love, we'll meet to part no more.'

Scene 131. As 126. Marie and Ophelia as in 126, St Clare standing right, Tom kneeling front right. Eva falls back on the pillow. All kneel and weep except St Clare, who leans against the bedpost and buries his face in his hands. While no one is looking at her, Eva sits up again, her face expressing joy. A group of small girls in white robes are superimposed on the bedhead (Figure 2.57). They gaze at Eva and beckon to her. She falls back on the pillow and they fade out. Everyone looks at Eva again. St Clare kneels and speaks to Eva. The superimposed girls reappear. Eva's spirit detaches itself from her inert body, turns and walks to the rear to join the girls (Figure 2.58). As they lead her away, she turns and looks back. All the spirits fade out. St Clare leans forward over Eva, and starts to cover her face with the sheet.

Scene 132. As 129. Topsy weeps, then exits right (Figure 2.59).

Scene 133. Long shot of the outside of the house. Assembled slaves kneeling with their backs to camera, waving their arms in mourning (Figure 2.60).

Subtitle 41. Topsy's offering.

Scene 134. Slight variant of 128. Topsy stands left holding a bunch of daisies. The door opens to reveal Tom. Topsy averts her eyes and thrusts the daisies at him (Figure 2.61). He takes them, she turns to go, but he calls her back, and leads her off into the bedroom.

Scene 135. Slight variant of 126. Eva dead in the bed. No one else is present except for Tom and Topsy coming from the door to the bed. Tom starts to put the flowers on Eva's breast, then hands them to Topsy, urging her to do it. Topsy kneels beside the bed right, reverently lays the flowers on Eva, then collapses weeping, her head in the bedclothes (Figure 2.62). Tom prays. A fade-out begins.[22]

2.60

2.61

2.62

Thus rather than gathering all the principals round Eva's bed and representing her ascent to heaven and their grief in one or two comprehensive tableaux, as in the stage versions and the Edison, the scene starts with the immediate family alone, and only gradually widens the circle. Tom is included before the death, but Topsy only enters Eva's presence some time later.

The ascent to heaven here, too, is strongly marked as Eva's vision, rather than as an allegory. The passage from the novel that inspired the stage representations of Eva's death does describe a vision:

The child lay panting on her pillows, as one exhausted,—the large clear eyes rolled up and fixed. Ah, what said those eyes, that spoke so much of heaven! Earth was past, and earthly pain; but so solemn, so mysterious, was the triumphant brightness of that face, that it checked even the sobs of sorrow. They pressed around her, in breathless stillness.

'Eva,' said St. Clare, gently.

She did not hear.

'O, Eva, tell us what you see! What is it?' said her father.

A bright, a glorious smile passed over her face, and she said, brokenly,—'O! love,—joy,—peace!' gave one sigh and passed from death unto life!²³

This emphasis on Eva's vision is much attenuated in the stage versions, however, which drew on the traditional representation of the apotheosis of the martyr in painting and drama, itself deriving from representations of the ascensions of Christ and the Virgin Mary. Such representations might appear as the vision of a saint, or even of the picture's patron, but more commonly they simply gave spectators a privileged view of an objective reality—perhaps a reality concealed from profane eyes, or only visualizable via allegory, but not simply a subjective vision. The stage versions of the death of Eva seem to share this objectivity, and the same is true of the Edison version. The Edison Catalog runs as follows: 'Eva points toward the sky telling her father that she is going there, and falls back dead. Uncle Tom and Topsy, who were standing at the foot of the cot, kneel in prayer while the angel appears, takes the spirit of Eva and ascends.' It is the action described at the beginning of the first sentence in this description rather than that in the second that is illustrated in the Catalog by a still captioned 'Eva's Vision'.²⁴

Nineteenth-century staging tradition did have methods of representing visions, and the devices deployed were often indistinguishable from those used in objective apotheosis scenes. Thus Mathias's vision at the end of Act 1 of *The Bells* was achieved by a 'sink and rise', dropping part of the set representing the street wall of the inn into a stage sloat, raising part of it into the flies, and revealing, behind a scrim giving the appearance of a cloud, Mathias (acted by a double) pursuing the Polish Jew's sled; while his dream of being tried for the murder in Act 3 was represented by raising a black cloth from behind the transparent gauze depicting the rear wall of his bedroom to reveal the ghostly courtroom beyond.²⁵ What constitutes

these as visions is an appropriate narrative context and their visibility to one character alone (in addition to the audience, of course). Such devices were rapidly adapted into early cinema, which, before 1910, regularly superimposed or matted in a second scene over the main scene to represent a vision.²⁶ Here too, narrative context distinguished a vision from an objective supernatural being. If the ascent of Eva to heaven in the Edison version of *Uncle Tom's Cabin* is not a vision, because Eva has had her vision, but the spectator has not been able to share it, and she is dead before the angels appear to take her to heaven, the appearance of the spirit of Eva to the dying Tom in the same film is at least compatible with the representation of a vision. In the World version, the status of a vision is extended to the other stage apotheosis. Eva's vision before death is vouchsafed the spectator, so when the angels reappear after her death to lead her spirit away, this seems to be a continuation of the vision by a now disembodied Eva (Figures 2.57 and 2.58). The supernatural paraphernalia of the stage versions have been subjectivized.

The World version thus presents some filmic 'equivalents' of the tableau, such as the iris out on the Harrises' arrival in Canada, or the use of cuts into medium shot on Cassy holding Tom after his beating, and Tom and Eva in the garden. Although these devices might be considered 'cinematic' in and of themselves, and indeed the cut-in clearly derives from the emblematic close-ups found in earlier films, they also preserve the pictorial integrity of the canonical tableau and in this sense harken back to the stage versions. In the case of Little Eva's death, however, the tableau is transformed beyond recognition. Not only is Eva's vision subjectivized, but the film emphasizes the separation among characters traditionally gathered, motionless, around the bedside. The use of editing is somewhat different from that in *The Social Secretary* example, in which the film cuts into medium shots or close-ups to present the reactions of characters all within a single room. In the World *Uncle Tom's Cabin*, the characters are represented as in different spaces: Topsy at the window and Tom at the door outside the bedroom. The dissection of the scenic space is thus given in the construction of the sets themselves. Given this construction of the sets, the filmmakers seem to have gone out of their way to structure the scene differently from the canonical stage picture, and to present a temporal succession of grieving characters rather than a static moment of general grief. In other instances the film similarly transforms the canonical tableaux not simply as a function of continuity editing, but also through changes in camera angle and shot scale which heighten the sense of spatial fragmentation. Paradoxically, even the use of spectacular staging in depth, which is quite pronounced in this film, can contribute to the effect of this transformation.

Like the Vitagraph version of the same scene, the moment in which Tom bids his family farewell is characterized by a dispersal of significant elements, although in this case the film also employs a rather spectacular use of staging in depth. In Scene 77 this is achieved by having Tom exit off screen while his children come on. Tom kisses Chloe while Haley taps on

his shoulder. As Tom exits front right (Figure 2.63), his children run in from under an arch rear left which emphasizes the movement from background to foreground (Figure 2.64). Haley also exits off right. The children gather around Chloe, all gaze off right and wave sadly. The decomposition of the tableau continues, with Tom's departure from young George Shelby distributed over three shots interrupted by titles (Scene 78, Subtitle 27, Scene 79(*a*) and (*b*)). Scenes 78 and 79(*a*) are long shots showing Haley's carriage, facing front. Haley and Tom approach the carriage and are followed by George, who runs over a bridge front right (Figure 2.65). The last shot of the segment (Scene 79(*b*)) is a slight high-angle medium shot of George, who looks after Tom off right, weeping (Figure 2.66). This cut-in seems to function quite differently from the closer view of Tom and Eva in the garden. The lat-

2.63

2.64

2.65

2.66

2.67 2.68 2.69

2.70 2.71 2.72

2.73 2.74 2.75

ter held all of the tableau elements together, the use of the iris and the closer framing emphasizing the image's significance. In contrast, the shot of George weeping is but one element in a series that has been presented in linear succession.

In the sequence of Eliza crossing the Ohio, the decomposition of the unified space of the tableau is quite marked. Recall that the Vitagraph version already breaks up this action, presented in one shot in the Edison version, into three. At the end of the first shot, Eliza jumps on to an ice floe; a title follows, then the film cuts to the slavers and dogs remaining on the river bank; after another title, we see Eliza arrive safely at the other shore, aided by Phineas. In the World version Subtitle 21 announces Eliza's arrival

and her determination to cross the river. The sequence ends with Subtitle 22, introducing Phineas as her rescuer and a shot of Phineas leading her to his house. In between there are eight shots alternating between Eliza requesting help from the ferryman, and eventually running across the river, and Haley and other slavers mounted on horseback, with bloodhounds, on the riverbank.

Not only is the action broken up over more shots than in the Vitagraph, but also the World is shot on location, which introduces another order of spectacle (for the World version of the crossing of the Ohio see Figures 2.67 to 2.76, which appear here in the order of the sequence of shots in the film, and compare with the same scene in the Vitagraph, Figures 2.38 to 2.40, and the Edison, Figure 2.28). Like the Edison, the Vita-graph crossing of the Ohio employs a set: a painted backdrop in the background with a strip of real water across the middle ground containing moving papier mâché ice floes. As we have noted, the foreground of the set is dressed differently for the last shot of the segment, to indicate the opposite shore of the river.

Location shooting permits the filmmakers of the World version to create a much more varied sense of landscape. Thus, the shots of Eliza at the ferry landing are framed very differently from those showing the traders at the same location. Scene 51(a) (Figures 2.67 and 2.68), in which Eliza negotiates with the ferry-man, is a slightly high-angle long shot, with a largely frozen river across the rear, and a boat moored to the bank. Scene 51(b) (Figure 2.69) is a high-angle very long shot, which shows Eliza on the edge of the ice rear right, as she leaves the shore and begins jumping from floe to floe. Scene 52 (Figure 2.70) shows the arrival of the slave-hunters and bloodhounds at the river's edge. The framing is markedly different from that of Scenes 51(a) and (b) (Figures 2.68 and 2.69) of Eliza at the ferryboat landing; we see a row of buildings in the rear right, and the corner of a pile of lumber juts into the right foreground. In Scene 54 (Figure 2.72), a return to the slave-hunters, the framing has been altered again; the camera has moved closer to the men in the midground, so that the lumber is no longer visible and the buildings in the background are cut off. This composition emphasizes the outlines of the dogs, horses, and mounted riders, all looking off left, after Eliza.

There are pronounced variations in shot scale as well as background and composition in this sequence. Two of the shots of Eliza on the ice, Scenes 53 and 57, are high-angle long shots in which her figure fills about one-half of the frame (Figures 2.71 and 2.75), but there are also two extreme long shots, Scenes 51(b) and 55, in which her figure appears much smaller, dwarfed by the landscape (Figures 2.69 and 2.73). There may even have been a link between variation in figure size and the cut 'across' the river, so that the actress is very far from the camera in Scene 55 (Figure 2.73) as Eliza recedes from the view of the slave-hunters, and then is shown closer to the camera in Scene 57 (Figure 2.75), as she approaches Phineas on the opposite shore, the action announced in Subtitle 22 which follows it.

In one sense, in its use of landscape and evocation of the river's width, the World version recalls the spectacular effects that were engineered for the crossing of the Ohio in at least the big-budget theatrical renditions of the tableau. The stage directions in the Aiken version note that the full depth of the stage should be used to represent the Ohio, a distance that could run up to 60 feet in a major metropolitan theatre, and could be made to look much larger through masking and the painting of drops in perspective.[27] The Hermann recommends the creation of false perspective in this scene; the stage directions in the published play suggest that a small girl be substituted for the actress playing Eliza, and a child for Phineas, to increase the sense of depth and make the opposite shore of the Ohio appear farther away. In contrast, the sense of depth is relatively limited in the Edison version, as Eliza moves right to left in a line running between the moving backdrop and the forestage. Even in the Vita-graph, which stages the scene with movement from foreground to background, the space between the forestage and the backdrop remains confined. But while the crossing of the Ohio in the World version is the first of the film versions to approach or rival the spectacular stagings of the theatrical tradition, it does not simply reconstitute the elements of a theatrical spectacle in this scene; it exploits the ease with which the cinema alters viewpoint, introducing subtle variations of background from shot to shot as well as a 180-degree cut to the 'other side' of the Ohio. This kind of mobility of viewpoint is suggested in the Vita-graph version as well, through the device of changing the foreground of the Ohio river set, and indeed this film does contain true 180-degree cuts in at least one scene.[28] However, these 180-degree cuts are of a kind that can be called 'centripetal', the camera remaining outside the space of the action, all of which appears in all of the shots, viewed from opposite sides. In the World film's editing of Eliza crossing the Ohio, the 'centrifugal' type of 180-degree cutting more common in later, classical filmmaking is deployed: the camera stands in the middle of the field of action, and looks outward at different fragments of it in turn—the pursuers on one bank of the Ohio, viewed from near the shoreline, and Phineas running down the bank towards the camera and the opposite shoreline to help Eliza and Harry to his house. Thus, in the World version, the move to location shooting in com-

2.76

2.77

2.78

2.79

2.80

2.81

2.82

2.83

2.84

bination with the larger number of shots allows the filmmakers to traverse the spectacular deep space and to exercise the potential for pictorial variety to a much greater degree than was achieved by the Vitagraph filmmakers.[29] Other, traditionally spectacular, tableaux are treated in the same way in the film, exploded into a succession of striking, and strikingly varied, shot set-ups.

The scene on a rocky pass may be divided into two segments. The first is comprised of an alternation between two groups: George, Phineas, Jim Vance, Eliza, and Harry on a rock platform high on a mountain, and the posse led by Marks and Loker in the gully below. George and Phineas exchange shots with the members of the posse, the lawyer Marks gets scared

and flees on his donkey, and Loker begins to climb the cliff face. This segment comprises ten shots (Scenes 95 to 101(c) shown in Figures 2.77 to 2.86). The second segment cuts around the group on the rock platform with two interposed shots of Loker alone. Loker makes his ascent. George realizes the group is out of ammunition just as Loker reaches a hollow directly beneath them on the platform. George strikes Loker with a revolver butt and the slave hunter rolls down the cliff to the bottom of the gully. A cutaway shows Marks escaping on his donkey. This segment comprises seven shots (Scenes 102 to 103(f) shown in Figures 2.87 to 2.93).[30]

The first segment includes cuts from extreme high angle to extreme low angle, and a great variety of

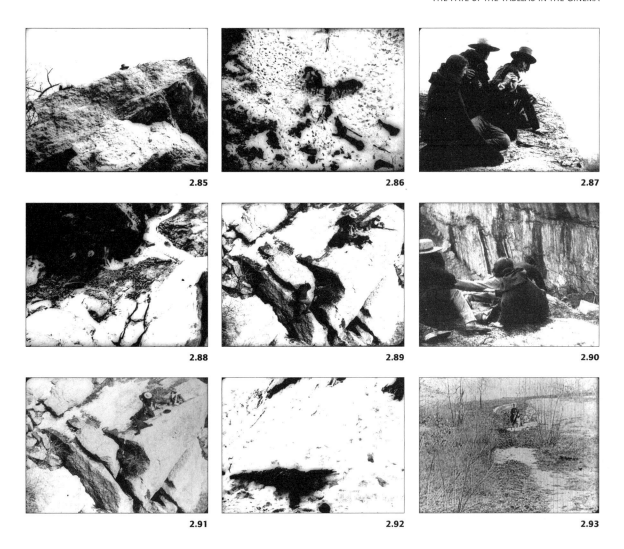

2.85   2.86   2.87

2.88   2.89   2.90

2.91   2.92   2.93

camera positions. Although there is one long shot, straight on, of the posse (Scene 99, Figure 2.82), most of the shots of the posse are high-angle long shots taken from the rocks above (Scene 95, Figure 2.77; Scene 97, Figure 2.79). A more extreme variant of this set-up is almost vertical (Scene 101(a), Figure 2.84), and a somewhat closer shot from the same vertical angle (Scene 101(c), Figure 2.86) shows Loker starting to climb. The group on the top of the rocks is shown from a number of positions: initially, shot from behind in a slight high angle, looking out on the snowy landscape beyond (Scene 96, Figure 2.78); then in a very low angle, the point of view of a rifleman looking over the barrel of a gun and firing at George and Phineas's heads visible just over the lip of the rock

(Scene 98(a), Figure 2.80); then in a very high-angle long shot, looking down on the rocky platform from an even higher position on the rock face (Scene 98(b), Figure 2.81); and later, at the same angle as the point-of-view shot, a somewhat closer view showing George and Phineas returning fire (Scene 101(b), Figure 2.85). The spectacular mobility of viewpoint is exemplified in the changes in camera angle between five shots, Scenes 98(a) to 101(a), the first the very low-angle shot looking up at the fugitives from the point of view of the rifleman (Figure 2.80), the second a very high-angle shot of the fugitives on the platform (Figure 2.81), the third a horizontal shot taken from a position on the gully floor (Figure 2.82), the fourth a return to the rifleman's very low-angle point of view

71

(Figure 2.83), and the fifth an almost vertical very long shot down on the posse in the gully (Figure 2.84). There is a similar variety of shot set-ups in the second segment. Without going into the same degree of detail, it can be said that this variety derives from the flexibility with which the film cuts around the group of fugitives on the platform. The scene on a rocky pass thus depends on visual and dramatic contrasts established over the sequence of shots rather than a unified and compelling picture which might approximate a tableau.

In the nineteenth century, the use of the tableau as a form of punctuation was pronounced, extending even beyond the theatre to verbal forms such as the novel, in which striking moments were often described as static pictures, to ordinary conversation.[31] Yet, as the example of *Uncle Tom's Cabin* indicates, the cinema frequently modified the theatrical tableau in favour of a more continuous rhythm of narrative development. This is evident relatively early, as in the truncated tableaux of the Edison version, in which the actors quickly resume their movements or, in the scene-end tableaux, when the film immediately cuts to the next shot. Similarly, one of the strategies of the Vitagraph version is to introduce epilogues after strong tableaux which militate against the sense of a pause. At the end of the first reel, for example, the image of Tom posed over the slaves in a blessing is followed by the movement of the carriage as Tom exits frame right and the scene closes on the Shelbys. The tendency to 'smooth over' the breaks in the action upon which the theatrical tableau was predicated became even more marked with the development of rules for scene dissection. Such editing conventions favoured the linear representation of significant elements through cutting in or around a space rather than the creation of composite or summarizing 'pictures'. Moreover, the distribution of narrative action across a series of shots gave filmmakers the opportunity to establish momentary pauses for description or emphasis without necessitating a definitive interruption. A concatenation of brief descriptive shots, a protracted alternation between characters, a cut away to a close-up, could underscore a meaning or a gesture without bringing the story to a complete halt. Thus, as continuity editing became part of the cinema's narrative armature, the tableau was dissolved into the sequence.

But, as Tom Gunning has suggested, editing carries within it the seeds of new forms of discontinuity—a capacity to interrupt the continuity of an action for the purposes of creating suspense or making a gesture stand out from the flux of the actor's movements. In an analysis of Biograph's *After Many Years* (1908), Gunning discusses a cut from the shipwrecked Enoch Arden about to kiss a locket given him by his wife, to her in England thinking of her lost husband. He argues this cut is akin to the sense of discontinuity attendant upon a theatrical tableau; it arrests the movement of Enoch's kiss and in so doing produces a heightened sense of its significance.[32] Gunning suggests that Griffith's innovative editing in *After Many Years* was inspired by the disjunctive style of stage melodrama—the quick scene changes, the freezing of the action, the creation of strong effects of shock or suspense—a style Gunning describes, with reference to Benjamin's essay on Brecht already cited, as an 'aesthetics of astonishment'.

While the cross-cutting between distinct spaces in the early Biographs is clearly disjunctive, especially when the cut is used to interrupt a gesture, one might argue that this is not the case for later continuity editing in which matches on action are precisely one way of smoothing over shot transitions.[33] That is, it is the more eccentric aspects of Griffith's editing style which might be said to bear an affiliation with melodrama, while the editing patterns in a film like the World *Uncle Tom's Cabin*, which more closely approximate classical norms, linearize melodrama's disjunctive style, including its deployment of the tableau. But this is too simple.

The mobility of viewpoint characteristic of the World *Uncle Tom's Cabin* could itself be used to punctuate the continuity of the action in order to generate shock effects or create moments of heightened allegorical or dramatic significance. For example, while the action takes place in continuity in the scene on a rocky pass, the film cuts between extreme high and low angles in a way which emphasizes the fragmentation of the space and the compositional contrast between shots. The use of the point-of-view shot from the bottom of the gully exacerbates the purely formal shock of these cuts, by providing for a dramatically sensational moment when the rifleman is shot by the fugitives, his hands momentarily thrown up into the frame before he falls dead. Another relevant example is the opening sequence, in which a number of whites post a notice of reward for the capture of Jim Vance while he is hiding in the tree above them. The sequence of shots is as follows:

Scene 1(*b*). Long shot of a road running from rear right to front right with a fence parallel to it and a large tree midground left. Whites mounted on horseback ride from rear to midground along the road and stop at the tree. One man dismounts holding a poster (Figure 2.94).

Scene 1(*c*). Insert of the wanted poster being nailed to a fence post with the butt of a gun. The poster promises a reward for the capture of Jim Vance, 'runaway nigger' (Figure 2.95).

Subtitle 1: Jim Vance.

Scene 2(*a*). Low-angle shot of Vance, framed from knees to head as he lies stretched horizontally along the branch of the tree (Figure 2.96).

Scene 2(*b*). Vance's point of view looking down on the heads of the whites, i.e. an almost vertical high-angle shot. The man on the ground remounts and they all begin to turn their horses (Figure 2.97).

Scene 2(*c*). As 1(*b*). The riders turn and ride away from the camera (Figure 2.98).

Scene 2(*d*). As 2(*a*). Vance cautiously works his way backwards along the branch, moving left (Figure 2.99).

The film thus abruptly thrusts us into the midst of a perilous situation without any exposition. It leaves Vance just as abruptly, as the next shot is Subtitle 2, introducing Tom and George Shelby. While there is no freeze in this sequence, it does perform functions analogous to the tableau. The incident epitomizes slave life in the South, bringing the elements of the narrative conflict together in a way which is not subject to much narrative preparation or development. Further, the elements of conflict are heightened through their graphic treatment. They do not assume the form of a single unified picture, of course, but the contrasting angles and the use of optical point of view help to evoke the state of threat and panic. The cut from Scene 2(*a*) to 2(*b*) (Figure 2.96 to 2.97), from low to high angle, is in part motivated by character point of view, and in this resembles the scene on a rocky pass. Like that example, too, we are given the point of view of a character who is not well known to us, though his naming in the poster and a subtitle suggest he will be more than a mere extra; it is not, however, a question of creating empathy, but of cutting to a vantage-point which will immediately maximize the sense of danger and suspense. The jump from Scene 1(*c*) (Figure 2.95) to the subtitle and then Scene 2(*a*) (Figure 2.96) functions the same way, suddenly revealing Vance's presence to the spectator and his proximity to the slave-hunters below.

2.94

2.95

2.96

2.97

2.98

2.99

2.100   2.101   2.102

2.103   2.104   2.105

Thus, the World version uses editing and other compositional devices specific to film to approximate the powerful summarizing and heightening effect of a tableau. Moreover, it does so for an incident which does not appear in the book or in any of the stage versions and has no previous history of such pictorial representation. Another sequence akin to the opening with Vance depicts Tom, Emmeline, and Simon Legree's trip by steamboat up the Red River to Legree's plantation. While the steamboat motif has theatrical precedents in the sensation scenes involving views of boats on the Mississippi, we have found no stage pictures nor tableaux concerning the disembarkation of Legree and his slaves. Like the Vance episode, then, the depiction of this incident clearly does not rely on theatrical representational strategies while at the same time it achieves some of the effects of the stage tradition: the drawing out of a situation by emphasizing the potential conflicts and moral contrasts between the characters. The sequence of shots is as follows:

Subtitle 47. Up the River to Legree's plantation.

Scene 144. A quay with a gangplank leading up to the steamer off front right. Legree is seated at the end of the plank, watching as Tom leads a line of slaves on left and off up the plank (Figure 2.100). The last of this line is Emmeline. Legree rises and embraces her, then points for her to go off up the plank.

Scene 145. Very long shot of the Mississippi. A real stern-wheeler paddle-steamer sailing right to left. Pan left (Figure 2.101).

Scene 146. The bow of the steamer moving right to left, with its name, 'OMAHA', painted on it. Tom and several slaves seated in the bow with Legree (Figure 2.102).

Subtitle 48. Cassy, the slave, Legree's housekeeper.

Scene 147. A hilly green with houses surrounded by picket fences to the rear, and a levee across the front. Slaves are sitting on the bank, waiting. Cassy stands in medium long shot looking off front centre. Cassy prays (Figure 2.103).

Subtitle 49. 'God help the poor wretches he is bringing to this hell on earth.'

Scene 148. As 147. The slaves point off front centre (Figure 2.104).

Scene 149(a). A different view of the bow of the 'Omaha', with Tom, Emmeline, and slaves sitting down. Legree, upright, waves his hat off front left (Figure 2.105).

Scene 149(b). 180 degrees from the angle of 147. Cassy stands in medium long shot front left, back to camera, with the slaves seated front centre. The 'Omaha' is approaching on the river rear right. Cassy shades her eyes to look at the steamer (Figure 2.106).

Scene 150. In the foreground the group on the steamer, with the levee in the far rear. Emmeline and Legree are stand-

2.106

2.107

2.108

2.109

2.110

ing front left and right in medium long shot. The slaves and Cassy are visible on the levee rear centre (Figure 2.107). Legree grabs Emmeline.

Scene 151. Variant of 149(*b*). The steamer is rear left nearing the levee while Cassy waits front right (Figure 2.108). A gangplank is lowered on a crane to front left. The slaves carry grain sacks from the steamer across the gangplank and off front left (Figure 2.109). Legree stands with Emmeline in the bow rear left, until the last of the slaves has disembarked, when they follow, Legree staggering drunkenly. At the top of the plank he greets Cassy. Emmeline exits front left, then re-enters at Legree's command. Legree introduces her to Cassy (Figure 2.110). Pan left. Emmeline, Cassy, and Legree exit left. (The shot is 117 feet 11 frames long in NFTVA.)

Unlike the scene on the rocky pass or the crossing of the Ohio, the time of this sequence is not continuous. The journey up river is initiated in Scene 144 (Figure 2.100). Scenes 145 and 146 (Figures 2.101 and 2.102) have a largely descriptive (and spectacular) function, at most they summarize the time of the boat's passage. The film then introduces Cassy and cuts to the time of the disembarkation, Cassy and the other slaves react to the boat's appearance (Scene 148, Figure 2.104), and Legree waves to them in response (Scene 149(*a*), Figure 2.105). Another series of shots

then emphasize the stately grandeur of the steamboat's movement towards the shore. Scene 149(*b*) (Figure 2.106) cuts around to the back of Cassy and the other slaves, so that the boat is shown rear right moving towards the figures in the foreground. Scene 150 (Figure 2.107) is a new angle on the characters on the boat—the previous Scenes 146 and 149(*a*) (Figures 2.102 and 2.105) have shown the characters gathered in the bow—but now we see a side view in which the shore is visible in the background. In Scene 151 (Figures 2.108 to 2.110), whose composition is similar to 149(*b*) (Figure 2.106), we see the boat come in, the gangplank lowered, and the slaves come off in single file. What is impressive here is not simply the use of a real paddle steamer, but the flexibility of the changes of camera position. The film cuts 180 degrees around Cassy and the other slaves, so that we can gauge the boat's movement from their position on shore.

Perhaps the most striking thing about this sequence is its redundancy. The only new narrative material it contains is the introduction of Cassy, who appears in all but one of the shots following the title which names her, but does nothing after her prayer for Legree's victims. Three of the shots show Legree pawing Emmeline. Unlike the alternations in the scenes of Eliza crossing the Ohio and the fight in the rocky pass, the 180-degree cutting here is of the centripetal type, increasing the repetition: the camera remains outside the arena of the action, looking in, so all the significant characters are in each shot together. Finally, Scene 151 (Figures 2.108 to 2.110) is very long held—118 seconds at 16 frames per second, in a film with an average shot length of 10 seconds. This shot, which might be expected to climax when Legree introduces Cassy to the woman with whom he intends to supplant her, simply ends with all three exiting together. All the elements of a tableau are present: the wretchedness of the new arrivals, Cassy's mixed feelings at seeing her master and his new favourite, Legree's lust for Emmeline and anticipation of triumph over Cassy, mingled with trepidation at her response, Emmeline's grief, disgust, and terror at Legree. A single tableau expressing each of these character's feelings and their moral significance in a grouping of attitudes is easy to imagine. But the presence of all these elements in this shot is no more than an unmarked continuation or repetition of their presentation in the sequence. The shot is not qualitatively different from the ten which precede it; what could conceivably have been the components of a theatrical tableau are effectively dispersed and reiterated over the entire group of eleven shots. However, this is not a smooth integration of narrative action with narrational commentary on it, such as we might expect from the classical narrative cinema. The redundancy and the anticlimactic nature of the sequence in general and the final shot in particular retain the suspension characteristic of the stage picture, where the action stops while its significance is presented.

The World *Uncle Tom's Cabin* makes fluent use of what were to become standard devices of classical continuity editing: centrifugal 180-degree cutting, optical point of view, and a tendency evident throughout the film to use a relatively large number of shots, and to dissect the scenic space into highly varied shot set-ups. While such techniques entailed the abandonment of some, if not all, of the conventional tableaux, they also provided new ways of securing what Gunning calls shock effects, interrupting or punctuating the continuity of the action to underscore important dramatic situations. Cutting to characters outside Eva's room during the deathbed scene, cutting across the Ohio with Eliza, establishing an alternation between the top and the bottom of the rocky pass, the film reproduced the canonical tableaux of the old play with a new panoply of cinematic techniques. The fact that the World version used the same techniques to similar effect in scenes without clear theatrical precedents, such as the posting of the notice for Jim Vance and the trip up the Red River, suggests that it may be possible to speak of an autonomous development of pictorial effect in film, one which goes beyond the straightforward adaptation of certain plays. In what follows then, we will turn from consideration of a specific theatrical device and its filmic equivalents to consideration of how a broad range of pictorial effects associated with methods of acting and staging in the theatre contributed to the development of strategies for handling *mise-en-scène* in the early feature, having an influence beyond and apart from the range of theatrical adaptations.

1. Other versions which we do not treat here include ones by Lubin, 1903, 1 reel; by Thanhouser, 1910, 1 reel; by Imp, 1913, 3 reels; by Kalem, 1913, 2 reels; by Paramount, 1918, 5 reels; and by Universal, 1927, 13 reels. There are also a number of parodies, e.g. *Uncle Tom without the Cabin*, Paramount, 1919, 2 reels; *Uncle Tom's Caboose*, Universal, 1920, 2 reels; elaborations on characters from the book, such as *Topsy and Eva*, Feature Productions for United Artists, 1927, 9 reels; and many films in which characters assist in the staging of an adaptation of the novel, from *An 'Uncle Tom's Cabin' Troupe*, Biograph, 1913, 1 reel, to *The King and I*, Fox, 1956, 133 minutes, via *Dimples*, Fox, 1936, 78 minutes. See William L. Slout, 'Uncle Tom's Cabin in American Film History', *Journal of Popular Film*, 2 (1973), 137–51.

2. Frank Kessler and Sabine Lenk, ' ". . . levant les bras au ciel, se tapant sur les cuisses".' Réflexions sur l'universalité du geste dans le cinéma des premiers temps', in Roland Cosandey and François Albèra (eds.), *Cinéma sans frontières/Images across Borders, 1895–1918* (Lausanne/Quebec: Payot-Lausanne/Nuit blanche éditeur, 1995), 133–45.

3. In *D. W. Griffith*, 249, Tom Gunning discusses several tableaux in *A Corner in Wheat*, including one of men on a breadline in which the actors remain static for the duration of the shot, resembling a 'freeze frame'. We have not seen anything comparable to this last example in any other film of the period, nor can we relate this shot to a previous iconographic tradition.

4. The National Film and Television Archive dates one of these films, an Italian-language print entitled *Vita e passione di Cristo*, to 1906, the other, an English-language print entitled *The Life of*

Jesus Christ, to 1914. As the individual tableaux of these films were sold separately, and Pathé remade different tableaux at different times, dating individual prints of the Pathé Passion is notoriously difficult. It seems to us more likely that the NFTVA's earlier version is that released in 1902, the later that released in 1907. See Henri Bousquet and Riccardo Redi, *Pathé Frères: Les films de la production Pathé (1896–1914)*, part 1: [1896-1906], *Quaderni di Cinema* 8, no. 37 (Jan.–Mar. 1988), 79–81 and Henri Bousquet, *Catalogue Pathé des années 1896 à 1914*, [part 2] *1907–1908–1909* (Paris: published by the author, 1993), 4.

5. This scene is absent from the print circulated in the USA by the Museum of Modern Art. For a description and still, see the shot breakdown in Pierre Jenn and Michel Nagard, 'L'Assassinat du Duc de Guise', *L'Avant-Scène Cinéma*, no. 334 (Nov. 1984), 72.

6. Frank Woods, 'Reviews of Licensed Films . . . *Gold Is Not All*', *New York Dramatic Mirror*, 63, no. 1633 (9 Apr. 1910), 17; cit. Eileen Bowser, *The Transformation of Cinema 1907-1915*, vol. ii of *A History of American Cinema*, ed. Charles Harpole (New York: Scribner's, 1990), 88–9.

7. Bowser, ibid.

8. Booth, *Victorian Spectacular Theatre*, 83, writes of Augustus Harris's 'obsession' with processions in his Drury Lane pantomimes; see also Allen, *Horrible Prettiness,* 17–18.

9. In surviving prints, this shot is the last in episode two, and would therefore be the natural place for a scene-end tableau. Its slightly anticlimactic character suggests, however, the possibility that a subsequent shot in the temple showing her consigned to the flames in the temple has been censored, as certain sequences were in the reissue print from which current prints derive. See Paolo Cherchi Usai, '*Cabiria*, an Incomplete Masterpiece: The Quest for the Original 1914 Version', *Film History*, 2, no. 2 (June–July 1988), 155–65.

10. Burch, *Life to Those Shadows*, 193–6.

11. Méliès began to use dissolves to link scenes in *Cendrillon* (Cinderella) in 1899, his first multiple-scene film sold as a single unit, and he continued to do so for most scene transitions throughout his career. Porter took up the same device at Edison, in films such as *Jack and the Beanstalk* (1902). In such dissolves, any characters left in scene often freeze in something like a tableau, but the transition rarely lasts longer than a second or two, and the appearance of new visual material simultaneously distracts attention from the tableau function. Trick films provide instances of another sort of pseudo-tableau also related to the possibility of splicing lengths of film together, when actors had to hold a pose while the camera was stopped and restarted after changing some aspect of the scene for a magical transformation. The poses adopted would often be similar to those of stage tableaux (where one of the constraints was the need for poses actors could retain for a significant length of time), and as all the actors rarely arrived at a pose absolutely simultaneously, it was almost impossible to sustain the illusion of continuity of movement through the transition.

12. Charles Musser suggests, both in *Before the Nickelodeon: Edwin S. Porter and the Edison Manufacturing Company* (Berkeley: University of California Press, 1990), 242, and in *The Emergence of Cinema: The American Screen to 1907*, vol. i of *A History of the American Cinema*, ed. Charles Harpole (New York: Scribner's, 1990), 349, that the Edison Company hired a travelling Uncle Tom troupe for the film, but in neither place does he offer any supporting documentation. It would hardly have been necessary to hire a constituted troupe, however, as so many of the small-time actors available for hire would have known the play well. It should be said that many settings, groupings of actors, and tableaux look very like cut-down versions of the stage photographs of the William A. Brady New York production of 1901 (see Stephen Johnson, 'Translating the Tom Show: A Comparison of Edwin S. Porter's 1903 film and William Brady's 1901 Stage Production of *Uncle Tom's Cabin*', paper presented at Celebrating 1895, a Conference held in Bradford, July 1995). For an approach to the Edison film version employing a very different method and reaching rather different conclusions from ours, see Janet Staiger, *Interpreting Films: Studies in the Historical Reception of American Cinema* (Princeton, NJ: Princeton University Press, 1992), 101–23.

13. See Ch. 3, n. 21, above.

14. This description assumes that the film as first issued was ordered as the Paper Print in the Library of Congress is ordered, an order which also corresponds to the descriptions in Edison catalogues. The other print we have seen, in the National Film and Television Archive, London (deriving from a copy in the Museum of Modern Art, New York), has the scenes in an order bearing no relation to the traditional sequence of the action, presumably as a result of a broken print being incorrectly respliced at some time; more important, it consistently inserts its titles into the scene more or less at the point where the action described in the title begins, a reordering we presume is an exhibitor's or collector's deliberate re-editing. Here, as in other quotations from film intertitles, we have followed the spelling of names found in the title, but in all descriptions of films and plays we have used that found in the original novel.

15. Edison Films, Catalog Supplement no. 175, May 1903, in Musser's microfilm collection. The cross mentioned in the vision of Lincoln freeing the slaves is not visible in the NFTVA print or the Library of Congress Paper Print version, and this vision is followed in both prints by one not described in the catalogue, showing two soldiers in the uniforms of the North and the South reconciled by an angel of peace.

16. See Ben Brewster, '*Traffic in Souls*: An Experiment in Feature-Length Narrative Construction', *Cinema Journal*, 31, no. 1 (Fall 1991), 40–1.

17. We have seen two prints of this film. The National Film and Television Archive print is a copy of one in the Dansk Filmmuseum, Copenhagen, with Danish titles, but otherwise closely corresponding to the plot summaries of the film in the trade press. The second is a print belonging to Murray Glass, deriving from a reissue by the 'Empire Safety Film Co.', according to its opening title. This is apparently a version re-edited for home viewing, in six parts rather than the original three, and with many interpolated titles and some interpolated footage. We have based our descriptions on the National Film and Television Archive print (our shot numbers refer to this print), with occasional references to the Murray Glass print when it contains clearly authentic footage missing from the NFTVA print.

18. For plot summaries see 'Stories of the Films . . . *Uncle Tom's Cabin*', *Moving Picture World*, 7, no. 6 (6 Aug. 1910), 314; and Frank Woods, 'Reviews of Licensed Films . . . *Uncle Tom's Cabin*', *New York Dramatic Mirror*, 64, no. 1650 (6 Aug. 1910), 26. The latter has a particularly careful account of the reel ends.

19. The first title in this sequence is our translation of the Danish one in the NFTVA print, the second follows one of the Vitagraph titles

interpolated in the NFTVA's print of the World version discussed below.

20. Since this was written, we have seen a fifth print, a 16-mm one in the Cinémathèque Française. We were not able to study this in as much detail as the others, but it is clear that it derives from the same reissue as the Grapevine video, with fewer later modifications, and a certain amount of original footage not in any other version, particularly in the sequence of the auction after St Clare's death.

21. We should like to thank Pat Loughney for providing us with a copy of this script.

22. The surviving prints differ more or less from the script, all but NFTVA placing Scenes 129, 132, and 133 differently, and all but LoC1 breaking up the very long Scene 131 with cutaways and titles.

23. Stowe, *Uncle Tom's Cabin*, 427–8.

24. Edison Films, Catalog Supplement no. 175.

25. Leopold Lewis, *Henry Irving and 'The Bells'*, 34, 49, 62, 67, 84 n. 21, and 91 nn. 10–14. For stage visions more generally, see Vardac, *Stage to Screen*, 34–5 and 38–9.

26. Book-ending the vision scene with dissolves or fades was a less common alternative.

27. See Ch. 8, below, and Vardac, *Stage to Screen*, 2–4.

28. Shots 12–16, where Eliza overhears the sale of Harry and Uncle Tom, alternating shots of the Shelbys' parlour, with Eliza just visible through the sliding doors rear centre, and shots of her behind the doors in the adjoining room, with the characters in the parlour visible through the crack between the doors.

29. For a discussion of the effect of location shooting on film style between 1909 and 1915, see Bowser, *Transformation of Cinema*, 162–5.

30. In the first of these segments, NFTVA lacks one of the shots in the other three prints, and it is in a slightly different order. It should be said that this is one of the few sequences in the film that leaves room for doubt as to the precise correlation of the script and the shots in the surviving prints.

31. For an example from a novel, see Stowe, *Uncle Tom's Cabin*, 286–7: 'The group that stood in various attitudes, after this communication [the news of Loker's recruitment of a posse to pursue the Harrises], were worthy of a painter. Rachel Halliday, who had taken her hands out of a batch of biscuit, to hear the news, stood with them upraised and floury, and with a face of the deepest concern. Simeon looked profoundly thoughtful; Eliza had thrown her arms around her husband, and was looking up at him. George stood with clenched hands and glowing eyes, and looking as any other man might look, whose wife was to be sold at auction, and son sent to a trader, all under the shelter of a Christian nation's laws.' For the everyday use, see the examples from the *Oxford English Dictionary* and Walter Benjamin referred to above.

32. Gunning, *D. W. Griffith*, 114–16.

33. Ibid. 115.

ACTING

LADY HAMILTON was one of the originators of the late eighteenth-century art of 'attitudes', a branch of amateur theatricals which comprised the assumption of a succession of poses usually reminiscent of classical statuary or painting. It seems quite likely that she learned many poses, and the techniques of manipulating the draperies and shawls required for them, from the artist George Romney, for whom she worked as a model during the years 1782–6.[1] While Romney's *Lady Hamilton at Prayer* derives from a Christian, not a classical tradition, the model's dress and pose resemble her later attitudes and seem typical of them (Figure 3.1).[2] The pictorial elements of the pose have been carefully worked out: the eyes look upward to express devotion but the face is gracefully tilted to the model's right and down, to contrast with the rest of the body and to provide the spectator with a good view of the features; the little fingers have been bent to differentiate the fingers of the hands in prayer, and to give an impression of lightness and repose. The effect of the pose is reinforced by the way the painter has handled the light. It seems to come from the upper left corner, to which her gaze is directed, and falls full upon her face while

the play of light on the hands also helps to differentiate the fingers. It is both an evocation of an invisible divine presence and a way of showing off the model's posture to great advantage. The ersatz quality of the painting according to the canons of present-day taste lies precisely in these qualities of the pose and the composition. What is ostensibly a private moment of religious contemplation appears much too clearly directed outwards in the creation of an 'effect' for a spectator, its formal elements are too controlled, its significance too emphatic.[3] But attitudes such as this, organized with great attention to compositional elements as well as to the expression of dramatic situations, formed a cornerstone of late eighteenth-century and nineteenth-century acting technique. An understanding of these techniques is a precondition for one of the evolution of film acting in the 1910s.

Our insistence on the importance of such pictorial elements for film acting in this period may seem anomalous. The traditional account is that film acting rapidly departed from the 'large' stereotyped gestures suited to the scale of the stage and associated with early nineteenth-century theatrical practice, adopting a more modern style which relied upon 'small' restrained gestures and facial expressions more appropriate to the close framings that the cinema permitted.[4] In an influential recent study of acting styles at Biograph, *Eloquent Gestures*, Roberta Pearson has attempted to trace the eclipse of what she calls the 'histrionic' style, which relied on stereotyped postures and attitudes, in favour of the 'verisimilar' style which aimed to adhere to conventionalized notions of 'real' gesture and action. She argues that by 1912 the verisimilar style had largely replaced the histrionic, at least among the most acclaimed actors at Biograph. In our view, the actor's assumption of poses and attitudes was much more important and was important for far longer than this, and other, accounts suggest. In what follows, we begin with a discussion of how gestures and attitudes functioned in nineteenth-century acting traditions, seeking to arrive at a more precise definition of pictorialism in acting. We then turn to the question of how this tradition was taken up and transformed within European and American filmmaking traditions.

Actors struck attitudes even when they were not in a tableau. The concern with postures, and the attempt to control how the actor looked while standing or moving on stage, became pronounced in the mid-eighteenth century and persisted until well into the early twentieth. Of course, acting style did not remain invariable throughout this period, but however acting and staging practices changed, the assumption of attitudes and poses remained an important part of the actor's technique. It should be noted that our efforts to generalize about an acting tradition that covers such a long time-span works against some of the best recent theatre history which has concentrated on reconstructing specific productions, and documenting the activities of particular theatres and companies. None the less, we have been struck by the strong continuities underlying the discourses on acting in this lengthy period, continuities which derive from a vivid concern with the stage picture. For example, the eighteenth-century performance practices described by Dene Barnett were largely geared to suiting gesture to words; in his sources one finds little discussion of the creation of the sort of wordless tableaux advocated by Voltaire, Diderot, and others.[5] Yet, even within the rhetorically oriented performance styles still frequently deployed for tragedy and for declaiming verse in the eighteenth century, one finds frequent admonitions to the actor to imitate paintings and statues in postures on-stage, and, as Barnett documents, great concern with finding striking visual correlates for verbal expressions.[6] Here we will argue that such postures and attitudes persisted in the nineteenth century, despite the shift to a much less exclusively verbal theatre.

The coherence of pictorialism as a tradition emerges most strikingly in the contrast with present-day acting methods from which it is quite remote. We will argue that the advent of naturalism and the new drama of Ibsen, Shaw, and Pinero represents a definitive break with the actor's traditional concern with the stage picture (indeed, William Archer's attacks on acting geared to 'picture-poster situations' in the name of the new drama provides some of the best descriptions of the older aesthetic and acting methods). But even if pictorialism begins to appear dated to the most advanced theatre practitioners at the turn of the century, the older tradition did not simply disappear. For example, Delsarte's acting system, which was based on the teaching of poses, was still being taught by Gustave Garcia at the London Academy of Music in the first decade of the twentieth century, and the evidence from films we will adduce later shows that these traditions were still alive a decade later throughout Europe.[7]

We would also like to distinguish what we are calling pictorial styles of acting from pantomime. Although contemporary works on pantomime such as Charles Aubert's *L'Art mimique* of 1901 do include examples and discussion of attitudes, we take pantomime to be more specifically concerned with the substitution of gesture for dialogue.[8] One can find examples of pantomime in silent film, especially in the early years in which actors often resort to it to convey story information. However, the practice also came in for criticism, as by Frank Woods in 1909:

The old pantomime sought to convey ideas by motions as if the persons were deaf and dumb. The natural action of the silent play also entered largely in the development of the plot, but detail ideas were indicated by unnatural movements of the hands. For instance, if an actor desired to indicate to another that he wanted a drink of water he would form his hand in the shape of a cup and go through the motions of drinking. Pantomime of this sort is still seen too often in picture playing, but the tendency is to get away from it, the idea being that the nearer to actual life the picture can be made to appear the more convincing it must be to the spectators. The modern director of the first class will now avoid the unnatural hand pantomime as much as possible and will indicate the wish for a drink of water, for instance, by having the player do some plausible thing that will convey the desired idea. The player wishing to ask for drink may hand a glass to some one with a natural motion, or he may indicate the water pitcher by a simple movement of the hand, or he may appear to ask a question, which, followed by the fetching of the drink, clearly and reasonably shows what the request has been.[9]

Woods is objecting to pantomime as opposed to stage business as a means of story-telling. And we would

agree with Kristin Thompson's assessment that pantomime in this sense does indeed play a much less prominent role in film acting in serious drama by the middle 1910s.[10] However, what we would call pictorial styles of stage acting encompass a much broader range of gesture than this idea of pantomime. Given the resources of the legitimate stage, a character would not have to mime, but could simply ask for a drink of water; she would probably not accompany the request with a marked pose unless the situation called for emphasis, for example, if she was about to put poison in the drink.

The important point, for us, is to move away from the kind of linguistic analogy which posits a one-to-one relationship between attitudes and speech as is the case in Wood's example where the actor's hand gesture means 'I want a drink.'[11] Poses and attitudes in the general sense which interests us were conventionalized and did carry significance, but they are probably best understood through analogy with the music which, as noted above, always accompanied nineteenth-century popular theatre. Like music, posing was used to underscore dramatic moments, to convey and heighten emotions, to elongate and intensify situations. Poses are best understood therefore, not as a lexicon, but as a way of managing the stage picture, a visual repertoire that was deployed in relation to specific narrative contexts. A given conventionalized pose, for example an actor placing hand upon forehead in despair, needs to be analysed not simply in terms of its conventionalized meaning, but more importantly, in terms of how the gesture is realized and how it fits within the overall visual design of the scene. It is these points which we intend to pursue here: how poses and attitudes functioned as an integral part of an actor's preparation for a role (indeed, of the training of actors in general), and how they provided a means of blocking scenes for individual actors and the ensemble.

1. Holmström, *Monodrama*, 110–40.
2. Ibid. 120 and figures 45:2 and 45:11, Holmström points out two examples of Lady Hamilton in poses deriving from Christian iconography in Friedrich Rehberg's drawings of her attitudes. *Lady Hamilton at Prayer* is part of the Iveagh Bequest, and can be seen at Kenwood House, Hampstead, London.
3. This analysis of why the painting of Lady Hamilton violates modernist canons of taste is, of course, indebted to Michael Fried's distinction between theatricality and absorption, already discussed in Ch. 1.
4. In an interview in 1914, D. W. Griffith enunciated one of the earliest versions of this position, arguing that the use of the close-up permitted a more 'restrained' style of acting that was 'closer to real life'. See Robert Welsh, 'D. W. Griffith Speaks', *New York Dramatic Mirror*, 71, no. 1830 (14 Jan. 1914), 49 and 54; repr. in George Pratt, *Spellbound in Darkness: A History of the Silent Film*

(Greenwich, Conn.: New York Graphic Society, 1966), 110–11. There are many recent variants on this argument, including James Naremore, *Acting in the Cinema* (Berkeley: University of California Press, 1988), 38–9; and Janet Staiger, 'The Eyes Are Really the Focus: Photoplay Acting and Film Form and Style', *Wide Angle*, 6, no. 4 (1985), 14–23.

5. It is perhaps worth mentioning that Barnett's starting-point is a search for contemporary accounts of acting to assist modern opera singers in the authentic performance of eighteenth-century opera. The performance practices he documents accompanied not simply speech, but also recitative and song. In comments on an earlier draft of this book, David Mayer has insisted to us on the importance of the fact that not just opera but much straight drama in the nineteenth century was accompanied, for part if not all of the performance, by music, as were film screenings in the early twentieth century. All our discussion of pictorial acting assumes these conditions.

6. For many examples of admonitions to imitate paintings and statues see Barnett, *Art of Gesture*, 122–7 and esp. 161–312 for the various and inventive connections between words and gesture.

7. For a discussion of Gustave Garcia's Delsarte-based textbook *The Actor's Art* see Stephen R. Macht, 'The Origin of the London Academy of Music and Dramatic Art', *Theatre Notebook*, 26, no. 1 (Autumn 1971), 19–30.

8. Charles Aubert, *L'Art mimique suivi d'un traité de la pantomime et du ballet* (Paris: E. Meuriot, 1901).

9. Frank Woods, ' "Spectator's" Comments', *New York Dramatic Mirror*, 62, no. 1612 (13 Nov. 1909), 15; for a similar complaint about pantomime see C. H. Claudy, 'Too Much Acting', *Moving Picture World*, 8, no. 6 (11 Feb. 1911), 288–9; and J. Searle Dawley, then director for Famous Players Co., interviewed by Robert Grau, in *The Theatre of Science: A Volume of Progress and Achievement in the Motion Picture Industry* (New York: Broadway Publishing Co., 1914; repr. New York: Benjamin Blom, 1969), 258–9.

10. Bordwell *et al.*, *Classical Hollywood Cinema*, 189–92.

11. For discussions of posing according to linguistic paradigms, see Pearson, *Eloquent Gestures*, 21–6; and Kessler and Lenk, 'Réflexions'.

THE frequency with which eighteenth- and nineteenth-century actors were enjoined to study statues and paintings, and to practise poses, and the consistent use of illustrative drawings in manuals on acting and oratory stand in sharp contrast with present-day training methods, and help to signal the degree to which acting was conceived along pictorial lines. Dene Barnett's extremely useful compilation of rules governing posture, gleaned from eighteenth- and early nineteenth-century European books on acting, makes it possible readily to document the insistence on copying poses from the other arts.[1] To take only a few examples, Franciscus Lang, in a work of 1727: 'I assert, that it can be of the greatest use, if one contemplates frequently, and diligently, the pictures of skilful painters, or statues carved by masters (most of all to be sure [those] of skilful Actors, and also of sacred Orators), so that by the contemplation of these, one may train one's own imagination properly, and thus may strive to imitate the images imprinted on one's mind in living action also.'[2] And, in his acting manual of 1827, Johannes Jelgerhuis writes: 'In general one will note in the Ancient figures, curves which are invaluable in the forming of graceful positions, to

be looked at with attention; I hope that these instructions will have shed light in your understanding, and demonstrated with what kind of eye these masterpieces of time-honoured sculpture should be observed, and how the mind must work in order to profit from them for use on the Stage.'[3] Similarly, from later in the nineteenth century, in Henry Neville's section on gesture in an 1895 work addressed to students of rhetoric: 'We term attitude the position adopted at the end of the walk, or when standing still; and this requires very careful study. The elder Kean was so perfect a master of his art that when he first walked on the London stage, and took his position in the centre without speaking a word the audience recognised in him a genius. We may be aided in our selection of appropriate attitudes by attending picture galleries. The painter paints attitudes; his mind is cultivated to record them; they are the significant objects of his art.'[4] Such advice is seconded by the use of illustrations of postures and significant gestures in a range of acting and public-speaking manuals. Jelgerhuis is unique in actually having been a painter, and hence able to draw examples of good and bad posture that fit precisely with the text of his lectures, but one also finds illustrations of attitudes, sometimes adopted from other sources, in Henry Siddons's *Practical Illustrations of Rhetorical Gesture and Action* (where the drawings are adapted from the earlier German work by Engel), Antonio Morrocchesi's *Lezioni di declamazione e d'arte teatrale*, Neville's already cited work, and in Delsarte's system of oratory and the various acting manuals derived from this, and many others.[5]

Neophyte actors were thus encouraged to think very carefully about their body on stage in pictorial terms, even to the point of practising attitudes in front of a mirror. In contrast, a naturalist acting teacher such as Stanislavsky rarely talked about how the actor on stage would look to the audience. Rather the preparation of the actor involved getting students to relax their muscles so as to be able to move freely on stage, doing exercises to improve their concentration, and various techniques for analysing a role in psychological terms and promoting identification with the part. Thus, in a discussion of the actor's gait in the Moscow Bolshoi Theatre studio at the end of the 1910s, Stanislavsky asserted that the walk should develop without forethought in a relaxed and natural way from the actor's conception of the part. His greatest concern was that the actor should not develop a self-consciousness about his body that would break his concentration, so that in the midst of a scene he would become 'hampered by' his feet. He remarks, in the context of criticizing an actor's gait:

Gait is in general one of the weakest points of actors. For instance, of all the actresses I have seen, there was only one whose manner of walking on the stage I personally liked, and even then many people disagreed with me. But no actor's part, as the centre of the audience's attention, ever suffered from it. Why then did the actor's gait spoil everything in this particular instance? Because it constrained and hampered the actor himself. His attention was not fixed on the problem on his part.[6]

Attention to the walk as such can thus be detrimental, even if it leads to an attractive or graceful gait, because it may interfere with the actor's internal identification with the character. Stanislavsky has a much stronger rebuke for an actor who, during a rehearsal of Massenet's *Werther*, assumes a pose:

But let us go on. How do you behave after having seen and realised the frightened and confused state of the woman, of the Charlotte you are in love with and into whose house you have rushed so violently? You are an educated man, a man of the world, a man who is used to the society of ladies, that is to say, who possesses civility, courage and strength. And you can't manage a bow, a smile, a tender look for the woman you love? Is it natural to freeze like that at the door? If you had seen Charlotte lying dead in the room, I could have understood and justified your petrified pose. But now there is no reason for your petrified state. And how long do you intend standing there like that? A minute? Two minutes? Five minutes? Half an hour?[7]

The pose is seen as a violation of the psychological logic of character action, a point where the actor loses touch with his part and lapses into a self-conscious stance directed towards the audience.

Perhaps because of the contrast with later acting methods, some historians have concluded that the importance accorded to poses and attitudes in the pre-naturalist nineteenth-century theatre means that actors then were not concerned with character psychology and acting methods were not geared to the creation of what we would consider psychological realism.[8] Certainly the nineteenth-century acting manuals do not place the same emphasis on the *actor's* psychology, and on the process of identifying with a part, that Stanislavsky does. None the less, it seems clear that throughout the period with which we are concerned, a variety of conceptions of psychology and/or physiology provided a basis for the methods of acting associated with pictorialism.[9] For example, in connection with the frequently repeated rule that gesture should precede speech, Franciscus Lang writes:

Now the reason for this effect, is that the parts of the body move more quickly to perform their task by way of the passions, than the mind to its task by way of reason. Moreover it is easier, to show something by a sign, than to utter words, since the mind must devote itself more to the latter, than to the former. Indeed the passions are marshalled without intermediary by the imagination, which flows into them. But the words, as though in the workshop of the emotions, ought first to be worked out by the intellect, until the things which have been inwardly conceived may be expressed in due form through speech. An example from nature. In a harpsichord the keys are pressed first, before the plucked strings give out a sound. So it is in man. The first realisation of something may be in the imagination: this moves the passion, and the limbs, before reason works, and discloses the inward emotion in words. The actor therefore imitates this natural way, so that he anticipates the word by the gesture.[10]

Like the harpsichord, the body is conceived mechanically, producing gestures and poses almost automatically in response to the 'applied force' of the emotions. By imitating the postures which have a natural derivation in the emotions, the actor is sure of stirring a sympathetic response in the audience. Charles Le Brun's 1698 lecture to the French Royal Academy of Painting and Sculpture on facial expression is often cited as an early attempt to codify expressive gesture and to give it a basis in the science of physiognomy. The lecture was accompanied by drawings which appear in many subsequent acting volumes.[11] Both Joseph Roach and Louis James have traced the lines of scientific argument which posited various sorts of connections between specific emotional states and expressive gestures, from Le Brun to Johann Caspar Lavater's illustrated and much adapted *Essays on Physiognomy* (1797), through Darwin's *The Expression of Emotions in Man and Animals* (1872), illustrated with photographs.[12]

Delsarte's late nineteenth-century system of oratory can also be seen as partaking of a similar set of assumptions about the physiological basis for the manifestation of the emotions in gesture, and hence their power to affect an audience. In deriving what he refers to as the 'semeiotics' of gesture, he begins by observing the human form in various situations in real life. Thus, he claims that he found it difficult to act surprise until he felt a spontaneous shock in which he 'naturally' discovered the way to hold his hands; similarly, his research on hand position led him to compare the way the thumb of the hand is held on cadavers versus children at play.[13] It should be noted that although Delsarte uses the word 'semeiotics' in relation to the gestural signs which he proposes to analyse, these signs were, in the terms of a later Saussurian semiotics, motivated and not arbitrary ones. Delsarte, like the other commentators on acting within this tradition who came before him, sought for and found a natural or physiological basis for the postures and attitudes that were taught and practised. The passions were thought to find natural expression in gesture; in so far as the actor could mobilize these gestures, either through literally re-experiencing the relevant emotions himself, or simply through assuming their outward manifestations, he was likely to strike a resonating chord in his audience.[14]

Moreover, actors and critics throughout this period clearly aimed to provide a convincing representation of character psychology. Holmström, for example, notes that Mlle Clairon, an early advocate of the actress's use of facial expression based upon the physiological manifestation of the passions, also emphasized the need to differentiate between characters on the grounds that 'the passions take different expressions in different people, depending on social position, nationality, age, etc.'.[15] And the failure to achieve a convincing portrayal of character was often grounds for criticism. Wilhelm von Humboldt, writing to Goethe in 1800 about the skill of French tragic actors in achieving pictorial effects and the beauties of what he called 'gestural acting', expressed reservations about the style because a sense of interiority in the representation of character was sacrificed. He argued that the French actor

shows and paints the whole state of the soul, feelings, passions, decisions, but not the heart itself, torn by feelings, overpowered by passions, steeled to bold and sudden decisions. But how could the actor represent what is not representable in its essence? Of course, he can only show us the externalizations, but there is undeniably a mood in human beings in which, in the closest combination of all feelings and opinions, everyone feels an individual being wholly and purely. If the actor can adopt this mood, if he can make voice, facial expressions, gestures stem only from it, he will evoke the same mood in us, and what happens in every great artistic effect will happen—the spectator will see more than the artist was directly able to represent.[16]

Pictorial gesture then is 'external' but it could and should spring from the 'internal' seat of all emotions and, in the very best acting method, would provide the spectator with an illusion of 'depth', an intuition of the character from which the individual passions and postures spring.

Humboldt's remarks can be taken as evidence of a real concern with character psychology, an interest which he takes to be typically German and opposes to the French tragic actor's concern with the external and merely visible. None the less, it is in our view a mistake to interpret this as evidence of two distinct approaches to acting. Almost all of the commentators that we have read, German or otherwise and including Humboldt himself, thought that *internal states should be externalized in gestures and attitudes*. One frequently finds the objection raised against particular performances that they are focused on external elements to the detriment of a sense of internal processes or psychological motivation. But in practice this seems to mean little more than that the observer found the performance in question unconvincing. For example, specifically objecting to Henry Irving's acting style in the role of Mephistopheles in his well-known production of *Faust*, Coquelin writes:

Of course picturesque detail is not to be despised, but it should never become the object of exclusive attention, and above all, no picturesque trait, however natural, should ever be taken as the starting-point of a role. It is the *character* that is the starting-point of everything. If you have assimilated the essence of your personage, his exterior will follow quite naturally, and if there is any picturesqueness, it will come of itself. It is the mind which constructs the body.[17]

Note that Coquelin does not here dispute the premiss that picturesque detail expresses character, but merely argues that the actor's understanding of the 'internal' aspects of a character should come 'first' in the creation of a role. Obviously this is something that is quite difficult to judge in performance. Hence Louis Calvert's evaluation of one of Coquelin's most famous roles, Cyrano de Bergerac: 'It seemed to me that Coquelin, with all his superb technique, was concerning himself merely with the externals and superficialities, the visible attributes of Cyrano, instead of feeling him.'[18] In our view, it is not useful to attempt to explain the pictorial tradition in acting in terms of a lack of interest in character psychology, or an opposition between internal and external approaches to character. Like their modern successors, actors in the pre-naturalist theatre found psychological justifications for what they did on stage (although of course in the naturalist theatre and after actors appealed to radically different kinds of psychology), valued the representation of interior states, and were sometimes found lacking in their representation of those states. What distinguishes pictorial styles of acting, then, is that actors were encouraged to think about how they looked on stage through a training process in which interesting poses were

sought out, most frequently borrowed from painting or sculpture, and in which gestures or systems of gesture as codified in the acting manuals were studied and practised. Presumably many actors received a similar but less formalized training simply by watching others on the stage, and associating certain attitudes with certain moments in certain roles.

The assumption of poses served multiple functions in the management of staging and blocking in this period. Frederick Marker has emphasized the important fact that up until the 1860s, and in some cases even later, there were very few rehearsals as well as real problems disciplining actors to attend rehearsal. For example, at mid-century in the Danish Royal Theatre, the number of rehearsals for a new production averaged between six and eight, even for plays with elaborate scenic effects and newly written music. Marker concludes, with many others, that the modern idea of the director as the person responsible for controlling the *mise-en-scène* and the one in charge of the visual design of a production did not hold in the pre-naturalist theatre, where responsibility for managing the *mise-en-scène* was much more decentralized.[19] Actors were thus largely charged with working out the details of their own movements on stage, and managing how they looked within the stage picture. As Thomas Rede cautions in 1827 in *The Road to the Stage*: 'All theatrical people that know their business (no matter how many may be engaged in the scene) form a picture; to understand the consequence of dressing the stage, people should pay a visit to a private theatre, where, from the straggling manner in which the performers stand, some stuck close together, others at the extreme corner of the stage from each other, etc. etc., as if uncertain of their ultimate place of destination, the whole effect is marred.'[20] Within this context the utility of acting styles based upon stereotyped poses and attitudes is clear. Such styles would have helped actors to plan out their own movements and expressions, and moreover to anticipate what others were likely to do in a scene, facilitating management of the ensemble.

There are several indications of the way in which attitudes were used to plan staging. Most obviously, they functioned expressively to mark situations. Humboldt writes of Talma that 'He practices the art of drawing, and his acting shows that every situation he thinks of appears to his imagination as a pictorial image.'[21] In 1879, a reporter who had attended one of Bernhardt's rehearsals noted: 'Her acting has always shown that she has a keen sense of the beauty of pose. She gets the full plastic as well as histrionic value of a situation.'[22] Dupont-Vernon recalls a performance of *Le Crime de Faverne* by Frédérick Lemaître in which 'at the end of an act in which he had been shaken by contradictory impressions, he summed up the whole situation at his exit in one brilliant gesture. In this gesture, which was at once quite simple and sublime, he gathered together the whole genesis of the scene.'[23]

A similar account of the relation between attitude and situation, although coloured by a rather different aesthetic evaluation, is given in William Archer's wicked caricature of romantic acting in *Hernani*. The precision of the example makes it worth quoting at length:

The scene is Spain, the hot-bed of romance; the characters, a king in disguise, a Castilian hidalgo, an Arragonese bandit. The King, hidden in a cupboard, overhears and then interrupts a love-scene between the bandit and the betrothed wife of the hidalgo: Situation First. Just as the rivals are crossing swords, the hidalgo thunders at the locked doors and enters: Situation Second. He makes a noble speech, concluding thus:—

Don Ruy Gomez (à ses valets)—
  Écuyers! écuyers! à mon aide!
  Ma hache, mon poignard, ma dague de Tolède!
  (Aux deux jeunes gens)
  Et suivez moi, tous deux!
Don Carlos (faisant un pas)—
  Duc ce n'est pas d'abord
  De cela qu'il s'agit. Il s'agit de la mort
  De Maximilien, empereur d'Allemagne.
  (Il jette son manteau, et découvre son visage
  caché par son chapeau.)
Don Ruy Gomez—
  Raillez-vous? . . . Dieu! Le Roi!
Doña Sol—
  Le Roi!
Hernani (dont les yeux s'allument)—
  Le Roi d'Espagne!

Situation Third—and what a situation! What attitudes for all concerned! The king drawing himself up with superb gesture; Ruy Gomez passing from rage to astonishment, and then bending before his liege lord; Doña Sol shrinking back in surprise and dread; and Hernani couched, as it were, for a spring, his eyes blazing forth in sudden hate from the gloomy background of the Gothic chamber![24]

While of course this does not describe an actual performance, it does give a plausible account of how a group of actors working within the romantic tradition might approach such a big scene. The scene is broken down into parts defined by the disguised King's entrance, Don Gomez's entrance, and the recognition of the King, reversals or recognitions which mark the passage from one dramatic situation to the next. For each situation, each actor in the ensemble strikes at least one pose. Archer's description assumes the importance of pictorial contrast already discussed in relation to the tableau, but here it is accorded to the linear succession of poses—the changes in attitude assumed by Ruy Gomez in the course of the recognition—as well as the final static picture—in the contrast between Doña Sol who shrinks back in fear while Hernani looks ready to spring forward in an aggressive posture.

As in the hypothetical case of *Hernani*, actors often seem to have assumed attitudes upon their entrances. Jelgerhuis, for example, writes: 'To come onto the stage, in whatever character, I hold it to be necessary and useful that one choose a certain Attitude, to comply with the great lesson of Karel van Mander's Painting Book, never without stylishness.'[25] A star who would be expecting applause at his or her first entrance would hold an attitude to allow time for it, as in the cases already discussed of Irving's first entrance in *The Bells* and the poor opera singer in *Werther* rebuked by Stanislavsky. Humboldt also noted that French tragic actors exited in attitudes, unlike their German counterparts,[26] and the discussion of Lemaître's acting already cited suggests that this tradition continued until well into the nineteenth century.

Henry Siddons provides a good indication of how a scene could be planned out as a series of attitudes. He discusses a scene from the opera *Alceste* in which, having already pledged to the gods that she is willing to die in order that her husband may be spared, the Queen is overcome by fear, believing that she already hears the underworld shades who have come to take her. Siddons describes the appropriate attitude of weakness caused by fear (Figure 3.2):

The last attitude of an actress charged with such a part should accompany this expression with a degree of faintness almost approaching to annihilation, with her face averted

Despair

Pub by Sherwood Neely & Jones Nov.1 1821

3.2

Enthusiasm

Pub by Sherwood Neely & Jones Nov.1 1821

3.3

from the spot whence the terrific sounds are supposed to arise: she should now and then cast a timid and furtive glance, as if fearful of beholding the dreaded spectres: the reversed hands, which she had opposed to them, ought to preserve their former direction; but she should not appear to have force or courage sufficient to give any degree of tension to the muscles, so that, feeble and trembling, they may afterwards drop lifeless by her sides.[27]

However, immediately after this, Alcestis changes her mind and reiterates her devotion to her husband and her vow in the 'second invocation of the infernal gods'. In this attitude (Figure 3.3): 'The countenance of Alcestis should be fixed on the ground, because she is invoking the infernal deities; her body should bend forwards; her step ought to be grand, her arms extend, and each open eye to seem bursting from its orbit: the whole countenance should beam with a species of haggard inspiration.'[28]

The problem which Siddons goes on to discuss is

how to make the transition from one attitude to the next, how to bind together sentiments and attitudes which are extremely different, and how to motivate the repetition of the musical motif associated with the vow itself. The solution he proposes is to interpose two attitudes in between the first and the second, so as to make the change in the Queen's countenance and posture more gradual. The intermediate postures make use of Parthenia, the Queen's sister. After her expression of fear upon hearing what she imagines to be the shades, the Queen should rest on Parthenia's breast, lifting one arm and drawing it across her forehead (Figure 3.4), demonstrating 'the sentiment of the disorder which troubles her soul'. Then, in response to her sister's tender plea to abandon her vow, the Queen should express displeasure and finally tear herself away from her sister's arms (Figure 3.5), now ready to reiterate it. Siddons concludes: 'By this means the repetition of this devotion will be found not only perfect, but the hurried leap from one

Distraction & Persuasion

Pub by Sherwood Neely & Jones Nov 1821

3.4

Persuasion repulsed

Pub by Sherwood Neely & Jones Nov 1821

3.5

sentiment to the other will be totally avoided; and what, without this prudent precaution, might have appeared a useless ornament or a mere misplaced musical luxury, becomes an admirable and expressive trait in the character of Alcestis.'[29] This is one of the few discussions we have seen of how attitudes could serve as the basis for blocking out a scene, although in Antonio Morrocchesi's *Lezioni di declamazione e d'arte teatrale* there is a similar sequence of plates to illustrate Pylades' false report of Orestes' death to Aegisthus in Alfieri's *Oreste*.[30] Not only the expression of particular emotional states, but also the relation of the poses to the music and the problem of how to make a graceful and logical transition from one pose to the next would have had to be considered. Although they do not approach the clarity of Siddons's directions, we have found early twentieth-century stage manager's libretti in the Tams-Witmark music library in which it is proposed that the singers be left free to improvise a series of

attitudes in tandem with the music in key scenes or arias, indicating the viability and persistence of this way of approaching the problem of staging.[31]

The interest in how actors made the transitions between attitudes is also indicated by Garrick's well-known party piece performed at the salon of Baron d'Holbach in Paris during his visit in 1763–4 in which he poked his head out from behind a screen and illustrated various passions in rapid succession.[32] In about the same period, Lessing also commented on the skill required of an actor who had to 'change from one emotion to another and must make this dumb transition so naturally that the spectator is not carried away by a leap, but by a series of rapid still perceptible gradations'.[33] It seems important to stress the complex effects that could be achieved by modulating attitudes, and thereby preparing for the largest and most striking effects, since this style of acting is often caricatured on the basis of the acting manuals as merely the assumption of isolated, highly stereotyped poses. But the single pose was only one building block in the architecture of the scene.

In the example from *Alceste* Parthenia poses in tandem with the Queen, and the process of acting for the ensemble must have involved the orchestration of a number of attitudes on the part of the various actors. The procedure we have outlined of breaking plays down into situations which were then illustrated by a number of highly stereotyped postures would have helped actors to plan and co-ordinate their movements without much aid from a director, and without many rehearsals. Writing of the acting ensemble in 1750, Riccoboni explains:

Several Actors, who ordinarily each have a different character, and whose situation is never the same, must keep in their Playing a certain rapport which prevents them from being inharmonious to the ear, or eyes, of the Spectator. They can be compared to Musicians who sing a piece in several parts; each utters different sounds, but all together create one same harmony. . . . In the gestures and movements of all the Actors the same harmony should be found, as in the tones of their voice. Elementary care makes the thing extremely easy. Let each one examine in what position he finds himself with regard to the others. Whether he should show superiority or respect in his position, whether it is proper for him to audaciously face the one who is speaking, or avoid meeting his eye, and keeping to the rule that movements of one lead on to those of the other, and that all keep exactly within the situation where the scene should place them.[34]

With each actor watching the rest of the cast, and adjusting his or her pose in accord with the situation and the poses of the others, it would have been possible for individual actors to manage the look of the ensemble. Jelgerhuis also recommends that actors mutually adjust their poses, here in order to insure the proper contrasting attitudes:

And if one's eye is drawn to a chorus of attendants in a Tragedy, who mostly all stand thus [with arms folded?] from bad habit, then that position is even more to be avoided, I abandon it immediately, as soon as I see, that one or other of my fellow artists, assumes it for a while, as nothing is more ugly, than for two Actors to stand alike, because contrasts must hold in the whole of the tableau, as well as in *one* particular personage; we must learn to see this, as we stand in a scene, because if it is bad enough that a whole suite stand with arms folded, think then what you get when the principal persons also make much use of it.[35]

In the manuals, actors are frequently enjoined to act and especially gesture in response to the dialogue of others so as to ensure a unified stage picture.[36] The manuals also insist that the most important characters should visually dominate the scene although then as now one supposes that actors sometimes tried to upstage each other, and to make themselves more prominent within the stage picture. The *Dictionnaire dramatique*, defining the term *jeu de théâtre*, recommends: 'In this last case [with several actors on stage], verisimilitude requires that the degrees of their expression are suited to the degree of interest which their Characters take in the action which takes place on the stage. In the images which the Play offers us, the same as in paintings [*tableaux*], the leading figure should always have the advantage over the others of principally holding the eye.'[37] Similarly, Thomas Wilkes writes:

It is his business in all cases to observe nature and propriety; it is observable that in all capital paintings, there are a few principal figures which more remarkably strike the eye, and by that means throw the attendant figures into their proper distance; in like manner, on the Stage, the leading figures or personages in a scene, should, by their dignity of action, throw the attenting characters into their proper shade of inferiority; and, then the whole, like a fine painting in perspective, will be all graceful and harmonious.[38]

The idea of the overall stage picture, and the rules laid down for preserving its compositional harmony, and appropriate relation to the dramatic action, thus served as a guide for organizing the efforts of the ensemble in which actors worked independently to a large degree.

Attitudes thus facilitated staging in a number of ways. They were used expressively to mark situations. They provided a way of managing entrances and exits. Conceiving of the scene as a series of attitudes permitted the individual actor to work up to the strongest ones and to plan out how he or she would effect the transition from one important posture to the next. They also offered techniques for managing the ensemble by positing the principles of contrast between different actors' poses and of a hierarchy whereby the spectators' attention was directed to the most dramatically important figures on the stage.

Pictorialism in acting, the traditions of actor training and of staging which we have outlined here, are often defined in opposition to a realist or naturalist style. The terms have become so vexed, especially in regards to film, which is often simply assumed to be naturalistic as a photographic medium, that they require some comment. Appeals to realism or some idea of a 'natural' style appear frequently in contemporary discussions of acting but it is often difficult to discern what is meant by them. The problem is compounded when these terms are taken up by present-day historians who interpret them in the light of twentieth-century conceptions of acting without posing the question of the ways the appeal to realism functioned within the context of nineteenth-century theatrical discourses and assumed importance as a criterion for judging acting. In our view, there are several such ways. With one exception these do not presuppose a rejection of or departure from pictorial elements in favour of some other style.

Most important in the eighteenth century, and for at least half of the nineteenth, was the opposition between beauty and expressiveness. The acting manuals continually stress the importance of grace, decorum, and good bearing in the actor's movements and gestures on stage. Rémond de Sainte-Albine notes that the passions 'must be portrayed with vivacity on the face of the Actor. They must not disfigure it. . . . Affliction should not be rendered hideous, instead of its being rendered interesting.'[39] The *Encyclopédie méthodique* invokes Lessing's discussion of this question with regard to the visual arts by recommending that the actor study the Laocoön as an example of how to maintain grace and beauty 'even in the extreme situations of tragedy'.[40] Lessing himself argues that as acting, in contradistinction to the plastic arts, is transitory, the actor may permit himself 'the wildness of a Tempesta, the insolence of a Bernini', provided that these attitudes are carefully treated: 'It [the art of the actor] must not remain in them too long, it must prepare for them gradually by previous movements, and must resolve them again into the general tone of the conventional.'[41] Ever practical, Jelgerhuis gives instructions for how to die, be stabbed, pray, sleep, and sit at a table in despair with good bearing.[42] He advises that even supposedly 'clumsy' characters, such as a farmer and his wife, be portrayed with grace.[43] Obviously, these comments apply only to tragedy, and in comedy the grotesque as opposed to the picturesque was tolerated and even required.

Within the context of the concern to idealize or formally contain expressive gesture, violations of decorum and good bearing were often described as 'realistic', and indeed criticized as such. While scholars such as Dene Barnett see the insistence upon good bearing as typical of the eighteenth century, the notion of realism which is opposed to it certainly survives into the nineteenth.[44] Boucicault invoked such a conception of realism when he unfavourably compared Bernhardt's playing of the death scene in *Adrienne Lecouvreur* with Rachel's performance of the same scene. He recalled that Bernhardt went into convulsions, writhing on stage, while Rachel simply clung to her young lover and died gazing into his eyes with 'no vulgar display of physical suffering except in her repression of it'.[45] Bernhardt is thus criticized for having sacrificed beauty to expressiveness. Of course, one could also accept this idea of 'realism' as a positive value, and justify violations of the accepted canons of decorum and the rules of graceful posture on these grounds, as indeed Zola does when he praises what he calls 'Romantic' acting as an advance over classical styles.[46] But whether actors were praised or criticized for being realistic in this sense, there is no reason to assume that they had thereby abandoned the interest in pictorial effect in acting. One may have an expressive gesture, and one that is significant in terms of a narrative situation, without having a formally beautiful pose. Bernhardt's performance in *Adrienne Lecouvreur* presumably fits in this category, and perhaps one definition of the romantic performance style, as opposed to its eighteenth-century precursors, might be a tendency to push in the direction of expressiveness at the expense of compositional harmony and graceful posture.

A second way of using the terms 'realism' or the 'natural' which also seems to derive from the late eighteenth century advances them as positive terms in opposition to an overly affected or mannered style of acting. Humboldt noted that the French connected the term 'nature' with the ideas of simplicity, ease, and restraint, a position which in this passage he does not seem entirely to share.[47] However, later in his letter to Goethe, he criticizes some French actors in very similar terms:

Acting here is so often mannered, a failing of which even the best actors are not entirely free. Sometimes they are mannered in the pictorial part, one sees attitudes that do not advance the meaning of the speeches, or a protraction of others that conflicts with nature, or a sudden interruption and change which taste here perhaps finds piquant, but which merely disturb anyone who wants to see all movements arise from a single source alone. Another kind of mannerism is exaggeration and an inadequately measured gradation of expression; a third, which is admittedly uncommon among the good actors, but which I find the most offensive, is the repetition of certain gestural tirades, so to speak, which one actor copies from another, and which become a sort of theatrical commonplace.[48]

This kind of argument appeals to nature as opposed to the overly wrought. 'Nature' figures as part of an argument for a 'plainer' pictorial style, without rapid or drastic changes in attitude, or long, extended holding of poses.[49] It is part of an argument for a style which does not call attention to the conventional or stereotyped aspect of the poses, which is apparently what Humboldt objected to when it became obvious that one actor was copying another's postures. Again, in our view, this is a complaint which exists within the confines of the pictorial style; it is not a rejection of posing as such but rather a call for economy and simplicity within its terms.

A conception of a 'natural' acting style similar to that evoked by Humboldt can also be found in the late nineteenth century, even after a new conception of naturalism, deriving from Zola, had begun to circulate. For example, elucidating the very different ideas of nature which had influenced actors since Garrick, Constant Coquelin explained his own position as a rejection of the 'extremes' of both romanticism and naturalism in Zola's sense: 'Just as I would not allow any departure from truth on the plea of picturesque effects, so I would not permit a representation of commonplace or horrible things on the pretext of reality. I am always on the side of nature and against naturalism. . . . What I mean by art that is natural in the modern sense is equally remote from both these extremes. It is classic rather than romantic, for everywhere it regards limit, everywhere it shuns violent antitheses.'[50] Coquelin argued for the importance of mid-nineteenth-century theatrical conventions, both conventional declamatory styles and picturesque effects, but also that

good actors should use and judiciously vary the conventions in relation to the demands of genre (he distinguished between tragedy, melodrama, and comedy) and of particular roles. This is not necessarily an argument for simplicity or a plain style, since, for example, he argued that melodrama required a certain degree of exaggeration, but the argument appealed to 'nature' as a principle of limitation or restraint on the way the actor deployed a recognized body of theatrical conventions.

Coquelin's reference to Zola signalled yet a third important meaning of the term 'nature'—naturalism. In so far as Zola's naturalism was associated with the representation of 'commonplace or horrible things', it obviously pertained to the first usage of the term discussed above. But it cannot be reduced to it. Boucicault seems to have found Bernhardt's death scene in *Adrienne Lecouvreur* overly 'commonplace and horrible', but this does not make her a 'naturalist' actress in the sense of the tradition defined by Zola or Ibsen. While a comprehensive account of naturalist theatre is beyond the scope of this work, it is necessary to indicate how, in our view, naturalism represented a departure from pictorially oriented styles.

The important feature of naturalist acting as it developed in the 1880s was not that it encouraged actors to approximate real life, or even some conventionalized notion of the real. Rather, in their staging practices the great naturalist directors and actors were willing to abandon not only graceful movement and posture, but also highly emphatic and expressive gesture. In striking attitudes, the actor traditionally summed up an emotion or narrative idea for the audience in the form of one or more compelling 'pictures'. But in the naturalist theatre, incidental activity, stage business, became much more important than the telling gesture or pose as a way of organizing the actor's activity on stage. There are many well-known instances of the importance accorded to mundane stage business within this movement. For example, Strindberg's stage directions for the pantomime scene in *Miss Julie* involve the cook, Christine, doing the dishes, cleaning up the kitchen, and curling the bangs on her forehead with a curling iron. Similarly, in the 1905 Moscow Art Theatre production of *Ghosts* described by Frederick and Lise-Lone Marker, Stanislavsky staged the opening scene, in which exposition is provided by a conversation between Regine and her father the carpenter Engstrand, by having the carpenter on stage from the start of the act, busy fixing the lock on the garden door.[51] Comparable methods were devised for handling the ensemble. The Markers report that in William Bloch's definitive staging of *An Enemy of the People*, the director gave fifty-three extras specific 'identities' and bits of purposeful stage business.[52] Clearly all of these examples have actors performing activities which bear some relation to character or atmosphere, but they are not purposefully designed to produce a pleasing composition, nor to epitomize an emotion or situation as, for example, Lady Hamilton's attitude epitomizes religious devotion in George Romney's painting.

Along with the highly elaborated use of stage business, the naturalist theatre of the 1880s fostered an 'underplayed', even opaque acting style. For example, the naturalist director Otto Brahm commented approvingly on the performance style of Rudolf Rittner, one of the actors hired when Brahm took over the administration of the Deutsches Theater in the 1890s:

I had the impression of something which gained extraordinary clarity from its very insignificance: I saw him simply go out a door, nothing more. He had read a letter from his Musotte, and as he mulled it over, filled with its mournful tidings, he walked off, without any ceremony—I think I have never seen anything like it. Since our whole former style of acting required an appearance of volition, of careful attention to detail, the 'effective exit' was one of the weightiest requirements of this school. Every step was defended like the retreat from a battlefield, the actor holding every eye on himself until the last. The significance of Rittner's exit consisted in that he simply went out, adding nothing. This delighted me and in this little action I saw symbolized the whole revolution of our new method of presentation.[53]

We take Duse's famed performances of Ibsen as representing an extreme within this general tendency. Duse's acting is consistently described in terms like 'restrained' or 'non-melodramatic', which we take to mean a marked absence of emphatic elements, including gestures and attitudes. Writing in 1927, Arthur Symons described her style as 'the antithesis of what we call acting', and contrasted it with that of Henry Irving, characterizing Irving's as 'dramatised oratory', which 'crystallises into an attitude, dies upon a long drawn-out word', while Duse's performance style was 'like the art of Verlaine in French poetry; always suggestion, never statement, always a renunciation'.[54] Indeed, even the arch-Ibsenite William Archer bemoaned the levelling effect of her 'dread of melodrama' in her performance as Nora in *The Doll's House* in London during 1892. He complained that her reactions were so minimal in the scene in which Krogstad points out the discrepancy between the date of Nora's father's death and the date on which he supposedly countersigned for her loan, that the audience did not even get a sense of her surprise. Tracy Davis suggests that Archer was expecting Duse to start, and palpably to demonstrate her fear through explicit gestures.[55]

Although one can certainly find examples of productions of Ibsen with other actresses which were praised for their pictorial beauties, and indeed even a famous tableau in *Hedda Gabler*,[56] the naturalist theatre pioneered by Ibsen and others and developed by actresses such as Duse eventually fostered a real departure from those eighteenth- and nineteenth-century styles of acting which aimed to produce marked pictorial effects. Ibsen's plays themselves place a great deal of weight on the idea of repression—the inability of characters to express or in some cases even understand the situation in which they find themselves.[57] The point is underscored by Minnie Maddern Fiske, the American actress who made her reputation as a naturalist in Ibsen's plays, speaking of *Hedda Gabler* in an interview with Alexander Woollcott:

To Hedda the very sight of Lövborg standing there on the threshold of her drawing-room brings a flood of old memories crowding close. It must not show on the surface. That is not Ibsen's way. There are others—alien spirits—present, and Hedda is the personification of fastidious self-control. She has sacrificed everything for that. No, it may not show on the surface, but if the actress has lived through Hedda's past, and so realized her present, that moment is electrical.[58]

The actor's refusal to provide the audience with pronounced and significant poses would seem to be ideally suited to this kind of dramaturgy which works by the indirect representation of a hidden past, and the repression or containment of feeling. In contrast, pictorial styles as we understand them were geared toward the powerful and direct expression of interior states, and toward making dramatic situations as clear and intense as possible through the orchestration of pose and gesture.

We should note that in our view naturalist acting techniques did have an influence on some film acting, an influence we discuss below in connection with the great Swedish director and actor Victor Sjöström. However, this influence is not as pronounced as has sometimes been asserted or supposed, and we would like to stress the daring involved in adopting this kind of refusal of pictorial effect in the medium of silent film. Naturalist theatre was famously wordy, and to some extent the emphasis on the language compensated for the opacity of gesture and action typical of the acting style. It required considerable sophistication to adapt it to the new medium.

1. Dene Barnett, 'The Performance Practice of Acting: The Eighteenth Century, Part I: Ensemble Acting', *Theatre Research International*, 2, no. 3 (1977), 157–86; 'The Performance Practice of Acting: The Eighteenth Century, Part II: The Hands', *Theatre Research International*, 3, no. 1 (1977), 1-19; 'The Performance Practice of Acting: The Eighteenth Century, Part III: The Arms', *Theatre Research International*, 3, no. 2 (1978), 79–93; 'The Performance Practice of Acting: The Eighteenth Century, Part IV: The Eyes, the Face and the Head', *Theatre Research International*, 5, no. 1 (1980), 1–36; 'The Performance Practice of Acting: The Eighteenth Century, Part V: Posture and Attitudes', *Theatre Research International*, 6, no. 1 (1981), 1–32. Many of the same passages also appear in his remarkable book *The Art of Gesture*. Although both articles and book are concerned with the eighteenth century, several sources, including the fascinating and amply illustrated manual by Johannes Jelgerhuis, *Theoretische Lessen over de Gesticulatie en Mimiek: Gegeven aan de Kweekelingen van het Fonds ter Opleiding en Onderrigting van Tooneel-Kunstenaars aan den Stads Schouwburg te Amsterdam* (Amsterdam: P. M. Warnars, 1827; repr. Uitgeverij Adolf M. Hakkert, 1970) date from the early nineteenth century and seem to us to apply to acting practices in this period as well.

2. Franciscus Lang, *Dissertatio de actione scenica cum figuris eandem explicantibus et observationibus quibusdam de arte comica* (Munich: Typis Mariae Magdalenae Riedlin, 1727), 42; cit. Barnett, 'Performance Practice', v. 2.

3. Jelgerhuis, *Theoretische Lessen*, 70; cit. Barnett, 'Performance Practice', v. 2.

4. Henry Garside Neville, 'Gesture' in Hugh Campbell, R. F. Brewer, and Henry Neville, *Voice, Speech and Gesture: A Practical Handbook to the Elocutionary Art* (New York: G. P. Putnam's, 1895; repr. in Granger Index Reprint Series, New York: Books for Libraries Press, 1972), 121.

5. See the already cited works and Antonio Morrocchesi, *Lezioni di declamazione e d'arte teatrale* (Florence: Tipografia all'insegna di Dante, 1832). Various acting teachers published their versions of Delsarte's system, with illustrations; one of the most important in America was Genevieve Stebbins, *Delsarte System of Dramatic Expression* (New York: Edgar S. Werner, 1886). See Macht, 'Origin of the London Academy of Music', for a discussion of Delsarte's influence in England.

6. Konstantin Stanislavsky, 'The System and Methods of Creative Art', in *Stanislavsky on the Art of the Stage*, trans. David Magarshack (London: Faber and Faber, 1950), 215. The essay derives from notes taken by auditors of a series of lectures given in the studio of the Bolshoi Theatre, the Moscow opera house, between 1918 and 1922.

7. Stanislavsky, 'Five Rehearsals of *Werther*', in *The Art of the Stage*, 280.

8. To take just two examples, see Susan Bassnett, 'Eleonora Duse', in John Stokes, Michael R. Booth, and Susan Bassnett, *Bernhardt, Terry, Duse: The Actress in her Time* (Cambridge: Cambridge University Press, 1988), 138; and Pearson, *Eloquent Gestures*, 21, on the stylized nature of the histrionic code, and p. 31, on the kinds of psychological complexity associated with realism.

9. See, for example, Roach, *Player's Passion*, 59, speaking of eighteenth-century theories of acting: 'The seminal interplay between the plastic arts and theatrical theory—in particular, the actor's fascination with pictures and statues—corresponds, directly, as we shall see, to the interaction between art and science that encouraged the most advanced thinking in this period. In turn, the theatrical theorist's tendency to enumerate the physical signs of the passions and his desire to notate their transitions stemmed logically from current developments in physiology and psychology.'

10. Lang, *Dissertatio*, 46–7, cited in Barnett, 'Performance Practice', IV. 8.

11. See, for example, Michel Gareau, *Charles Le Brun: First Painter to King Louis XIV* (New York: Harry N. Abrams, 1992), 99, which shows Le Brun's drawing of five rows of eyes, used in his lecture to illustrate the expressive aspects of the eye and eyebrow, and compare with the similar drawing, used almost 200 years later for the same purpose, in Neville, 'Gesture', 149.

12. Louis James, 'Was Jerrold's Black Ey'd Susan More Popular than Wordsworth's Lucy?', in David Bradby, Louis James, and Bernard Sharratt (eds.), *Performance and Politics in Popular Drama: Aspects of Popular Entertainment in Theatre, Film and Television, 1800–1976* (Cambridge: Cambridge University Press, 1980), 6–7; for another discussion of the importance of Le Brun and related theories on the emerging pictorial style, see Holmström, *Monodrama*, 29–32.

13. François Delsarte, *Delsarte System of Oratory* (New York: Edgar S. Werner, 1893), Episode 1, pp. 388–9, and Episode 2, pp. 401–11.

14. Roach, *Player's Passion*, 78–92, traces out the prolonged debate concerning the conundrum of 'internal' versus 'external' theories of acting: some argued the actor must first inwardly feel the emotion that he is to portray, others argued that the actor's simple performance of the relevant physical gestures would awaken the requisite feeling in himself and his audience. For Roach, Diderot's formulation of this problem remains the definitive one for the nineteenth century.

15. Holmström, *Monodrama*, 32.

16. Humboldt, 'Französische tragische Bühne', 394.

17. Constant Coquelin, 'Actors and Acting', in *Papers on Acting II: The Art of Acting, a discussion by Constant Coquelin, Henry Irving and Dion Boucicault*, Publications of the Dramatic Museum of Columbia University, in the City of New York, 5th ser. (New York: Columbia University Press, 1926), 11.

18. Louis Calvert, *Problems of the Actor* (New York: Henry Holt, 1918), 131–2.

19. Frederick J. Marker, *Hans Christian Andersen and the Romantic Theatre* (Toronto: University of Toronto Press, 1971), 166–8; see also Edward J. West, 'Histrionic Methods and Acting Traditions on the London Stage from 1870 to 1890', Dissertation, Yale University, June 1940, pp. 39–43 and 69; Bettina Knapp, *The Reign of the Theatrical Director: French Theatre, 1887–1924* (New York: Whitston, 1988); Helen Krich Chinoy, 'The Emergence of the Director', in Toby Cole and Helen Krich Chinoy (eds.), *Directors on Directing: A Sourcebook of the Modern Theatre* (Indianapolis: Bobbs-Merrill, 1976).

20. Leman Thomas Rede, *The Road to the Stage; or, The Performer's Preceptor* (London: J. Smith, 1827), 41, cited in Barnett, 'Performance Practice', i. 180.

21. Humboldt, 'Französische tragische Bühne', 379.

22. Alb., 'A Rehearsal at the Française', *Time* (June 1879), 350, cit. John Stokes, 'Sarah Bernhardt', in Stokes *et al.*, *Bernhardt, Terry, Duse*, 34.

23. H. Dupont-Vernon, *Diseurs et comédiens* (Paris: Paul Ollendorf, 1891), 238.

24. *About the Theatre*, 308. A prose translation of the passage might run as follows: *Don Ruy Gomez (to his servants):* Squires! Squires! Help me! My axe, my dagger, my Toledan blade! (*To the two young men.*) And follow me, both of you! *Don Carlos (taking a step forward):* Duke, we have other business first: the death of Maximilian, Emperor of Germany. (*He throws down his cloak and reveals the face concealed beneath his hat.*) *Don Ruy Gomez:* Are you mad? . . . My god! The King! *Doña Sol:* The King! *Hernani (his eyes lighting up):* The King of Spain!

25. Jelgerhuis, *Theoretische Lessen*, 38, cited in Barnett, 'Performance Practice', v. 9.

26. Humboldt, 'Französische tragische Bühne', 386.

27. Siddons, *Practical Illustrations*, 347.

28. Ibid. 348.

29. Ibid. 350.

30. Morrocchesi, *Lezioni*, 255–7 and figures 17–38, illustrating his own performance of a speech in Act 4, scene 2 of *Oreste* in Vittorio Alfieri, *Tragedie*, ed. Nicola Bruscoli (Bari: Laterza, 1946), i. 363.

31. The Tams-Witmark music library is the major US clearing house for performance rights for opera, operetta, and musical theatre. A collection of libretti and musical parts for material now out of copyright is held at the John Mills Music Library at the University of Wisconsin-Madison. For many productions the holdings include a stage manager's score with staging instructions. The date at which most of these annotations were made cannot be established with certainty, but most of the material in the University of Wisconsin's holdings was acquired by Alfred Tams between the mid-1880s and 1920. The stage manager's guide for Donizetti's *Lucia di Lammermoor* notes that in the aria Lucia sings after her first entrance with her maid in Act 1, scene 2, p. 33, 'Lucy should portray the emotion the words express facially and physically

with hands and face and especially eyes, and the two girls should come to an agreement as to what they will do on the different phrases; if they have enough interest in the scene to make it go, as far as it rests on their efforts. It is well worth the trial and so we leave it in their hands.' A similar kind of notation is found in the stage manager's guide for Sir Julius Benedict's *The Lily of Killarney*, for the scene in which Danny Mann sings an aria about his willingness to kill Eily, opposite p. 144.

32. For a discussion of this incident and the commentary it provoked on the part of Diderot and others, see Roach, *Player's Passion*, 111, 127, 138.

33. Gotthold Ephraim Lessing, *The Hamburg Dramaturgy*, trans. Helen Zimmern (New York: Dover, 1962), from no. 17 (June 1767), p. 46.

34. Riccoboni, *L'Art du théâtre*, 79, cited in Barnett, 'Performance Practice', i. 178–9; for a discussion of the ensemble along similar lines, but related to the mid-nineteenth-century handling of the ensemble, see Frederick and Lise-Lone Marker, 'Fru Heiberg: A Study of the Art of the Romantic Actor', *Theatre Research*, 13, no. 1 (1973), 31.

35. Jelgerhuis, *Theoretische Lessen*, 90, cited in Barnett, 'Performance Practice', i. 183.

36. Barnett, 'Performance Practice', i. 175–80.

37. De la Porte and Chamfort, *Dictionnaire dramatique*, ii. 117, cit. Barnett, 'Performance Practice', i. 184.

38. Thomas Wilkes, *A General View of the Stage* (London: J. Coote, 1759), 170, cit. Barnett, 'Performance Practice', i. 184.

39. Pierre Rémond de Sainte-Albine, *Le Comédien*, rev. edn. (Paris: Vincent fils, 1749; repr. Geneva: Slatkine Reprints, 1971), 149, cit. Barnett, 'Performance Practice', iv. 21.

40. Nicolas Étienne Framéry and Pierre Louis Ginguené (eds.), *Encyclopédie méthodique, musique* (Paris: Panckoucke, 1791), vol. i, article 'Action', p. 49; cit. Barnett, 'Performance Practice', v. 3–4. The reference is of course to Lessing's *Laocoön*, first published in 1766.

41. Lessing, *Hamburg Dramaturgy*, from no. 5 (May 1767), 19.

42. Jelgerhuis, *Theoretische Lessen*, 56–64; cit. Barnett, 'Performance Practice', v. 24–9.

43. Ibid. 53; cit. Barnett, 'Performance Practice', v. 17–18.

44. Barnett, *Art of Gesture*, 91–4 and 139–45; see also Frederick Marker, *Hans Christian Andersen*, 184, on what he calls the 'neoclassic ideal of *Schöne Wahrheit*'.

45. Dion Boucicault, 'Coquelin-Irving' in *Papers on Acting II: The Art of Acting, a discussion by Constant Coquelin, Henry Irving and Dion Boucicault*, Publications of the Dramatic Museum of Columbia University, in the City of New York, 5th ser. (New York: Columbia University Press, 1926), 59–60. But compare Boucicault's account of Rachel's performance with that given in Laurence Senelick, 'Rachel in Russia: The Shchepkin-Annenkov Correspondence', *Theatre Research International*, 3, no. 2 (1978), 103, in which the critic Pavel Vasil'evich Annenkov describes Rachel's performance of this death scene in Russia in 1853 as having involved her writhing in convulsions and raving so that many women had to leave the auditorium. The discrepancy between the two accounts may be due to a variation in Rachel's performance of the part over time, or a lapse of memory by Boucicault, or, more interestingly, changing theatrical conventions which could have made Rachel look 'restrained' to Boucicault in the light of Bernhardt's performance style. In any case, our use of the example does not ride on the accuracy of Boucicault's mem-

ory—we cite it as indicative of how he understood the notion of realism and the limits of decorum on stage.

46. Émile Zola, 'From *Naturalism in the Theatre*', trans. Albert Bermel, in Eric Bentley (ed.), *The Theory of the Modern Stage* (Harmondsworth: Penguin Books, 1968), 349–72.

47. Humboldt, 'Französische tragische Bühne', 387–8.

48. Ibid. 396.

49. For a similar complaint about over use, and overly mannered use, of gesture see Lessing's discussion of hand movements, *Hamburg Dramaturgy*, from no. 4 (May 1767), 16–17. In the middle of the nineteenth century George Lewes cautioned against both overacting, adopting a bombastic or exaggerated manner in an effort to achieve an effect, and underacting, adopting a manner so close to 'natural' behaviour that the audience did not register any effect at all, so that the character appeared dull and flat. See 'On Natural Acting', in *On Actors and the Art of Acting* (London: Smith, Elder & Co., 1875; repr. New York: Grove Press, 1957), 103.

50. Coquelin, 'Actors and Acting', 37–40.

51. Frederick and Lise-Lone Marker, *Ibsen's Lively Art: A Performance Study of the Major Plays* (Cambridge: Cambridge University Press, 1989), 105.

52. Ibid. 130.

53. Otto Brahm, 'Die Freie Bühne in Berlin', *Berliner Tageblatt* (16, 18 Oct. 1909); repr. in *Kritiken und Essays*, sel., introd., and ed. Fritz Martini (Zurich: Artemis Verlag, 1964), 524; cit. Marvin Carlson, *The German Stage in the Nineteenth Century* (Metuchen, NJ: Scarecrow Press, 1972), 224.

54. Arthur Symons, *Eleonora Duse* (New York: Duffield & Co., 1927), 7; cit. Bassnett in Stokes *et al.*, *Bernhardt, Terry, Duse*, 157.

55. Tracy C. Davis, 'Acting in Ibsen', *Theatre Notebook*, 39, no. 3 (1985), 113–23.

56. See Davis, ibid., and Frederick and Lise-Lone Marker, *Ibsen's Lively Art*, 169.

57. Meisel, *Realizations*, 8, makes a similar point about the differences between nineteenth- and twentieth-century dramaturgical traditions in terms of their assumptions about the possibility of representing emotion: 'The actor's challenge always has been to externalize feeling and thought, including that within which passeth show. Only recently in the Western tradition have we accepted the convention that true feeling is always inarticulate and ultimately inexpressible. The earlier convention took for granted a full expressibility in language and behavior; that is, the convention admitted and demanded a direct externalization, with all the analytic simplification that entailed.'

58. Alexander Woollcott, *Mrs. Fiske: Her Views on the Stage* (New York: The Century Company, 1917), 64–7.

THE study of theatre history, at least as regards the nineteenth century, consists in the reconstruction of performances we cannot directly know. But in the case of film we have access to the performances, a fact which sets the historian new problems of analysis, and complicates the process of comparing the two in so far as it involves comparing disparate kinds of evidence. The seeming disadvantage of theatre history, that our sense of performance style must be derived largely from contemporary accounts and reviews, is also an advantage in that the evidence comes to us filtered and to an extent interpreted by viewers already imbued with a sense of the theatre and the performance practices that we seek to reconstruct. If a reviewer says that Sarah Bernhardt 'gets the full plastic as well as histrionic value of a situation', one is justified in assuming that he recognized poses in what he saw her doing on stage, even if more research is necessary to try and determine what those poses were, and why they were singled out for praise. In the case of cinema, however, we are frequently left on our own to describe and analyse the performance which has been reproduced in such detail; we need to isolate its significant moments, to

find ways of becoming sensitive to the parameters of a style quite remote from present-day film acting. The real difficulty of learning how to watch the acting of this period, evident to anyone who has tried to teach 1910s cinema, is indicative of this historical distance.

When we do have contemporary accounts of film acting, these are usually found in the trade press. (The respectable cultural press largely ignored film until the end of the 1910s.) Such accounts demand much more careful reading than they have been accorded by most modern commentators. Much of the discussion of acting in the trade press turns out to be impossibly vague when examined closely, and this problem is confounded by the fact that the trade press is, precisely, a corporate press. It hopes to advance the cause of the cinema as a whole, not to champion some of its products and damn the rest. Every article praising an aspect of the films of one production company will always be balanced by a matching article praising those of another equally strongly. Moreover, from very early there is a tendency to champion film over theatre and, in the USA, with some exceptions such as the early Film d'Art productions, to champion American films over those of Europe.[1] Hence it is too easy to select quotations to support, say, a claim for a change in film acting or a contrast between film and stage acting, while ignoring all the other quotations which would undermine it or without taking into account the institutional biases of the trade press as such. Only the most precise accounts of what the commentators see on the screen can be taken seriously, and even then they have to be considered very carefully in the light of the actual performances that we can examine in surviving films.

The problem, then, is to register when and how actors are adapting pictorial stage traditions to the cinema. Most immediately, in our case, the problem is how to recognize a pose when we see one. The difficulty becomes clear if we consider the question of the length of time that an actor must stay in a position for it to qualify as a pose. In this regard, a comparison with what we know about the pace of theatrical acting is instructive.

It seems clear that the pace of the acting differed according to genre—comedy was played faster than tragedy—and according to individual style—for example, Garrick is reported to have had a livelier style than did the Kembles.[2] Moreover, the few indications that we have about the length of the poses in tragedy and serious drama imply that the pace of acting changed over time. Dene Barnett suggests that although repose was a valued attribute of eighteenth-century acting style, the pace of declamation in tragedy and the recitatives of opera was quite rapid in comparison with present-day performances of such works.[3] The practice of varying gesture in accordance with the word or phrase, as opposed to the sentence, also implied that there was at least potentially a great number of gestures for each speech.[4]

By the end of the nineteenth century, the tempo of such acting seems to have slowed considerably. Yeats provides one of the most precise accounts of the length of the poses in a description of the performances of Sarah Bernhardt and Édouard de Max in *Phèdre* in London in 1902:

For long periods the performers would merely stand and pose, and I once counted twenty-seven quite slowly before anybody on a fairly well-filled stage moved, as it seemed, so much as an eyelash. The periods of stillness were generally shorter, but I frequently counted seventeen, eighteen, or twenty before there was a movement. I noticed, too, that the gestures had a rhythmic progression. Sara [*sic*] Bernhardt

would keep her hands clasped over, let us say, her right breast for some time, and then move them to the other side, perhaps, lowering her chin till it had touched her hands, and then, after another long stillness, she would unclasp them and hold one out, and so on, not lowering them till she had exhausted all the gestures of uplifted hands. Through one long scene De Max, who was quite as fine, never lifted his hands above his elbow, it was only when the emotion came to its climax that he raised it to his breast. Beyond them stood a crowd of white-robed men who never moved at all, and the whole scene had the nobility of Greek sculpture, and an extraordinary reality and intensity.[5]

It is hard to tell how typical Bernhardt's style is here and whether it represents a more general change in the tempo employed for classical French tragedy. But one does find other reports of long-held poses.

Paul Ranger provides the example of Mrs Siddons in the role of Euphrasia in Arthur Murphy's *The Grecian Daughter* (1772). Having stabbed Dionysius in the fifth act, Mrs Siddons 'slowly sank to her knees, stretched upward the arm which had driven the fatal knife into the tyrant's chest and so remained for five minutes to the accompaniment of quiet sobbing from the audience'.[6] This does not seem very plausible to us, and the description by Friedrich Wilhelm von Hassel on which it is based might rather be read as suggesting she was wordless for five minutes while executing a series of poses expressing her complex reactions to the murder.[7] However, Shaw did commiserate with Ellen Terry about a scene in *King Lear* where Irving's performance of Lear's awakening was so protracted as to force her to hold a pose for the same time.[8] There are certainly other instances of actors prolonging poses to make a picture at scene-ends. With regard to French tragedy, Humboldt notes that 'one often sees attitudes protracted that would follow one another more rapidly in our country. Thus, at the end of a significant scene, the actor leaves the stage with as it were protracted gestures, where we would not tolerate someone, say, walking away with upraised arms and wanting to hold them up until he is lost to the spectators' view. If something like this did happen in our country it would at least happen violently and rapidly, but here it always has the hesitant calm characteristic of all aesthetic poses.'[9] In the middle of the nineteenth century, Fru Heiberg was often praised for the plasticity of her style, but Frederick and Lise-Lone Marker record one occasion when a reviewer, speaking of her performance in Oehlenschläger's *Dina* (1842) demurred: 'When Colonel Walter has proposed to Dina, she stretches forth her arm to show him the ring which Ulfeldt has placed on her finger. Walter rushes out, but for some time after his exit she remains standing with her arm stiffly outstretched. This is presumably meant to indicate her absorption in her sorrow, but it is unnatural because of the effort the pose must cost her.'[10] The reference to the effort the pose costs the actress would suggest that it was held for a considerable period.

Boucicault also advised remaining in a pose: 'Another thing is, do not let your gesture be too short. It seems that some cannot give the appropriate gesture. They say, "Go away!" [*with a quick gesture*]. They cannot rest long enough in a gesture. You do not know how long you can rest upon a good one. It tires you, but it will not tire the spectator.'[11] It should be noted that while film scholars sometimes assume that melodrama was acted at a quick pace we have seen no evidence that poses were not held for just as long in this genre—indeed, this citation from Boucicault suggests otherwise. Moreover, the particular importance of music in melodrama would have allowed scope for long and marked posing, since music helps to give rhythm to the actor's movement, and covers over brief cessations in the action.[12]

In the case of cinema it seems clear that poses, like the tableaux in the film versions of *Uncle Tom's Cabin*, were not normally held for anything like the length of time of, for example, Bernhardt's poses in *Phèdre*. Certainly the way of *elaborating* poses which Yeats describes, in which Bernhardt moved her hands from one breast to another until she had 'exhausted all the gestures of uplifted hands', bears a strong resemblance to some kinds of film acting in the 1910s (see, for example, the discussion of Borelli's acting below). But we have rarely seen an actor pause for more than a few seconds. Thus, in our efforts to analyse this acting style, the time of the pause could not be the sole criterion for defining a pose or attitude. Instead we have looked for the following:

1. There is a slight pause in the actor's movement when the film is viewed at the correct speed of projection (remember Humboldt's term, cited above, of a 'hesitant calm'—*zögernde Ruhe*);

2. The actor assumes a stereotyped posture;
3. The posture expresses the character's interior state or in some other way clearly and directly relates to the dramatic situation;
4. The posture is systematically iterated and varied by the actor;
5. The blocking of the actor's movement, or of the acting ensemble, clearly leads up to the pose or leads from one pose to the next.

Obviously the frame stills used in this chapter do not 'prove' the existence of an attitude, since they represent no more than one-sixteenth of a second of the actual time of the performance. Rather, they are used to facilitate the work of description.

Poses in the sense proposed above appear in a wide range of silent film. Perhaps the most systematic attempt to describe how they function is Roberta Pearson's discussion of what she calls the 'histrionic code' of film acting at Biograph in the period between 1908 and 1912. While we find Pearson's analyses of individual films compelling, we believe the theoretical terms of her argument misrepresent pictorial styles of acting on the stage and make it difficult to understand the various ways poses were adapted to film.

Pearson defines the histrionic code in opposition to the verisimilar code. The former does not aim to create psychologically complex characters, nor an effect of realism, while the latter does. The former frankly admits its theatricality—the actor palpably 'acts', striking conventionalized poses and attitudes—while the latter eschews such self-consciousness, favouring stage business and byplay with props. But we have tried to indicate the difficulties of defining pictorialism in acting simply in opposition to realism. Nineteenth-century discourses on acting appealed to concepts of realism quite frequently, and often in ways which did not preclude an emphasis on attitudes and posing, but simply served to reinforce notions of expressiveness, restraint, or decorum that were not clearly specified as such.

We find the calls for realistic or subtle acting in the film industry trade press similarly amorphous. In general, with the possible exception of Frank Woods, the trade press does not provide enough detail about what actors were doing on screen, or what they should have been doing, to provide a fruitful definition of realism.[13] Albert Goldie's 'Subtlety in Acting', for example, argues that self-conscious acting is bad, but he does not specifically mention poses or attitudes, and it is not clear if posing would necessarily be seen as self-conscious in his terms.[14] In her memoir 'Growing up with the Movies', Florence Lawrence is somewhat more specific, criticizing an unnamed stage actor who appeared in a feature in the following terms: 'The actor I speak of would strike a pose in nearly every other scene which seemed to ask, "Now am I not the handsome lover?" or "Don't you think I'm some hero?" '[15] However, it still is not obvious whether Lawrence is objecting to what she sees as the stage actor's narcissistic showing off, or if any pose, even an expressive one linked to character or situation, is in her view inappropriate for film acting. Recall that Humboldt, who tremendously admired Talma's pictorial style of acting, none the less criticized 'mannered' or 'exaggerated' poses which became obvious as such.[16] The problem is not simply how to interpret Lawrence's language here, but more generally that analysis of the film industry trade discourse in terms of an opposition between posed and realistic styles of acting is logically fraught. Because people strike poses in real life, often quite conventional ones, even an avowed advocate of 'realistic' acting might admit some poses on the grounds that they were 'lifelike'. For example, a *Moving Picture World* critic like Goldie was not likely to comment adversely on an actor playing the part of an Italian immigrant who used large, vivid, and fully extended gestures, given that the lack of 'subtlety' would be motivated by ethnic stereotypes. Stanislavsky himself was willing to admit that the actor in *Werther* could strike a pose upon his entrance to Charlotte's cottage provided there was sufficient motivation, that is, supposing he had discovered her corpse. Even a very strict commitment to realism can accommodate poses in certain narrative contexts. Moreover, there does not seem to be a principled way to determine from the reviews or commentary when an actor is being criticized for posing as such, and when the issue of posing is raised simply because a particular attitude was found inappropriate or unconvincing.

But of course we do not have only the reviews. We have at least some of the films, and this evidence suggests that there was posing throughout the years 1908–12 and beyond, even as the trade press praised realistic acting. Pearson's own analyses of films

suggest that what she has defined as two distinct codes coexisted, and that well into the 1910s Biograph actors continued to use poses alongside elements such as stage business or the employment of props. For example, she notes that, in the otherwise 'verisimilar' film *His Lost Love* (1909), the actors fall into poses during the climactic scene in which the wife discovers her husband's adultery.[17] She finds a similar mixture of the two codes in Henry Walthall's performances in the films *Thou Shalt Not* (1910) and *The Avenging Conscience* (1914), and indeed throughout his career.[18]

Our examples, taken from a European context, confirm Pearson's observations that actors use attitudes more prominently in some scenes than in others. *Le Homard* (The Lobster; Léonce Perret, 1912), a part of Gaumont's Léonce series, represents typical comic acting of the period, which involves a great deal of complex pantomime, as well as attitudes and gestural asides to the camera. In the film, Suzanne (Suzanne Grandais) quarrels with Léonce (Perret) over his refusal to purchase an expensive lobster from a local fisherman. He then pretends to go out fishing for lobsters on a stormy night while in fact having made arrangements to buy them. He finally returns home and, with much mugging to the camera, pretends that he is exhausted and suffering from cold after having spent a difficult night at sea. The revelation of his deception leads to a quarrel which is only resolved by the fact that he must rescue the seabathing Suzanne by removing an offending crustacean from her posterior. While Perret and Grandais employ vivid and expressive gestures, these often take the form of a rapid 'dialogue', gestures expressing exasperation or reproach exchanged between man and wife during their quarrels. The only attitudes notably held in the film occur during what is for Suzanne (but not the spectator) a potentially tragic moment; during the long night that Suzanne awaits Léonce's return, Grandais poses, first at the window looking out to sea, then in her bedroom, on her knees in prayer (Figure 3.6). The contrast between the comic and the serious tone is particularly shown up later in this scene when, through a split screen composition, the film composes a triptych showing Grandais on the left, in an attitude of prayer, the sea in the middle of the frame, and Perret on the right, seated comfortably at the movies, and laughing with glee at the Gaumont comedy on the screen (Figure 3.7).

Note that Perret does not hold a pose in the triptych; this is reserved for Grandais's expression of grief and remorse. It is as if Grandais's acting in *Le Homard* falls out of the comic mode in order to convey Suzanne's state of mind. In general, it seems quite clear that genre was an important factor in determining whether or not the actors choose to adopt attitudes, and the length of time the attitudes were held. Serious drama called for a slower style than comedy, with more pronounced poses and gestures (this was true on the stage as well as film, as Coquelin's discussion of theatrical genres already cited indicates). One tends to find the longest and most marked posing in historical or costume pictures such as *L'Assassinat du Duc de Guise* (1908) or *Quatre-vingt-*

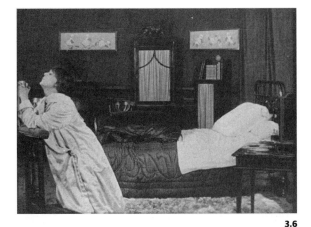

3.6

3.7

treize (1914–21), or sentimental stories, especially those dealing with dignified, upper-class characters such as *Ma l'amor mio non muore!* (1913). Pearson notes a similar division in her survey of Walthall's films for Biograph, with one of his most 'histrionic' performances being a historical romance, *The Sealed Room* (1909).[19]

But even within serious films, poses become more pronounced at climactic moments, as if the actors are 'saving' them for the big scenes. That is, posing is determined by situation as well as by genre. One of the clearest examples we have seen of this tendency is the Danish film *Klovnen* (The Clown, 1917). Joe Higgins (Valdemar Psilander) is the clown in the travelling circus run by Mr and Mrs Bunding in which their daughter Daisy (Gudrun Houlberg) is the bareback rider. Joe and Daisy are in love, and when a major impresario offers Joe a big city contract, he makes it a condition of accepting that the Bundings accompany him. Two years later he is a great success and has married Daisy, but Daisy is courted by Count Henri. One day after his performance, Joe sees Henri kissing Daisy in the mirror in the green room of the theatre. He goes home in despair and finds Daisy there waiting for him. He asks her if she loves the Count; she says yes, so he tells her to go to him. The plot then takes a predictably unhappy turn. After the Count tires of her, Daisy tries to return to Joe, is rebuffed by her father, and commits suicide. Having forgiven Daisy on her deathbed, and mourning her loss, Joes goes downhill himself, and is working in a cheap circus when he meets the Count once again and kills his old rival before expiring.

The scenes of Joe's happy life—the courtship of Daisy, eating dinner with the family, the back-stage preparations for their acts in the travelling circus—are all done at normal tempo and without marked posing. However, the whole tempo and style of the acting alter after Joe sees Daisy and the Count kissing in the mirror. The shift is particularly evident in the confrontation between the two at the house which follows Daisy's departure from the theatre (the titles are translations from the Danish ones in the print):

1   A salon in Joe's palatial mansion: the anteroom brightly lit rear centre and right, with a closed glass portière at the top of a short flight of steps; a bay window left; a small table, chair, and settee front centre. Houlberg is sitting on the settee, her head on her hands on the table.

3.8

3.9

3.11

3.12

3.14

3.15

3.10

3.13

3.16

Psilander enters from the rear right, opens the portière, looks at Houlberg (who does not yet look at him) and stops (Figure 3.8). He staggers slowly down the steps, then comes forward more quickly, pauses midground right, crosses to stand between the chair and the settee, with his right hand on the chair back. He speaks. Houlberg raises her head with a start, looks up, and leans slowly backwards as he leans forward to her. She apologizes (Figure 3.9). She leans forward again and looks off right. He leans down and seizes her hand. She rises. He releases her hand and steps back, briefly wringing his hands. Without looking at him, she looks down at the table as he leans back towards her, his fist on the table (Figure 3.10). He speaks.

2 Title: 'Daisy, do you love him?'

3 Cut-in to medium shot. Psilander is in profile left, Houlberg's head is raised. She very slowly nods assent, then wipes tears from her eyes. Psilander looks off front centre vacantly in grief. He puts his hand on his forehead (Figure 3.11).

4 As 1. Cut on action. Psilander with hand to forehead, Houlberg looking down left front (Figure 3.12). Psilander backs unsteadily to stand with his right hand on the chair back. He speaks to her. She turns to him, starts, and looks him full in the face. He comes forward and leans on the table.

5 Title: 'Then you have only one thing to do; go to him!'

6 As 1. Houlberg turns quickly to face front left and puts her left hand to her heart. She leans over to front right in agony (Figure 3.13). Psilander comes forward, raises his hands as if to grasp her shoulders but drops them again. He retreats round the settee, his left hand on its back. He points listlessly off left (Figure 3.14). She tries to face him, raises her arms halfway in appeal, drops them again, turns to face front right, then back again, and passes in front of Psilander and off left slowly. Psilander watches her go, makes a full gesture of appeal off left, raising his hands to head height (Figure 3.15). He leans back and puts his hands on his head. He turns to front left, pulls his hands down the sides of his face and leans slightly forward (Figure 3.16).

The plot is nominally advanced in these six shots. Daisy decides to part from Joe, but with regret, and Joe's agony at the loss is reaffirmed. However, much more important story events occur in the prior discovery scene in the green room, or a subsequent scene in which Bunding disowns his daughter, thus preparing for his later dismissal of her after she has repented, and her suicide. In contrast, this scene is almost entirely devoted to extending and elaborating upon the situation put in place by Joe's discovery of the betrayal. The acting does not operate to further the action, but to delay it—to maintain the situation and exploit its emotional resonances, before the next turn of events. Our sense that the pace of the acting slows down here is partly a function of the length of the shots (the six shots comprise 173 feet or 2 minutes, 53 seconds at 16 frames per second), partly one of the tempo of the action, as, for example, in Psilander's pose at the top of the stairs and the slow movement from the background to the foreground in shot 1. The gestures and poses adopted by the actors tend to be iterative expressions of grief; this also helps to provide a sense of long duration in the scene, since the succession of poses does not provide us with new information about the characters or events, but merely a variation on what we already know. After this scene, the acting never returns to the rapid and unmarked gestures of the early scenes; as the plot shifts to a serious and sentimental register, the acting style changes in accordance with it.

Because posing was keyed to genre and situation, and effectively coexisted with other, more fluid, uses of gesture, it does not make sense in our view to define it theoretically as opposed to realism, or historically as a precursor which was eventually superseded by a realistic acting style. This is not to deny, however, the observation by Pearson, Gunning, Thompson, and others that acting style changes in American films in the period from 1908 to 1912. For us, the questions are somewhat different. How did the actors in the newly forming stock companies in 1907–8—actors largely trained in the theatre—adapt pictorial traditions to film? How did their style change in relation to later developments in film technique?[20]

In this connection it is worth iterating the conditions which impinged on film acting as opposed to the stage in 1908. There was no spoken dialogue, and the whole register of diction and the voice was lost. There was no live audience whose reaction to and understanding of a scene could be gauged. The relatively great figure/camera distance which was the norm in this period meant that the actor was shown full figure but relatively small and on what was usually a small screen (see Chapter 9, below). The 'speed' of the one-reel film required that a complex sequence of actions be conveyed in a relatively short span of screen time as compared with any but the most brief

one-act play or vaudeville playlet.[21] In response to these conditions, a theatrically trained actor moving into film at this time might well have been motivated to develop a more emphatic style than he had formerly employed on stage. Several points about acting in the 1908–9 Biographs can thus be explained not as a direct carry-over of popular stage traditions, but rather as an attempt to adapt these traditions to the specific requirements of the new medium.

For example, one aspect of acting in the 1908–9 period is what Pearson categorizes as overly emphatic uses of gesture. She argues that actors in the early Biographs often adopt poses with fully extended arms or legs, as in the discussion of Griffith's own acting in *Rescued from an Eagle's Nest* (1908).[22] In one instance, this tendency is evident even in the use of the hand and fingers. Pearson contrasts two proposal scenes in which the principal actor makes his appeal by placing a hand upon his chest, one, *The Voice of the Violin* (1909) with Arthur Johnson, the other, *A Summer Idyl* (1910) with Henry Walthall:

Because Walthall stresses his gestures less than Johnson, the performance does not connote the same degree of theatricality. This becomes clear in comparing the way each actor places his hands on his chest. Johnson uses both hands with the palms flattened, to modern eyes parodying a lover declaring himself, as the pose absolutely reeks of theatricality. Walthall places one hand lightly on his chest, the palm slightly raised and fingers slightly cupped. Though Walthall employs a conventional gesture, the lack of emphasis reduces the deliberate self-consciousness of the histrionic code.[23]

While we would agree with Pearson that actors often use fully extended limbs during 1908–9, we would dispute her claim that this kind of posing is simply carried over from pictorial acting styles in the theatre (although, of course, bad actors were everywhere). The fully outstretched hand position adopted by Arthur Johnson in this example would have been anathema to most nineteenth-century teachers of acting. What she characterizes as the 'slow and graceful' movements typical of Walthall's performance in *A Summer Idyl* are much closer to the way in which we understand the elements of pictorial style in the theatre.[24]

As we have noted, the late eighteenth-century and nineteenth-century acting manuals repeatedly stress the importance of grace and good bearing; they also specifically recommend against fully extended limbs. For example, in his lesson on hand position, Jelgerhuis argues that the fingers should always be gracefully curved, to give 'play and contrast' to their position. He cautions against either one of two extremes:

I used to know a very good speaker on the Stage, who out of unthinking habit, always appeared with crooked fingers; what a wretched habit! I hope, that this example will be enough, to draw your attention to it, so that you will always avoid it.–Yet don't think, Dear Students! that the hand hanging down with straight fingers can wholly redress this, no, although better than with crooked fingers. . . . For the hanging arm, and the free and unforced hand, there must be play and contrast in the posture of the fingers, to make it look elegant, to give it looseness, freedom and decorum.[25]

Similarly, he characterizes a fully extended arm as 'without grace, stretch[ed] out like a pole' and cautions against movements involving both hands and arms together unless 'one adopts them purposely, in order to become ridiculous'.[26] Riccoboni also tells students to avoid having both arms equally extended, and raising them to the same height. He cites a 'well enough known rule' that the hand should not be raised above the eye, adding the caveat that 'when a violent passion carries him away, the Actor can forget all the rules; he can move with despatch, and lift his arms even above his head'.[27] Riccoboni's remarks suggest that actors could use fully extended, and thus relatively emphatic gestures, but only sparingly, and in accordance with extreme situations. Recall that Yeats makes just such an analysis of Édouard de Max's performance in *Phèdre*, in which he apparently saved his biggest gesture for the climax of the scene: 'Through one long scene De Max, who was quite as fine, never lifted his hands above his elbow, it was only when the emotion came to its climax that he raised it to his breast.' Lessing's remark already cited about wild or baroque gesture also suggests the importance of modulating such gestures in a sequence; he argued that they could be made acceptable if the actor prepared for them and finally resolved them into more harmonious poses.

The sequence already discussed from *Klovnen* provides a good example of the way in which emphatic gesture could be controlled through the modulation of poses. The actors adopt a series of attitudes expressing grief. These are 'smaller' in shot 1, with Psilander posing far in the background, or, after he has come forward, leaning on a chair or table for support, with Houlberg turning away from him. The scale changes in shot 3, a medium shot, so that facial expressions can be emphasized with very little movement on the part of the actors, as in Houlberg's small nod of her head in affirmation to the question whether or not she loves the Count. The scene returns to the long-shot framing and builds to the largest gestures in shot 6: Houlberg's attitude in which she puts her hand to her heart and leans her body away from Psilander to the right to express her grief, and Psilander's attitude, in the same shot after her exit, in which he extends his arms and raises his hands to head height, and then later, when he pulls his hands down the sides of his face (Figures 3.13, 3.15, and 3.16).

In sum, the extended gestures of the Biograph actors described by Pearson were not the inevitable result of stage practices, but particular applications of them—in some cases without enough care to prevent clumsy postures, and in others without the calculation and timing by which experienced stage actors built up to 'big' or pronounced poses. Aside from inexperience or incompetence, we attribute this kind of posing to difficulties already adduced in the period before 1912—particularly problems of coping with the small scale of the actor's image in the typical long-shot framings, and the effort to make a story clear in a restricted amount of time to an audience that the actor could not play to nor get reassurance from directly.

Clearly then, another constraint on actors in this early period was the demand for a swift pace. Pearson discusses this, as does the perceptive Frank Woods in a 1910 'Spectator's' column in which he asserts that 'the most marked change that has taken place in the style of picture acting in the last year or two has been in the matter of tempo' and praises Biograph acting for the 'deliberation and repose' in its recent films.[28] Again, the fast tempo Woods disapproves of does not seem to be a direct carry-over from the theatre, since all the evidence we have seen about the length of poses there suggests that they were held for much longer than they ever were in film. In the same column, Woods attributes the emphasis on speed to the novelty of the moving picture itself: 'Everything had to be on the jump. The more action that could be crowded into each foot of film the more perfect the picture was supposed to be.' The limitation of length in the one-reel film may also have contributed to the relatively swift pace of film acting. This is how we would interpret Florence Lawrence's recollection about her differences with Griffith over acting tempo:

What seemed to annoy us 'Biographers' very much and hold us back from achieving greater artistic success was the speed and rapidity with which we had to work before the camera. Mr. Griffith always answered our complaint by stating that the exchanges and exhibitors who bought our pictures wanted action, and insisted that they get plenty of it for their money. 'The exhibitors don't want illustrated song slides,' Mr. Griffith once said to us. So we made our work quick and snappy, crowding as much story in a thousand foot picture as is now portrayed in five thousand feet of film. Several pictures which we produced in three hundred feet have since been reproduced in one thousand feet. There was no chance for slow or 'stage' acting. The moment we started to do a bit of acting in the proper tempo we would be startled by the cry of the director: 'Faster! Faster! For God's sake hurry up! We must do the scene in forty feet.'[29]

The problem then, was not simply that the exhibitors wanted 'action' in every foot, but that such a rapid pace was considered necessary if all the relevant action was to be conveyed in the requisite length.

Perhaps as actors and directors such as Griffith mastered the one-reel form, that is by the date of Woods's column in 1910, it had become possible to 'slow down' to some degree. Note, however, that six months before he praises the deliberation and repose of Biograph actors, Frank Woods criticizes the final scene of the same company's *All on Account of the Milk* (1910) with the comment: 'The last scene appears to degenerate into farce, and to be acted hastily and with too little dramatic effect, due, perhaps, to the lack of film space.'[30] In general he praises the acting in the film (by Mary Pickford, Arthur Johnson, Mack Sennett, and Blanche Sweet) and we assume that the problem of 'film space' to which he refers is that the filmmakers were forced to rush the last scene to ensure that the film was the proper length. Even if Woods is wrong in his guess about what happened at the end of this specific film, the comment suggests that he was aware of the lack of 'space' on

the reel as a problem for actors. We would argue that it continued to be, and, as compared to the early feature, actors in the one-reel film were given many fewer opportunities to dwell on situations, to hold poses or develop elaborate sequences of them. A three-minute sequence of the sort described in *Klovnen*, in which almost nothing happens at the level of the plot, would be extremely difficult to accommodate within a sixteen-minute movie.

Our attempt to search out the most accomplished and technically elaborated examples of pictorial styles has thus led us to focus primarily on the early feature film. But at the same time this periodization introduces a new limitation or constraint on pictorial acting, since by this point the editing options open to filmmakers begin to interfere with the actor's performance in ways that would not have been imaginable in the theatre. As Tom Gunning has argued in relation to the example of *After Many Years* already cited, editing can potentially disrupt and re-configure the actor's pose and gesture. Cross-cutting of the kind in *After Many Years*, and, later, the kinds of scene dissection which Gunning discusses in relation to *The Lady and the Mouse* (1913), effectively displace some of the actor's traditional functions, providing filmmakers with other means of directing the spectator's attention within a space, regulating the pace of a scene, expressing emotion, and underscoring dramatic situations.[31] This possibility is evident as well in the scene of Little Eva's death in the World version of *Uncle Tom's Cabin*, in which the various expressions of grief on the part of the actors are directed and controlled by the editing pattern which alternates between the bedroom and the various spaces outside it. In contrast, in the theatre this regulation of the spectator's attention would have been structured largely through the acting of the ensemble, through the actors taking turns, the gesture of one setting off or leading to the gesture of another in what Riccoboni compared to 'musicians who sing a piece in several parts'. Editing could thus at least partially fulfil functions which had previously been fulfilled by the actor(s) through the generation of pictorial effects. This is not to say that film editing could not coexist with posing and pictorial styles; but it is to say that a highly edited film could more easily support bad pictorial acting, or non-acting, or a more reduced, i.e. less emphatic, style.

Pearson argues the latter case. In a careful comparison of *After Many Years* (1908) with *Enoch Arden*, she shows how the later version of the same story requires fewer gestures, and less extended ones, because *Enoch Arden* can rely on more cross-cutting and glance/object editing to convey important information about story events and character states.[32] But moving away from the example of the Griffith Biographs, we would also suggest that highly edited films could help to accommodate very bad, or at least inexperienced, acting (see the discussion of *A Fool There Was* below).

Indeed, while Biograph films are usually praised by reviewers in the trade press when they are discussing acting specifically, discussions of Biograph's fast-paced editing usually elicited complaints about its effect on acting style. One review of *A Girl's Stratagem* (1913) notes 'The action is held in pretty closely to its center of interest, and the scene-making searchlight snaps back and forth from one actor to another and seems to pick out the different elements of the situation almost simultaneously. This is a speedy method and makes the picture, as a whole, clear at the expense, now and then, of the acting. The scenes change so fast that the players now and then seem all arms and hands.'[33] And from a review of *The Hero of Little Italy* (1913): 'There is a good story in this picture and the producer has made it exciting. As it approaches its climax, the scenes, flashed back and forth, keep the action concrete and almost breathless. But this playing for the thrill is not the best use of the motion picture camera; for in such there is almost no individual acting—everything goes to situation, nothing to character.'[34] Epes Winthrop Sargent reports on Dr Stockton's experiment in 1912 counting the scenes in over twenty one-reel and split-reel films by various manufacturers, with most companies having what he considered high cutting rates (the one Biograph on the list is the fastest cut). Sargent quotes Stockton's opinion of this tendency: 'It looks very much as if Edison and the foreigners were the only ones not bitten by the lightning bug, with the result that his releases are, to my mind, the only ones that are really drama. The others have lots of action, but no acting and no chance for any.'[35] The point is that not only did editing *permit* the actor to do 'less' in terms of posing and gesture, but the pace of a highly edited film *required* it.

1. On the claim that film is a distinctive medium, and superior to theatre, see, for example, Louis Reeves Harrison, 'Alas, Poor Yorick!', *Moving Picture World*, 19, no. 13 (28 Mar. 1914), 1653; or Maurice Tourneur's claim, in ' "Photo-drama is a Distinct Art," Declares Tourneur', *Motion Picture News*, 13, no. 4 (Jan. 1916), 516, that he 'cares little for the traditions of the speaking stage as applied to pictures', when in fact most of his 1910s features are theatrical adaptations. The claim that American films are morally and/or aesthetically superior to European ones does not become commonplace until after 1910. See for example '*Temptations of a Great City* [*Ved faengslets Port*], A Special Release that has been Successful in Europe', *Moving Picture World*, 8, no. 24 (17 June 1911), 1367; repr. in Pratt, *Spellbound in Darkness*, 118–19.
2. Paul Ranger, 'I Was Present at the Representation . . .,' *Theatre Notebook*, 39, no. 1 (1985), 19.
3. Barnett, *Art of Gesture*, 158–60 and 167; Barnett, 'La Vitesse de la déclamation au théâtre (XVIIe–XVIIIe siècles)', *XVIIe Siècle*, 128, no. 3 (July–Sept. 1980), 319–26.
4. Barnett, *Art of Gesture*, 348–57. Recall Morrocchesi's 22 plates illustrating a speech of 16 lines in a tragedy.
5. Cited in Stokes, 'Sarah Bernhardt' in Stokes *et al.*, *Bernhardt, Terry, Duse*, 58–9.
6. Ranger, 'I Was Present', 19–20.
7. See John Alexander Kelly, *German Visitors to English Theaters in the Eighteenth Century* (Princeton: Princeton University Press, 1936), 145–6, citing Friedrich Wilhelm von Hassel, *Briefe aus England* (Hanover: Ch. Ritscher, 1792), 92–100.
8. Michael Booth, 'Ellen Terry' in Stokes *et al.*, *Bernhardt, Terry, Duse*, 114. Booth indicates that Terry found the slowness of Henry Irving's pace on stage a problem, and discussed it in her correspondence with Shaw, who complained about the tent scene in *King Lear*, where Irving 'kept you waiting in an impossible pose for five minutes between "I will not swear" and "these are my hands" '. It is not clear how literally we should take the timing here.
9. Humboldt, 'Französische tragische Bühne', 386.
10. Cited in Frederick and Lise-Lone Marker, 'Fru Heiberg', 27.
11. Dion Boucicault, with an introduction by Otis Skinner, *Papers on Acting I: The Art of Acting*, Publications of the Dramatic Museum of Columbia University, in the City of New York, 5th Ser. (New York: Columbia University Press, 1926), 35.
12. David Mayer, 'Nineteenth Century Theatre Music', *Theatre Notebook*, 30, nos. 22 & 23 (1976), 115-22; id., 'The Music of Melodrama', in David Bradby, Louis James, and Bernard Sharratt (eds.), *Performance and Politics in Popular Drama: Aspects of Popular Entertainment in Theatre, Film and Television, 1800–1976* (Cambridge: Cambridge University Press, 1980), 49–63.
13. Frank Woods consistently complained about actors looking at the camera, and in one of his columns he specifically objects to posing in the sense of standing or speaking to the camera, and thereby acknowledging its presence. See ' "Spectator's" Comments', *New York Dramatic Mirror*, 67, no. 1736 (27 Mar. 1912), 24.
14. Albert Goldie, 'Subtlety in Acting', *New York Dramatic Mirror*, 68,

no. 1769 (13 Nov. 1912), 4; and for a confused account of whether or not film acting should be emphatic see Hanford C. Judson, 'What Gets Over', *Moving Picture World*, 8, no. 15 (15 Apr. 1911), 816.

15. Florence Lawrence in collaboration with Monte M. Katterjohn, 'Growing up with the Movies', *Photoplay*, 7, no. 2 (Jan. 1915), 103.

16. Humboldt, 'Französische tragische Bühne', 396.

17. Pearson, *Eloquent Gestures*, 62.

18. Ibid. 110–11 and 119.

19. Ibid. 105.

20. Charles Musser, 'The Changing Status of the Film Actor', in *Before Hollywood: Turn-of-the-Century American Film* (New York: Hudson Hills Press, 1987), 57–62, gives 1907–8 as the date of the formation of the stock companies, a time when the demand for story films had increased to the point that it was no longer practicable for the major producers to hire actors only on a per-day basis. Lawrence, 'Growing up', 96, refers to the formation of the stock company at Biograph in 1908. Many in the Biograph stock company had stage experience; see Pearson, *Eloquent Gesture*, 83–4, on Griffith making the rounds of the theatrical agencies. The extent to which theatrically trained actors predominated in other motion-picture stock companies is indicated by the biographies of members of the Vitagraph stock company in Anthony Slide, *The Big V: A History of the Vitagraph Company*, rev. edn. (Metuchen, NJ: Scarecrow Press, 1987), 134–55.

21. On the latter two conditions see Thompson in Bordwell *et al.*, *Classical Hollywood Cinema*, 189–92.

22. Pearson, *Eloquent Gestures*, 27 (on the unchecked histrionic code with fully extended gestures as typical of 'melodramatic' acting), 79–81 (on Griffith's acting as an example of this style), and 2 (for another example of these sorts of fully extended gestures).

23. Ibid. 40–1.

24. Ibid. 41.

25. Jelgerhuis, *Theoretische Lessen*, 97–8; cit. Barnett, *Art of Gesture*, 98.

26. Ibid. 89 and 87; cit. Barnett, 'Performance Practice', iii. 82–3. In *The Art of Gesture*, iii, 132, Barnett suggests that this remains a problem for performers today: 'One of the worst (and most common) examples of the lack of pictorial contrasts is to have both hands raised to the same height and equally extended; this always looks gauche and lacking in grace and proportion.'

27. Riccoboni, *L'Art du théâtre*, 13–14; cit. Barnett, 'Performance Practice', iii. 84. For similar comments about the possibility of extending gesture, and raising the arms above the height of the eyes in moments of passion, see Barnett, *Art of Gesture*, 107–8.

28. Pearson, *Eloquent Gestures*, 27, seems to assume that 'melodramatic' acting on the stage as well as the 'unchecked histrionic code' employed by Biograph actors was fast-paced; see also pp. 80 and 87 on Griffith's preference for 'fast acting'. Frank Woods's remarks appear in his column ' "Spectator's" Comments', *New York Dramatic Mirror*, 63, no. 1641 (4 June 1910), 16; repr. in Pratt, *Spellbound in Darkness*, 84.

29. Lawrence, 'Growing up', 107. Note that Pearson, *Eloquent Gestures*, 87, has abridged this quotation to remove the reference to the thousand-foot reel and the comparison with the feature film. She also interprets this quotation differently, assuming that Griffith's preference for 'fast' acting derived from the fact that he had still not abandoned habits acquired in the theatre and his preference for the 'histrionic' code. We think the full quotation amply demonstrates the specific cinematic need for speed in this period, i.e. that scenes had to be completed within the requisite number of feet given the limitation of the one-reel film.

30. Frank Woods, 'Reviews of Licensed Films, . . . *All on Account of the Milk*', *New York Dramatic Mirror*, 63, no. 1622 (22 Jan. 1910), 17; repr. in Anthony Slide (ed.), *Selected Film Criticism 1896–1911* (Metuchen, NJ: Scarecrow Press, 1982), 4–5. Woods's review of *The Merry Wives of Windsor* (Selig, 1910), 'Reviews of Licensed Films', *New York Dramatic Mirror*, 64, no. 5177 (30 Nov. 1910), 30, makes a similar point: 'The part of Falstaff was adequately taken, although it suffered like all the rest from the necessity of hastening the action to make it fit into the allotted time.'

31. Gunning, *D. W. Griffith*, 113–14 and 262–70.

32. Pearson, *Eloquent Gestures*, 63–74.

33. 'Comments on the Films, . . . *A Girl's Stratagem*', *Moving Picture World*, 15, no. 12 (22 Mar. 1913), 1219; reprinted in Pratt, *Spellbound in Darkness*, 104.

34. 'Comments on the Films, . . . *The Hero of Little Italy*', *Moving Picture World* 16, no. 3 (19 Apr. 1913), 279; repr. in Pratt, *Spellbound in Darkness*, 105.

35. Epes Winthrop Sargent, 'The Photoplaywright: Scenes and Leaders', *Moving Picture World*, 13, no. 6 (10 Aug. 1912), 542; repr. in Pratt, *Spellbound in Darkness*, 101–3.

Chapter 7

The Pictorial Style in European Cinema

DR Stockton's reference to the slow-cut European films as giving scope to the actor is instructive. Florence Lawrence similarly mentions European films, recalling that the release of the Film d'Art productions distributed by Pathé made a big impact on American actors and directors and inspired the 'Biographers' to request that Griffith allow them to do 'slow acting'.[1] And, from a European perspective, Yuri Tsivian has pointed out that in the 1910s advocates for the advancement of a specifically Russian school of filmmaking argued that it was necessary to avoid the 'fidgety' American style of acting. Another Russian manifesto discusses the importance of slowness in the following terms:

In the world of the screen, where everything is counted in metres, the actor's struggle for the freedom to act has led to a battle for long (in terms of metres) scenes or, more accurately, for 'full' scenes, to use Olga Gzovskaya's marvellous expression. A 'full' scene is one in which the actor is given the opportunity to depict in stage terms a specific spiritual experience, no matter how many metres it takes. The 'full' scene involves a complete rejection of the usual hurried tempo of the film play. Instead of a rapidly changing kaleidoscope of images, it aspires to *rivet* the attention of the audience on to a single image.[2]

The rapid development of editing techniques in America, and the fact that American films were consistently faster cut than European ones throughout the 1910s meant that the two film acting traditions developed differently. Given their lengthy takes and tendency to employ deep staging in long shot, European films of this period necessarily relied more upon the actor and the acting ensemble to provide dramatic emphasis. This mode of filmmaking also gave the actor the time to develop elaborate sequences of gestures and poses. European film actors were thus in a relatively better position than their American colleagues to adapt and refine the performance practices associated with pictorial styles in the theatre. Given these differences, we have chosen to privilege European examples in our description of pictorial styles, and to refer to American films for purposes of contrast in the context of a discussion of the effects of editing.

It is not altogether surprising that a diva film like *Ma l'amor mio non muore!* depends on elaborate sequences of poses and attitudes. But what we would like to indicate here is the extent to which Lyda Borelli's performance in this film is dependent upon and facilitated by the lengthy takes and staging in depth which are typical of European cinema more generally.

The film uses large-scale sets with doors/alcoves or stairs at the back, with one set, the heroine Elsa Holbein's dressing-room, having a large triple mirror which shows the entrance door off right. While there are some cut-ins to medium shot, there is no shot-reverse-shot, cross-cutting between simultaneous actions, or high fragmentation of a single scene. There is basically one set-up per space—important entrances and exits in the dressing-room are shown in the mirror without cuts, for example. The final scene is the one exception to this rule: the other scenes of singing are seen from behind her on the stage looking out at the audience, but the final scene shows Elsa on the stage from behind her lover in the audience and then cuts round to a new position on the stage. Aside from the cut-ins to medium shot, characters are usually shown full-figure in the large sets, with the camera a little below eye level and nearly horizontal throughout.

A good indication of Borelli's style is the scene in which Elsa (Lyda Borelli) discovers that her lover Max (Mario Bonnard) is really the heir to the Duchy of Wallenstein (he has been staying incognito near Lake Locarno to recover from a serious illness), and decides to leave him. Elsa, whom Max knows by her stage name Diana Cadouleur, is in fact the daughter of a Wallenstein general who committed suicide when plans of the country's fortifications entrusted to him were stolen by a spy. News of Max's liaison with an actress has reached his father, who dispatches a messenger to call Max back home. The messenger is a former friend of Elsa and her father, Colonel Theubner (Emilio Petacci).

The scene is essentially one shot although interrupted by an insert of the letter. One of the conventions of the diva film is to create scenes in which the diva is left alone to express her reaction to the big situations—a way of directing attention to the star's performance. The last part of the scene provides one of these 'star turns' in which Borelli is alone on camera. Excluding the insert, the scene described here takes approximately 5 minutes at 16 frames per second.

68 Salon in Max's villa. A piano front left, a table midground right, stairs rear centre rising to a landing across the

rear, with a conservatory far rear centre. Bonnard is seated at the piano facing left, with Borelli standing beside him, both framed from head to foot (in their closest framings, characters come forward until they are cut off at the shins). They stop playing to talk, looking at the music. She rests a hand on the back of his head, briefly leans down and rests her head on his. Keeping her hands on his head and shoulders, she crosses round behind him to stand on his left, thereby making space on the right for the servant.

The servant enters through the right background entrance and walks down the stairs to Bonnard. Borelli moves to the centre foreground, stands back to camera but turned slightly towards Bonnard, her left hand cupped and resting on her breast. Bonnard reads the card handed him by the servant while Borelli moves to stand behind him, but he places the card down on the piano where she cannot see it. He makes a face expressing annoyance, and dismisses the servant who exits background right. Bonnard gets up as his mistress's banter restores him to a good humour; he stands left, Borelli right, so that they are facing each other in profile.

Petacci enters background right, and the lovers separate and stand back to camera so that Petacci is clearly visible coming down the stairs between them (Figure 3.17). Although her back is to camera, Borelli visibly starts at Petacci's entrance, hunching up her shoulders. As Petacci approaches Bonnard, she turns left into profile and drops her hands which had been clasped at her breast (Figure 3.18). To indicate her surprise and anxiety, she backs away from the two men, moving to the right edge of frame. Petacci bows to the Prince, and hands him the letter. Bonnard turns to the camera to read it. Petacci steps back from Bonnard respectfully looking downwards. He then sees and recognizes Elsa. He raises his eyes, opens them wide in surprise and drops his jaw slightly (Figure 3.19). He gives her a brief nod.

69 Insert: Max's father's letter, presumably reproving him for his affair with a notorious actress.[3]

70 As 68. Borelli raises her right hand very slightly from the hip, turning the hand and opening the fingers in a gesture imploring Petacci not to reveal her identity (Figure 3.20). Bonnard looks furious, drops the envelope, and crumples the letter. He turns back to camera, and walks up the stairs, exiting left, followed by Petacci. Borelli remains foreground right, back to camera, one arm folded at chest height, the other raised to head height as she watches them leave.

The section in which Borelli is alone on camera may be divided into three parts. The first segment consists in the confirmation of Elsa's growing suspicions

3.37

3.38

3.39

3.40

3.41

3.42

Nielsen's typical use of heavy dark make-up around the eyes and eyebrows helps reinforce. Although it is not possible to document it from our stills and written notes, we also have the sense that Nielsen's performance is more slowly paced. That is, she will rest for a longer period on a climactic pose, such as the moment when she leans far over to the left in shot 3.

Although operating within the framework of the diva film, Nielsen differs from Borelli in her willingness to introduce comic or 'low' gestures into the gestural soliloquies typical of this acting tradition. Borelli's style, which pushes in the direction of the utmost grace and almost balletic complexity, is motivated in part by the character she plays in *Ma l'amor mio non muore!*—an aristocratic lady, a great prima donna. Recall the use of the daintily moistened handkerchief to seal the envelope. Nielsen rarely plays refined upper-class characters of this sort, but rather working-class girls, gypsies, and down-and-out actresses on the make. These sorts of parts both call for and permit some rather daring alterations of acting style, daring from the point of view of the dignity and grace to which the diva usually aspired.

Nielsen's deliberate introduction of vulgar poses and gestures is most obvious, of course, in her comic roles. In *Engelein* (Little Angel), Nielsen plays Jesta, a 17-year-old who must pretend to be 12 as part of her family's plan to make her birth appear legitimate to her rich American uncle (her parents did not actually get around to marrying until Jesta was 5). Spending the summer pretending to be a child at her uncle's chateau, Jesta falls in love with him, and must stand by and watch as another visitor, scheming to get his money, aims to entrap him in marriage. Convinced that she is sure to lose out to her rival, Jesta decides to commit suicide, writes a note, and then leaves it with a flower for her uncle to find. The sequence is to some extent a 'serious' one—the character is sad and does plan to kill herself (although of course this situation is resolved comically). Like the other two letter scenes already discussed, it concentrates on the actress alone, although the action is split over two locations, Jesta's room and her uncle's office. Writing the note in her own room, her rear end gets stuck in her chair, which has been designed for a child and is thus too small for her (Figure 3.43). The scene in her uncle's office encompasses bits of business—such as Jesta kissing her uncle's pipe in affection—with gestures

motivated by her persona as a naughty child. At one point she wipes the flower that she is going to leave for her uncle on her dress (Figure 3.44), at another point, she scratches her knee (Figure 3.45). The comedy thus depends upon deliberate clumsiness, and violations of the rules of 'correct' lady-like behaviour.

What is particularly interesting about Nielsen, however, is that she does not limit this kind of acting to comedy but introduces such vulgar elements into her performance of more serious parts. In *Die arme Jenny* (Poor Jenny), for example, Jenny, a working-class girl seduced by an upper-class man, tells off her lover after he has refused to recognize her in public. The boyfriend tries to apologize as Nielsen stands immobile for eighteen seconds with hands on hips, elbows sticking out, right hip bent out, and left knee bent in a pose which amply justifies the previous title's characterization of her as a *Proletariermädchen* (Figure 3.46). She breaks the pose and reacts violently when he attempts to touch her, sending him away by pointing into the distance. After he leaves, she leans quite far to the left, shouting insults after his retreating figure (Figure 3.47), but this pose is followed immediately by an attitude expressing grief, as she sits and breaks into tears (Figure 3.48). Later in the film, in the scene of Jenny's thirtieth birthday party, one finds the same repetition of gestures which express her physicality and low-class status, intermixed with the kind of grieving gestures that are evident in *Die weisse Rosen* and *Ma l'amor mio non muore!* Nielsen sits with legs splayed out, smoking a cigar and drinking (Figure 3.49). She gets up and dances with her second lover, now presumably her pimp, quarrels rudely with another dancer who bumps into her, and collapses rather drunkenly in a chair front right. The pimp gets a paper and begins to read as she belches, her head resting on her hand (Figure 3.50). But, upon hearing from the pimp that her seducer has got married, she sits straight up, her hand falls and her face expresses grief (Figure 3.51). As the party-goers gather round she pretends to laugh and coarsely toasts the couple, but then, unable to bear it, she staggers drunkenly from the café.

The examples of Lyda Borelli and Asta Nielsen indicate the range of styles of acting that fall under the rubric of pictorialism, and further demonstrate the difficulty of explaining these styles in terms of a simple opposition between pictorialism and realism. Although Nielsen was trained at the Danish Royal Theatre and would certainly have been familiar with the naturalist stagings of Ibsen and others performed there, her film acting is much better understood, we believe, in terms of the adoption and transformation of the histrionic tradition of the diva. Within this context, it might be observed that her performance style seems more 'realistic' than that of a Borelli. But this effect of realism is primarily the result of the deliberate mixing of comic and tragic acting modes, and, in tandem with this, a movement away from stories about refined upper-class types in favour of lower-class characters who are usually presented as spontaneous and physically unrestrained. 'Realism',

then, derives from Nielsen's willingness to violate the expectations of grace and ladylike de-corum which surrounded the diva, or at least to alternate the more typical gestural soliloquies that one finds in a film like *Die weisse Rosen* with other sorts of expressive gesture. It does not, however, presuppose a rejection of or departure from pictorialism as such.

The examples discussed so far have concerned an actress alone, or as the central point of attention in a scene. But the handling of the ensemble within the European filmmaking tradition provided a different set of staging problems, concerning how the spectator's attention was directed when action was staged in depth with a group of actors. Shot 68 of *Ma l'amor mio non muore!* (see above) demonstrates some of the

3.43

3.44

3.45

3.46

3.47

3.48

3.49

3.50

3.51

possible difficulties. Theubner enters, Elsa recognizes him and registers surprise and anxiety. After delivering his message to the Prince, Theubner sees her and also registers surprise. This action is handled in a single take, and the staging of this scene in particular makes it difficult to notice the byplay between the two actors—at least for modern viewers used to the classical style. Elsa's surprise must be conveyed with Borelli's back to camera, since she must be turned away from the spectator to 'see' Petacci enter at the rear. Later in the scene, just as Petacci looks up and recognizes the true identity of the Prince's mistress, Bonnard, in the foreground of the shot, turns to face camera and reads the letter from his father, expressing displeasure. It is thus quite possible that the spectator will watch Bonnard in the foreground, missing out on what the other actors are doing (indeed, this happened to us on our first few viewings).

In the American cinema in its classical phase, this kind of situation is handled through spatial fragmentation, cutting to a series of reaction shots. This is the case in the scene from *The Social Secretary* discussed in part 2, the discovery of Mayme in the notorious Count's bedroom. In the hunt breakfast scene in *The Whip* (discussed in detail in Chapter 10, below), Tourneur handles the villainess's surprising declaration that she is engaged to the hero in a similar way, cutting to reaction shots of the hero Brancaster and his true intended Diana, the villain Sartoris, and, after Brancaster has left the shot, Diana surrounded by sympathetic friends, and so on. This simplifies the acting problem considerably, since all the actor has to handle is his or her own facial expression. Even in this regard, less is more: the repetition and variation of facial expressions established in the pattern of cutting itself helps to convey the emotions of the various members of the group.

Even in the American cinema, however, cutting of this sort does not become common until the mid-to-late 1910s. Earlier American films frequently adopt a different tack, placing the most narratively important character in the foreground of the shot, i.e. somewhat closer to camera than Bonnard's position as he reads the letter in *Ma l'amor mio non muore!* In *The Warrens of Virginia*, for example, the Northern hero (House Peters) waits in the home of his Confederate sweetheart (Blanche Sweet) for news of the battle which will make it clear to her and to her family that

he has been operating as a spy. For much of the scene, the hero is positioned in the foreground and is also lit with a floor-stand arc off left which emphasizes his features. Sweet, supposedly waiting anxiously for news about the outcome of the battle, moves from a position beside him through the midground to the door at the back, and later in the scene Confederate soldiers, including her own wounded brother, enter the door with the news of the betrayal (Figure 3.52). Given this composition, Sweet's movements and the later entrances of other characters through the door at the rear of the set never detract from Peters's expressions and gestures. Similar staging can be found in the two-reel film *Red and White Roses* (Vitagraph, 1913). The vamp Lida (Julia Swayne Gordon) is shown in a hotel suite seducing her victim, the politician Morgan Andrews (William Humphrey) in the same foreground position—although she retreats to midground at one point to pose by the eponymous red roses (Figure 3.53). In a later scene, in which the politician discovers that Lida has been paid off with a necklace to seduce him and destroy his career, he paces angrily front to back centre, while she remains still, front right, facing camera (Figure 3.54).

Of course, stage actors have always come downstage to the footlights in order to utter important lines. But this kind of blocking has a much more pronounced effect in the cinema. As will be discussed in more detail in Chapter 9, below, the depth of the playing area in the cinema is much greater than that of the stage, and entails a much greater range of differences in scale—an actor at the nine-foot line appears much 'bigger' and closer to the spectator than an actor would in the theatre, while actors in the background of a shot in depth appear much 'smaller' and farther away. Thus, the nature of cinematic space gives the actor in the foreground much more relative prominence than the actor at the footlights. Even apart from editing then, in many American films compositional elements specific to cinema were brought to bear on the problem of directing the spectator's attention in the ensemble.

In Europe, however, filmmakers were more likely to retain the long-shot framings in which actors were shown full figure. And, given the tradition which evolved there of staging complex action in depth, they developed other strategies for directing the spectator's attention: most typically, careful blocking

3.52

3.53

3.54

and timing of the action of each actor in the group. One important way to highlight a particular action or gesture was simply to get other actors, or objects, out of the way at the relevant moment. Take for example, the Film d'Art production of *La Tosca* (1909), featuring Cécile Sorel, Alexandre, and Le Bargy of the Comédie Française. In the famous scene in which Tosca (Sorel) kills Scarpia (Le Bargy), each character carries out actions without being observed by the other. Scarpia apparently writes an order that Cavaradossi's execution be faked, and gives Tosca a safe conduct for herself and her lover, but he actually signals his lieutenant to ignore the order for the fake execution. Tosca agrees to sleep with Scarpia in order to save Cavaradossi, but then plans his death. It is important that the spectator understand the plotting of each character in the action which leads up to the murder. Cécile Sorel and Le Bargy manage this by taking turns, giving each other prominence in alternation.

The set represents Scarpia's bedroom, with double doors rear right, a desk to their right, a bed rear left, a cupboard with candlesticks rear left, and a prie-dieu with crucifix rear centre. There is a table midground left, with glasses, carafe, and knife, and a couch front right. After having concluded the bargain, Le Bargy hands an order to the lieutenant at the rear doors, instructing him that Cavaradossi's firing squad is to use blanks. To represent Tosca realizing that she must now fulfil her part of the bargain, Sorel collapses in horror on the couch front right. Although the couch is in the foreground, Sorel remains very still and with head downward, so that the eye is directed to the rear of the set and the byplay between Le Bargy and the lieutenant. Le Bargy gestures, countermanding the order, and the lieutenant expresses understanding and exits. Le Bargy comes forward, pulls Sorel to her feet, and embraces her. She demands that he write a safe conduct.

He goes to the desk rear right and begins writing. At this point, Le Bargy has head down and is busy writing in the rear, leaving Sorel the focus of attention in the midground. Sorel goes to the table midground left and picks up a glass of water. After an insert showing the contents of the safe conduct written by Scarpia, the film returns to the same scene. She drinks the water, then assumes a pose indicating that Tosca has seen the knife and conceived her plan (Figure 3.55). She goes to front left, and turns to face Le Bargy,

3.55

3.56

3.57

3.58

hiding the knife, which is visible to the spectator, behind her back (Figure 3.56).

Le Bargy rises and shows her the safe conduct. She goes to him and having seen it, stabs him in the heart. They struggle, he seizes the knife, pursues her to front left. Then he staggers back towards the door to call for help. Sorel runs to the rear and blocks the doorway with arms open wide (Figure 3.57). Although her pose at the doorway is held and thereby given emphasis, Sorel then takes the knife from Le Bargy and moves off rear left, letting Le Bargy move to midground centre. His gestures then become the focal point of the scene as he tiptoes forward (Figure 3.58), falls on to the couch front right, then rolls off it, and finishes up lying on the floor, head to camera, his arms stretched out.

The rest of the scene does not concern us here, but

it should be noted that it involves prototypical diva acting—the female star, now alone except for the corpse, performs the stage business which became canonical in Bernhardt's performance of Sardou's play, with requisite postures.

The blocking up to the point of the murder thus provides a kind of alternation in which each actor is featured at the moment he or she performs significant bits of business or attitudes. One of the important aspects of blocking in this kind of filmmaking is finding plausible business or attitudes for the actor who is *not* to be the focus of attention, and finding ways for actors to move smoothly in and out of prominence. In *La Tosca* this is done by having each actor look downwards or obscure their face at a point in the scene in which they are not supposed to be noticed; as well as by utilizing the depth of the set to differentiate the actor in the foreground from the actor in the background.

A related blocking strategy, but concerning objects rather than other actors, may be found in another Film d'Art production, from 1910, *La Fin d'une royauté* (The End of a Royal Line), with Berthe Bovy of the Comédie Française, and Blanche Dufresne and M. Clément of the Théâtre Sarah Bernhardt. In this scene, the Dauphin (Bovy), imprisoned with Marie Antoinette (Dufresne) and two ladies-in-waiting, is separated from the Queen by Revolutionary officials.

The set is a poor room in the Temple, with a barred window high in the rear centre wall, a door rear left, and a bed rear right in which Bovy sleeps at the beginning of the scene. There is a table front centre with two chairs and a stool on which the Queen and her ladies-in-waiting sit. At the entrance of the Revolutionaries, Dufresne and the ladies-in-waiting move to the door rear left. In response to the Revolutionary leader's written order (shown in an insert), Dufresne assumes a pose of refusal, with open arms (Figure 3.59). The scene continues with byplay between Dufresne refusing, the ladies-in-waiting pleading, and the Revolutionaries insisting that Louis must be taken. Then Bovy wakes up, is dressed by the ladies-in-waiting, and before being carried out, assumes a group pose with the other actresses, kneeling in front of the bed to pray (Figure 3.60).

It is necessary to get the chairs and table that were in front of the bed out of the way in order to prepare for the formation of this tableau, and this is done through the work of the ensemble.[4] One chair is moved back before the ladies-in-waiting go to the door to respond to the Revolutionaries. Other furniture is moved at the same time as Bovy's costume change. In response to the Queen's order to prepare Louis for departure, the ladies-in-waiting move the table to left of the bed. One exits left, the other goes to rear right of the bed with stockings. The first lady-in-waiting re-enters with clothes, then moves the stool from front centre to left of the bed. One chair remains in which Dufresne sits while the ladies-in-waiting put on Bovy's jacket, sash, and coat.

This business prepares the set for the tableau of prayer, as well as subsequent postures that follow the exit of the Revolutionaries with the Dauphin, in which all kneel and weep in the area front centre, burying their faces in the bedclothes. Obviously the

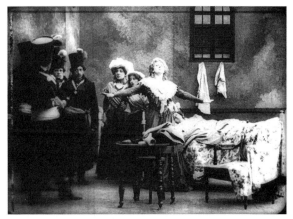

3.59

3.60

dressing of Louis also has important narrative functions—the respect with which he is treated by the ladies-in-waiting contrasts with a later scene, in which he is made to work and serve at table for soldiers and other citizens. Moreover, the dressing routine helps to delay the moment of leaving, extending the situation of the impending separation of mother and son. But alongside its narrative functions, the stage business performed by the ensemble is integrated with, and put at the service of, the formation of attitudes. The actresses simply and unobtrusively move objects out of the way, opening up a playing space, and a prominent position, for these attitudes.

The examples cited of ensemble acting are fairly early ones, and the actors remain full figure and relatively far from the camera. But many European features of the mid-to-late 1910s encompass action closer to camera (with the actors' feet 'cut off') and hence mobilize the range of scalar values found in the American films as well. They also incorporate more frequent cut-ins to medium shot. None the less, the kind of ensemble acting described above persisted, and was able to exploit the cut-in, and the greater sense of depth made possible by the use of the foreground space. The high point of the pictorial style in film acting of the 1910s may well not be the gestural solos of the solitary diva, but these extended gestural duets or trios, in which the movements of the ensemble are orchestrated in depth, with actors sometimes trading off expressive gestures, sometimes coming together to form group poses or tableaux.

A scene in Evgenii Bauer's *Korol' Parizha* (King of Paris, 1917) in which the Duchesse de Diernstein (Emma Bauer) attempts to dissuade her son Jean Hiénard (Mikhail Stal'skii) from fighting a duel with her lover provides an outstanding example.[5] Jean is alienated from his wealthy widowed mother and has been living independently of her as a sculptor in Paris. Obliged to visit her in Deauville to request a loan to help a sculptor friend, Frégose, get married, he discovers she is receiving the attentions of a young adventurer, the so-called Marquis de Prédalgonde, nicknamed the King of Paris. Investigating Prédalgonde with the help of a friend of his mother's, Lucienne Maréchal, Jean discovers he is the pawn of a shadowy underworld figure, Raval' Venkov (Rascol in the novel). He confronts Prédalgonde with his discovery, in order to persuade him to leave Paris and give up his suit of the Duchesse. Prédalgonde refuses, and insults the Duchesse. Jean slaps him and Prédalgonde challenges him to a duel. That night, Venkov attempts to murder Jean, but Frégose shoots him dead. Learning of the imminent duel from Lucienne, the Duchesse goes to Jean's studio to beg him not to fight.

This scene has a duration of 3 minutes, 46 seconds at 16 frames per second (excluding the intertitles and inserts there would have been in the original).

1 Jean's studio apartment. Midground right are stairs leading off and up with a mirror behind them. Rear left, there is a vestibule with a nude statue and an outer door beyond. Large windows cross the right rear. There is a bed midground left, and a chair front right.

The shot begins with the actors alternating attitudes within a deep space composition. In doing so, they necessarily shift the position of prominence from background to foreground and back again.

Stal'skii stands front right in medium long shot facing off front right, but very still. Bauer enters rear left, stops and poses (Figure 3.61). Stal'skii turns to the rear and reacts to her presence; she then drops her coat from her shoulders (Figure 3.62). The actors then move to midground and embrace, forming a group pose (Figure 3.63).

2 Cut in, same angle. Bauer and Stal'skii embracing in medium shot. He turns slowly to look off front centre, she to look off front left (Figure 3.64).

3 A slightly longer-framed variant of 2. Bauer goes and sits in the chair front right, facing front left. Stal'skii comes to the left arm of the chair and leans over her. He speaks and then straightens up (Figure 3.65).

4 Extreme high-angle very long shot of a clearing in woods. Seconds are pacing out the duelling ground.

The next shot utilizes deep space and the principles of alternation found in shot 1, except with Bauer now in the foreground.

5 As 1. Stal'skii is standing midground left, facing rear left. Bauer rises from the chair in the foreground and totters to front centre as he turns to look at her. She turns to face him, with her back to camera, and holds out her arms in a gesture of appeal (Figure 3.66). He runs to embrace her but stops and puts his hand on his heart to indicate that his honour is at stake (Figure 3.67).

This is a relatively small gesture, and is performed far from the camera, but because Bauer is turned away and still when it occurs, it is not in much danger of going unnoticed. Then it is Bauer's turn to express distress.

Bauer turns slowly away to face front left and puts her hands to her cheeks. Stal'skii looks off front left and wrings his hands in regret. Then he turns away from her as if to reiterate his refusal to abandon his duty. He walks further into midground left, facing left, with his back to the camera. Bauer backs to the chair and leans on it (Figure 3.68).

The actors then come together again to form group poses.

Stal'skii turns, comes to front centre, and faces her with his back to the camera (Figure 3.69). They clasp hands, and she kneels. Tilt down (Figure 3.70).

3.61   3.62   3.63

3.64   3.65   3.66

3.67   3.68   3.69

3.70   3.71   3.72

3.73   3.74   3.75

6 Similar to 2. Tilt up as he raises her, then sits her down in the chair (Figure 3.71). He kneels beside her, to the left of the chair, facing the camera. He stands up.

7 Stal'skii stands facing the camera in medium long shot. Jump cut, reframed to the left in which he appears in profile, facing her. She looks up at him (Figure 3.72). He kneels, the pose echoing Bauer's gesture in shot 5 and being similarly accompanied by a tilt down. They embrace. He makes a vow. He rises. Tilt up.

The content of the vow is not clear from the print or easily deducible from the novel. Stal'skii's exit follows his vow. Like Borelli's exit in the scene in Max's villa in *Ma l'amor mio non muore!*, it utilizes the depth of the set to the full, but unlike the diva film it involves both actors in important ways.

> Stal'skii leaves Bauer in the foreground, turning and walking to the midground. He pauses in his exit, prolonging the moment by turning to face her and posing (Figure 3.73). He then runs to the vestibule for his hat and stick and exits rear left.

Meanwhile Bauer's gestures become more prominent.

> Bauer rises and follows him into the depth of the shot, pausing in the midground, and gesturing with back to camera and arms stretched out towards him as he exits. Stal'skii then reappears briefly outside the window at the rear of the set, moving left to right, while Bauer puts her hands on her head (Figure 3.74). Bauer goes to the foot of the bed.

8 Cut-in, same angle: Bauer in medium shot at the bedpost. Facing front left, she clutches the bedpost with her left hand, holding her right hand out in front of her (Figure 3.75). Her breast heaves, her right hand drops out of frame, and she lowers her eyes. Fade out.

The final cut-in, like shots 6 and 2, follows upon the composition in depth, allowing a concentration upon Bauer's facial expression.

One of the most interesting aspects of *Korol' Parizha* is the way in which cinematic devices like the use of depth and the cut-in are put in the service of acting in a pictorial style. Throughout the scene, the moments in which the actors alternate poses are articulated through foreground/midground contrasts. Deep staging is used to orchestrate a whole series of poses and attitudes—Stal'skii walks into the midground to strike poses in shots 5 and 7 for example. Further, Stal'skii's reappearance in the window in shot 7 spec-

tacularly caps this use of depth, the principle of separating the actors into two planes of action being varied with the employment of a playing space even farther removed from the camera.

Editing and camera movement do not limit the scope allowed to the actor but rather follow from the actor's gestures. All three of the cut-ins serve to emphasize an attitude or facial expression—the actors looking off in different directions as they embrace in shot 2, Bauer kneeling to ask forgiveness at her son's feet in shot 6, and her facial expressions after he has departed in shot 8. The tilts are similarly cued to the gesture of kneeling which each actor makes in turn.

The kind of ensemble acting found in *Korol' Parizha* can be found throughout Bauer's œuvre; other prominent examples of actors trading off gestures include a scene in *Deti Veka* (Children of the Age) in which the young bank clerk tells his wife he has lost his job, and a scene involving three actors, in *Nemye Svideteli* (Silent Witnesses, 1914), in which the serving maid, herself in love with her master, finds his fiancée embracing her lover. A similar employment of the ensemble, although perhaps not so slowly paced, can also be found in other European films, and in genres as diverse as the Danish science fiction film *Himmelskibet* (The Space Ship, 1918), in the scene in which Captain Avanti confronts the villain David Dane in the space ship, and at various climactic moments in Feuillade's thriller *Judex* (1917), as for example in the pronounced alternation of attitudes that occurs in the scene in which Judex confesses to his mother, the Countess de Trémeuse, that he is in love with Jacquelyne, the daughter of her sworn enemy.

The scene of Fantine's death in Capellani's *Les Misérables* (1912) provides another example, which demonstrates how the alternation of attitudes among the actors is combined with the formation of tableaux by the group. Fantine (Marie Venture), ill and dying, is terrified by the appearance of Javert (Henri Étiévant), who has previously tried to arrest her, and who has followed the disguised Jean Valjean (Henry Krauss) to her bedside in order to arrest him.

> Krauss leans over talking to Venture who lies in bed, midground left. Suddenly, the door midground right opens and Étiévant enters, standing on the threshold. Venture sees him and assumes an attitude expressing terror. Étiévant folds his arms over his cane forming a barrier as if to prevent his prisoner from leaving the

room. Venture points to Étiévant, and maintains this pose. Krauss turns, keeping his back to Étiévant and moves to front centre, then turns again, glances at Étiévant, turns back to face front. All of the actors then hold their positions in a tableau.

Krauss makes gestures as if to reassure the patient. Étiévant comes to front right, and puts his right hand on Krauss's left shoulder. Krauss signals him to be calm, but Étiévant grabs his lapels. Venture, terrified, sits up in bed. Étiévant discloses to the sick woman the true identity of her protector, a thief and run-away convict. Venture throws her hands up. Tableau. While Étiévant and Krauss remain still, she clutches her bosom, falls in two movements and collapses, dead, her eyes open, one arm fully extended to the left.

As if by main strength Krauss forces Étiévant to rear right, picks up a chair, and breaks it on the floor to give himself a counter-weapon against Étiévant's stick. He points, gesturing for Étiévant to get out. Tableau. Étiévant then goes to stand in the doorway rear right, Krauss drops the chair leg, turns to Venture.

In a film like *Les Misérables* the ease with which actors move in and out of tableaux, pose both individually and in groups, allows for the control of blocking in interesting and subtle ways. The postures of the actors can be varied to form striking visual compositions, to help structure the sequence of actions in the take by calling attention to certain gestures or areas of the frame, and to drive home specific dramatic situations in a series of punctual moments. To an even greater degree than in the diva's gestural soliloquy, then, ensemble acting in the European cinema performed functions which were fulfilled by editing in the American cinema: singling out important aspects of a scenic space, providing a structure of alternation and repetition within scenes. Of course editing did not rule out ensemble acting in America, any more than the shorter average shot lengths ruled out the gestural soliloquy of the isolated actor, but in both instances actors were given less time and less scope for posing.

In the American cinema, which even by the early 1910s approximated more closely the modern conception of one idea per shot, actors had to make do with one or two poses per take. *An Official Appointment* (Vitagraph, 1912) provides a good example of the American tendency to limit the duration of the scene even in a film without the kind of extended cross-cutting which provided the swift cutting rates

for Griffith's films at Biograph. Charles Kent, who plays the principal role as well as directing, had a distinguished stage career from 1875 until 1906. He began acting in films because he lost his voice.[6] His character, that of an elderly, aristocratic Southern Colonel, motivates Kent's extremely dignified carriage, evident in his frequent bowing and other polite gestures, a trait made fun of by other characters in the film. It is a tribute to Kent's grace and skill that his courtly bearing, while noticeable, never appears overdone even in the face of parodies of it by other actors.

Colonel Armistead has sold off the last of his possessions and travelled to Washington with his loyal servant Amber (Harold Wilson) in hopes of receiving a government post. The post is not forthcoming, and Amber must play his fiddle and beg in the streets to get enough money to pay the rent. A letter, apparently from the Secretary of State, finally arrives offering him a job. The letter is in fact a forgery, the result of a practical joke, a fact which contributes to the film's unhappy end.

The scene in which the Colonel receives the letter is in one take, but relatively brief (approximately 1 minute at 16 frames per second). It is preceded by a title: 'The joke is taken seriously.'

Colonel Armistead's sitting-room has a window with lace curtains on the rear wall, and a door in the left wall at the rear. A large stuffed armchair is foreground left beside an off-screen fireplace (the flickering light is visible), and a table with chair is midground right where Kent, in dressing-gown over his shirt, waistcoat and tie, sits having morning coffee (Figure 3.76). His landlady enters with the mail, rear left, and gives it to Wilson. Wilson brings the letter to Kent at the table. Still chewing, Kent takes the letter and looks at it. He wipes his mouth with a napkin held in his right hand, holding the letter in his left and looking at it. He gets up. He walks to foreground right, while Wilson comes to midground left, behind the armchair. Kent rips open the letter, unfolds it, while Wilson clasps his hands. Kent reads, holding the letter in his left hand. Kent then executes a series of poses. He puts his right hand on his heart (Figure 3.77), then staggers back, fully extending his right arm and resting it on top of the chair back (Figure 3.78). He recovers, looks off left, lifts his right arm high above his head (Figure 3.79), then brings it down, thumping his chest twice with his fist. At the finish of this thumping gesture, he very swiftly points behind him (Figure 3.80). Wilson then goes to rear

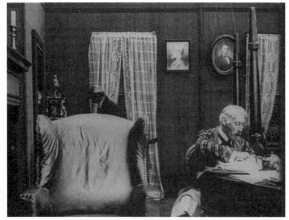

3.76

3.77

3.78

3.79

3.80

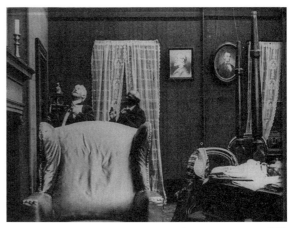

3.81

right, while Kent turns left into profile still reading the letter. He turns away from camera and moves into midground, still reading. Wilson brings him his coat, helps him take off his dressing-gown. Kent folds up the letter as Wilson helps him into a frock coat. Moving toward rear left, Kent takes his hat and stick from Wilson. At the door, he stops, faces front left, puts his left hand, still holding the letter, on his heart. He inclines his head back. Meanwhile, Wilson also inclines his head back and holds up open hands at chest height (Figure 3.81). Kent and Wilson exit.

The fast tempo here is a matter of a narrative deadline rather than inexperience on the part of the actors. The scene is hurried in that, from the time he receives and reads the letter, the Colonel is eager to be off to the offices of the Secretary of State to accept his appointment. The business of getting up while still eating at the breakfast table, and later of exchanging the dressing-gown for frock coat, hat, and stick, are all directed towards this narrative goal. None the less expressive gestures are interposed with these bits of business, most prominently when Kent is in the foreground position beside the armchair, but also at the end of the scene, when the two actors pose before exiting. One does find attitudes then, but not very many of them when considered in relation to the European examples discussed above, and they are delivered on the run, pictorial acting's equivalent of American fast food.

As Griffith's experiments with cross-cutting began to make the shot the unit of construction of the scene, or more commonly of the sequence, the opportunities for expressive gesture and posing became still more restricted. Attitudes in the late Griffith Biographs are few and far between, although they are often heightened because of their isolation and the editing structure within which they are placed. Blanche Sweet's performance in *The Painted Lady* (1912) seems an appropriate example, as it has been discussed by Russell Merritt as an early demonstration of bravura acting in Griffith, one of the careful orchestrations of emotional climaxes for which his leading actresses became renowned.[7] The story concerns the elder of two daughters who follows the precepts of her repressive father (Charles Hill Mailes) and does not paint her face. While most of the young men at an ice-cream social prefer her younger sister (Madge Kirby), who does use make up, the older girl

meets and is courted by a stranger (Joseph Graybill). Later, forbidden to see him by her father, she meets the young man clandestinely and reveals aspects of her father's business to him. When the young man, face disguised with a kerchief, attempts to rob her father one night, she threatens the intruder with a gun and accidentally kills him. The discovery that she has shot her lover drives her mad.

The scene of the murder and discovery takes place in eighteen shots with two titles, the action largely split between two rooms (our breakdown actually begins with the shot in which Graybill begins to force open an exterior window, but for brevity we begin here with shot 12, after she has got the gun and when she enters the study for the first time).

12 Long shot (as 3). The heroine's father's study. There is a chair rear left, an alcove with bookcase and picture rear right, a window on the right side wall, and, near the rear and on the same wall, midground, a desk. The door is midground left. There is a table left front and a chair front centre. Sweet enters through the door and Graybill rises. She holds out her free hand, pointing, briefly, in the direction of the window. As he advances towards her, she points several more times in that direction. He grabs the gun and they struggle, backs to camera. He is shot, staggers towards the front and falls into the chair front centre, his head, facing upwards, resting on the table. She approaches the corpse slowly, gesturing towards the window (Figure 3.82). There is a marked change of attitude indicating that she realizes he is dead. Sweet's eyes widen in horror, she clutches her face with her left hand, retreats rapidly to lean against the door midground left, and rests her right hand against it (Figure 3.83). She moves out of the door, lifting her left hand high above her head.

13 Medium long shot (as 4). Hall. Stairs going up and off midground centre. The door leading to the study is in front of the stairs, to the right. A chair and cupboard are partly visible beyond the stairs, rear left. Sweet backs out of the door, still holding the gun, turns back to camera and lifts both her hands above her head, calling for help (Figure 3.84). She turns around, first facing left, then towards camera, then right, her left hand in a fist held at chest height. She starts, opening her mouth and raising both her hands slightly higher, as she looks through the doorway, right (Figure 3.85).

14 As 3. Sweet approaches the corpse, gesturing to the window. She removes Graybill's hat with her right hand, which still holds the gun. Giving her left arm an abrupt shake, she pulls down his kerchief, revealing his face.

Sweet's face remains neutral at this discovery, she moves one shoulder slightly (Figure 3.86).

15 As 4. Madge Kirby enters down the stairs. She screams. Mailes enters front right.

16 As 3. Sweet stands near the body, right hand held to mouth. Mailes enters and stands to her right, Kirby to his right. Mailes gestures, bringing his left hand to chest height. Two more men rush in and stand behind him. He explains what has happened, gesturing with open hands. He picks the dead man up by the lapels. Meanwhile, Sweet removes her hand from her mouth, her lips tremble and a tear rolls down her cheek. She then becomes relatively more active, tearing Mailes's hand off the body (Figure 3.87). She clutches at her breast with her right hand. She turns to the corpse, rests her right forearm on the chair back, and left hand on the corpse's chest. She

smiles down at him. With her left hand she taps her chest to indicate he was her lover. She turns to her sister and pantomimes painting her face (indicating that she did not do so, did not have to in order to win him). Then she looks down at him, assumes a sorrowful expression. Mailes puts his arms around her and pulls her away from the body. She puts her left hand to her head as he leads her out the door (Figure 3.88).

17 Title: Shattered.

18 As 4. Mailes and Sweet enter through the door. He takes the shawl and puts it around her shoulders. She smiles and addresses her (imagined) boyfriend off front right (Figure 3.89). Her father holds her, his hands on her shoulders, horrified. He turns her to face him, pleads with her. She turns back to front right, smiling, then begins to frown, then opens her mouth and stares wide-

3.82   3.83   3.84

3.85   3.86   3.87

3.88   3.89   3.90

eyed in the stereotypical 'madness' expression (Figure 3.90). She leans back and Mailes supports her. He clasps her to him.

A single gesture or a small number of them are contained within each shot, obviating the need to repeat and vary poses, and helping the actress to engineer transitions from one pose and emotional mood to another. Thus, there is only one pose when she realizes she has killed the masked intruder at the end of shot 12, followed by a cut, while shot 13 similarly makes room for only two, the call for help which also functions as an expression of horror, with hands raised above head, and then the turn and start at the sight of the body. Shot 16 obviously allows for more extended posing, and indeed an alternation between Mailes, whose gestures dominate at the beginning of the shot, and Sweet, whose gestures dominate at the end. But note that even here, the shot is basically concerned with one idea, the revelation of the dead man's identity both for Sweet (although this began previously when she unmasked him at the end of shot 14) and more importantly for her family. The transition to the next situation, the heroine's madness, is not effected in this shot, but through the interpolation of the title (shot 17) and then the cut to the space outside the study. The framing in shot 18 is closer than in 16, permitting Sweet to act out her madness with smaller gestures, and isolating her from the group in the previous shot. But it also means that the division of the scene into distinct moments is largely out of her hands. We do not see Sweet 'become' mad. She leaves the study conflicted, defiant, and sorrowful, in shot 16, and the title 'shattered' prepares us for the change at the beginning of shot 18. The actress's work in shot 18 is limited to pantomiming the conversation which indicates her mental state, and then assuming the final expressive gesture which caps this point.

As we have already indicated, in one-reel films like *An Official Appointment* or *The Painted Lady* a great deal of action had to be packed in, so it may not be surprising that such films do not allow for extended series of poses. But the tendency to limit the lengths of individual takes, and the number of events or ideas presented in each take, becomes if anything more pronounced in early American features. Griffith's features in particular provide single poses or significant gestures, often isolated in close or medium shots, to drive home the point of a character's reaction to a scene. The well-known repeated shots of Mae Marsh pulling at her handkerchief with her teeth during the highly edited scene of her husband's trial for murder in *Intolerance* are indicative of this trend.

One might think that *A Fool There Was* (Frank Powell, 1915), which depends upon and repeatedly asserts the fascination of the Vampire (Theda Bara), would move closer to the lengthy takes and performance style of the diva film. But most of the film is comprised of short scenes with only minimal time for posing, which alternate between the Vampire and the hapless husband (Edward José) on the one hand, and his wife (Mabel Fremyear) and child (Runa Hodges) on the other. The predilection for brief scenes holds true even in one of the big situations of the film when the moral opposites are brought together, and the wife and Vampire confront each other face to face, so that no cross-cutting is necessary. The husband, having been abandoned by the Vampire and now an alcoholic, is visited by his wife and is about to leave with her to return home. There is a cut to the exterior of the house which shows the Vampire arriving to reclaim her victim and threatening Tom, a family friend (Clifford Bruce). Cut back inside:

> Fremyear and José are standing together back to camera at the door, about to exit. Bara appears outside the door; they separate, Fremyear moving left and José right. She enters and poses in the doorway, staring left at Fremyear. Fremyear and José both fall back further, José leaning against the doorjamb, hands shaking and head bowed. Bruce appears behind Bara in the doorway. Bara looks right, at José, then back left at Fremyear again. Fremyear points at Bara and addresses a question to her husband, who nods his head. Bara moves right, leans towards the husband, and rests her right hand on the doorjamb above him, in a sexually aggressive posture. He leans backwards, his pose also held. She puts her left arm around his neck and kisses him. Bruce enters the room, takes Fremyear by the arm and leads her out of the doorway while she sobs. The Vampire lifts her head and looks left, out the doorway, watching them leave and laughing in triumph. José collapses on his knees in front of her and kisses her hand. She looks down at him, then inclines her head back and looks off left again. The pose is held.

While Bara poses several times in the doorway, sometimes along with the other actors, the poses are not varied or elaborated. There is virtually no prolongation of the duration of the situation by pictorial means, as could have been easily motivated either by representing the husband as torn between the two, unable to make a choice, or by representing the wife as unwilling to leave. The way this particular scene is structured is partly a function of the fact that Powell utilizes the typical Griffithian shallow staging so that everyone is clustered at the door, precluding larger movements and new groupings of the actors. We also suspect that the actress would have had difficulty handling a lengthier take; all the publicity that accrued to the persona of Theda Bara notwithstanding, Theodosia Goodman was neither a Lyda Borelli nor a Blanche Sweet. But the point is that in Europe even a bad director working with a bad actress would have had a much more extended scene here, with many more, and more varied, attitudes. One can imagine what Bauer would have done with it. That Powell dispenses with a situation like this so quickly is an important indication of the kind of scene construction typical of the early American feature. (Of course, directors such as Griffith did prolong situations, but by cross-cutting, not by gestural means.)

There were American directors such as Cecil B. De-Mille and Maurice Tourneur who were celebrated in the trade press during the 1910s for the beauties of their respective visual styles, and who, despite relatively high cutting rates, seem closer than Griffith does to European conceptions of the scene, and the traditions of theatrical pictorialism. The American cinema should not be reduced to Griffith; it obviously encompassed a range of degrees of scene dissection and accommodation to pictorial styles of acting. None the less, because Griffith stands as an early prototype of shot-based scene construction, he represents *in extremis* a tendency that had profound effects on American film acting as a whole in the period. For both features and the one-reel film, the principles of scene construction and developments in editing techniques entailed reduced forms of pictorial acting styles. American acting tended to be faster in tempo than most European acting and more restrained, partly because actors did not have the time to build up to the very largest gestures, and partly because there was less necessity to rely on the actor to provide emphasis at climactic moments.

One might, then, argue that acting in American films became more 'naturalistic', in the sense that it offered reduced opportunities for posing. But it is not clear, to us at any rate, that American acting should in general be called 'naturalistic' in the sense of being deliberately non-emphatic, an alternative discussed above in relation to Duse's performance style. This is not merely quibbling over terms, since it raises questions about the range of acting styles available in the 1910s—more or less emphatic, more or less pictorially inclined—and also the degree to which pictorial elements survive in the case of Griffith, a director often said to be at the forefront of developments of acting technique in the USA.

We have noted that Duse's performances were sometimes referred to as 'non-melodramatic' or 'restrained' by critics, and that in one instance she ran the risk attendant upon this kind of reduction of gesture, when the critic William Archer complained that she did not 'put over' an important point in *The Doll's House*. There is one moment in *The Painted Lady* which seems to approach this method: in shot 14 when Sweet unmasks the corpse and then remains without significant facial expression (Figure 3.86). There is a similar moment in *The Mothering Heart* (Griffith, 1913), when Lillian Gish remains absolutely calm as she receives the news from the doctor that her baby is dead. In a later shot, showing her walking in the garden, her face also appears still. But, these moments of calm appear as such precisely because Griffith tends to isolate discrete moments of scenes in discrete shots. If we look at the scenes as wholes, it becomes clear that the absence of expression occurs only temporarily, the actress briefly withholding expressive gesture only to give vent to it again. In both of these cases, the heroine's calm stands in contrast to previous outbursts—in the case of Sweet, the horrified pose assumed when she realized the intruder had been shot dead, and in the case of Gish, her hysterical attempt to hold on to her child when the doctor first appeared to examine it. Moreover, in both cases, the calm precedes another outburst and moment of emphatic gesture—Sweet's madness in shot 18 of *The Painted Lady*, and the second shot in the garden in *The Mothering Heart* in which Gish flays at the rose bushes with a stick. No doubt these poses and gestures are relatively brief when compared to the gestural soliloquies of a Lyda Borelli or an Asta Nielsen. But, in the context of Griffith's editing, and, in *The Painted*

Lady, his use of titles to effect transitions, these minimal gestures have a great deal of dramatic force. The effect of this mode of filmmaking is anything but non-emphatic.

Thus, we want to chart out a third alternative—in contrast to both Griffith and the examples of European filmmaking discussed so far—which pursues the renunciation of expressive gesture much more aggressively. The Swedish director Victor Sjöström has helped to define this option for us, and was one of those who most systematically explored naturalist technique in this sense. His *Ingmarssönerna* (The Ingmarssons, 1919) is very concerned with the subjective experiences of its central character, yet the actors, including Sjöström himself in the title role, hold the use of expressive gesture to a minimum.

The story of *Ingmarssönerna* is essentially one of a decision that has to be made by Little Ingmar Ingmarsson, a Dalecarlian farmer from a locally respected family. His common-law wife, Brita (Harriet Bosse), whom he could not afford to marry because of a series of bad harvests, has killed their child at birth in rage and shame at her unmarried state, and been sent to prison for infanticide. Her sentence is now over. Respectable local opinion, including Ingmar's own mother and Brita's parents, assumes that Ingmar will reject Brita, so her father has arranged for her to emigrate to America. Ingmar must decide whether to go along with these plans. He goes to the city and meets Brita as she comes out of prison. As her ship to America does not leave for some time, he drives her back to the village. It is Sunday, and she wishes to join the villagers at church. They go into the church, are mortified by the congregation's stares, and flee before the sermon. When they reach Ingmar's farm, his mother says she will leave if Brita enters. Brita begs to go back to the city, and Ingmar starts to drive her there. On the way they meet the congregation returning from church, so Ingmar turns into a side road. As he does so, he is hailed by the postman, who gives him a letter. He drives a little way into the trees, then stops and looks at the letter. It is from Brita. She tells him it is a letter she wrote in prison which he was not supposed to receive until she had gone to America, and begs him not to read it. He insists on doing so, and discovers that she had come to love him. He then confesses to her that he continues to love her. Meanwhile, the pastor has

gone to the Ingmarsson farm and congratulated Ingmar's mother on Ingmar's courageous decision to take Brita back. Embarrassed, the mother sends servants to look for the couple, and they are found and return to congratulations all round.

The story thus turns crucially on decisions and feelings internal to the characters: Brita's rage turning to love, Little Ingmar's conflict between the social and moral dictates of his community and his own conscience. In order to support the psychological inflections necessary for this story, and yet allow for the extremely reduced acting style, the film resorts to a number of other devices: a frame story in which Little Ingmar's question of conscience is directly posed to his ancestors in heaven in a dream; other visions, e.g. of the folk wedding there might have been; large numbers of prolix titles which often tell what people are thinking; and a fast-cut editing style that approaches classical continuity in the use of eyeline matches (see, for example, the scene in which Brita's parents tell her she must marry Little Ingmar, which has classically correct matches for three characters who are moving about a table). These devices permit Sjöström to convey strong, and complicated, emotional and psychological states while at the same time employing spare and simple gestures.

The scene in which Little Ingmar reads Brita's letter provides an example of this style. The scene is 9 minutes 34 seconds long at 16 frames per second, and consists of 78 shots, of which 27 are titles and 1 the insert of the letter. This breakdown begins with shot 28 of the scene, shortly after the letter insert, and Little Ingmar's reading of the letter. The scene takes place in a wood, with a dirt road through tall trees. The titles are translated from the original Swedish.

28 The trap is standing facing front, with the horse front right. Bosse is seated in the trap facing front, Sjöström standing to the left of the trap. He goes to the trap, stands front left, grabs her right arm and shakes her. She looks off front right.

29 Title: 'Is it true that the letter says that you love me?'

30 Medium long shot from the front of the trap. Bosse is sitting in the left seat, Sjöström standing to her left, holding her arm. She looks down off front right. He shakes her (Figure 3.91).

31 Title: 'Does it say in the letter that you love me?'

32 Same angle as 30, vignetted medium shot of Sjöström (Figure 3.92).

3.91

3.92

3.93

3.94

3.95

3.96

33 Same angle as 30, vignetted medium shot of Bosse (turned a bit to the right). She looks at her lap (Figure 3.93).

34 Title: 'Yes.'

35 As 33.

36 As 32. He thrusts her hand off right. His face breaks up. He screams.

37 Title: 'So you are lying! So you are lying!'

38 As 30. She has turned to face him, he looks at her. She speaks.

39 Title: 'God knows I prayed to him every day to get to see you before going.'

40 As 33.

41 As 32. He cries out.

42 Title: 'Where are you going?'

43 As 32.

44 As 33. She looks wearily off front right, speaks.

45 Title: 'I suppose I am going to America.'

46 As 33.

47 As 32. He looks down right.

48 Title: 'Like hell you are!'

49 As 32.

50 As 33. She turns to look off left at him, and laughs.

51 As 32. He turns to front left, his face working (Figure 3.94).

52 As 16. He staggers off front left (Figure 3.95).

53 Long shot of the trap facing right across the rear. Bosse in the trap looking at Sjöström as he staggers then falls headlong towards the camera (Figure 3.96).

54 Title: Now it was his turn to weep.

55 Long shot at 90 degrees to 53. Sjöström lying on the ground, his head to the right, weeping.

56 Title: She was so happy she did not know how she should behave so as not to laugh out loud.

57 As 53. Bosse gets down from cart, comes to the left of Sjöström's head front left, sits down on the ground, takes off his hat and strokes his head.

This segment, like the scene as a whole, is dominated by medium shots, which show either the two characters together or one of them individually. There is a high degree of repetition, the extent of which is not immediately apparent from this short segment. For example shot 30, which shows them together in the trap, is a variant of shot 1, a composition repeated in shots 3, 5, 7, 9, 11 (slightly turned to the right), 13, 15. Within the segment, the vignetted shots of individual characters, shots 32 and 33 (Figures 3.92 and 3.93) are both repeated: shot 32 six times, shot 33 five times. These shots have precedents in shots 18 and 19 and following. The scene is thus largely composed of medium shots which regularly alternate with titles following every one or two of the images.

The actors typically remain poker-faced in the medium-shot framings. The whole point of the scene, at least until shot 57, is that each character is trying to withhold the display of emotion—Brita because she does not want to force a socially unacceptable marriage on Little Ingmar, Little Ingmar because he does not want to force himself on her for a second time. The neutral or contained facial expressions are thus to be read as repressed emotions. Their hesitation or despair is often represented through the direction of their glance, rather than through facial expression. Thus, Bosse looks away from Sjöström in shots 30, 33, 44 when she is trying to deny her feelings for him.

There are moments of expressive gesture, although without extended elaboration, as in Sjöström's grimaces in shots 36 and 51 (Figure 3.94). And such expressions stand out the more forcefully against the backdrop of the previous shots in the sequence, in which characters have seemed so impassive. But note that these momentary outbursts are transitional moments, they do not come at the end of the discovery, epitomizing the meaning of this moment. Indeed, after Little Ingmar comes to the full realization that Brita loves him, the actor collapses on the ground, crying, in long shot and without our being able to see his face (Figure 3.96). Certainly this suggests the idea of a powerful emotion, but it does not directly display the character's reaction to the new situation to the spectator. The title which informs us that Brita is trying not to laugh out loud is similarly indicative of the level of repression still operative in the scene at this point.

The sequence from *Ingmarssönerna* is remarkable for the absence of pictorial effect at the level of acting; it does not heighten, or even always mark out, changes in dramatic situation in this way. The stylistic differences between this film and one like *Korol' Parizha*, films made within two years of each other, should be apparent. At every point in the scene with mother and son before the duel, the Russian film depends on the actors striking elaborate series of poses and attitudes so as to convey a sense of their emotions, and to organize the rhythm and pacing of the scene. The scene is also structured through the repetition of elements such as the actor's movements from foreground to background, which take place within the 'shot'. In contrast, not only do the actors express little with their faces and bodies in *Ingmarssönerna*, but all of the important dramatic transitions in the scene are distributed across a large number of shots and titles, the repetition and variation of which account for the structure of the scene as a whole. Paradoxically, there is a gain for the actor in this, since very minimal gestures—a glance off camera, or slight shake of the shoulder when a man is ostensibly crying on the ground—seem to carry a great deal of signifying weight.

The relation between *Ingmarssönerna* and acting in the American features, such as those by Griffith, remains somewhat more difficult to specify. In so far as Sjöström's reduced style depends upon a high cutting rate, it is closer to Griffith than to Bauer. On the other hand, Griffith's films often provide the spectator with 'telling' facial expressions, and poses, a point highlighted by the editing and use of titles. In so far as the films aim to clarify and heighten the characters' reactions to situations, a process frequently capped by the actor's gesture if not entirely dependent upon it, they are closer to Bauer than to Sjöström. Thus, Griffith does not reject pictorially oriented acting styles so much as he 'tames' them, so that they can fit the tempo and discursive logic of the

edited sequence. Whereas Sjöström uses editing, among other devices, to pursue the possibilities of an anti-pictorial and non-emphatic style.

In place of a simple binary opposition between naturalism and pictorialism then, we would emphasize that 1910s cinema encompassed a range of acting styles which incorporated pictorial elements to a greater or lesser degree. These elements, which include not only gestural soliloquies, but also methods for focusing attention on specific characters or bits of business in ensemble scenes, and for blocking out scenes for two and three actors with the requisite poses and tableaux, became relatively more important in the case of filmmakers who did not pursue the option of shot-based scene construction, that is for most Europeans in the 1910s. They do appear in the shot-based scene construction typical of the Americans, but they are certainly much attenuated. Our present-day tendency to see marked pictorialism in acting as 'hammy' or vulgar, our inability to appreciate its grace, sometimes even to understand the ideas emphasized in this way, is a function of the predominance of reduced acting styles made possible by the development of classical editing techniques which have entailed much greater interest in and attention to the shot at the expense of the complex pictorial elements within it.

1. Lawrence, 'Growing up', 107; another example of admiration for the Film d'Art actors may be found in a review of *L'Assassinat du duc de Guise* by Thomas Bedding, 'The Modern Way in Moving Picture Making', *Moving Picture World*, 4, no. 11 (13 Mar. 1909), 294–5; repr. in Slide, *Selected Film Criticism*, 12–13: 'The scenes of the Assassination show accuracy of costume, accessories, archaeological and other details; the grouping, and what we commonly call the *mise-en-scène* are perfect; the acting such as only long and careful rehearsing under a master mind can produce. From this point of view, and I speak from experience of the Paris, London and New York stages, I have no hesitation in pronouncing the film in question as an ideal piece of stage craft in the way of silent drama.'

2. *Proektor*, 20 (1916), 3; cit. Yuri Tsivian, 'Some Preparatory Remarks on Russian Cinema', in Paolo Cherchi Usai, Lorenzo Codelli, Carlo Montanaro, and David Robinson (eds.), *Testimoni Silenziosi: Film russi, 1908–1919/Silent Witnesses: Russian Films, 1908–1919* (Pordenone/London: Edizioni Biblioteca del-

l'Immagine/British Film Institute, 1989), 28–30; see Tsivian's entire section on the deliberately slow tempo of Russian films, pp. 26–34.

3. Unfortunately, the original intertitles of *Ma l'amor mio non muore!* do not survive; the longest print we have seen (that of the Milan Cineteca) has new titles composed by the restorers, and the English-language print in the Museum of Modern Art, deriving from an earlier stage in the Milan restoration, translates the Milan titles. These titles leave gaps in the plot, but, more important, we think they may at times falsify the action. Here these prints reconstruct a text of the letter which suggests that the Grand Duke knows that Diana Cadouleur is really Elsa Holbein, daughter of the supposed traitor to Wallenstein. As we note below, Theubner is visibly shaken when he recognizes Elsa. He might not be in the Grand Duke's confidence, but it seems more plausible to suggest that the letter simply reproves Max for a liaison with the notorious actress Diana Cadouleur.

4. Marvin Carlson suggests that actors moving furniture to vary the

stage composition began in France in productions of Scribe's plays at the Comédie Française in the 1840s, and was further developed by Montigny at the Théâtre de la Gymnase in the 1850s. See 'French Stage Composition from Hugo to Zola', *Educational Theatre Journal*, 23, no. 4 (Dec. 1971), 366–7 and 372.

5. The print we have seen, deriving from the negative preserved by Gosfilmofond, Moscow, lacks titles. The complex plot is difficult to follow without them, so our reading of the story is tentative and indebted to the novel *Roi de Paris* by Georges Ohnet on which the film was originally based. Our spelling of most of the character names also derives from this source. Gosfilmofond has added opening titles to the reconstructed print which give cast lists and character names in Russian, derived from contemporary publicity for the film. With a few exceptions, these seem to be Cyrillic transliterations of the character names in the novel. See Georges Ohnet, *Roi de Paris*, from the series *Les Batailles de la Vie*, 8th edn. (Paris: Paul Ollendorff, 1898). Yury Tsivian is currently attempting to restore a subtitled print of the film, using the novel as his source.

6. Slide, *The Big V*, 144.

7. Russell Merritt, 'Mr. Griffith, *The Painted Lady* and the Distractive Frame', *Image*, 19, no. 4 (Dec. 1976); repr. in Marshall Deutelbaum (ed.), *'Image': On the Art and Evolution of the Film* (New York and Rochester: Dover Publications and International Museum of Photography, 1979), 147–56.

STAGING

Iɴ his history of British theatrical scenery, Richard
Southern refers to the nineteenth century as 'a century of change'.[1] On the contrary, we largely treat the
period between the middle eighteenth and the early
twentieth century as a single block, taking what a historian of nineteenth-century theatre would see as a
period of variation and change as essentially constant
and homogeneous. This difference is partly one of
perspective. Historians have a vested interest in
change in their objects; we ourselves are probably second to none in insisting on the rapidity with which
film style changed in the relatively short period we
are dealing with in the 1910s, and on national and
even individual variations in filmmaking practice
during the same period. When considering the influence of theatre on cinema during these years,
however, we are less interested in immediate
connections, such as a filmmaker's attempt to imitate a particular stage production or a fashionable
theatrical trend, than in such filmmakers' general
sense of what was theatrical, what might, if translated somehow into film, raise film to the recognized
aesthetic status of the legitimate stage. We would
argue none the less that this homogenization is not

just a matter of perspective; it reflects a conception of the theatrical that emerged in the middle of the eighteenth century, continued unchallenged until the middle of the nineteenth, and survived in all but very narrow circles of theatrical activity until well into the twentieth.

This periodization is hardly novel, of course. Southern himself goes on to note that: 'The eighteenth century has seen the consolidation of the system of changeable scenery as part of the spectacle of the show; throughout the nineteenth century changeable scenery will remain as the scenic principle of the time, but towards the end—at the dawn of our present period—it will lose a feature that once was essential to it, for the changes will no longer be visible.'[2] Southern's last point will be discussed further below, but in other respects this suggests a basic constancy in the period we take as that of the pictorial stage.

Our dates also correspond to those suggested by the subtitle 'David Garrick to D. W. Griffith' of *Stage to Screen*. However, while accepting Vardac's chronological limits, we have rejected his characterization of this period, and hence his account of its origins and demise. Without trying to pinpoint precisely the beginning, we would locate it at the point at which the spectacular staging characteristic of musical drama—masque, opera, ballet—in the seventeenth century was applied to spoken drama, tragedy, and comedy. Both of these had hitherto been acted either (in England) in front of the proscenium arch on a long forestage, with the scenery forming a generally appropriate background, or (in France and Italy, where forestages were shorter) in unchangeable standing sets representing palaces or streets. By the middle of the eighteenth century, acts and even scenes in tragedies and comedies began to be played before changeable scenery more specifically appropriate to the action of that scene (in France such divisions characterized by their own scenery began to be called *tableaux*); this scenery increasingly included practicable elements and thus became a location for the action rather than a mere background—indeed increasingly participated in it, with breaking bridges, volcanoes, and other active elements of the décor. Other significant changes noted at the time were: the shift from the usually axial backdrops of the musical stage to oblique views (attributed in France to Servandoni, but best illustrated in surviving designs by the work of the Bibienas); the abandonment of the traditional cloud border for extensions of the wings carrying architectural elements beyond the upper limit of the field of view and closing in the tops of settings with architectural borders (interiors) or tree branches (exteriors); the extensive adoption of ground rows to conceal the stage floor (attributed in England to de Loutherbourg); and finally the use of receding series of cut cloths or *fermes* so that a relatively light backdrop is viewed through a series of frames progressively darkening to the front (sometimes attributed to Daguerre, and certainly a basic principle of his dioramas as well as his stage sets, but already found in de Loutherbourg's sets for the Drury Lane Theatre).[3]

Such sets are often counterposed (as 'romantic') to the everyday contemporary room sets, sometimes ceilinged box sets, furnished with real modern furniture, used by Madame Vestris, for example, for domestic comedies at the Olympic Theatre in London in the 1830s. Vestris's quest for consistency within her settings and between the setting and the action has led to her being considered as the progenitor of a line leading, via the Bancrofts, to a fully-blown naturalism.[4]

The problem with this view is that it tends to turn the history of theatre in the nineteenth century into a steady evolution from romanticism to realism to naturalism, with symbolism and then the various twentieth-century theatrical avant-gardes as a reaction to this whole trend. On the contrary, we would see theatrical pictorialism as much more persistent, and naturalism as constituting the radical break, but one which affected a much narrower range of theatrical practice, leaving most of both popular and respectable early twentieth-century theatre still holding to the pictorialist line. There certainly was a desire for enhanced stage illusion in most nineteenth-century theatre. But this desire was not for a perceptual identity between what was seen and heard on the stage and everyday experience outside the theatre. As has been discussed in relation to realism in Chapter 1, theatrical illusion was a matter of the utilization of specific devices, rendering rather than simulating reality in Chion's terms,[5] and the constitution of what were recognizably pictures in the sense we have used this term was part of that rendering. What distinguished the naturalist theatre was not so much an increase in the degree of perceptual identity, i.e. that it looked 'more real' than previous kinds of theatre, but, rather, the rejection of the explicit solicitation of the audience involved in offering them a recognizable stage picture. This rejection is clear in the following remark of Stanislavsky's:

The usual impression is that a director uses all of his material means, such as the set, the lighting, sound effects, and other accessories, for the primary purpose of impressing the public. On the contrary. We use these means more for their effect on the actors. We try in every way to facilitate the concentration of their attention on the stage.[6]

Illusionism *for the audience* is of no importance to Stanislavsky:

Imagine a beautiful set, designed by some artist highly gifted in the use of colour, line and perspective. You look at the set from the auditorium and it creates a complete illusion. And yet if you come up close to it you are disillusioned, you are ill at ease with it. Why? Because it is a set made from the painter's point of view, in two and not in three dimensions, it has no value in the theatre. It has width and height but lacks the depth, without which, as far as the stage is concerned, it is lifeless.[7]

The conformity of this idea with Stanislavsky's insistence that the actor should ignore how he looks to the audience, discussed in Part 3, is obvious. In both acting and staging, pictorial theatre concentrates on the effect what happens on the stage has on an audience, on how the stage looks to the audience; naturalism is focused on the action as such, freed as far as possible from any consideration of appearance to an audience. Although naturalism achieved this with what can be considered a whole series of illusory techniques, and by a very rigorous distinction between the stage and the auditorium (the 'fourth wall' and *Guckkästchen-theater* pilloried by twentieth-century theatrical reformers), there is a direct line between this conception and the quasi-abstract ramps, curtains, and stairs of twentieth-century avant-garde staging, where the stage is simply a place of action, one which became able to include the audience again, as participants rather than onlookers. On the other hand, for many nineteenth-century audience members, actors, and directors who went to, acted in, and produced naturalist plays, they 'looked real', and hence could still be conceived as an extension of pictorial theatre. It is perhaps for this reason that theatrical naturalism was able to function as a crossroads, both between

pictorial theatre and modern theatre, and between nineteenth- and twentieth-century distinctions between respectable and popular theatre.

Yet this same ambiguity makes it only too easy for modern commentators to read naturalist staging, and especially the critique of it produced by the early twentieth-century theatrical reformers, back into what we would see as 'normal' nineteenth-century theatre. Thus, when Christopher Baugh summarizes the transformation brought about by Garrick and de Loutherbourg as 'a change from theatre as a participatory and rhetorical event to a theatre of passive spectacle',[8] we would endorse the opposition between rhetoric and spectacle, but not that between participation and passivity, which seems an anachronistic attempt to bring the spectacular stage into the sights of anti-naturalistic guns. Whether or no the audiences for French neo-classical drama, English Restoration comedy and their coevals (for which we might adopt Allardyce Nicoll's name, the 'baroque and its legacy')[9] were noisier than those for nineteenth-century theatre, more participation does not seem inscribed in baroque dramaturgy. The latter is more rhetorical in so far as more of the action is conveyed in the characters' speeches, but these are mostly overheard by the audience, as they are in later theatre; even asides are only indirectly addressed to the audience, and they, of course, flourished in nineteenth-century pictorial theatre. On the other hand, while, as the earliest proponents of pictorial theatre emphasized, in that theatre action is conveyed visually rather than verbally, the pictures involved are not, *pace* Diderot, pictures that pretend the audience is absent; there is a highly conscious complicity between a stage presenting a picture and an audience admiring it in what could be quite appropriately called a kind of participation.

Contrast Stanislavsky's dismissal of illusion with a passage in which Percy Fitzgerald condemns the idea that

the closer reality is imitated, the more nearly effect is produced. . . . The scenic artist . . . paints falsely to produce a true effect. The inexperienced goes up to a scene, and is amazed at the coarseness and roughness—the absolute no-shape and no-colour—all streak and daub. Yet the artist has in his own mind a finished picture utterly dissimilar, and sees it as a result all the time.[10]

Fitzgerald's insistence that illusion is always an 'effect', a kind of magical transformation by the audience of 'no-shape and no-colour' into a beautiful picture, might seem old-fashioned, and, indeed, much of his theatrical commentary is nostalgic for an earlier era. This makes his response to an 1880 innovation all the more interesting.

In that year, the Haymarket Theatre was redesigned so that the front of the stage coincided completely with the proscenium arch, and a gilded and moulded frame, like a picture frame, surrounded the proscenium opening. This innovation is discussed by most historians of nineteenth-century British theatre, and seen as emblematic of the character of that theatre. Thus, for Michael Booth: 'The union of stage and painting was publicly and officially consummated when Squire Bancroft had a 2-foot wide picture-frame moulded and gilded right round the proscenium of the Haymarket in 1880, the bottom of the frame corresponding exactly with the front of the stage. Other theatres followed suit.'[11] For many commentators, this is seen as the fulfilment of a tendency to exclude the spectator implicit in pictorial theatre from the beginning (what Allardyce Nicoll, generalizing a phrase of Richard Wagner's, calls the 'mystic gulf').[12]

In his 1881 book *The World behind the Scenes*, Percy Fitzgerald, too, was enthusiastic:

In the New Haymarket, as altered and recently reconstructed by Mr. Phipps, Mr. Bancroft, the manager, has introduced a novel arrangement which favours the view here given. A rich and elaborate gold border, about two feet broad, after the pattern of a picture frame, is continued all round the proscenium, and carried even below the actors' feet. Some singularly pleasing effects flow from this. There can be no doubt the sense of illusion is increased, and for the reason just given; there is no borderland or platform in front; and, stranger still, the whole has the air of a picture projected on a surface. There is a dreamy softened air about the whole that is very pleasing.[13]

The 'view here given' refers to a long polemic against the forestage, clearly still a living part of the theatre in England. Thus, here Fitzgerald seems to be celebrating the transformation of the proscenium opening into a window on to a represented world, in a conception of staging shared with naturalist theatre.

Other passages from the same chapter suggest, however, that Fitzgerald rejects elements of naturalistic scene design. He attacks the box set because the realism of three of its walls draws attention to the absence of the fourth. 'It will be seen that this supposes quite a fallacious theory of the relation of the audience to the scene, and assumes that the fourth side of the room has been conveniently removed to allow them to look in and see what is going on.'[14] And he criticizes the use of cutaway practicable multiple-room sets:

'Jonathan Bradford, or the Murder at the Roadside Inn,' produced at the Surrey in 1833, was one of the earliest of those curious attempts at dividing the stage into various rooms.... The precedent has been followed a good deal since, more particularly in dividing the stage into two rooms. But it would seem that nothing is gained by this device; and, indeed, anything mysterious or effective that is thus presented loses in illusion by the clumsy air of the mechanical arrangement. The more the stage is considered as 'the scene'—a sort of generality, as one would speak of 'the country'—the more will the sense of illusion be carried out. But if we become literal and circumstantial, i.e. present a 'room' with sides and ceiling, the fourth side removed to let us look in, the joining with the outer world becomes too palpable. The true theory should be that we are in the room, which encloses us all; and all action and plot should be arranged on this basis.[15]

In his hostility to box sets, the 'fourth wall', and décors with multiple practicable interiors, Fitzgerald is a supporter of the 'traditional' rather than what Vardac might consider the 'proto-cinematic' theatre. He is, indeed, as noted above, conservative and nostalgic in much of his commentary, disliking particularly the gas lighting that he felt clashed with the painted shadows on the flats. It might seem a mere inconsistency therefore that he should praise the 1880 novelty of the picture-frame stage, and approve the disappearance of the forestage. But the praise is for the same properties for which he preferred the old flats and wings to the box set—the pictorial effect, and an increase in the power of the illusion, with 'illusion' here having a meaning rather distinct from 'real'.

Much of Fitzgerald's criticism of excessive realism is devoted to the inconsistency between real and artificial elements in it—'There must be a consistency in this mysterious stage world, and all must be of a piece'[16]—and it is in the name of just such consistency that he praises the picture-frame stage and denounces the forestage (a criticism that was not new, for Fitzgerald supports it with a quotation from Francesco Algarotti's *Saggio sopra l'opera in musica* of 1763).[17] However, in the construction of an essentially unreal décor capable of summoning an audience's participation in an illusory effect, what a particular spectator finds 'jarring' will depend on his or her taste, and Fitzgerald's is clearly too fastidious to accommodate a melodrama like *Jonathan Bradford*. Within as generically and socially diverse a field as nineteenth-century pictorial drama, the point at which particular spectators' belief in the scenic illusion would break down in response to particular productions of particular plays can be expected to differ. Thus, plays such as *Jonathan Bradford* should not be considered unpictorial (*a fortiori*, not proto-cinematic) simply because Fitzgerald found the multiple-room sets undermined the illusion for him. Multiple-room sets are perfectly compatible with stage pictures, indeed, as we shall see, they do not disappear with the rise of a cinematic ubiquity based on editing. On the other hand, the Bancrofts' picture-frame stage should not be used to align pictorial theatre with a 'realist' as opposed to a 'conventional'

staging. Rather one should look for stage pictures that solicit audience participation in an illusory effect, often with a contradictory mixture of devices.

The Bancrofts' innovation also suggests a cinema screen—many early screens were surrounded on all four sides by a moulding recalling a picture frame. In our examination of staging, we take the analogy between stage and screen picture as our guide rather than the question of realism or the lack of it. In order to understand both theatre and cinema in pictorial terms, that is, to give more than a pejorative connotation to the idea of theatre and cinema as spectacle, as *opsis* in Aristotle's sense, they have to be considered as optical machines. One needs to understand, in concrete detail, the practical and technical aspects of staging—the limitations of the playing area, the use of real depth, and the construction of perspective. Moreover, as we will emphasize in the chapters which follow, while both media could be vehicles for pictorialism, the optical differences between them ensure that pictorial staging in theatre and cinema posed the producers of plays and films with very different problems.

1. *Changeable Scenery, its Origin and Development in the British Theatre* (London: Faber & Faber, 1952), 249.
2. Ibid. 249.
3. See Pierre Sonrel, *Traité de scénographie, évolution du matériel scénique, inventaire et mise en œuvre du matériel scénique actuel, technique de l'établissement des décors, perspective théâtrale, autres scènes en usage* (Paris: O. Lieutier, 1943), 76–8; and Christopher Baugh, *Garrick and Loutherbourg* (Cambridge: Chadwick-Healey in association with the Consortium for Drama and Media in Higher Education, 1990), slide 29: 'The Cavern at Castleton or Peak's Hole, sections of scene model for *The Wonders of Derbyshire*, Drury Lane Theatre January 1779', and the commentary on pp. 74–6.
4. See, for example, Sybil Rosenfeld, *A Short History of Scene Design in Great Britain* (Oxford: Blackwell, 1973), 111–15.
5. Chion 'Quiet Revolution', 71–2; see Ch. 1, pp. 7–8 above.
6. *An Actor Prepares*, trans. Elizabeth Reynolds Hapgood (New York: Theatre Arts, 1936), 173; cit. Denis Bablet, *Esthétique générale du décor du théâtre de 1870 à 1914* (Paris: Éditions du Centre National de la Recherche Scientifique, 1965), 114. The idea became a naturalist truism, expressed more pithily by Frank Napier in *Curtains for Stage Settings: A Practical Guide to Their Use with the Necessary Adjuncts* (London: F. Muller, 1937), 9 (cit. Southern, *Changeable Scenery*, 99), as 'The fundamental purpose of scenery is to help the actor and nothing else.'
7. *An Actor Prepares*, 171.
8. Baugh, *Garrick and Loutherbourg*, 10.
9. Allardyce Nicoll, *The Development of the Theatre, A Study of Theatrical Art from the Beginnings to the Present Day*, 5th rev. edn. (New York: Harcourt Brace Jovanovich, 1966), ch. 7.
10. *Principles of Comedy and Dramatic Effect*, 28–31.
11. Booth, *Victorian Spectacular Theatre*, 11. Compare Rosenfeld, *Scene Design*, 116: 'The logical conclusion of a picture stage was reached by the Haymarket in 1880, when the forestage was abolished and the proscenium surrounded by a gilded frame.' The Bancrofts' innovation had already been discussed by Richard Southern in 'The Picture Frame Proscenium of 1880', *Theatre Notebook*, 5 (Apr. 1951), 59–61. It is also noted by Martin Meisel, *Realizations*, 44.
12. Nicoll, *Development of the Theatre*, 201–2. Wagner took the phrase from a letter of 26 Nov. 1865 from the architect of his projected Munich theatre, Gottfried Semper. See Carlson, *German Stage*, 182.
13. Fitzgerald, *World behind the Scenes*, 20–1.
14. Ibid. 10.
15. Ibid. 37–8. For the set in *Jonathan Bradford* and the playtext of the scene there enacted, see M. St Clare Byrne, 'Early Multiple Settings in England', *Theatre Notebook*, 8 (1954), 81–6; and Peter Winn, 'Multiple Settings on the Early Nineteenth-Century London Stage', *Theatre Notebook*, 35 (1981), 17–24.
16. Fitzgerald, *Principles of Comedy and Dramatic Effect*, 31–2.
17. Francesco Algarotti, *Saggio sopra l'opera in musica* (Livorno: Marco Coltellini, 1763; repr., ed. Annalisa Bini, Lucca: Libreria Musicale Italiana Editrice, 1989), 76: 'The actors should necessarily stand beyond the stage opening, within the scenery, far from the spectator's eye; they too should form part of the sweet illusion which governs everything in stage representations.' Cit. (in a slightly different translation) Fitzgerald, *World behind the Scenes*, 20.

Chapter 8
Pictorial Staging in the Theatre

Pictorial staging can be thought of as a historically restricted theatrical style. Nevertheless, no more than cinematic pictorialism can it be considered independently of the machinery that allowed it to be realized. At the heart of this machinery is the stage in the literal sense. This stage is very different in construction from that in most modern theatres, and, despite important national differences that will be discussed below, remarkably uniform from the late baroque period to the beginning of the twentieth century.[1]

The most basic feature of this stage was its floor. This was almost always made of wood, and sloped gently down from the back wall of the theatre to the footlights at the division between stage and orchestra pit, usually extending a little beyond the proscenium arch in a short forestage that sometimes carried forward the rake. This floor had between two and four stories of substage space beneath it, and was divided in very complex ways by openings running across the stage, perpendicular to the axis of stage and auditorium. Indeed, so few were the axial structural elements of these stages, especially those in the French style, as to constitute a serious structural weakness,

so that they tended to creep forward under their own weight.[2] The basic transverse units were numbered from front to rear and called 'entrances' in England, 'plans' in France; the number varies according to the size of the theatre and the depth of each entrance, but that depth had to be large enough to allow characters and stage furniture to come and go.

In French and most other continental-European stages (see Figures 4.1–4.3, Clément Contant's illustrations of the plan, transverse, and longitudinal sections of a 'French-system' stage containing a closed décor),[3] the plans were divided into two zones, the 'rue', a relatively wide band of the stage, with a floor made up of 'trappes' that could be slid aside to allow characters and three-dimensional furniture or properties to enter from below stage; and between each rue, a number of much narrower 'fausses rues', made up of 'trapillons' or little traps, that could also be slid aside so that a flat piece of scenery could be raised through the slot thus created. The two or three fausses rues between each rue were separated by 'costières', narrow slots running right across the stage. In the first substage storey below, there was a corresponding iron rail on which ran two-wheeled 'chariots' support-

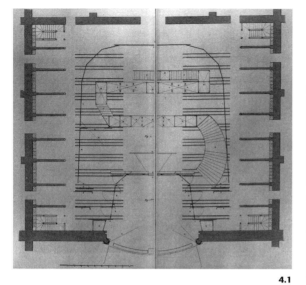

4.1

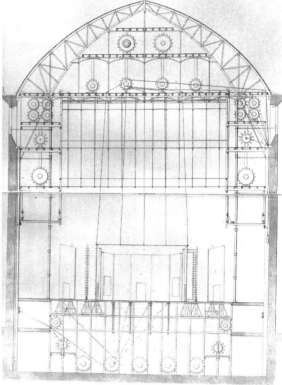

4.3

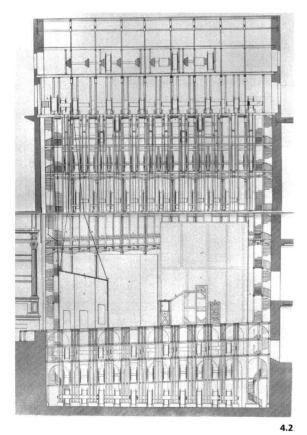

4.2

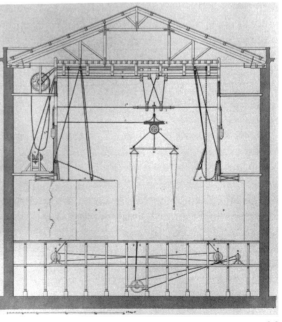

4.4

ing a mast that came up through the slot. '*Châssis*' or wing flats (sometimes hinged or raked) were hung on the masts in two large *chariots* on either side of the stage; smaller pieces of scenery could be hung in the same way on masts in removable small *chariots* between the main *chariots*. The presence of more than one *costière* between each *rue* allowed for wings to be removed and replaced simultaneously in an open-stage scene change, in a well-equipped theatre entirely by machinery, powered essentially by counterweighted pulleys. Beneath the first substage storey the lower storeys housed the windlasses, counterweights, and other machines that moved the stage floor, raised and lowered elements of scenery through it, and moved the chariots from side to side.

English and American stages (see Figure 4.4, Contant's cross-section of an English-system stage) had 'bridges' corresponding to the *trappes* making up the *rues*, and 'sloats', 'slotes', or 'cuts' across the space between the wings, corresponding to the *fausses rues* and accommodating flat scenery such as ground rows. Instead of *costières* for the wing flats, however, they had a system of 'grooves'. Flat battens with a number of raised tongues and hence grooves between them were bolted to the stage floor in the wing area on either side of the stage, usually parallel to the stage front, more rarely slightly obliquely, raked towards the rear centre of the stage (wings in oblique grooves better concealed the off-stage area in the wings from laterally placed audience members, but made the stage less accessible by sight, hearing, and in entering and exiting, and hence hindered the performance; they were also more difficult to paint in effective perspective). Above each bottom groove, a corresponding top groove was bolted to the floor of the first fly corridor above the wing. The bottom grooves could be removed entirely if they were not to be used; the top grooves were hinged and could be folded up if they would obstruct a hanging border or ceiling cloth, or be visible to the audience. Wing flats were slid on from the wings in these grooves (which were lubricated with graphite); the multiple grooves, like the multiple *costières*, allowed simultaneous withdrawal and replacement of different sets of wings, sometimes mechanically (though less commonly than with French stages). In the seventeenth and eighteenth centuries, at least one set of grooves towards the rear of the stage ran right across, and was used for

the two-leafed 'rear shutters', the perspective-painted vista that closed the back of a scene; these rear shutters could be changed, like the wing shutters, and slid apart for a 'discovery' scene. By the end of the eighteenth century, the rear shutters fell into disuse, usually being replaced by a hanging backcloth. Around the same time, the bottom grooves began to be abandoned, the wing flats resting directly on the stage, only their tops held by a groove. By the end of the next century, the top grooves too had fallen into disuse, and flats of all types were supported by weighted props behind them. The term 'grooves' had always also been used to indicate a stage depth ('the first grooves', etc.), and this use survived the disappearance of actual working grooves.

Above both French and English stages was a fly-tower in which scenery painted on cloths was hung, either unfolded, if the tower was high enough, or folded or rolled if there was too little height to contain a whole drop. Above the wings on either side of the stage were several storeys of fly corridors, housing the ropes that controlled the cloths, and catwalks linked the fly corridors, enabling stage-hands to reach snagged lines or cloths over centre stage. The top floor (or floors) ran right across but was more an open grid than a continuous floor. It housed the machinery needed to handle the movement of the cloths and special effects like flying characters and apotheoses.

Scenery thus consisted of back-cloths; 'borders' or *frises* (short cloths representing sky, ceilings or tree-tops, blocking discovery of the fly area); shutters and large flats (*fermes*) raised through sloats or *fausses rues*; 'ground rows' or *terrains*, short flats raised through sloats or *fausses rues*, representing surface features such as ground, water, sloping hillocks, fences, etc.; wing flats, either in grooves or on masts; and set pieces, *ad hoc* constructions of flats, platforms, and other elements resting directly on the stage floor.

As we shall see, hardly any of this complex machinery was adopted by early filmmakers in their studios. However, filmmakers, like pictorialist theatrical producers, saw themselves as presenting to audiences pictures of spaces in a represented world through a more or less fixed frame, and hence many of their problems were analogous to those of their theatrical contemporaries, however different their technical means. Comparisons and contrasts with the cinema will serve as our guide in our examination of the stage as a pictorial machine.

Perhaps the most basic characteristic of the live stage that needs to be thus compared and contrasted with its cinematic equivalent is the scalar fixity of the former. The audience sits in front of a stage on which real actors are deployed within a small range of distances from those spectators, and they remain so for the whole of a performance. Stages and auditoriums differ in size, so the actual distances and ranges will vary from performance to performance, but the basic spatial set-up is constant. It is not hard to imagine ways in which this scalar homogeneity might be differentiated. For example, pantomimes and *féeries* such as *Alice in Wonderland* and the many versions of *Gulliver's Travels* surrounded actors representing people magically shrunken or magnified, or naturally Lilliputian, with sets or costumes representing plants and insects grotesquely magnified. However, even in such exceptional examples, the rule in pictorial theatre was that 'the natural size of the human body should be the unchanging unit of measurement', a rule whose absence in the film version of *Quo Vadis?* was deplored by Felix Salten, as we have seen.[4] Despite this protest (and as the fact that it could be made suggests), early filmmaking was by no means free of scalar constraints, but technically there is nothing to prevent the film picture representing objects at any scale whatsoever. From very early the moving-picture camera was used at a wide variety of distances, and with even a relatively wide range of focal-length lenses, resulting in pictures at a very wide range of scales.

Second, the stage is wide. Again, particular theatres differ considerably in how wide the proscenium opening is, varying from the 20 feet cited by Vardac for the Wagner Opera House in Garrett, Indiana, via the 23 feet of the court theatre at Weimar under Goethe, the 30 feet of the 1792 Royal Theatre in Copenhagen, the 35 feet of Carl Friedrich Schinkel's Neues Schauspielhaus in Berlin (1820) and the Britannia, Hoxton (1858), the 38 feet of the 1812 Drury Lane Theatre, London, the 47 feet of Louis Sullivan and Dankmar Adler's Auditorium Theatre, Chicago (1889), to 53 feet for the Paris Opéra (completed 1875).[5] However, in all these cases, even for the back seats, the stage occupies a considerable part of the spectator's field of view, and allows many people to stand side by side across it. It was possible to narrow the playing area with shutters or curtains (the French had a set of side and top cloths immediately behind the proscenium, the *manteau d'Arlequin*, which could usually be adjusted in this way) and Hubert Herkomer advocated and introduced in his Bushey theatre a mechanically variable proscenium.[6] However, collections of scene designs and, later, stage photographs, show how rare and slight such modification was. Even 'scenes in one' or 'carpenter's scenes', the scenes acted before a backdrop in one of the front grooves while a set scene was changed behind them, usually occupied the full stage width. As a result, every environment in a play tended to be more or less the same size, however this might contradict the dramatic context. Denis Bablet notes the absurdity of this in relation to the décor for Faust's cabinet in the Paris Opéra's production of Gounod's opera in 1892, and that the same objection had been raised by a contemporary critic to the setting for the same scene in the production of 1869.[7] He does not point out that the same remark might be made of Ménessier's décor for Act 2 of Antoine's 1902 production of *La Terre*, a barn interior, which the stage photograph reproduced in his figure 29 shows to be more than 30 feet wide (compare the cramped spaces of all the interior scenes in Antoine's 1918 film from the same novel). The film director Urban Gad remarked how different theatre and film were in this respect:

Cinematic décor is more real than theatrical scene painting, its dimensions are genuine and not obtained by painted perspective—but its greatest advantage over theatrical décor is that it can represent *small* spaces. Everyone knows the theatre's failings in this respect. A play demands a small confined room, the action presupposes it, the dialogue refers to it; and what do we see: a hall, larger in height and breadth than a banqueting room. Why? Because the theatre uses every inch of the auditorium for seats, right up to the roof, from where nothing at all would be visible if the décor were really of low height, because the *manteau d'Arlequin* (usually a flat cloth) would conceal everything happening on the stage. Similarly, spectators at the sides would see nothing if the décor were really as narrow as the prescribed small room requires. The cinema is quite different; the thousands of eyes of the spectators are all pressed to the one tiny peephole of the camera, so one can make one's settings as small and narrow as one wishes.[8]

Moreover, characters tend to be spread across the

great width of the theatrical stage. One reason for this is, as Gad noted, the relative breadth of the auditorium, and the need to provide as good a view of the action on stage (and as good a 'picture', i.e. as effective a composition) as possible to as many members of the audience as possible. A broad shallow grouping of a number of characters in a tableau such as those described in Chapter 3, above, is visible to a wide arc of spectators, and reasonably preserves its significant composition for most of them. Hence the typical promptbook representation of a scene-end tableau, such as the one at the end of act one of *The Whip* (London, 1909):[9]

CROWD grouped around precipice at back
RAYNER
LADY D holding BRANCASTER's head on her knee
BRANCASTER

BEVERLEY	SARTORYS
LADY ANTROBUS	HARRY
LAMBERT	MYRTLE

Furnishings and practicable elements of the set are similarly arranged to facilitate these wide compositions. This is illustrated by the photograph of Act 2 scene 3 of *The Whip*, the Great Hall at Falconhurst, with the banqueting table set for the Hunt Breakfast (see Figure 4.77, below).[10] The set is slightly oblique (the corner opened up to much more than the right angle it is supposed to represent), with the table parallel to its longer wall, i.e. at a very low angle to the front of the stage. Compare the set for the same scene in the 1917 film of *The Whip*, where the table's foot is at the bottom of the stairs, and, in the only overall views of the room we get, is photographed down its length to the stairs in the far rear (see Figure 4.78, below).

Depth is somewhat more complex. Many nineteenth-century stages were quite deep, though the tendency in the design of new theatres was to make them shallower. Pictorial theatre inherited the buildings (or at any rate the sites, as the actual buildings were destroyed by fire fairly regularly) of baroque theatre, and musical theatre in the seventeenth and eighteenth centuries required very deep stages (the stage of the Salle des Machines, built in Paris in 1662, was 141 feet deep).[11] The Comédie at Lyons, built in 1756, was 52 feet deep from the proscenium arch to the rear wall of the stage, with a room beyond that wall that could be opened to give a further 10 feet. The

Britannia, Hoxton (1858), was 60 feet deep. The Opéra's stage was 88 feet deep, with a possible extension of 68 feet. On the other hand, the Weimar court theatre was only 34 feet deep with a 16-foot extension, and the Munich Künstlertheater of 1908 only 31 feet with a 7-foot extension.[12] The baroque theatre used its very deep spaces for 'scenes of relieve': the area beyond the rear shutters (often only half way to the rear wall of the stage), and especially the extensions (in the later theatres usually used as rehearsal rooms or storage spaces behind the stage with large doors linking them to the stage proper for the rare occasions they were brought into play to extend it) were not occupied by actors, singers, or dancers, but by recessions of perspective-painted flats and set scenes representing spectacular vistas.[13] Garnier included an extension in his design for the Paris Opéra which usually served as a rehearsal and warming-up room for ballet dancers but which he conceived might be used for pyrotechnic effects, its remoteness and separability from the stage helping protect the audience from the danger of fire.[14]

However, the uses that could be made of this depth were limited. It is a defining feature of the pictorial tradition that the action should take place in the décor and not in front of it, as had been characteristic of baroque theatre with changeable scenery. But a whole series of pressures tended to drive the action to the front of the stage, and helped to retain small forestages through most of our period.[15]

One of these pressures came from lighting. Whereas most of the stage machinery described by Sonrel in 1943 differed little from that discussed in the corresponding sections of the *Encyclopédie*,[16] his account of stage lighting is entirely devoted to incandescent electrical lighting. Lighting is the area in which stage technology changed most during the nineteenth century. In the eighteenth century, almost all the light on stage came from the house lights, which remained fully lit throughout the performance, supplemented by smaller chandeliers on stage and the row of footlights at the front of the stage. From its beginnings, pictorial staging was associated with changes in lighting, as patent oil lamps (Argand lamps or *quinquets*) replaced wax candles. De Loutherbourg used coloured gauzes as gels for groups of these suspended behind wing flats to produce night and day effects on the front of the flat behind.

Such lights were necessitated, apart from particular spectacular effects, by the fact that the footlights also increased in brightness, and hence without additional light from the wings, shadows of each wing flat would appear on the one behind, hindering the illusion of the three-dimensional features painted on these flat cloths. Thus, although the picture beyond the proscenium became much brighter, it remained dark relative to the forestage, and this continued to be the site of most of the action. Moreover, the new lamps also increased the overall brightness of the auditorium, in turn necessitating brighter footlights and stage lights. Objections to the footlights because of the unnatural direction of their source were common from the beginning of the nineteenth century. Thus Jean Baptiste Pujoulx complained:

The illusion arising from the truthfulness of the scenery is one of the major ways to increase the theatrical illusion; but it is only too true that, despite the talent of our painters and machinists, we are still in the infancy of this art, if, as I believe, the art of providing scenery for a theatre is simply that of transporting on to the stage the various effects of nature. The main error, the one that destroys any kind of truth, arises from the nature of the illumination. Seeing the beam of light that rises from the actor's feet, would one not say that he is lit by the fires of Tartarus? What! In our fields, in houses, the light always comes to us from heaven, yet we are eternally condemned in the theatre to receive it only from hell!

But Pujoulx immediately goes on to point out that to abolish this unnatural effect, house lights would have to be lowered during the performance of the play:

No, this method is nothing but obstinacy, and it is only persisted in because everything is sacrificed to that part of the building in which the spectators serve as spectacle for each other, whereas everything should be sacrificed to illusion on the stage. The intensity of the illumination in our theatrical auditoriums has increased so much that, in order to be able to light the stage proportionately, the number of quinquets has had to be doubled, and yet the décor seems less well lit than it used to be. I believe, and have long argued, that the brilliance of the auditoriums and the clarity necessary for the scenery could be reconciled by adapting to the chandelier a simple machine whereby it could be veiled during the play, casting only a gentle light; this would restore to the stage its necessary clarity; it would of course be unveiled again between the acts.[17]

The introduction of gas lighting at the end of the 1810s in England, a few years later on the continent, made possible a great increase in the amount of light falling on the stage beyond the proscenium arch and the flats and drops forming the picture there. If Pujoulx was right, and it was already possible to dowse an oil-lit chandelier, gas certainly made it much easier to change the level of the house lights to suit the action.[18] It was not until late in the century that it became customary to follow Pujoulx's advice and lower the house lights to very low levels except during intervals. Wagner did this at the opening of the Bayreuth Festspielhaus in 1876, but Irving was still seen as an innovator in England when, at the beginning of the 1880s, he played scenes at the Lyceum with reduced house lights, and lowered them as far as gas lights could be without going out during open-stage scene changes.[19] Nevertheless, it became not uncommon to play night scenes under blue light and with the house lights lowered, creating a pictorial illusion of darkness instead of the traditional mimed one.[20] As a result, it became possible for the action to be visible beyond the proscenium. However, as Fitzgerald noticed, because the individual gas jets were a relatively weak light source, they had to be used in large numbers, constituting large-area and hence very diffuse sources. The effect of such diffuse overall light is visible in the many films of the first fifteen years of moving pictures which employ similarly diffuse light sources (diffused sunlight or mercury-vapour lamps); they yield good figure moulding but no true shadows. Often the effect of the brighter light was to show up the artificiality of the chiaroscuro shadows painted on sets which had been convincing when dimly visible under oil lamps.[21] Limelights and electric arc lamps provided strongly directional sources which did create true shadows, but they could rarely be located at the represented source of the light, and hence inhibited free movement on the stage, in so far as such movement draws attention to the real source.[22] These problems were not solved by the move to incandescent electric light occasionally supplemented by arcs or limes which began at the end of the 1880s, but these lights combined greater flexibility in control and placement with much less encumbrance of the stage floor with piping, helping to free the actors' movement.[23]

Advances in lighting did thus make the depth of

the stage more available as an arena of the action rather than a pictorial background. Other factors continued to pull in the opposite direction. Francesco Algarotti deplored the tendency of opera singers to advance beyond the proscenium, but recognized that one of the reasons they did so was the poor acoustics of the stage.[24] By the end of the eighteenth century, most metropolitan theatres had fly-towers tall enough to hold full scene drops suspended over the stage without folding or rolling, as well as equally deep substages to hold *fermes*. Most of the power of the voice was thus lost unless the singer or speaker stood near the front of the stage, as, in opera, the principal singers still largely do.

More important than this, however, is the problem of the visibility of action deep in the stage. Many of the audience are seated well to the side of the axis of the stage, and also well above it (and some even well below it). Spectators in the upper galleries see rather little of the back wall of a modest box set, let alone an effect 50 feet from the proscenium. Even if such an effect is within their sight lines, any visual composition arranged in depth changes greatly with changes in its angle of view, so the deeper the arrangement of significant figures and scenic elements on the stage, the more different it looked to the spectators in seats remote from the 'centre of vision' to which perspective effects were addressed.

This brings us to perhaps the most decisive feature of pictorial staging that inhibited free movement in the depth of the stage. Even a stage as big as that of the Paris Opéra was often called on to represent spaces larger and deeper than the stage itself. This was achieved by using the techniques of both artificial and natural (or aerial) perspective to give an illusory sense of depth of any magnitude desired. Such techniques work very well, even for spectators who are not at the true centre of the perspective projection, so long as the picture itself is flat, as the painted backdrop is (and the cinema screen—hence its success in this respect). However, painted spaces are not practicable. False perspective was also applied to the real three-dimensional space of the stage, using fairly straightforward adaptations of the standard devices for constructing artificial perspective on flat picture planes. Assuming that the wings represent parallel receding lines—the two sides of a street, or receding bays in a Gothic interior—a real distance is chosen for

the represented infinite horizon, and a horizon height selected. The inner edges of the wing flats should then be on two lines that meet at that horizon line. If the base of a wing is supposed to be level with the one in front of it, but further behind it than it actually is, it also has to be higher. To ensure that the foot of each wing is the correct distance above the horizontal level of the front of the stage, that stage should ascend evenly from its front edge to the horizon, being cut off, however, by the rear wall of the stage, or by suspending the grade before the horizon is reached. Thus the rake of the stage, a structural feature not normally variable from production to production, is (theoretically) established by the rules of *perspectiva artificialis*. As Peter Nicholson put it in his article on 'Scenography' in the *Cyclopaedia, or Universal Dictionary of Arts, Sciences and Literature* (1819):

That part of the stage which lies before the curtain is generally horizontal, but the part which lies beyond the curtain is made to incline upwards. The reason of this is, that if the plane of that part of the stage which lies within the theatre were parallel to the horizon, it could only then appear as any other floor or pavement, and every object placed upon it being of its true size and shape, the whole would only be a geometrical model of what is intended to be represented without reference to the rules [of perspective], as there could be no apparent fore-shortening in this case, but what was the natural effect of direct vision, and thus nothing upon the stage would appear of any larger extent than what that floor or piece of ground might contain, and the whole appearance of the theatre could be no other than that of a room, wherein the real objects were placed in their true dimensions and situations; but the art of constructing a theatre is making it appear of greater extent than it is in reality, and thus giving it a more ample and extended prospect; the stage or ground should be made to appear enlarged, and the distance between one object and another increased; not merely as a picture painted on a flat wall, but as something more real and solid; and thus in a space which is only the size of a room, whole countries, towns, villages, &c. may be exhibited, and the objects may be made to appear as remote as may be conceived in nature.[25]

In very deep baroque stages the rake usually stopped at the rear shutters, the floor of the stage being horizontal thereafter, but invisible to the audience (and of course bare of actors). Andrea Pozzo in his *De perspectiva pictorum et architectorum* of 1693 turns a practical account of scene design on such a stage into an extraordinary baroque conceit. The diagram

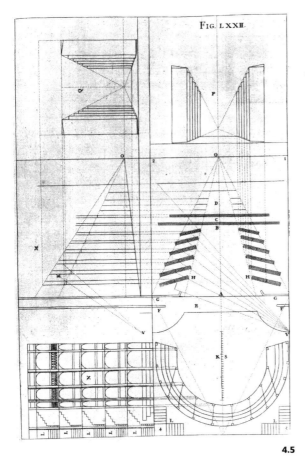

FIG. LXXII.

4.5

result, when the back shutters are opened for scenes of relieve or long scenes, the whole universe can be represented on the stage (in three dimensions, not just as a flat painted vista), and elements of scenery in the back-stage become infinitesimally small and represent infinitely large objects as they approach the rear wall of the theatre.[26]

By the time of Nicholson's *Cyclopaedia* article, scenes of relief in the baroque sense had become obsolete, and the back shutters had lost their 'discovery' function, indeed, were usually replaced by a rolled or flown backcloth, so Pozzo's rear stage seemed simply a waste of space:

But as it is not necessary that the place of the eye should be confined to the extremity of the house, but be nearer to the centre of that part which is allotted to the spectators, so that the inconveniency necessarily arising from different situations out of the true point of sight may be more equally distributed among the company, and the effect of the scenery be generally exhibited to more advantage; so neither is it necessary that the centre of contraction should fall exactly on the opposite wall, but rather at a distance beyond it, to prevent the too quick decrease of the back scenes; whereby a considerable part of the depth of the theatre might be rendered useless: it being evident, that the nearer the centre of contraction is to the curtain, the quicker is the decrease of the back scenes, which become so small, that the theatre behind them is of no farther use for the scenery.

In conformity with this conception, it became the norm to use a rake that implied a horizon line beyond the rear wall and to carry the rake to that wall, abolishing the rear shutters.[27]

A rake was nearly universal in nineteenth-century stages. All the theatres illustrated in Clément Contant's *Parallèle des principaux théâtres modernes de l'Europe* of 1860 have one. The theatre architect Edwin O. Sachs, writing in 1898 in the third volume of his *Modern Opera Houses and Theatres*, notes that 'all our [i.e. English] stage floors, with one exception, are laid to the same "rake", namely with a fall of one half inch to every foot from back to front,[28] and it is strange how accustomed actors and dancers become to this sloping floor, and how "all at sea" they are if, by any chance, they have to perform upon a level platform'.

Sachs goes on to note that 'horizontal stages have been introduced in other countries, and recently by Herbert Beerbohm Tree in "Her Majesty's" Theatre, London'.[29] Nevertheless, only two European theatres

illustrating the basic perspective plan of a theatre (Figure 4.5) shows a room divided exactly into two squares by the proscenium arch, with a semicircle of galleries of seating in one half and a stage in the other. The stage is divided half-way up by the grooves for the rear shutters, which point he calls the 'poscene' (*proscenium* or *postscænium*, i.e. the rear stage, or rather the area behind the *scænium* or façade of the stage house). Between the poscene and the proscenium arch are six pairs of oblique wing grooves; beyond the poscene are four further pairs of grooves parallel to the stage front. The constructed horizon is placed precisely at the back wall of the stage, where the lines joining the ends of the grooves on either side meet (what Nicholson called the 'centre of contraction'), while the 'centre of vision', the viewing-point from which the stage so constructed presents perfectly a window on to the represented world, is symmetrical to it at the rear wall of the auditorium. As a illustrated in the three volumes of his book have flat stages, the Munich Opernhaus and the Raimund Theater, Vienna.[30] In 1900, Sachs himself replaced the stage of the Covent Garden Theatre in London with a horizontal one, and one of the most influential early twentieth-century German theatres, the Munich Künstlertheater, designed by Max Littmann and opened in 1908, had a horizontal stage.[31] Later in the century the flat stage became the rule. In 1939, Richard Southern states categorically that 'a stage floor should be flat. Stage rake is a tradition connected with perspective scenery.' After dismissing various purported advantages of the raked stage (all unlinked to the rules of perspective), and enlisting the support of a German authority, he notes the difficulties box sets present on a raked stage—'The side flats of all chamber sets must be shaped at the bottom to suit the rake, hence those built for one side of the stage will not suit the other, nor can they be used at the back of the set'—and that 'on a raked stage scene handling by means of trucks is far more difficult'.[32] Although many modern stages allow tilting of various parts of the stage floor, and can thus create a rake if one is desired, in practice the basic rule now is that a stage is flat.[33]

While commentators at the beginning of the nineteenth century, not only Peter Nicholson, but also Johannes Jelgerhuis,[34] clearly linked the stage rake to the problem of theatrical perspective, as did the theatre historian Southern after its demise, there seems to have been much less awareness of this connection as the turn of the century approached. Charles Garnier discusses the architectural problems of the stage and the problems of stage perspective in his *Le Théâtre* of 1871, but nowhere mentions the rake, although the stage of the Paris Opéra, which was being built to his design as the book was written, has a rake of 5 centimetres per metre.[35] Sachs believed the function of the stage rake was simply to make the actors visible from the pit: 'The slope of the stage is . . . by no means a necessity. . . . It is only a question of arranging the "sighting lines" of the auditorium to enable the occupants of the area to see the actor as he retires "up" the stage'.[36] In the same vein, when discussing the flat stage of Her Majesty's Theatre in 1897, a correspondent for *The Builder* attributes the general prevalence of the rake to 'the height of the "float" of the footlights, which was liable to hide the feet of the performers', and even claims that 'the perspective ef-

fect of a rising stage is always unfortunate'.[37] The last remark might just be the result of an architectural journalist who is not a theatre specialist getting the wrong end of the stick. It might also be a reference to the growing problem of the treatment of simple box sets on an inclined stage, discussed in more detail below. At any rate, it seems clear that, well before the rake began to be abandoned in new theatres and when stages were rebuilt in old ones, its original purpose had faded from many theatrical practitioners' awareness.[38]

Pozzo's 1693 plan is, of course, concerned with the standard baroque setting with symmetrical wings and a backcloth. As we noted above, at the beginning of the pictorialist period, such simple axial stage plans tend to be replaced with more asymmetrical ones, with more varied buildings set at various angles to the stage axis. Such settings are much more spatially vague, to some extent relaxing the problem of their precise perspective recession, and hence demanding a much less strict correspondence between the rake and the perspectival construction of the stage picture. Similarly, the use of multiple ground rows and 'dioramatic' vistas through holes in cut cloths or *fermes* largely concealed the stage floor, and thus made its precise rake much less critical. Natural or aerial rather than artificial perspective—a succession of planes lighter in colour and more brightly lit from front to rear—became the key to the illusory representation of great depth on a relatively shallow stage. Hence, presumably, the amnesia about the original function of the rake.

One of the problems of the raked stage, however, was that it was an architectural feature of the theatre, and, until the development of hydraulically supported stages late in the nineteenth century, could not easily be varied from scene to scene or even from production to production. As Emanaud puts it, 'the slope of the stage floor is given *a priori*'.[39] It is noteworthy that none of the guides to stage perspective that we have consulted offers a derivation of the appropriate rake from perspective principles; they all simply state that 'the stage rake in most theatres is such and such' (although, as we have seen, the figures they give for 'such and such' can differ considerably). With a fixed stage rake, the only way to retain correct perspectival proportions and yet vary the distance of the constructed horizon behind the front of the stage is to raise or lower the horizon line (since a higher line will meet the raked stage or its virtual product further back, and vice versa). Nicholson suggests this as an appropriate procedure, but for others, e.g. Jelgerhuis, the level of the horizon is determined by the eye level of a 'best seat', either an actual preferred seat, or a position such that the maximum number of seats will be close to the centre of vision. Under this construction, the rake of the stage functions as a kind of magnifying glass, establishing a fixed relationship between the true and apparent size of any perspectively precise décor.

This is not a serious problem with settings represented as large, but it becomes so as soon as one wants to represent one as small. As we have suggested, in exterior settings, and even in romantic interiors like grottoes or ruins, the mathematical precision of artificial perspective can be displaced by the vaguer system of natural perspective. Even architectural elements were traditionally fudged by, for example, treating perspective below the horizon line orthogonally, i.e. representing supposedly receding parallel horizontal lines below eye level on frontal flats as parallel to the horizon, and concealing the feet of the flats with furniture and ground rows.[40] Simple contemporary room sets, however, can be cheated in such ways much less easily. With them, the disadvantage of the raked stage is not simply Southern's one that the necessarily raked bottom of oblique flats makes them usable in only a single position, but also that right angles have to be opened up to make the back wall appear to recede further, so either the room is excessively confined for the actors, or it appears very large to the spectators.

Closed décors, with highly oblique side flats rather than the traditional receding array of frontal or only slightly oblique wings, and ceiling cloths rather than borders, began to appear in France and perhaps in England at the end of the eighteenth century.[41] They were treated in perspective like everything else on the stage, and when the side flats were hung on masts in chariots in the costières, as on a French stage, the machinery to handle them differed little from that for any other kind of setting. In England, as the side flats could not be held in the grooves, they were necessarily set scenes, and were more difficult to change, so they contribute, along with the practicable set pieces of the sensation scene, to the increasing elaboration

and length of scene changes. However, it is clear from the growing attention to the constructions for perspective projection on to oblique flats in the later nineteenth-century treatments of stage perspective, that they were also increasingly a design problem. In effect, the raked stage makes it impossible simply to reconstruct a real space on the stage (unless one can somehow demonstrably incorporate the rake into the space, i.e. represent the stage floor as sloping, which with such low-angle slopes is obviously very difficult). It is thus radically incompatible with the Stanislavskian conception of décor as essentially for the actors. There is a connection between the abandonment of the raked stage in the twentieth century and the importance of box sets to quasi-realistic early twentieth-century décor.

Algarotti noted one of the problems of the perspective stage. Entrances and exits must be made near the front (he assumes that all the action will take place there), or else the contrast between the diminutive size of the supposedly distant doorway and the actual size of the actor becomes too glaring:

Characters are seen only too often coming from the rear of the stage, because that is where the entrance to the scene is usually placed; and everyone must have noticed the awkwardness of this and the offence it presents to the eye. The apparent size of an object depends on the size of its image combined with the judgment we make as to how distant it is. Thus, given an image of the same size, the object will be seen as bigger the further away it is judged to be. Hence characters who approach from the back of the stage seem to be towering giants; the perspective, and the artificiality of the scene causing them to be judged to be much further away. And these giants diminish and become dwarfs as they come forward, closer to the eye. The same is true of supernumeraries, who one would rather not see so far back that their shoulders or even their waists are the same height as the capitals of the columns; the result is to destroy the scenic illusion.[42]

As the reference to the capitals of columns indicates, Algarotti is talking about what might be called the artificial perspective stage. When quoting this passage, Fitzgerald remarks, 'This perspective fashion, that of lines of columns, trees, and houses, etc., diminishing to a central point, led to the destruction of illusion,'[43] implying, uncommonly for him, that the modern theatre had surpassed this problem. But it is still basically applicable to the stage of natural perspective. Garnier noted:

Thus, in distance effects, great care is taken never to allow the actors to go further upstage than a certain distance from the backcloth, and they are made to restrict themselves to the fore parts of the stage, where the sets still have more or less the real dimensions of the objects represented, and in every case, even in a big theatre where there is no lack of space, soloists and crowds hardly ever go more than fifty feet from the proscenium opening.[44]

There were certain ways to extend the action into the depth of the stage, thus avoiding the tendency for the picture to become a mere background. Jules de la Gournerie stated that 'the shortest extras or even children can be made to occupy the back rows',[45] and, as we have seen in Part 2, the stage directions for Charles Hermann's 1853 London version of *Uncle Tom's Cabin* suggest that when Eliza Harris crosses the half-frozen Ohio River, she should be carried off on a moving ice floe, and then a child representing her should reappear in the rear at the other bank, to be rescued by another child representing Phineas Fletcher. According to Denis Bablet, the executioners in one scene in the 1835 première of Meyerbeer's *La Juive* were played by children for the same reason.[46] Georges Moynet describes a production of *Die Walküre* at the Paris Opéra in the early 1890s in which the Valkyries were seen riding through a distant cloudscape in the sky, disappearing off left, then entering left on foot on the practicable rocks nearer the front of the stage. The distant figures were papier mâché horses mounted by children rolling down an incline between two cloud flats (see Figures 4.6–4.8).[47] Dummies or models alone were also used, if the motion could be allowed to be so stereotyped as to be performed by an automaton. The same technique was much more frequently employed with vehicles such as carriages, automobiles, and railway trains, which appear first in the rear as miniature models, exit, and then re-enter the same side of the stage full-size and containing practicable compartments with live actors in them. In all these cases, the exit and entrance is required, since the miniatures have to stay in the same plane, as do the full-size figures further forward; hence all the movement is lateral.

Indeed, as Algarotti and most other people who discuss the problem remark, the scalar discrepancies of perspective stages are aggravated by movement in depth. As long as characters remain in the same plane, unless there is some immediate and grotesque standard of comparison, like Algarotti's columns, these discrepancies will not be anything like so visible as if they move from the rear to the front or vice versa. The avoidance of an open central stage floor leading from the front of the stage to the backdrop, blocking it with set scenery, ground rows, and cut cloths, a precondition of the natural-perspective system, also made it difficult for actors to move up the stage without zigzagging obliquely across it or exiting and re-entering. Much movement on nineteenth-century pictorial stages must have resembled the toy theatres of the epoch, in which a figure that has been pushed on at the Right Upper Entrance on the end of a stick or wire must perforce re-exit RUE before it can re-enter R1E. This establishes the action on stage as a series of planar arenas entered laterally rather than a single space in which characters can move freely backwards and forwards. Thus, the prevalence of false perspective, whether this was predominantly artificial or natural, further inhibited movement in depth, so that the principal actors spent most of their on-stage time at the front of the stage, with crowds of extras essentially lined up behind them.

That pictorial staging should involve these questions of both two-dimensional and three-dimensional space is obvious; perhaps less so are the temporal aspects of such staging. The 'tableau' in Pougin's sense of 'certain material divisions in works which are complicated in their staging', and defined by a 'change in the setting' is a relatively long-lasting picture. At the other extreme, 'tableau' in his final sense, the stage picture discussed at length in Part 2 of this book, is much more brief. Even in the sense of 'picture' that this chapter has been concerned with, the picture as the décor in general, temporal characteristics shorter than the whole material division of a scene occupying a single setting are important.

First, even where the picture does not change during the scene, the points at which it is most significant and where most attention is drawn to it will vary. The commonest such point is the beginning of the scene. We referred earlier to the stage direction in the 1890 play *Men and Women* calling for the timing of the rise of the curtain on the third act by a clock striking midnight: 'At the eighth stroke the curtain is raised, being timed so as to reveal the whole stage picture on the twelfth stroke.'[48] In Donizetti's opera *Lucia di Lammermoor* (1835), there is a long purely

4.6

4.7

orchestral passage at the beginning of Act 1, scene 2, in which the music paints a picture of the fountain in the castle garden by moonlight, which the spectators can also admire on the stage (the Tams-Witmark prompt script in the Mills Music Library of the University of Wisconsin-Madison shows a setting consisting of foliage wings and borders, steps to a terrace in front of a 'fancy garden drop' at the rear, and steps to the castle stage left, with a practicable fountain with a light in it stage right), before the characters enter and the action-advancing singing begins. The sort of inconsistencies complained of by Algarotti and Fitzgerald often arose because of switches of attention of this kind—a wholly consistent picture would give way, say, to the entrance of an out-of-scale character at an upstage doorway, but most members of the audience were now preoccupied with the advance of the plot and did not find the inconsistency illusion-shattering.

As well as pictures constituted by an empty stage with a spectacular décor, there were also many occasions when crowd scenes constituted pictures. The cotton-picking scenes in *Uncle Tom's Cabin*, discussed in Part 2, evolved into full-scale dance scenes, recalling the role of the ballet in grand opera and *féerie*; these can also be considered as populated pictures. The same pictorial function is performed by the processions so popular in spectacular historical drama.

Such processions had a tendency to grow in scale in order to increase the spectacle as far as resources would allow, with the result that large-scale productions multiplied retinues to fill the stage and arrayed them in more and more glorious costume, often with little attention to narrative motivation. In Shakespeare's *Richard III*, to the stage direction 'Enter the corse of Henry the Sixth with Halberds to guard it, Lady Anne being the mourner, attended by Tressel, Berkeley and other gentlemen' (Act 1, scene 2), Edward Capell in 1768 added 'slenderly attended', as this is a hole-and-corner funeral. Yet Charles Kean's 1857 production at the Princess Theatre had a 'procession of monks with torches, priests with a golden cross, 59 bannermen and so on.'[49] Pierre Victor complained in 1827 about the multiplication of retinues in Comédie Française productions: 'Does this Mr Taylor claim the honour of having introduced extras from the Opéra to the Théâtre-Français and having had the idea of furnishing every new play with a suite of pages?'[50] Although the crowd scenes of the Meininger, the Duke of Saxe-Meiningen's theatrical company under the direction of Ludwig Chronegk, which toured German and then European cities between 1874 and 1890, presaged something new and had an enormous influence on naturalist theatre, they can also be seen as part of this tradition of the spectacular procession scene, and complaints about their distracting character echo similar complaints about Charles Kean's 'excesses'.[51]

Pictorial effects also crucially involved transformations of the stage picture. These, of course, varied very greatly in type. The most basic is the scene change itself. Richard Southern has given a history of the curtain, which can be summarized as follows.[52] From the beginnings of the enclosed theatre with changeable scenery, a front curtain was raised and lowered (or moved sideways across the stage) at the beginning and end of the performance, but originally all other scene changes were performed on the open stage. Towards the end of the eighteenth century, the longest units of a play, the acts, were separated by lowering a cloth for the duration of the interval, the so-called 'act drop', usually a flat cloth with an elaborately painted scene or allegory hung in the first grooves. Other changes continued to be made in full view of the audiences. As the nineteenth century progressed, and the time needed for each scene change increased,

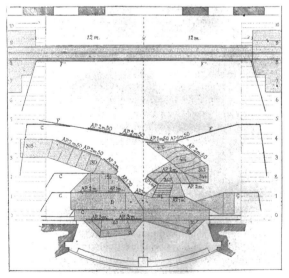

4.8

157

lights were lowered, sometimes to near darkness, to conceal the inter-scene on-stage activity, and soon the act drop was used for scene changes throughout. Finally, by the end of the century (when fire regulations also began to require the lowering of a safety curtain at some point in the performance), the modern practice of using the main curtains for act and often scene changes came into use.

With a décor consisting of wings, shutters, and drops, major scene changes could be carried out on an open stage with great speed, liveried stage servants rapidly removing and replacing the few pieces of practicable furniture needed for the scene, while other hands slid off the old wing flats and shutters and replaced them by new ones, and new drops were lowered in front of old ones. Better equipped theatres could carry out the whole process mechanically, a system of pulleys, winches, and counterweights enabling a single hand to move many flats simultaneously in their grooves or *costières*. Nostalgic nineteenth-century accounts are full of memories of the stage manager's whistle which signalled these near miraculous transformations of the scene. With growing numbers of increasingly elaborate set scenes, involving three-dimensional practical structures built on the stage floor rather than in grooves or *costières*, scene-to-scene intervals became longer and longer, despite the interpolation of simplified carpenter's scenes to enable the dismantling and setting-up of these sets to proceed while the play continued downstage of them. The length of the waits, and the interference caused by the noise of the scene setters during the inevitably dialogue-heavy carpenter's scenes, were standard targets of theatrical reformers by the end of the century. These problems led to a variety of experiments with mechanical means of reducing delays, like Steele McKay's elevator stage at the Madison Square Garden Theatre, New York, in 1879 (in which whole décors could be set up above the stage and lowered into position on it, whereupon the previous scene's would be dismantled below the stage), and the adoption from *kabuki* of the revolving stage at the Munich Residenztheater in 1897.[53]

Despite the more frequent use of the curtain, scene changes did not lose their importance for the pictorial tradition. They provided opportunities for the kind of opening tableaux discussed above, and the scene-end tableaux examined in Part 2, and rapid transformations of the stage picture remained a crucial part of spectacular and sensational drama.

One theatrical genre is almost defined by the persistence of the open-stage scene change, with the change in décor sometimes representing a change in place or time as in the standard scene change, more commonly with it standing for a magical transformation of the situation. This genre is that of the *féerie* or pantomime. Changes by simultaneously sliding off and on old and new wings and shutters in grooves or *costières* were accompanied by raising *fermes* from below the stage and lowering drops and the deployment of three-dimensional and practicable machines such as the '*grand bâti pour une apothéose avec parallèles*' illustrated in J. Moynet's *L'Envers du théâtre* and described by Booth,[54] as well as specialized devices designed for a particular effect in a particular production.[55] Scrims and transparently painted flats could also play a big part, changes in levels of lighting on either side radically altering their relative opacity, as in a diorama.

Such effects were not limited to this genre, however. Although the sensation scene in nineteenth-century drama is linked to the plot as the depiction of a particular sort of situation, it is also characterized by specialized staging that often corresponded very closely with the magical transformations of the *féerie*. This is true of those transformations which represented visions, such as that of the death of one of the *Corsican Brothers* in a duel, first seen in Act 1, then, from the other point of view, in Act 2, or the scene of Mathias's memory of the murder of the Polish Jew in *The Bells*, and the dreamt trial at the end of the same play.[56] It is also true of objective sensational events, the volcanic eruptions in *La Muette de Portici* (Paris Opéra, 1828, décor by Cicéri), *Masaniello*, and *The Last Days of Pompeii*, the escape from prison in Dion Boucicault's *Arrah-na-Pogue* (1864), the fire scene at the end of his *The Poor of New York* (1857), the marine collision of *The Price of Peace* (Drury Lane Theatre, 1900), the train crash of *The Whip* and so on.[57] In every case, an elaborate stage picture is rapidly transformed on an open stage, using a variety of scene-change devices: transparent décors for vision scenes, or a sink and rise, especially before the introduction of powerful arc lights which made it possible to achieve similar effects with transparent paint and light alone; a sink and rise extended into a wall 'panoraming' vertically for the prison escape in *Arrah-na-Pogue*; combinations of transparent décor, lighting, and burning lycopodium for fire scenes and volcanic eruptions; panoramas and treadmills for race scenes and the moving train of *The Whip*; finally the construction of elaborate practicable sets that could be moved as a whole—the deck of a yacht rocking in a storm before sinking, as in *The Price of Peace*, crashing automobiles and locomotives, as in *The Whip*. In all these cases, the effectiveness of the illusion is enhanced, even induced, by the intensity of the dramatic situation. Inversely, this also heightens the disappointment if the illusion should fail—hence the extremely contradictory reports of the success of these scenes in contemporary criticism, as noted by Vardac and others.

Rapid transformations were also deployed where the sensation was the product of a strong situation rather than the representation of a large-scale event. In *Alias Jimmy Valentine*, the play that Paul Armstrong adapted from O. Henry's short story 'A Retrieved Reformation', Act 3 ends with the eponymous hero having reformed and assumed the identity of Lee Randall, a respectable bank employee. He has just outbluffed his nemesis, the police detective Doyle, and persuaded him that he is not the notorious safecracker Valentine with the miraculous ability to open a safe by feeling the tumblers turning. As Doyle leaves, Valentine's former criminal associate Red Joclyn, now a watchman in the bank, rushes in calling 'Jimmy', to tell him that the owner's daughter Kitty is locked in the new bank vault, to which no one but her absent father knows the combination. Act 4 is set in the vault with the safe rear centre; Jimmy uses his skill to open the safe and rescue Kitty, watched not only by Doyle, but by his fiancée, Rose, from whom he has always concealed his criminal past. The set for Act 3 is a corner set of Jimmy's office; the scene transition is a brief curtain or possibly blackout (less than a minute according to playbills), during which the two walls of the set and Jimmy's desk and chairs are removed, and the lights and/or curtain go up to reveal the barred windows of a basement and the safe rear centre. The rapidity of the transition contributed to the high tension of the situation; as a reviewer put it: 'One of the tensest situations imaginable is produced when the scene magically changes to the cellar of the bank, and Randall accompanied by the bank watchman is seen in a state of feverish excitement

working in the semi-gloom to open the combination by the phenomenal sense of feeling with which nature has endowed him. From an open door the sleuth is seen watching the efforts of his prey, while in another door, contemplating the scene, stands Rose.'[58]

Sensation scenes were a speciality of melodrama. Even *Alias Jimmy Valentine* was treated by contemporary reviewers as a high-class melodrama.[59] However, equivalents, involving pictorial effects which changed over time rather than in an instant, existed in more respectable forms of theatre. An example is the slow changes of lighting that were a feature of David Belasco's productions throughout his career, and often written into the plays he wrote for other producers before becoming a director himself. These changes are usually motivated as 'astronomic' or 'meteorological' effects: sunrise or sunset effects in *The Girl I Left behind Me* (New York, 1893), *Madame Butterfly* (New York, 1900), and *The Girl of the Golden West* (New York, 1906); the moon appearing from behind clouds in *Men and Women* (New York, 1890); an eclipse of the sun in *The Wife* (New York, 1887). This kind of change was not invented by Belasco, of course. In 1875, Frederick Lloyds gave detailed descriptions of ways to create such effects using relatively simple lights and elaborately painted drops and transparent cloths.[60] In his own productions at the Belasco Theatre, however, Belasco achieved them by the use of incandescent electric lights of various colours on dimmers controlled centrally so that sets of lights could be coupled to dimmer shafts and raised and lowered simultaneously, or one colour raised and another lowered with a single rotation of the shaft. These effects, too, are linked to situations: the dawn in *The Girl I Left behind Me* is expected to bring the final, fatal Indian attack on the beleaguered fort, but in fact brings the rescuing cavalry; that in *Madame Butterfly* will end with the return of the married Pinkerton to the unsuspecting Cho Cho San to reclaim his son.[61]

Nineteenth-century staging is thus characterized by a stage picture of a relatively fixed and large size, with often great perspective-rendered depth. These perspective effects enforced a planar organization of the space, with little movement in depth and action distributed across the stage; the demand for visibility of the action to a widely distributed audience, and for a large proportion of the audience to see a relatively similar pictorial composition, drove the principal action to the front of the stage, as did problems of audibility. Despite the gradual suppression of the open-stage scene change during the nineteenth century, transformation effects remained a crucial element of pictorial staging in both comic and serious genres, and both popular and respectable theatre, but these transformations were tied to situational high points rather than to a simple change of place.

As we have often noted in passing, the optical properties of the cinema are very different, and create a very different kind of 'stage' for cinematic performance. Before examining the extension of the pictorial tradition to the cinema, we need to understand the nature of this cinematic stage.

1. For more detailed accounts and bibliography, see Southern, *Changeable Scenery*, and Sonrel, *Traité*.

2. See Georges Moynet, *La Machinerie théâtrale: trucs et décors* (Paris: Librairie Illustrée, n.d. [1893]), 20–1.

3. Clément Contant and Joseph de Filippi, *Parallèle des principaux théâtres modernes de l'Europe et des machines théâtrales françaises, allemandes et anglaises*, rev. edn. (Paris: Lévy, 1860 (first published 1842); repr. New York: Benjamin Blom, 1968).

4. Salten, 'Zu einem Kinodramen, Anmerkungen', 365.

5. See, for the Wagner Opera House, Garrett, Indiana, Julius Cahn, *Official Theatrical Guide* (New York: Publication Office, Empire Theatre), vol. i (1896–7), 275, cit. Vardac, *Stage to Screen*, 4–5; for the Weimar Hoftheater, Alexander Weichberger, *Goethe und das Komödienhaus in Weimar, 1779–1825: Ein Beitrag zur Theaterbaugeschichte, Theatergeschichtliche Forschungen*, established by Berthold Litzman, ed. Julius Petersen, no. 39 (Leipzig: Leopold Voss, 1928), 48 (Carlson, *German Stage*, 14, gives a width of 30 feet); for the Royal Theatre, Copenhagen, Contant and de Filippi, *Parallèle*, plate 76; for the Neues Schauspielhaus, Berlin, Contant and de Filippi, ibid., plate 46; for the Britannia, Hoxton, *The Builder*, 25 Sept. 1858, cit. Jim Davis (ed.), *The Britannia Diaries, 1863–1875: Selections from the Diaries of Frederick C. Wilton* (London: Society for Theatre Research, 1992), 14; for the Drury Lane Theatre, Contant and de Filippi, *Parallèle*, plate 38, and an original plan of Benjamin Wyatt's remodelled Drury Lane in the Victoria & Albert Museum, reproduced in Nicoll, *Development of the Theatre*, figure 202; for the Auditorium, Chicago, Dankmar Adler, 'The Chicago Auditorium', *Architectural Record*, 1, no. 4 (Apr.–June 1892), 415–34, repr. in William C. Young (ed.), *Famous American Playhouses 1716-1899: Documents of American Theatre History*, vol. i (Chicago: American Library Association, 1973), 298; for the Opéra, Paris, Charles Garnier, *Le Théâtre* (Paris: Hachette, 1871), 470, and Edwin O. Sachs and Ernest A. Woodrow, *Modern Opera Houses and Theatres*, 3 volumes (London: Batsford, 1896, 1897, and 1898; repr. New York: Benjamin Blom, 1968), vol. iii, suppl. 1: 'Stage Construction', 23.

6. For the *manteau d'Arlequin*, see Sonrel, *Traité*, 128 and Sachs and Woodrow, *Modern Opera Houses*, suppl. 1, p. 7, where Herkomer's proscenium is also discussed and illustrated. Rosenfeld, *Scene Design*, 143–4, also mentions Herkomer's innovation: 'He proposed a mobile proscenium so that the opening could be made large or small as occasion demanded, but this had already been done by means of sliding panels in the Drury Lane of 1842.'

7. Bablet, *Esthétique générale*, 27–8 and figure 5 (the 1892 décor by Philippe Chaperon). Of the 1869 one, by J.-B. Lavastre and

Édouard, Désiré and Joseph Despléchin, Paul de Saint-Victor wrote: 'The large size of the opening (*cadre*) is the thing that most harms the effect of the first scene. Who would recognize Faust's mysterious cell in this warehouse full of retorts, alembics and flasks, reminding one of the Physics Hall in the Exposition?' (cit. Charles Reynaud, *Musée rétrospectif de la classe 18, Théâtre, à l'Exposition Universelle Internationale de 1900 à Paris*, report of the committee of installation (Saint-Cloud: Belin Frères, 1903), 123, with an illustration of the setting on p. 124.

8. Urban Gad, *Filmen, dens midler og maal* (Copenhagen: Gyldendalske Boghandel/Nordisk Forlag, 1919), 122.

9. We are indebted to David Mayer for generously giving us a collated version of the script of *The Whip* including this tableau, which is not in the Lord Chamberlain's copy.

10. See also figure 7 in Booth, *Victorian Spectacular Theatre*.

11. Nicoll, *Development of the Theatre*, 180 and figure 206.

12. For the Lyons Comédie, see Sonrel, *Traité*, 95–6, and plate 34; for the Britannia, Hoxton, Jim Davis (ed.), *Britannia Diaries*, p. 14; for the Paris Opéra, Garnier, *Le Théâtre*, 470, and Sachs and Woodrow, *Modern Opera Houses*, iii, suppl. 1, p. 23; for the Weimar Hoftheater, Weichberger, *Goethe*, 48; for the Munich Künstlertheater, Sonrel, *Traité*, 101 and plate 39.

13. See Southern, *Changeable Scenery*, 57–81.

14. Sonrel, *Traité*, 97 and 129 n. 1.

15. Allardyce Nicoll's statement (*Development of the Theatre*, 159) that the forestage 'finally departed during the Victorian era' should not be taken to imply that it was moribund long before the end of the century. Marvin Carlson, in 'Hernani's Revolt from the Tradition of French Stage Composition', *Theatre Survey*, 13, no. 1 (May 1972), 1–27, and 'French Stage Composition from Hugo to Zola', argues on the basis of an extensive study of *livrets de mise-en-scène* (semi-published or archived accounts of the staging and blocking of plays rather than the hand-annotated stage manager's promptbooks familiar in the study of English and American theatre), that, between 1830 and 1880, there was a steady evolution from stagings dominated by lining up principal characters across front centre to a free deployment of all the depth of the stage. We have already indicated our scepticism of such evolutionism, and believe that (apart from a few passing remarks about lighting) Carlson ignores the pressures that continued to drive the action to the front of the stage throughout the nineteenth century. In particular, his reconstructed plans of sets take no account of the perspectival stage, and thus exaggerate the depth; compare them with Sonrel's extraordinarily shallow plans, which do.

16. The plates in the *Encyclopédie* are most easily available in Denis

Diderot and Jean le Rond d'Alembert (ed.), *Theatre Architecture and Stage Machines: Engravings from the Encyclopédie, ou dictionnaire raisonné des sciences, des arts et des métiers* (New York: Benjamin Blom, 1969).

17. Jean Baptiste Pujoulx, *Paris à la fin du XVIIIᵉ siècle, ou esquisse historique et morale des monumens et des ruines de cette capitale; de l'état des sciences, des arts et de l'industrie à cette époque, ainsi que des mœurs et des ridicules de ses habitans* (Paris: Brigite Mathé, 1801), 128–9 and note.

18. For the introduction of gas, limelight, and electric arc lighting in Britain, see Terence Rees, *Theatre Lighting in the Age of Gas* (London: Society for Theatre Research, 1978).

19. Booth, *Victorian Spectacular Theatre*, 96.

20. On baroque stages, the audience knew it was night from the narrative context and because the actors carried lanterns and felt their way round the stage. Such mime is as illusionistic (and as conventional) as the use of blue light (or silent film's use of blue tinting or toning) for the same purpose.

21. Fitzgerald, *Principles of Comedy and Dramatic Effect*, 30.

22. Id., *World behind the Scenes*, 16.

23. The incandescent lights installed in theatres during the nineteenth century had individual bulbs with a maximum of 16 candle-power, so they still had to be used in groups and thus constituted a diffuse source much like the gas lights they replaced; indeed, the basic light housings remained essentially the same. Georges Moynet regarded directional light as more or less inappropriate to the stage: 'Light falling parallel to one direction is impossible in the theatre, because the wings would cast shadows on each other, producing an extraordinary cacophony. . . . Light must come from all sides, so that shadows cancel each other out. This produces some rather odd effects. For example, a projecting pillar in an architectural décor is seen to cast a strong shadow on the wall it decorates. An actor comes and leans against this pillar, so common sense would suggest that his outline should be added to the shadow of the pillar, but if the shadow is painted, the actor, lit from above by the battens, from below by the footlights, and from each side by the wing lights, resembles that Hoffmann character who had sold his shadow. But the spectator ignores this detail. If he does notice it, he accepts it without a word, just as he accepts the dusty wooden floor, hatched by *costières*, splashed with the damp spirals of the watering can, which represents the burning sands of the desert, the flower-studded turf of the prairie, or the rich mosaics of the palace and the temple. It is just one more convention' (p. 240).

24. Algarotti, *Saggio sopra l'opera in musica*, 75: 'The forestage, on which the actors stand, means that they are advanced several feet into the pit. As this places the actors more or less in the middle of the audience, there is no danger that they will not be perfectly audible to everyone.' He maintained that the problem could be solved by an elliptical auditorium, but this seems dubious.

25. Peter Nicholson, article 'Scenography', in *Cyclopaedia, or Universal Dictionary of Arts, Sciences and Literature, Illustrated with Numerous Engravings*, ed. Abraham Rees, vol. xxxi (London: Longman, Hurst, Orne, and Brown, 1819). Most entries in the *Cyclopaedia* are anonymous, but the author of the article on 'Scenography' refers to himself by name. In 'Peter Nicholson and the Scenographic Art', *Theatre Notebook*, 8 (Oct. 1953 to July 1954), 91–6, William A. Armstrong notes that this volume of the *Cyclopaedia* was in fact first published in 1815, and explains that

Nicholson was a carpenter (in modern terms, something more like a 'timber construction consultant') and architect.

26. Andrea Pozzo (Puteus), *Rules and Examples of Perspective proper for Painters and Architects, &c.*, in English and Latin, English translation, from the edition in Latin and Italian published in Rome in 1693 by John James (London: printed for J. Senex and R. Gosling in Fleetstreet; W. Innys in St Pauls Church Yard; J. Osborn and T. Longman in Paternoster Row, n. d. [1709?]), figures 72–5, esp. 72, reproduced here. Nicoll reproduces two of Pozzo's beautiful designs for wings and shutters representing curved arcades as his figures 125 and 126. For more on Pozzo, and on the perspective-stage tradition more generally, see Günther Schöne, *Die Entwicklung der Perspektivbühne von Serlio bis Galli-Bibiena nach der Perspektivbüchern, Theatergeschichtliche Forschungen*, established by Berthold Litzmann, ed. Julius Petersen, no. 43 (Leipzig: Leopold Voss, 1933; repr. Neudeln, Liechtenstein, 1977).

27. The rake of the 1875 Paris Opéra stage continued to the back wall of the main stage, but not across the 22 feet of the rear stage corridor. The *foyer de la danse* which could be opened up as a further extension of 46 feet was raked like the stage, but in the opposite direction (see Sachs and Woodrow, *Modern Opera Houses*, ii, plate 4). It needed a rake, because this reproduced stage conditions for the dancers who used it for rehearsals and warming up.

28. Pozzo, by contrast, claimed that 'in laying the Floor of the Stage, this Rule is commonly observ'd, . . . that the Rise of the Floor . . ., be about a Ninth or Tenth Part of the Length' (figure 74). Nicholson criticizes Pozzo explicitly: 'The rule given by Pozzo for the declivity of the stage is too much, being inconvenient for the actors, and perhaps one foot in twelve is a much better proportion.' The anonymous author of the article on 'Dramatic Machinery' in the same *Cyclopaedia* (clearly not Nicholson, since the article contradicts the one on 'Scenography' in a number of points), on the other hand, states that 'it is usual to allow one inch of perpendicular ascent for every 36 inches of length from the front to the back of the stage'. Jules de la Gournerie's *Traité de perspective linéaire, contenant les tracés pour les bas-reliefs et les décorations théâtrales, avec une théorie des effets de perspective*, 2nd edn. (Paris: Gauthier-Villars, 1884), 194, remarks: 'The slope of stage floors . . . can go as high as 4 centimetres per metre.' The same figure is given by Maurice Emanaud in his *Géométrie perspective* (Paris: Doin, 1921), 360. These figures seem to suggest that stage rakes became less pronounced between 1700 and 1900, but also perhaps the *ad hoc* character of these 'rules'. An examination of the longitudinal sections of stages in Gabriel Pierre Martin Dumont's *Parallèle de plans des plus belles salles de spectacles d'Italie et de France* (Paris: published by the author, n.d. [c.1774]; repr. New York: Benjamin Blom, 1968), in Contant and de Filippi, *Parallèle*, and in Sachs and Woodrow, *Modern Opera Houses* (three works conceived as complementing and updating one another) suggests that, while a rake of around 1 in 18 remained the most frequent, in the later nineteenth century the median shifted from about 1 in 18 to about 1 in 25, largely because many European stages built in this period had rakes lower than 1 in 50, which we have never seen prescribed; such low rakes are not found at all in earlier theatres.

29. Sachs and Woodrow, *Modern Opera Houses*, iii, suppl. 1, p. 11.

30. See ibid. ii, plate 74 and iii, suppl. 1, p. 68. The Raimund Theater (1893) had an 'Asphaleia-system' stage, one in which all parts of

the highly divided stage floor were mounted on hydraulic supports that enabled them to be raised, lowered, and tilted at will (though not usually very quickly). The Munich Opernhaus (not completed when Sachs was writing) had a stage revolve. The most advanced American stages were already flat by the 1890s (Edward Kinsila saw this as one of the few theatrical innovations which crossed the Atlantic from West to East, see *Modern Theatre Construction* (New York: Chalmers, 1917), 70). The Chicago Auditorium of 1889 had a stage described as related to the Asphaleia system (Adler, 'Chicago Auditorium', 295); by no means all such stages were basically flat (Sachs discusses many, but the Raimund Theater is the only one whose longitudinal section shows no rake), but the Auditorium's seems to have been. This flat stage and other advanced features, such as the possession of a cyclorama, the lack of borders and, apparently, wings–'All scenic effects are produced by drops extending across the entire stage, perforated where necessary'–should not be taken as a token that staging at the Auditorium had moved beyond the pictorial tradition, since these drops were 'so treated as regards perspective effect as to produce all the illusions of closed stage setting' (Adler, ibid. 297).

31. Richard Leacroft, *The Development of the English Playhouse* (London: Eyre Methuen, 1973), 289; and Sonrel, *Traité*, plate 39.
32. *Proscenium and Sight-Lines: A Complete System of Scenery Planning and a Guide to the Laying out of Stages* (London: Faber, 1939), 38–9. Southern's authority is Friedrich Kranich, *Bühnentechnik der Gegenwart*, vol. i (Munich: R. Oldenbourg, 1929), 117 ff.
33. It is noteworthy that Henry Morgan's *Perspective Drawing for the Theatre* (New York: Drama Book Specialists, 1979) assumes that all stages are horizontal. The book is not a treatise on stage perspective in the sense of any of the earlier ones we have cited; it is simply an account of how to produce perspectival flat pictures of three-dimensional stage settings.
34. Jelgerhuis, *Theoretische Lessen*, 15–32 and plates 1 and 2.
35. Sachs and Woodrow, *Modern Opera Houses*, iii, suppl. 1, p. 24. Georges Moynet gives the rake of the Opéra stage as 'exactly 0.0492 metres per metre' (*Machinerie théâtrale*, 176), and does still link this rake to perspective effects: 'The *rues* and *fausses rues* are narrower than in most theatres, which, in combination with the fairly steep rake of nearly 0.05 metres per metre, aids the perspective of the décor and effects of depth' (p. 196).
36. Sachs and Woodrow, *Modern Opera Houses*, iii, suppl. 1, p. 11.
37. *The Builder*, 13 Mar. 1897, cit. Leacroft, *Development of the English Playhouse*, 251. The article on 'Dramatic Machinery' in the *Cyclopaedia* already attributes the rake entirely to the problem of the visibility of the stage: 'This inclination is considered to be of advantage to the vision lines, supposed to come from the eye of the spectator in the front of the house, to any given point in the stage. It particularly places it in the power of the architect to keep the back part of the pit lower, than could be done without injuring the vision, were the flooring of the stage horizontal.' This argument was not unknown to the proponents of stage perspective. Both Jelgerhuis (*Theoretische Lessen*, 22) and de la Gournerie (*Traité*, 194) note that the rake is sometimes steeper than the rules of perspective would recommend, because the stage front is lowered to increase the visibility of the stage from the pit.
38. In *Practical Guide to Scene Painting and Painting in Distemper* (London: G. Romney and Co., n.d. [1875]), 53–9, Frederick Lloyds discusses stage perspective fairly briefly and vaguely in relation to wings and borders, devoting much more precision to the perspective painting of backdrops. French treatises on perspective geometry continue to have sections on theatrical perspective until Emanaud's of 1921, but this seems to be because the topic became part of the standard curriculum in technical drawing courses rather than because the live theatre retained a strong sense of its importance. However, the fact that Sonrel includes a discussion of the practical problems of the perspective drawing of sets in his *Traité de Scénographie* of 1943 suggests that the tradition was more alive in France than elsewhere.
39. Emanaud, *Géometrie perspective*, 373.
40. De la Gournerie, *Traité*, 191; Emanaud, *Géométrie perspective*, 368; and Lloyds, *Practical Guide*, 53–4.
41. Pujoulx, *Paris à la fin du XVIIIe siècle*, 130–1 and note, refers to 'the closed rooms that have been tried in a number of plays,' but deplores the fact that 'wings still prevail, and I know of only one machinist who believes they [i.e. the closed décors] should be adopted all the time,' that machinist being Boulle. Southern suggests (*Changeable Scenery*, 236–7), on the basis of a 1769 print, that the opera *The Padlock*, as produced at Drury Lane in 1768, had a set with a back flat and two oblique side flats; as an exterior, it had no ceiling. *The Conquering Game*, produced by Madame Vestris at the Olympic in 1832, is more commonly taken as the first box set in England, but the only evidence of its having had a ceiling is a very conventional representation of one in the frontispiece of a published playtext. See James H. Butler, 'Early Nineteenth-Century Stage Settings in the British Theatre', *Theatre Survey*, 6, no. 1 (May 1965), 54–64, and Rosenfeld, *Scene Design*, 112 and plate 27.
42. Algarotti, *Saggio sopra l'opera in musica*, 67.
43. *World behind the Scenes*, 14.
44. Garnier, *Le Théâtre*, 253. See also J. Moynet, *L'Envers du théâtre: machines et décorations* (Paris: Hachette, 1873), 116: 'As the stage is occupied by living people, they cannot grow smaller as they move towards the rear, as the figures in a painting do. The scene painter takes the necessary precautions to prevent the actors encroaching on the remote and diminishing parts of his composition. He is obliged to invent obstacles so there is no offence against verisimilitude.'
45. De la Gournerie, *Traité* 194 n.; cit. Bablet, *Esthétique générale*, 32, n. 59.
46. Bablet, *Esthétique générale*, 32, n. 59.
47. G. Moynet, *Machinerie théâtrale*, 359–76. This was presumably the French première, at the Opéra, opening 12 May 1893.
48. De Mille and Belasco, *Men and Women*, 313.
49. Anthony Hammond, 'Introduction', in William Shakespeare, *King Richard III*, the Arden Edition of the Works of William Shakespeare (London: Methuen, 1981; repr. Routledge, 1994), 70. In the notes to the passage, Hammond adds: '[A. C.] Sprague has remarked that in the 19th and early 20th centuries the scene was so far misunderstood as to be turned into an immense ceremonial, with a funeral procession numbering 70 or 80. This would make the ensuing wooing scene absurd instead of merely outrageous.'
50. *Mémoire contre le Baron Taylor* (Paris: Ponthieu, 1827), 75; cit. Marie-Antoinette Allevy (Akakia Viala), *Édition critique d'une mise en scène romantique, indications générales pour la mise en scène de 'Henri III et sa cour' (drame historique en cinq actes, en prose, de M. A. Dumas) par Albertin, directeur de la scène près le Théâtre Français (1929)* (Paris: Droz, 1938; repr. Geneva:

Slatkine Reprints, 1976), 14.

51. 'Whenever it is possible in these Meininger productions to introduce shouting, ringing, singing, chanting, fighting, jostling, pushing, these are never under any circumstances omitted. Two citizens cannot begin a conversation without the bustle of a market-place erupting behind them, so that we are willy-nilly distracted from the important dialogue. When Brutus and Cassius take center stage to hold a council of war before the battle of Philippi, several archers of the advance guard at stage left engage in an exciting skirmish—imagine!—only about four or five steps from the war council of the leading generals!' (Hans Hopfen, 'Die Meininger in Berlin', in *Streitfragen und Errinnerungen* (Stuttgart: J. G. Cotta, 1876), 241; cit. Carlson, *German Stage*, 177). This critique of the Meininger's *Julius Caesar* as presented during their 1874 visit to Berlin goes on to compare their productions with the contemporary London stage, i.e. by implication with Charles Kean: 'If we want to find a country where no money is spared to deck the words of the play with every conceivable ostentation, with every archaeological finesse or mechanical marvel, we only need to look at England today, where dramatic art has sunk to the lowest level among European nations' (pp. 245–6).

52. Southern, *Changeable Scenery*, 163–76.

53. Nicoll, *Development of the Theatre*, 203.

54. J. Moynet, *L'Envers du théâtre*, 101, fig. 22; Booth, *Victorian Spectacular Theatre*, 80.

55. Georges Moynet gives descriptions of elaborate transformations of complex set scenes, such as a prison tower that magically changes into a flight of stairs (*La Machinerie théâtrale*, 122–40) and a ship that leave harbour, goes through a storm, and eventually founders (pp. 78–100).

56. Lewis, *Henry Irving and 'The Bells'*, 34, 49, 62, 67, 84 n. 21, and 91 nn. 10–14.

57. For *La Muette de Portici*, see Marie-Antoinette Allevy (Akakia Viala), *La Mise en scène en France dans la première moitié du dix-neuvième siècle* (Paris: Droz, 1938; repr. Geneva: Slatkine Reprints, 1976), 59 and plate 11; for an 1829 English production of *Masaniello* (first staged in 1827), Booth, *Victorian Spectacular Theatre*, 61; for *Arrah-na-Pogue*, Vardac, *Stage to Screen*, 25–9; for *The Poor of New York*, Booth, pp. 63–4, and Rees, *Theatre Lighting*, 149; for *The Price of Peace*, Dennis Castle, *Sensation Smith of Drury Lane* (London: Charles Skilton, 1984), 126, and Booth, figures 4 and 5; *The Whip* is described in more detail below.

58. 'The Plays of the Week', *New York Dramatic Mirror*, 63, no. 1623 (29 Jan. 1910), 6. Some of the playscripts we have seen call the final scene Act 3, scene 2 rather than Act 4, emphasizing the continuity of the action. According to a Wallack's Theatre (New York) playbill in the scrapbooks of the Daniel Blum Collection of the Wisconsin Center for Film and Theater Research (vol. 28 (1909–10), microfilm reel 4, frame 854), 'between Acts III and IV there will be an interval of but one minute.'

59. See Otis Colburn, 'Chicago Stage Gossip', *New York Dramatic Mirror*, 62, no. 1620 (8 Jan. 1910), 12, for the first staging at the Chicago Studebaker, 24 Dec. 1909, with Hal B. Warner as Jimmy; 'Plays and Players', *Hampton's Magazine*, 24 (May 1910), 701, for the staging by the same company at Wallack's Theatre, New York, 21 Jan. 1910; and 'Art, Music and the Drama', *Illustrated London News*, 136 (9 Apr. 1910), 536, for the Comedy Theatre, London, production with Gerald Du Maurier as Jimmy.

60. Lloyds, *Practical Guide*, 78–82, cit. Rees, *Theatre Lighting*, 133–5.

61. See Jacobs, 'Belasco, DeMille and the Development of Lasky Lighting', esp. pp. 408–12.

WE have noted the relative freedom of the cinema from the constraints of a constant scale based on the 'natural size of the human body'. However, this freedom long remained only a relative one. One avenue to the exploration both of the continuities between nineteenth-century theatre and early cinema, and of the differences between the staging traditions in the two media, is provided by the persistent demand that moving pictures should be 'life-size'.

The first public screenings of projected moving pictures in 1895 and 1896 were usually described as 'life-size' (or 'grandeur naturelle' in France). The immediate motive seems to have been to distinguish them from the moving pictures in Kinetoscope machines, which were seen as 'small' since they were viewed through a lens in a smallish box (though really it makes little sense to attempt to give a scalar description of a peep-show image, which is viewed without contextual cues with the eye focused at infinity). Thus *Le Radical* of 30 September 1895, reviewing one of the private previews of the Cinématographe Lumière, noted: 'Whatever the nature of the scene thus taken and however large the number of people thus caught in their daily activities, you see them again, natural size, in colour, with perspective, distant skies, houses, streets, and all the illusion of real life.'[1] Charles Musser reproduces a number of similar descriptions of the Vitascope projector's first appearances in New York: 'Life size presentations they are and will be, and you won't have to squint into a little hole to see them' (*New York World*, 28 May 1895); 'For two hours, dancing girls and groups of figures, all of life size, seemed to exist as realities on the big white screen which had been built at one end of the experimenting rooms' (*New York Journal*, 28 March 1896); 'In the Vitascope, the figures of the Kinetoscope are projected, enlarged to life-size, upon a screen' (*New York Mail and Express*, 24 April 1896).[2]

These early uses of 'life-size' clearly partake of journalistic hyperbole (note *Le Radical*'s reference to colour in the Lumière Cinématographe's pictures), and are not very reliable as accounts of actual practice. Moreover, the intention to differentiate projected images from the peep-show picture might suggest that all that is meant is 'large'. However, the notion of the film image as 'life-size' outlasts the period of competition between projection and peep show as outlets for moving images.

A question frequently asked of the writers of the

regular columns on projection matters that began to appear in the American moving-picture trade press at the beginning of the 1910s was this: how bright a projection lamp did a movie house need for a certain throw? The standard answer was that the throw was not the issue; what mattered was the size of the eventual projected image, equal-sized images needing the same amount of light at the source however near or far away. The experts consulted then, however, went on to say how large that image should be, indicating that projection lenses should be selected to give a 'life-size' picture. Thus, F. H. Richardson, in his 'Operator's Column' in the *Moving Picture World* in 1910 called for a 'ten foot by twelve foot (life-size) screen'; and, in an article on moving-picture house design in the *Architectural Record* in November 1915, John Klaber recommended 9 feet by 12 feet, to give an 'approximately life size' picture. Similarly, when discussing how close subjects ought to be photographed for the cinema, the same prescription appears; in the *Moving Picture World* in 1911, an anonymous polemicist stated that 'no figure should appear larger than life-size to the eye'.[3]

These articles in the cinematic trade press and architectural journals clearly carry more authority than the early journalistic comments as precise recommendations by technical experts to practising exhibitors and architects. Nevertheless, the prescription that figures on the screen should be life-size is an odd one, in several respects.

First, it is odd to present-day viewers, who are used to dealing with moving images of sizes varying from a fifteen-inch television screen to the thirty-foot screen in a metropolitan movie house. Devotees of 'real cinema' may argue that the experience of moving pictures requires a big screen, but everyone interprets film images in more or less the same way irrespective of their size. From such a standpoint, the answer to the question as to how large the screen should be is that it depends on the size of the auditorium; the bigger the latter is, and the further away, therefore, the average seat is placed, the bigger the projected image should be. This is, indeed, the prescription that begins to be given towards the end of the 1910s in the trade press, although screens remained small by modern standards throughout the silent period, even in very large houses.[4]

Second, it is odd in so far as the term 'life-size' is not commonly used for flat pictures. Most of the early citations for 'life-size' or 'life-sized' given by the *Oxford English Dictionary* apply it to sculpture, i.e. to three-dimensional representations; the earliest example for an ordinary picture is 'two life-size portraits on panels' in *Tess of the d'Urbervilles* in 1891. There are, however, two earlier citations for specialized kinds of picture: 'A life-sized cartoon', in 1847; and 'The Birds of America . . . containing 448 plates, life-sized and colored,' in 1879. Thus, the term and the related 'natural size' do have a longer history in connection with flat pictures when those pictures are technical drawings or scientific illustrations. Even without the term, it is clear that the idea has a much longer history in such contexts. Thus the plates in Christian Conrad Sprengel's *Das entdeckte Geheimniss der Natur im Bau und in der Befruchtung der Blumen* (Berlin: Friedrich Vieweg, Sr., 1793) have numbers next to each item included in the crowded image indicating a scale or ratio, such that '1/1' means life-size, '2/1' twice life-size, and so on.[5] However, such pictures, and especially these last examples, are pictures which make no attempt to represent space, except in so far as one leaf of a plant is in front of another. Although there have been attempts to introduce perspective renditions of space into botanical, zoological, and palaeontological illustration throughout its history, they remain exceptions, because of the scalar ambiguity they introduce into a picture which is intended to aid the recognition and classification of specimens. Paintings proper, however, while often classified in terms of their absolute size (from 'miniature' to 'monumental'), are not usually considered in terms of the relation between the size of the image and the size of what that image represents, precisely because, in a perspective tradition, that relation is a representation of the distance between the viewer and the people or objects represented.

However, the tradition of theatrical perspective discussed above gives a clear indication of what is meant when the flat image projected in a movie house is described as 'life-size'. According to Maurice Emanaud, on a perspectively conceived stage, 'the plane of the *manteau d'Arlequin*, which the actors keep close to, is the frontal plane of true sizes'.[6] In other words, objects in the plane of the stage opening are full size or life-size, whereas further back they should be smaller than life-size (which, of course, actors cannot usually be, except by the subterfuge of the substitution of children for adults mentioned above). Transferred to film, this means that the images of actors who appear to be in the picture plane (which is taken to mean actors who are in the front plane of the action, i.e. where 'the actors keep close to' as Emanaud puts it) should be full size, or about 6 feet tall.

The way moving pictures were taken (especially in fiction films, where conditions were much more controllable by the filmmaker than in actualities) and the way they were projected in the first twenty years of cinema broadly bear out this understanding of the relation between the audience and the figures on the screen. Before about 1905, the moving-picture camera was mounted on a tripod with its lens axis more or less horizontal and more or less at eye level. The actors were then told not to come closer to the camera than a line marked on the studio floor with chalk, a rope, or other objects, such that their feet remained in view, and the principals rarely retreated much behind the same line. Hence they occupied about half the height of the image when projected, with their heads half-way up the frame and their feet close to the bottom frame line, i.e. the bottom of the screen. Clearly, such a picture will be 'life-size' in the sense indicated if the screen is about 12 feet tall. The principal venue for projected films up to this date was the variety theatre—*café-concert* in France, music-hall in England, *Varieté* theatre in Germany, or vaudeville house in the United States—and such houses were often large, with a stage big enough easily to accommodate a screen 12 feet by 16 feet. The few pictures we have seen of such screens suggest they were of such a size.[7]

After 1906, however, the principal locations for film projection changed, from the large variety theatres to much smaller shop-front theatres, the theatres called 'nickelodeons' in the United States. Such theatres were shoe-box shaped, accommodated 50 to 299 seats in 15 to 30 rows, sometimes without a rake, and in big cities were often restricted in height by the upper floors of the multi-storey building whose ground floor they occupied.[8] Such venues could not easily accommodate a screen 12 feet high; optimal sight lines were usually achieved with one less than 9 feet high. Even the Omnia Pathé, Pathé's Paris flagship house, inaugurated in December 1906, had a

screen only 4 metres by 3.5 metres (13 feet by 11 feet 6 inches—but a 13-feet wide screen can only accommodate a picture 9 feet 9 inches high).[9] It is a striking fact that one of the very few nearly universal stylistic shifts in filmmaking between 1905 and 1909 is that the standard size of the principal actors on screen grew to fill the frame height, more or less. This was achieved by bringing the camera closer to the actors, and by lowering it or tilting it downward, or a combination of the two, so that the characters' heads are in the top quarter of the frame and their feet close to the bottom frame line. It seems plausible to suggest that, as screens became smaller, filmmakers adapted their methods to ensure that characters on typical screens remained 'life-size'.

However, as is well known, in the next few years the camera was often brought even closer to the actors than the distance guaranteeing a life-sized figure on a smallish screen. Unlike the earlier tendency, however, this was by no means universal, being much less marked in Europe than in the United States. It should be emphasized that we are not here talking about 'close-ups' in the modern sense of cut-ins from the main view of the scene. Closer shots of characters or objects in scenes which were shown complete for most of a film had been regularly used since at least 1900, when such shots were called 'magnified views'.[10] Although they become rare in dramatic films around 1908–9, they persisted in comedies and trick films, and were used in dramatic ones to convey emphatic narrative information (e.g. to show that the hero's cast-off mistress is injecting poison into candy destined for his new fiancée in *Drive for a Life*, Biograph, 1909) and in the opening and closing 'emblematic' shots discussed in Part 2. Here, on the contrary, we are talking about the standard framing of a dramatic scene. By 1911, the actors in such scenes occupied a position such that they were considerably larger than life-size on a 9-feet by 12-feet screen.

A larger-than-life-size image on a flat screen may be understood in three ways. The first can be called 'scalar relativism', and is the one we are most familiar with today. In this conception, however large or small the image is, from 1 inch to 20 feet, it is interpreted as a normal-sized person or a 9-inch elf in relation to the fictional context and the likely size of the décor surrounding it.

Second, the spectator can take his or her binocular perception that all of the picture is on the screen as the standard, and interpret the object's size accordingly, with the result that the image of half a man 5 feet high means that the picture is of a man 10 feet tall. Maurice Noverre records statements by Georges Méliès criticizing 'modern film technique' (i.e. the films of the 1920s) that suggest that this is how he tended to interpret closer shots: 'What is there to say . . . about . . . characters who suddenly grow larger or whose hands and feet become enormous so a detail can be made visible?'[11] Méliès clearly has his tongue in his cheek to some extent here, and perhaps 'understanding' or 'interpreting' are not the most appropriate terms for this spatial literalism. No one believed that they were supposed to think the medicine had made the kitten grow suddenly larger in the close-up of it which is introduced into *The Little Doctor and the Sick Kitten* (G. A. Smith, 1901), in the way they did think the inventor's head was supposed to be inflated in *L'Homme à la tête en caoutchouc* (The Man with the India-Rubber Head; Méliès, 1902). They simply found the larger views grotesque and objected to the sudden changes in scale from shot to shot. As an editorial in the *Moving Picture World* put it in 1909:

The figures in this picture [an unnamed recent film] arrested our attention. Or we should say a part of the picture. These figures were so large that they occupied the entire perpendicular dimension of the sheet, that is, the figures that were nearest to the camera. The consequence was that the people in the theatre had the idea that the film showed a story that was being enacted, or had been enacted, rather, by a race of giants or giantesses. A little later on in the course of the picture the figures had been photographed at a greater distance from the camera and were so less monstrous to the eye; while, in even a third part of the picture, the figures were so far away from the camera that they appeared of their natural size—an effect which was more agreeable to the audience. . . . Where the fault lay was in the disregard of uniformity of conditions evinced either by the photographer or by the producer, or both. If these figures had been photographed at equal distances from the camera, then they would have appeared of equal size on the screen, instead of varying between the dimensions of a Brobdingnagian monstrosity and Lilliputian pigmies.[12]

The problem was not so much how to understand these pictures, as how to take them seriously. As Felix Salten put it:

At one moment people appear larger than life size, at the next diminutively small. In one way or the other they are rendered grotesque, more or less like clowns. In the same narrow frame of the projection screen we see now an individual actor, overwhelming, all too close, all too magnified, a second later we see him shrunk down walking along a street, a dwarf among other dwarfs, and it becomes inconceivable that we could observe his acting, have it affect us seriously or comically.[13]

In the third understanding, the larger-than-life-size image can be interpreted as a normal-sized figure, but one that is closer to the spectator than the screen. In the case of the standard three-quarter-length framing that became typical in American and to a lesser degree European films around 1911, this meant that the figures seemed to hang in the air in front of the screen without feet.

The issue of 'cutting off the feet' and the unease it clearly aroused in many commentators,[14] should be considered in the light of the optics of the live stage. Audiences were quite familiar with actors coming closer to them than the plane of the *manteau d'Arlequin*, given the persistence of short forestages to the end of the nineteenth century. However, if larger-than-life-size figures are interpreted as closer to the audience than the screen, their lack of feet is a problem when there is no stage edge or footlight float to mask them. The cutting-off of the feet produces an ambiguity about how the image is to be interpreted. During the wave of 3-D films in the 1950s, it was normal to keep the actors behind the front plane of the picture, precisely to avoid this effect of figures lacking their lower limbs, yet floating in the air in front of the screen. Writing in 1953, Charles G. Clarke remarks:

Some readers may recall that in the very early days of filmmaking it was a hard and fast rule that the feet of the actor must always be shown. Audiences had to see what the characters were standing on! This seems ridiculous now that we are educated to seeing close-ups with no visible means of support; but it took many years to get audiences adjusted to this technique of the cinema. Likewise, it will take some time before audiences will accept persons or objects standing out in front of the screen in 3-D films, where in reality they belong. In time this will come about of course, but for the present it is probably better not to include objects too close to the foreground or ahead of convergence.[15]

Spectators in the 1900s and 1910s were undoubtedly accustomed to all three ways of thinking about images. When they looked at the illustrations of novels, or at monumental sculptures, they applied scalar relativism. But in the theatre, the other two were more familiar. Although different interpretations were used by audiences in the period, and scalar relativism gradually gained ground as the standard cinematic expectation, during the 1910s cinematic space was still in many ways more rigid, less plastic than it subsequently became. It was an extension of the space in the auditorium, as the stage space in a theatre is; in the closest views it even interpenetrated the auditorium space. The relative reluctance to cut within a scene and the even greater reluctance to change the angle of view can partly be understood in relation to this spatial rigidity.

Although most of the editing patterns typical of the cinema of the 1920s and later are already to be found in films made by 1911, these occurrences are usually isolated, both in the sense that the films in which they occur are rare, and in the sense that they are infrequent or unique in the films in which they do. By contrast, the typical classical narrative film has large numbers of examples of reverse shots, alternations, or cut-ins, and they occur in almost every film. Before 1917, the overwhelmingly preponderant editing patterns are of three types: filming the whole of an action in a single shot, with the front protagonists in either a long-shot or medium-long-shot framing; alternating between fragments of scenes to show two simultaneous actions, or two parts of a single action; and filming a scene as in the first type, but interpolating one or more closer views from the same angle as the main view. A fourth type might be added: filming a scene divided by a door or window by alternating between framings from either side of the partition at 180 degrees to one another; in very rare cases, the partition has such a large opening as to constitute a single space viewed from two sides. With the exception of this fourth type, therefore, the only fragmentation of a single space is the cut-in from a full view of the scene to a detail within it. It is worth adding that the same setting is also usually filmed from the same angle and in the same framing whenever it appears. The theatrical character of these patterns is obvious.

Despite all these homologies, film space presented a very different stage for actors from that of the live theatre. It is a space defined by the optics of cinematography, the basic parameters of which were established quite early in the history of the cinema, and once established changed very little.

First, W. K. L. Dickson at the Edison laboratories fixed the size and shape of the image photographed and projected in the cinema, a size and shape which lasted until the end of the silent period, despite various short-lived early experiments with wider film.[16] The film designed for the original Edison camera and the Kinetoscope viewing machine was the film nowadays called 35 mm, vertically fed from above into the camera and projector or viewing-machine gates, with sixteen frames to a foot, each frame occupying the full width between the two rows of sprocket-holes, and the full height pulled down by the claw for each exposure, i.e. each frame being one inch by three-quarters of an inch.[17] We have never seen any discussion of this choice of frame proportions, let alone an explanation for it, and it is an odd one for either a peepshow machine or a projection system, where the most efficient shape for the image (the shape making the best use of light from a point source) is circular, or, if the visual stability of a rectangular frame is desired, square. Most lantern slides were either round or square, and the frames in the earliest Edison experimental moving pictures were circular.[18] The 1.33:1 landscape image suggests that Dickson was looking for a broad picture reminiscent of a stage (proscenium arches are usually slightly taller than they are wide, but the top of the arch is filled in with drapery, so that the stage opening approaches the shape of the moving-picture frame).[19] Size and shape of the projected image became more or less fixed, varied only by such devices as diptychs and triptychs, and vignetting. Despite Salten's demand for a variable-sized frame, and Sergei Eisenstein's lecture to the Academy of Motion Picture Arts and Sciences in 1930 on the 'dynamic square' which proposes a variably shaped one,[20] for most of the time the frame projected on to the cinema screen is as fixed a value as the proscenium opening in the nineteenth-century stage.

A second characteristic of filmic space, and one in which cinema and theatre differed more strikingly, is a matter of lens optics. It is generally agreed that, in the 1900s, the standard lens for studio cinematography became a 50 mm one, or, as it was usually called in England and America, the 'two-inch lens'. By the late 1910s, this is evidenced by many sources. According to Urban Gad in 1919, 'lenses of 50 mm are most often used', and, in the 1917 edition of his *Guide to Kinematography*, Colin Bennett says, 'Kinematograph camera lenses range from two to six or more inches focus. Two inches is usual for work in the studio'.[21] Before the War, professional cinematographers were too few to constitute a market for technical manuals, they lacked the corporate self-consciousness to establish professional technical journals, and their training was solely 'on-the-job'. There is thus very little written evidence on the matter, and what there is seems to suggest a longer focal-length lens as the norm. In the 1913 edition of his manual, Bennett argues that 'for ordinary purposes, the focus of a kinematograph lens should be anything between two inches and three and a half inches, the shorter focus being more useful for topical filming in restricted situations, and the longer for scenic and artistic work, where there is plenty of elbow room at the camera man's command'.[22] In a 1914 article in the *Kinematograph and Lantern Weekly*, he is even more categorical:

The angle of the 3 in. kinematograph lens is, in fact, only about 19 degrees, which in the terms of the still view photographer, would be described as 'extreme narrow angle.' Yet the moving picture man has established it in his industry as a normal focus, and in this he has for once been absolutely in the right. The reason is that in order for a photograph to look natural the performance of the lens with which it was taken ought to approach as nearly as possible to that of the human eye. The angle included by the human eye when working at its best is never much over 16 degrees, so that it follows that a lens using only 19 degrees of view will give a much more faithful rendering than would one which included more than twice as much of any scene as the human eye could have observed at one moment from the like view point.[23]

And in the USA in 1911, David Hulfish also calls a three-inch lens the 'standard lens', and a two-inch one the 'wide-angle lens'.[24] The only contemporary reference we have been able to find to the two-inch lens as in regular studio use before 1917 is an exclamation from C. H. Claudy in 1908, and he clearly implies that such a lens was considered very short: 'Motion-picture people will tell you—some of them— that you can't have foreground sharp with the dis-tance. And they use lenses of a couple of inches in focal length!'[25]

Barry Salt notes that 'some people regarded a 3-inch lens as a standard lens during this period [1907–13], but this seems to be a reflection of newsreel and "topical" filmmaking attitudes rather than being the best professional practice in fictional filmmaking'.[26] 'Topical' is perhaps not the most appropriate term to use in this argument, because, as Bennett himself remarked, news cinematographers had the same preference for short lenses that news still photographers still do—they allow the photographer to work close to his subject and thus unblocked by bystanders with the minimum need to adjust focus. However, there is no doubt that Bennett's (and probably Hulfish's) readership was not the studio cameraman, but the cinema manager who had purchased a camera in order to be able to add local-interest films to his programmmes, and Bennett expected such cameramen to emulate the often self-consciously 'artistic' scenics as well as topicals.

Despite Bennett's further claim that most available cine-cameras could not accommodate a two-inch lens,[27] all the American advertisements for such cameras that we have seen suggest they came with a two-inch lens as standard, and all the cameras we have seen in film museums in America and Europe (which would mostly be such quasi-amateur models rather than true studio machines) seem to have a two-inch lens fitted.

More significantly, there is plenty of evidence that, in American studio filmmaking in the early 1910s, the standard front position for actors became 'the ten-foot line' or 'the nine-foot line',[28] and surviving films from the period usually have the actors in medium long shot (three-quarter height) in that front position. With a three-inch lens, an actor on the ten-foot line would be in medium close-up, a framing hardly ever used as the basic scene framing at this time; a two-inch lens would produce the characteristic medium-long-shot framing. It is possible that the manuals are conservative, and longer lenses were used earlier (the very long and narrow Edison Black Maria would seem suited to a narrow-angle lens, but it is hard to see how Méliès could have used one in his relatively short studio). Thus, a cameraman in the 1910s might think 'I usually use my wide-angle lens', rather than 'My standard lens is a two-inch one.' On the whole, it seems safe to claim that in practice the two-inch lens was the standard for studio cinematography by the end of the 1900s, i.e. as soon as actors began to come close enough to the camera for the choice of lens to have much impact on film staging and style.[29]

Although there is general agreement on this point, the reasons for the choice have rarely been discussed. In still photography, it was conventional to use a lens with a focal length equal to the diagonal of the photographic plate. This means that, if viewed from the centre of vision—the point at which the photograph would coincide with a view through a similar sized window on to the world originally photographed, i.e. a point the focal length in front of the photograph on a line perpendicular to it from the crossing-point of the diagonals—the resultant picture will more or less fill the spectator's field of vision. In other words, spectators are intended to view pictures from the 'centre of vision', i.e. from a distance equal to the focal length of the lens used (multiplied by any degree of subsequent magnification of the picture), and they are expected to choose a distance at which they can just see all the picture at once.[30] The diagonal of a one-inch by three-quarter-inch image is one inch and a quarter, appreciably less than two inches, let alone three, but a cinematic image photographed on 35 mm film with a two-inch lens and projected as an image 12 feet wide has a centre of vision 24 feet in front of it, which means that, in a nickelodeon, a reasonable proportion of the seats would be close to the centre of vision, i.e. close to the position giving the perspectively most 'correct' view, and this may thus be the explanation for the adoption of this standard. This is corroborated by C. L. Gregory in 1920: 'Lenses for general purposes [i.e. for still photography] are calculated for an angle of about 60 degrees. . . . As a motion picture is customarily viewed at a distance relatively greater than a still photo the angle of view averaging nearest normal is about 28 degrees, using the base and not the diagonal as a basis for calculation. This is the angle subtended by a two-inch lens on the standard ¾ by 1 inch aperture or picture frame.'[31]

The field of view of a moving-picture camera is a rectangular pyramid with its apex at the camera lens, and with the lens axis constituting the line joining the apex to the centre of its base (see Figure 4.9).[32] The cross-section perpendicular to that axis at any distance from the camera is a rectangle of the same proportions as the image that will be projected on to the screen, and every visible object at that distance within that rectangle and not blocked by something closer to the camera will appear on the screen, while nothing outside it will. With 35 mm film and a two-inch lens, the angle of the triangle subtended at the apex by the sides of this image rectangle will (as C. L. Gregory noted) be 28 degrees, that by the top and bottom 21 degrees. With a three-inch lens, the corresponding figures are 19 degrees and 14 degrees. The stage within which people and things that are going to be visible on screen must be deployed is thus a very tall pyramid, usually set more or less on its side, with its lowest face, the bottom of the field of view, intersecting with the ground a certain distance away from the camera, that distance depending on the height of the camera, its precise angle, and any declivity of the ground. A horizontal 35 mm moving-picture camera with a two-inch lens 4 feet 6 inches from the ground can show the full height of characters standing in the front plane 24 feet from those characters on a level floor (a horizontal one 3 feet from the ground will do so at 16 feet; one at eye level tilted down to do the same thing will be about 7 inches closer). Ten feet from the camera, the image rectangle will be 3 feet 9 inches by 5 feet; 40 feet from the camera, the image rectangle will be 20 feet wide, and its top will be 12 feet above the ground.

This field, narrow and low at the front and wide and high at the back, is the precise opposite of the characteristic stage playing space. For Peter Nicholson, 'the part of the theatre which is employed for the exhibition of scenery, is a recess from the great room where the spectators sit, and is in the form of a truncated pyramid, the base being what is called the

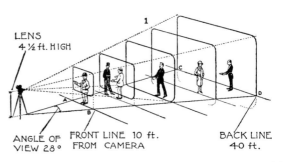

LENS
4 ½ ft. HIGH

ANGLE OF VIEW 28°   FRONT LINE 10 ft. FROM CAMERA   BACK LINE 40 ft.

4.9

curtain; and the vertex, which is the remote end of the pyramid, is called the point of contraction. The aperture, being thus diminished as it is more remote from the spectator, is of infinite advantage in representing an extended space in a small compass.' The perspective stage narrows as it recedes, in order to give the impression that the rear planes are further away than they are; but even a décor where the stage space is of exactly the same dimensions as the space represented effectively narrows towards the rear, since members of the audience in extreme positions on either side can see less of the rear stage on their side of the house, their view being blocked by the proscenium arch, side flats, and actors.

Thus, while for stage actors, the nearer they approach the footlights, the more room for manœuvre they have, for film actors it is the opposite. As Eustace Hale Ball put it:

The stage of the theatre is fan-shaped, with the curve of the fan—the apron or front of the stage, under the proscenium arch—as the place for leading action. The entire space across the stage, directly in front of the orchestra, can be used, and thus the actors have great latitude. It is exactly the reverse with the cinematographic camera. Its field is fan-shaped, but the eye of the camera is at the small end of the fan. The most important business must be performed as closely as possible to this fan-point, in order that the images may appear large and distinctly upon the film.... To work in the few feet allotted—amounting to a stage width of six or eight feet, at a distance of ten feet from the lens,—is a tremendous problem many times.[33]

On the other hand, the single viewpoint of the moving-picture camera solves the problem of blocking out positions so that the stage picture is visible (and reasonably similar) for as many of the members of the audience as possible, since anything which is visible to the camera is visible to all members of the cinema audience, however far to the side or above or below the screen they are sitting. Although film viewers in extreme positions see a distorted picture in which figures are laterally or vertically compressed, those figures have the same relationship to one another for the whole audience, however small their angular separation may have been for the camera. To repeat Urban Gad's words, 'the thousands of eyes of the spectators are all pressed to the one tiny peephole of the camera.' As a result, compositions can be used in which some important elements are very close to

the camera and some very distant without, as in the live theatre, presenting a very different picture to different parts of the auditorium.

Exploiting this unique viewpoint of the camera in stagings which place some elements of a setting much closer than others does, however, involve the possibility of exceeding depth of field, that is, that some of those elements will be out of focus, something which will not happen in the live theatre for members of the audience with normal or normally corrected vision. The historical significance of the emergence of a trend to exploit a very high depth of field in the American cinema in the 1940s and the technological feat this exploitation represented have perhaps made us overestimate the importance of the technical aspects of so-called 'primitive deep focus', but something should be said about it here.

First, until the end of the 1910s, almost all commentators expect a cinematic picture which is in sharp focus throughout. In 1919, Henri Diamant-Berger wrote: 'The sharpness of vision should be the same in every plane. At the present time, we are often shown very sharp foregrounds against soft horizons. If there is insufficient latitude to keep the horizon in focus, then such foregrounds should be avoided, or cheated, as can very easily be done.'[34] This insistence is remarkable, given the fact that the dominant style in late nineteenth-century still photography (and in early twentieth-century still photography, too, with the exception of a few avant-gardists) is the style known as 'pictorialism' (pictorialism here not having the broad meaning we are giving the term in this book, but rather signifying the introduction of painterly effects into photography, most of which encourage a softer image, either one whose overall definition is lower, or one in which all but the central subject is softened in the name of 'aerial perspective'). Urban Gad remarked on this contradiction:

It is a well-known fact that in photography effects have been striven for that come close to artistic productions. By appropriate shooting and later printing a softness of outlines and tones has been sought which is highly reminiscent of the personal stylization of nature by an artist. However, these means are inappropriate for cinematography, because technical difficulties make them impossible, and because films, as well as pictorial demands, must also meet dramatic ones. The pictures cannot be so painterly in tone that facial features, in the last analysis the only means by which film can attain access to the soul, are vague and confused. The pictures must be so clear and sharp that everything that helps to reveal mental activity can be clearly and vividly shown.[35]

In general, then, moving pictures were expected to be fully in focus throughout, and indeed, the most primitive form of film criticism is the complaint that the pictures are out of focus. However, this requirement was not usually as rigidly prescribed as by Diamant-Berger, nor was it rigorously adhered to. Yuri Tsivian notes that several early commentators deprecated the unselective nature of film images in terms that suggest they objected to the uniformity of focus. In the *New Review* in May 1896, O. Winter compared the moving pictures with Pre-Raphaelite paintings: 'Both the Cinematograph and the Pre-Raphaelite suffer from the same vice. The one and the other are incapable of selection; they grasp at every straw that comes in their way; they see the trivial and important, the near and the distant, with the same fecklessly impartial eye.' And the Russian cinematographer Alexander Digmelov, in his unpublished memoirs, cited an 1896 Russian newspaper article which complained about the moving pictures' 'lack of aerial perspective'.[36] In his 1913 manual, Colin Bennett argued that distant backgrounds should be thrown slightly out of focus to ensure good figure-ground separation for the subject of a film scene.[37] By the time Gad was writing, the very first examples of a cinematic 'soft style' were beginning to appear,[38] and he himself agrees that, once a clear view of the characters' faces has been given, 'in other shots one can use photographic means to enhance the mood of the scene; then effects lighting, half-lit faces and painterly effects of every kind are appropriate, in so far as they do not hinder, but help the actors' performances'.[39]

In practice, too, partly out-of-focus images were fairly common in the cinema of the 1900s and 1910s. Although in some insert close-ups the objects or faces were isolated from their environments against a neutral light or dark background, and in others the detail was placed very close to a wall flat or other background feature which could thus be kept in focus, simply filming such a detail from close up with a two-inch lens in the setting of the scene would almost always throw the background out of focus, and this was very often done. Even in longer basic scene framings, an out-of-focus background is not uncom-mon in films in the 1910s (e.g. in many scenes in *The Coming of Angelo*, Biograph 1913), and occasionally even principals are softer than their environment. In a deep-staged scene in *The Inherited Taint* (Vitagraph, 1911), the hero in medium long shot in the foreground is sharply focused, but the flirtation of his fiancée with another man that he is witnessing in the background is noticeably soft. In Georg af Klercker's *Kärleken segrar* (Love's Victory; Hasselblad, 1916), a whole scene in an automobile salesroom has the cars and one character in the background sharply focused, while all the other characters in the foreground are markedly blurred. Although one might conceive of reasons why this was done deliberately (the scene reintroduces the villain, the sharply focused background character), it seems more likely that it was a mistake on the part of the cameraman, but not one felt to be sufficiently serious to warrant reshooting.

As is well known, the depth of field of a photographic image, that is, the range of distances from the lens within which objects will appear in the photograph as sharply focused, depends directly on the absolute distance from the lens of the closest of those objects, and inversely on the focal length of the lens, and the lens aperture. Reducing the aperture reduces the amount of light admitted by the lens, and with a moving-picture camera the exposure time cannot be raised to compensate for this reduction to more than a value of about half the sixteenth of a second before which the frame is replaced in the gate by its successor. There is thus potential conflict between increasing depth of field and adequate levels of exposure, especially if the front plane of significant elements of the image is close to the lens.

However, in films of the 1900s and 1910s, this front plane is never, in the basic scene shots which are the ones which involve depth of staging, much closer than 9 feet from the camera in the United States, and usually even further away in Europe. With a two-inch lens, sharp focus (defined as a circle of confusion under 0.002 inches)[40] can be achieved from 9 feet to infinity at an aperture of f11 and from 9 feet to 30 feet at f5.6, and the standard apertures for studio shooting were within this range. Gad remarks, 'if one works in a Northern zone, where the quantity of light is limited, especially in an enclosed glass studio, the cameraman has to work with a wider aperture, which can easily lead to the background being blurred if the foreground is going to be sharp—as it should always be, as that is where the action takes place'.[41] But under most conditions, depths of field of this order presented filmmakers with no problems.[42] Indeed, in the passage referred to above, in which Colin Bennett advocated a shallow depth of field to isolate the significant plane from those in front and behind it—a common prescription in still photography—he remarks that this may not be practicable in moving-picture photography, because the high apertures required will necessitate reductions of exposure time to the extent of eliminating movement blur in individual frames, producing a stroboscopic effect in projection rather than the desired illusion of continuous movement.[43] In other words, his concern is that there is too much light to achieve low depths of field rather than that there is too little for high ones. It is thus not surprising that Gad is exceptional in perceiving serious technical difficulties in staging action in depth, especially given the fact established above that a certain amount of softness of the image was regularly tolerated.

There were, however, other aesthetic difficulties with such staging. The remarks by Winter and the Russian journalist cited by Digmelov, mentioned above in connection with 'aerial perspective', also involved the problem that as figures advanced towards or receded from the camera they seemed to change size in a grotesquely exaggerated way.[44] The same complaint was still being made in the 1910s by Salten: 'Our theatre has both a natural and an artificially illusory perspective. Film, on the contrary, is completely unperspectival. A photographed person who goes towards the background in a photographed room, say to the door, is already ridiculously small at the third step.'[45] As noted above, spectators in a nickelodeon-type theatre, and even many in the larger theatres of the 1910s, could well be sitting close to the centre of vision of the picture on the screen, and therefore, as far as the angle figures on screen subtended at the eye was concerned, the change as they move in depth was no more than it would have been seeing those figures in real life. In life, however, depth is also perceived via adjustment of the eye's focus, and stereoscopically via the different angle of view of each eye. Our knowledge of depth from these sources offsets the changes in subtended angle, so we

perceive the size of the images of figures moving in depth as changing less than it actually does. In the cinema these offsetting factors are absent, which in part accounts for the complaints about the supposedly exaggerated dwindling and expanding of cinematic figures as they recede from and approach the camera.

These constants of human perception are not the only issues in play, however. Modern spectators usually view screen images from a long way behind the centre of vision from which they were photographed (standard lenses have become progressively shorter over the history of the cinema, and cinemas have become larger, with the average seat further away from the screen), resulting in an effectively wider-angle picture, but we do not experience people approaching the camera as growing in size at a ridiculous rate. Rather, we are much more familiar with such wide-angle pictures than were spectators at the turn of the century, not only from the cinema, but also from the dissemination of newspaper photographs, often taken with relatively wide-angle lenses and habitually viewed from a distance many times the product of the focal length and the enlargement. Traditional paintings exaggerated aerial perspective to justify the scalar differences produced by artificial perspective. As noted above, movement in depth on the stage tended to be kept as oblique as possible, and when actors did move to the front or rear, their apparent size increased or decreased less than it would have had they moved as far as the stage perspective made them seem to. The earliest spectators thus found movement in depth in the cinema problematic, and theatrically based writers like Salten still had the same difficulties in the 1910s. However, the prevalence of staging in depth in films from all countries in the early 1910s suggests that ordinary spectators had already adjusted to 'wide-angularism'.

In practice, despite these optical disparities between theatre and cinema, the difference between the staging patterns in the two media is slight, so long as the film actors remain a long way from the camera, and the backdrop is set up only a short distance beyond them (or they never move more than a few feet from their front line). This is the space characteristic of much early fiction cinema, most notoriously that of Méliès. Even a film where characters approach to about 18 feet from the lens, such as

L'Assassinat du duc de Guise, can have sets relatively similar in disposition to stage sets, and its actors can behave on the film stage in much the way they might have acted in similar scenes in the theatre, although the stage implied is very small, in this case with a proscenium opening of only 10 feet (perhaps 12, if the very closest figures are thought of as on a short forestage).

Once, however, the front line of the action was brought closer to the camera, to the 'ten-foot line' in American films by 1911, usually not quite so close in Europe, the difference between the two stages became crucial. This is constantly mentioned by actors who moved from one medium to the other (as most did—very few cinema actors before 1917 lacked live theatrical experience). The confined nature of the front playing space made it difficult for actors to do much there; expressive movement was restricted, not necessarily by any concern for 'realism' or 'underacting', but simply by the need to stay in frame. As Victorin Jasset noted of American films in 1911, 'The Americans had perceived the fascination of facial expressions in close shots, and had resorted to them, sacrificing the setting and the scene as a whole when necessary to present to the audience the faces of characters who remain more or less motionless.'[46] If expressive movement is restricted, the same is even more true of any kind of physical action. These difficulties are very clear in the version of *Hamlet* filmed by the Hepworth company in 1913. In the exterior scenes, shot on a beach and in woods, the cameraman is forced into awkward pans in an often unsuccessful attempt to keep Johnston Forbes-Robertson in the scene. In the studio-shot interiors, the effect is much less marked, presumably because it was easier to arrange the acting areas in ways that forced the actor to keep to the visible field.

As this last example suggests, panning and tilting might be deployed to extend the area in which the actors could move. Panning tripod heads were introduced by 1900—the Biograph film taken of Dreyfus during his second court martial in Rennes in 1899 contains several pans which are both smooth and fast, which would be impossible without some kind of panning head, especially with the heavy 68 mm Biograph camera—tilting ones several years later, but the mechanisms remained relatively clumsy, utilizing ratchet and pinion drives with separate handles for vertical and horizontal plane movement.[47] It was particularly difficult to pan and tilt simultaneously. In practice if the camera had to follow, say, characters moving down a slope, pans and tilts alternated, producing a kind of zigzag stepped movement, which exacerbated the difficulty of co-ordinating the camera's and the actors' movements when close to the camera.

At more distant framings, pans were used in both France and America to extend the playing area laterally, adapting the panoramic backcloth of the theatre, but also the reframing pans used by actuality cameramen as soon as their tripods had panning heads, and the specialized actuality genre of the 'panoramic view', which was either a track, usually from a moving vehicle, or a large, even 360-degree pan over a landscape. *Cowboys and Indians Fording River in a Wagon*, an Edison film of 1904, follows its simple action in a real location with a long pan. In 1905–6, Pathé dramas and *féeries* included much more striking long pans over painted landscapes in certain scenes, most notably the walk from the miner's house to the pithead in *Au pays noir* (1905), and the hard-labour scene in *Au bagne* (Convict Life, 1905). In the former (see Figures 4.10–4.13), the pan convincingly conveys the transition from the street of a mining village to a relatively distant mine in open country; in the latter, the scene begins at the door from the prison building to the yard, the camera then pans left following a group of convicts who enter from the prison carrying a huge beam, stops when they put it down in the yard, then starts to move further left as another group of convicts enters front right carrying heavy sacks, and follows them until they climb a gangplank on to a ship moored by the yard. These are among the most striking shots in the whole of early cinema. The same technique is used in *Aladin ou la lampe merveilleuse* (Aladdin, or the Wonderful Lamp, 1906) to take the hero from the entrance to the underground cavern to the shrine housing the magic lamp and back again.

Much shorter pans and tilts which maintain the principal actors roughly in the centre of the screen, like those used in *Hamlet*, are much more common than these spectacular examples. These, too, are essentially reframing pans, maintaining the key characters centre screen. In the 1910s, European films in particular frequently pan between the rooms of a

4.10

4.11

4.12

4.13

two-room set, panning 'through' the wall or across a doorway. This is often used for scenes of overhearing (e.g. Sjöström's *Havsgamar* (Sea Vultures), 1916) but occasionally the dramatic function becomes more complex. In *Die Sumpfblume* (The Swamp Flower; Viggø Larsen, 1913), Sandra, who is modelling for the amateur sculptor Edgar von Schmetting in his Paris apartment, has a cast made of her foot in the studio; a pan right leaves the studio with the couple as they enter the dining-room. Von Schmetting later exits left back into the studio as Sandra explores the dining room. She opens curtains rear right, revealing an alcove with von Schmetting's bed behind. She exits through the curtains closing them behind her. Pan left to the studio to show von Schmetting at his desk. He rises, pan right as he returns to the dining-room. He looks around for Sandra, then, not seeing her, ad-

vances towards the curtains. The scene breaks off, whether because of a censorship cut in the Dutch print we have seen or as a deliberate ellipsis is unclear. Finally, there is at least one example where the reframing pan is taken much further. As well as having such pans in almost every scene, *Das Mädchen ohne Vaterland* (The Girl without a Country, 1912) has one scene that exploits their impossibility if the actors move independently of one another. Lieutenant Ipanoff's apartment in a central European fortress is L-shaped, with a window in the left-hand wall at the front, a door midground left in the front-facing wall, Ipanoff's desk front right, and, behind it, a sitting-room alcove rear right. When Ipanoff is confined to quarters for allowing Zidra, a gypsy girl, to see secret parts of the fortress, she steals past sentries to visit him, climbing into the apartment via the window.

After a while, there is a knock at the door. Zidra hides behind the window curtain and Ipanoff invites the visitor, a fellow officer, to sit with him in the sitting-room. Zidra, invisible from the alcove, comes out from behind the curtains and leaves by the door. Returning to the main room on a pretext, Ipanoff looks for her, and finds her gone. Later, having stolen plans of the fortress, Zidra returns to the room and hides behind the curtain again, coming out when the fellow officer leaves, and pretending to have been there all the time. The camera position and lens with which this décor is always shot cannot take in the area by the window and the rear right sitting-room simultaneously; when Ipanoff and his friend go off into the sitting-room, the camera must pan from one area to the other, producing an alternation within the shot reminiscent of the 'masking' frame André Bazin saw as characteristic of the film style of Jean Renoir in the 1930s.[48]

Renoir, of course, used tracking movements (movements in which the camera changes position as well as turning) to produce such effects, and such movements, too, are found in films in our period. Tracking movements were used to reframe moving characters, especially when they were moving in a vehicle. There are exceptional examples very early, but by 1913 they are common in both American and European cinema.[49] Tracks require elaborate preparation, and would not be used merely to give the actors a little latitude in a narrow stage, as pans were. In *Cabiria* (1914), however, tracks are used independently of the actors' movements, in relation to the sets. In the next few years directors everywhere include at least one spectacular tracking shot in their films, but in America they did not emulate Pastrone's displacement of the actors from the centre of attention, but, on the contrary, tracked in on or out from the principals in a scene, usually one that was spectacular in its most distant framing irrespective of the movement.[50]

Another much more uncommon solution is to use a wider-angled lens. Thus, the scene in the Holbeins' salon in *Ma l'amor mio non muore!* is filmed with a lens with a focal length of about 35 mm rather than 50 mm (see Figures 4.14 and 4.15). This produces a highly dynamic space, with strong scalar differences as characters move in depth in the three rooms visible from the camera's unchanging position, but a wide

middle ground, allowing some of the most important action to be staged laterally (Elsa and Sthar at the piano left, while her father and Colonel Theubner examine the plans in the alcove office right).

Ma l'amor mio non muore! also uses another method of extending the arena of action typical of European films in the 1910s, the staging of some of the action outside the space directly visible to the camera, but at a point where it is indirectly visible in a mirror in that space. As mentioned in Part 3, the set for Elsa's dressing-room includes a large three-pane mirror set up midground centre, and so placed that from the single camera position used for this set the central mirror shows the dressing-room door off right. In the first scene in this set, after Elsa's Paris début, a group of admirers follow her in from the door on the right. As she gets ready to change for her next number, the impresario Schaudard ushers them out, but one man sits

4.14

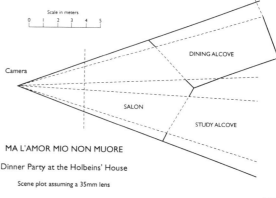

MA L'AMOR MIO NON MUORE

Dinner Party at the Holbeins' House

Scene plot assuming a 35mm lens

4.15

4.16

proprietorially on Elsa's sofa. When she becomes aware of this (seeing him in the mirror), she turns and asks him what he wants, whereupon he rises and tries to embrace her. She rings and her maid enters rear left (the door to her room is invisible behind the mirror). Elsa indicates that the gentleman is leaving, and the maid shows him out; he lingers as long as possible before, in the mirror, we see him shrug and exit. The same movement (but with the opposite emotional tone) is repeated in the last scene in the dressing-room. When Maximilian reappears in her dressing-room after she has tried to break off their relationship, he is first seen by Elsa and the spectators at the door, in the mirror (Figure 4.16). Later, when Elsa tells Maximilian that she will go back to him, he leaves to watch her performance, visible to the spectators in the mirror as he goes out of the door, while she, having said farewell, takes the poison that will kill her on stage a few minutes later.

The device had been used in Danish films since 1911; Barry Salt notes (and illustrates) an example from *Ved fængslets Port* (At the Prison Gates; Nordisk, August Blom, 1911); John Fullerton discusses the way Swedish directors used mirrors to extend the arena of action into the space occupied by the spectator without reverse-angle cutting, for example in *Mysteriet Natten till den 25:e* (Mystery of the Eve of the 25th; Hasselblad, 1917); and Yuri Tsivian has remarked on the importance of mirror shots for Russian films of the 1910s—*Korol´ Parizha* (1917) has a spectacular example, where a staircase in a ball scene has a mirror as one of its side walls, creating an almost unreadable space, even when one has seen the film several times

on an editing table.[51]

A more complex example is found in *Klovnen* (Nordisk, 1917), one in which the symbolic role of the mirror is as important as its purely spatial function. The clown Joe Higgins has achieved fame and married his sweetheart Daisy. His happiness is shattered when he catches his wife kissing a stage-door Johnny, Count Henri. The discovery scene takes place in the green room of the variety theatre where Joe is performing (see Figure 4.22). The wide double doors to the green room open directly on to the rear of the stage, blocked from the auditorium only by the backcloth. The wall opposite has a large mirror over the fireplace, used by performers to check their appearance immediately before their entrance. The sequence is as follows:

1   The stage-right wings of a variety theatre. Joe, left, in medium long shot, is offered a contract by an impresario, right, as he leaves the stage after his act. He signals off front left to the green room, and he and the impresario exit front left as pageboys enter rear left from the stage carrying the large bouquets retrieved after Joe's performance, which they deposit in the wings.

2   The green room, filmed from the stage side (Set-up A in the plan). A man in Chinese costume is examining his appearance in the mirror rear centre. The green room door, visible in the mirror, slides open from left to right, revealing Joe and the impresario. As the man in Chinese costume exits left, they come forward; Joe enters the directly visible space of the scene midground right in long-shot framing, and (in the mirror) the impresario closes the door behind them. The impresario enters the directly visible space midground right; a reframing pan left follows Joe and him across until only half the mirror is in shot rear right. The impresario helps Joe take off the outsize lute which is his principal prop. A stage hand enters rear left and re-exits, taking the lute with him. Three performers in evening dress, one a midget, enter rear left, cross to the mirror, examine their appearance (the midget has to be lifted to the mirror to manage this), and exit directly visible space front right. The impresario exits rear left. Joe comes to front left and reads the contract. In the mirror, the three performers can be seen to slide the green room door aside and exit across the left edge of the mirror, leaving the door open and showing the back of the drop across the rear of the stage. Joe sits on a table facing rear right, his eyes on the contract. A pan right brings the whole mirror back into view.

3   The stage-left wings (Set-up B). The Count and Daisy stand front centre in medium long shot, a wing flat behind them. Stage hands and firemen can be seen rear left look-

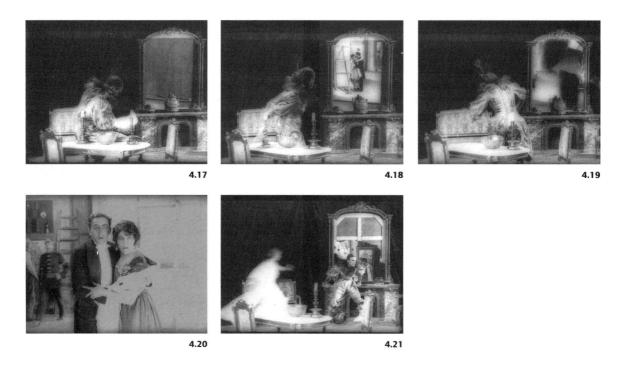

4.17　　　4.18　　　4.19

4.20　　　4.21

ing off right at the stage. One stage hand runs from rear left out front right. Daisy looks anxiously off front right (towards the green room). The Count makes a gesture of contempt in the same direction. He tries to kiss Daisy, but she turns violently away, saying she cannot. Finally, she yields and kisses the Count.

4 The same angle as 2, but closer in, showing the top of the table with Joe sitting on it front left, still in long shot, and the whole of the mirror (Figure 4.17). The backdrop visible in the mirror suddenly rolls up, revealing Daisy kissing the Count. Joe looks up and sees them (Figure

4.18). Aghast, he leans back, picks up a candlestick from the table, and hurls it at the mirror, which shatters (Figure 4.19).

5 As 3. Daisy and the Count look off front right in surprise (Figure 4.20). Daisy runs off front right.

6 As 4. Joe is standing in front of the mirror, by the fire-place, looking off midground right. In a remaining shard of the mirror, Daisy can be seen looking directly towards camera (Figure 4.21). The impresario and a dresser run in rear left and go to Joe. Daisy runs into directly visible space midground right and goes to Joe. Performers and stage hands run in from left and right as Joe pushes Daisy away and exits midground left. Daisy expresses her mystification to the impresario, then follows Joe off left.

The mirror here serves to emphasize Joe's seeing his wife's adultery, and, as is commonly the case with such devices, also draws attention to the partial and hence unreliable nature of a character's vision. Not that Joe is mis-seeing here—his wife really is about to commit adultery—but his overreaction to the sight makes any subsequent reconciliation with Daisy (as when she pleads with Joe in the scene analysed in Chapter 7, above) impossible, and ruins both their lives. However, the mirror does also serve a more strictly spatial function. It allows the viewer and what he sees to be staged in the same scene while retaining

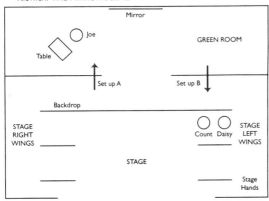

Klovnen: THE MIRROR SCENE

4.22

plausibility that the objects of the vision should be confident of their invisibility—not, that is, appealing to an arbitrary switch from invisibility to visibility such as is resorted to by Benjamin Christensen in the scene in *Det hemmelighedsfulde X* (The Mysterious X) discussed in the next chapter.

More typical and more important than these attempts to extend the playing area laterally is the exploitation of that area in depth, taking advantage of the visibility guaranteed by the single viewpoint. A simple form of this can be seen in theatrical adaptations, once directors and actors of these adopted the forward playing position. In *Shylock*, the 1913 Eclipse version of *The Merchant of Venice*, the casket scene and the trial scene are staged with Portia and the Doge, respectively, in the far rear, and Bassanio, and Antonio and Shylock, respectively, in the foreground position (Figures 4.23 and 4.24). The trial scene is an adaptation of a standard way of staging the same scenes in the theatre, e.g. Charles Kean's Princess Theatre staging of 1858 (Figure 4.25),[52] but with the playing space much deeper and narrower. The Hepworth *Hamlet* adopted the same kind of staging, using narrow aisles of fat romanesque pillars stretching deep into the rear for the scenes inside Elsinore castle. In Act 3, scene 2, the play-within-a-play scene, for example, the players' stage is located in the far rear, Claudius and Gertrude are seated front right facing left, Ophelia front left facing right with Hamlet sitting at her feet. This is a very traditional setting— compare H. Cuthbert's design for Kean's 1858 production[53]—except that characters and scenery have been brought in on either side at the front, leaving a long tunnel between the on-screen spectators to a remote view of the player's stage in the far rear. Chapter 10 of this book has several detailed accounts of deep-staged scenes in 1910s films.[54]

The single viewpoint of the cinema also affected the adaptation to filmmaking of illusory stage techniques. Although the architecture of the movie house did not restrict the space that could be represented on the screen in the way that of the theatre did what can be seen on the stage, and hence there was not the same need for a perspective stage, almost all interiors, and many exteriors representing exotic places or remote epochs, were still filmed in a studio, and the studio might well lack sufficient space to lay out the setting in its true three dimensions, or such

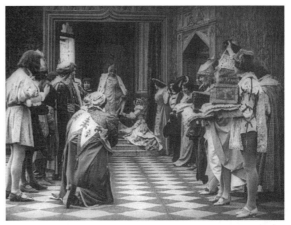

4.23

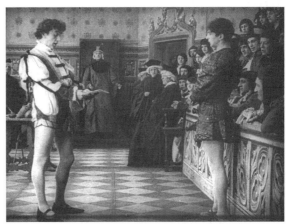

4.24

4.25

179

4.26

4.27

4.28

laying out was avoided to save expense. In such cases, illusory techniques continued, and continue, to be used.

Many early filmmakers built relatively small studios which divided the floor into an acting and a viewing area, for example, the Edison Black Maria and the rooftop stage built by the same company in New York in 1901, George Albert Smith's Hove studio in which a camera in the open air filmed action on a raised platform behind the large double doors of a barn, and, most notoriously, Georges Méliès, whose 1896 glass-house studio had a stage end which, by 1900, had acquired a few of the features of a *féerie* stage—two lines of traps, a single substage storey, a cantilevered frame from which drops could be hung, and possibly one set of *costières*.[55] Soon, however, larger studios were built, creating an entirely flexible floor space within a glass-roofed and walled shed, and the idea of filming action on a 'stage' at one end of the building disappeared. Pathé built such a studio in Vincennes in 1902 with a smaller dimension of 42 feet, and although the travelling crane suspended under the roof probably made it easier to hang large drops directly across the width, set scenes were built on the floor in any disposition convenient for light and the coordination of the simultaneous filming of several subjects.[56] The company erected an even larger studio at Montreuil in 1905. The studio built by the Vitagraph Company of America in Brooklyn in 1906 was of comparable size. Although such studios often had freight elevators for moving large elements of décor or furniture from storage, and these elevators are occasionally used as props in films (e.g. for the mine elevator in Pathé's *Au pays noir* of 1905), the relatively fixed elements of stage floor machinery (traps and grooves or *costières*) were abandoned as incompatible with the efficient deployment of studio space.

However, despite the abandonment of the fixed relationship between a camera and a 'stage' in almost all film studios after the turn of the century, many scenes continued to be filmed with backdrops perpendicular to the lens axis, painted, if the setting required it, with perspectival renditions of deeper space. Often such backdrops would be joined by short, usually splayed side wings, forming a shallow three-wall set. As the camera approached the action, however, such one- or three-wall sets began to give way to two-wall sets, with the two sides, often genuinely at right-angles, oblique to the lens axis. Such corner sets are found, for example, in the Vitagraph *Foul Play* of 1907 (Figure 4.26). Once characters act for large parts of the scene near the ten-foot line, the film stage cuts out of an interior space a narrow-based trapezium, leaving most of the walls invisible; these rooms are thus freed from the kinds of demands of plausibility associated with any theatrical chamber set. In a film like the Vitagraph *Daisies* (1910), the heroine's student lodging at Vassar has a most unlikely re-entrant corner immediately opposite the camera (Figure 4.27), and in the same company's *Wig Wag* of 1911, a room has a corner of considerably less than 90 degrees (Figure 4.28); such free sets are characteristic of filmmaking in short films in the early 1910s, when many rooms are only seen in a single framing which omits most of the space of the room, and most of the walls. A slightly different form of the same freedom from constraint in set construction is found in the features of Léonce Perret (e.g. *L'Enfant de Paris* (Child of Paris), 1913—see the illustrations below—and *Le Roman d'un mousse* (The Story of a Cabin Boy), 1914), where big rooms, often in wealthy homes, are created by raising rear lobbies up flights of steps, and arranging furnishings in groups, each separately lit, often with practical arcs in light fittings on the set, the darkness swathing much of the rest of the space concealing its rather perfunctory character.

A further consequence of the closer approach of the camera is a change in the way certain perspective effects are achieved. In the Pathé *féerie La Légende de Polichinelle* (The Legend of Mr Punch) (1907), in a scene where Polichinelle, pursued by the staff of the toy store whence he has escaped, runs off into the distance, the actor representing him (Max Linder) runs into scene front right in front of a painted backdrop of a hill (Figure 4.29). He exits right slightly further back, running up a ramp concealed by a ground row representing the rocky base of the hill (Figure 4.30), then a model version of him re-enters right and runs off left up the slope of the hill, as his pursuers enter front right and point towards the model (Figure 4.31). This is exactly the way the ride of the Valkyries was handled in the Paris Opéra production of *Die Walküre* discussed by Georges Moynet, mentioned above. This theatrical approach to illusory depth persists in a

4.29

4.30

4.31

4.32

4.33

later scene where Polichinelle escapes the same pursuers by running over a bridge across a chasm. The chasm runs from rear to front centre, and is in fact a fairly steep slide from the horizon down off bottom of frame, but represents a long canyon, with a castle on one side in the far distance. After he has crossed the bridge and his pursuers have been foiled by its collapse (Figure 4.32), Polichinelle goes to the rear and falls on to the slide, disappearing off the bottom of the picture. As he goes to the rear, his nearly constant height destroys the perspective effect of the distant castle (Figure 4.33).

The unique viewpoint of the cinema allowed a different approach to such illusions. Méliès had already exploited it to produce an expanding human head in *L'Homme à la tête en caoutchouc*, in which a man (Méliès himself) lying on a trolley with only his head visible to

camera was pushed up a slope towards that camera, and the resultant picture superimposed on another view of Méliès and a second actor in a constantly framed laboratory in which a decapitated human head is blown up with bellows. This device was adapted in *féeries* such as *Aladin* (Pathé, 1906, see Figure 4.34) and *Le Petit Poucet* (Tom Thumb; Pathé, 1909) to create giants by running a ramp up the bottom face of the visual pyramid and allowing certain actors to stand further forward than the basic front line; as their feet are on the same level in the frame as the rest of the cast, the larger size of their image is interpreted as a larger actual size. Conversely, films like *En avant la musique!* (Forward, Music!; Pathé, 1907) have characters near the front in medium long shot, framing an empty space revealing far to the rear other characters, who are thus made to appear Lilliputian (Figure 4.35).

Deployed as a more concealed illusion, such kinds of staging lead by the end of the 1910s to the characteristic filmic way of combining a flat perspective painting and a three-dimensional arena of action to give an illusion of a much greater space than the action was actually shot in, that is, the glass shot. Here the painting, instead of being a backdrop to the three-dimensional scene, is in front of it, painted on glass relatively close to the camera (as close as sustainable depth of field will allow) and the action is seen through transparent parts of the glass picture. Crude forms of the glass process go back to 1907; glass matte shots, in which the painted scene and the action are combined by superimposition (thus avoiding the depth of field problem), were perfected by 1911, and were in regular use in the USA by the end of the 1910s.[57] The same kind of effect can be achieved using models. Thus a train crash in *Le Manoir de la peur* (The Manorhouse of Fear, 1927) has the train pass obliquely across the rear from right to left, beginning to curve to the front as it exits; the train then reappears left nearer the front now moving in the opposite direction, and falls from the broken viaduct front right. The train that crossed the rear was a real, full-sized train; the one that crossed the front and crashed was a model much closer to the camera than the real train.[58]

Thus the moving-picture camera set very different parameters for the representation of space from those that had governed the stage since the eight-

4.34

4.35

barely half the size of even that of a small variety theatre. Given the relatively small size of cinematic screens, staging actions in the cinema in ways closely modelled on those of the theatre was possible only if the theatrical 'stage' photographed was very small by the standards of popular nineteenth-century theatre, particularly as defined by those genres (whether sensational melodrama or the costume dramas of Irving and Belasco) which depended upon spectacle. The early cinema solved this problem by moving rapidly away from a theatrical model of stage space and creating new forms where characters were brought forward to a position near the camera in which they were seen as very close to the spectators in an arena only a few feet across. This resulted in a space which was narrow at the front and wide at the back. The monocular viewpoint shared by all the spectators also allowed complex composition in depth. Action could be staged along lines parallel to the lens axis; indeed, it had to be if many characters were to be seen simultaneously without reducing the principals to dwarfish size. Editing also allowed the alternation of such close views with much longer shots in which characters appeared much less than life-size, but natural scenery and monumental architecture could be shown in full, in a way impossible on stage except in the outdoor arenas used for pyrotechnical drama (which could not handle the more intimate scenes, too). This flexibility also made it possible to show humble surroundings where appropriate without absurd discrepancies of scale.

Despite all these differences, the ways filmmakers used their apparatuses to present space for dramatic purposes can be shown to return to and rework stage conventions. By the 1910s, the cinema was technically highly independent of the theatre, but its treatment of space is more profoundly indebted to theatrical models than the editing-based accounts of film history would suggest.

eenth century. The theatrical stage was broad at the front and narrow at the rear, and the multiple viewpoints of the audience and the perspectival cheating of the actual stage space hindered movement or immediate interaction of characters parallel to the axis of the stage; the main action occurred at or near the proscenium arch, and was arranged across the stage. The cinematic screen, by contrast, was narrow—

1. 'Le Cinématographe: Une merveille photographique', *Le Radical* (30 Sept. 1895); repr. in Georges Sadoul, *Louis Lumière*, Cinéma d'aujourd'hui no. 29 (Paris: Seghers, 1964), 117–18.
2. Musser, *Emergence of Cinema*, 96 and 116–17. There is one curious exception. Reporting on the same event as the last of these quotations, the debut of the Vitascope at Koster and Bial's, the *New York Times* of 24 Apr. 1896 stated: 'The moving figures are

about half life size.' (In 'The Motion Picture Theater and Film Exhibition 1896–1932', Ph.D. thesis (Northwestern University, Evanston, Ill., 1980), 9, Charlotte Herzberg says 'the vaudeville screen was continually referred to as . . . framed like a picture with half life-size figures', but she only gives this one example, and we know of no others.) *The Times* reporter may have been more careful than his colleagues, but he may also have been confused by the knowledge that one's image in a mirror subtends half its dimensions on the mirror surface, and hence self-portraits tend to do the same on the picture plane, and other portraits follow suit—essentially implying that the sitter is the same distance behind the picture plane as the viewer is in front, but at any rate producing pictures of heads half the size of real human heads. The picture of the Koster and Bial's show of April–May 1896 reproduced from the National Archives by Musser in *Emergence of Cinema*, 117, does show what seems to be a rather small screen. On the other hand, the advertisement for the Milwaukee Academy Theater's presentation of the Vitascope in the *Milwaukee Sentinel* for 26 July 1896, reproduced in *Emergence of Cinema*, 125, shows a screen with dancing girls on it, and a live presenter standing next to the screen. In this case, the dancing girls are the same height as the presenter. Both these illustrations are drawings rather than photographs, of course.

3. *Moving Picture World*, 7, no. 9 (27 Aug. 1910), 470; John Klaber, 'Planning the Moving Picture Theatre', *Architectural Record*, 38, no. 5 (Nov. 1915), 540, cit. Richard Koszarski, *An Evening's Entertainment: The Age of the Silent Feature Picture, 1915–1928*, vol. iii of Charles Harpole (ed.), *History of the American Cinema* (New York: Scribner's, 1990), 10; 'Too Near the Camera', *Moving Picture World*, 8, no. 12 (25 Mar. 1911), 634.

4. For an early example, Colin Bennett in 'Knotty Points Answered', *Kinematograph and Lantern Weekly*, 20, no. 447 (18 Nov. 1915), 71, recommends a 10 to 12 foot wide screen for a throw of 45 feet, and a 15 to 19 foot wide screen for a throw of 80 feet. In 1917, the architect Edward Kinsila grafts the two schemata together: 'The size of a picture depends upon the distance of the throw and the amperage of the light. A twelve-foot picture is considered "life size." A well lighted picture of this size should be the limit for a fifty-foot throw, a fifteen-foot picture for a seventy-five-foot throw, and for a hundred-foot throw or longer any size that may be brilliantly illuminated and that will not show living figures that appear from the rear seats much larger than normal' (p. 106).

5. See Wilfrid Blunt and William T. Stearn, *The Art of Botanical Illustration*, rev. edn. (Kew: Royal Botanical Gardens, 1994), plate 48.

6. Emanaud, *Géométrie perspective*, 373.

7. For example, the advertisement mentioned above, reproduced in Musser, *Emergence of Cinema*, 125. As far as one can tell from a drawing, the screen here is about 14 feet by 18 feet. The same picture was reproduced as part of the heading of the notepaper of the New York Vitascope Company (see Musser, *Emergence of Cinema*, 132). *Scientific American* of 17 Apr. 1897 includes a drawing of 'The Biograph at work in a New York theater' showing a truly monumental screen, able to show a locomotive 'life size', let alone a person (reproduced in Musser, *Emergence of Cinema*, 182). Finally, the movies projected on a vaudeville stage in the Edison film *Uncle Josh at the Moving Picture Show* (1902) include life-size figures (but they would have to, or the story would not work).

8. In the USA, the numbers were partly determined by city ordinances which called for more stringent licensing conditions for theatres than for amusements or common shows, the difference being determined by capacity. See Herzberg, 'Motion Picture Theater and Film Exhibition', 38, no. 39.

9. For the Omnia Pathé, see the elevations submitted with the application for building permission, reproduced from the originals in the Archives of the City of Paris in Deslandes and Richard, *Histoire comparée du cinéma*, 496 and 499.

10. '*Grandma's Reading Glass*. A most successful film. Grandma is sewing, and her little grandson amuses himself by viewing the surrounding objects through her large reading glass. Circular and magnified views are shown of the objects he beholds, viz. the works of his watch, the canary in its cage, his grandma's eye, the cat's head, etc.' (*Charles Urban Trading Co. Catalogue*, Nov. 1903, p. 106). The film so described, George Albert Smith's *Grandma's Reading Glass*, was first advertised in September 1900.

11. Maurice Noverre, 'Le Gala Méliès', *Le Nouvel Art cinématographique*, 2nd ser., no. 5 (Jan. 1930), 71–90; cit. Deslandes and Richard, *Histoire comparée du Cinéma*, 468–70.

12. J. P. Chalmers and Thomas Bedding, 'The Factor of Uniformity', *Moving Picture World*, 5, no. 4 (24 July 1909), 115–16. The same objection had been raised against lantern slides by Duncan Moore in 1894: 'Pictures exhibited much above their normal size have a more or less grotesque appearance, especially if containing figures. . . . The screen proclaims their unreality, which is at once strikingly apparent' ('Size or Realism?', *Optical Magic Lantern Journal and Photographic Enlarger*, 5, no. 58 (1 Mar. 1894), 56; cit. Burch, *Life to Those Shadows*, 89).

13. Salten, 'Zu einem Kinodramen, Anmerkungen', 364–5. Yuri Tsivian discusses the nature of this objection at length in his book *Early Cinema in Russia and its Cultural Reception*, trans. Alan Bodger (London: Routledge, 1994), esp. pp. 131–4 and 199–201. Among other examples he cites (p. 131) the Russian critic E. Stark, who, like Salten, objects that the variation in scale makes it impossible to appreciate the acting: 'The directors are clearly people with no idea of artistic taste: the slightest hint of emotion in a scene and for some reason they immediately shoot figures and faces enlarged almost to twice life size. Imagine what it is like to see a huge nose, a vast mouth, monstrous lips, all leering down at you. And when all these bits of a face belonging to a visitor from outer space begin to move, to express profound emotion—well, the sadder the scene is meant to be, the more grotesque and totally ridiculous is the effect' ('S nogami na stole', *Teatr i iskusstvo*, 39 (1913), 770).

14. See H. F. Hoffman, 'Cutting off the Feet', *Moving Picture World*, 12, no. 1 (6 Apr. 1912), 53.

15. 'Practical Filming Techniques for Three-Dimension and Wide-Screen Motion Pictures', *American Cinematographer*, 34, no. 3 (Mar. 1953), 107. Although Clarke makes no distinction between people and things in his prescription, it seems clear that people without feet are more problematic than furniture ditto. *Dial M for Murder* (1954), almost entirely set in a single apartment, furnishes that apartment with a large low three-piece suite, thus ensuring that in most of its closer shots of characters, the bottom of the screen and the stereoscopically perceptible frontmost plane is filled by the top of a couch or armchair, thus concealing the disappearance of the characters' feet off the bottom of the picture. Non-stereoscopic films in the 1910s often put furniture in the frontmost plane for the same reasons.

16. The most important of these is the Biograph 68 mm film also introduced by Dickson and intended to provide a picture quality that would outdo Edison filmmakers and others, like the Lumière brothers, who had adopted standard Edison-type film.

17. Fred H. Detmers (ed.), *American Cinematographer Manual*, 6th edn. (Hollywood: ASC Press, 1986), gives the dimensions of 0.980 inches by 0.735 inches for non-squeezed photography where the camera aperture fills the four-perforation area and the full space between perforations. This format is now used by cinematogra-

phers only for special effects duplication (and for restoring silent films, of course), and in the early years of cinema, there were no prescribed standards. The difference between these figures and 1 inch by ¾ inch is an allowance for slight variations in registration in cameras and projectors.

18. See Musser, *Emergence of Cinema*, 62–72.

19. Richard Southern notes in *Changeable Scenery*, 177–82 and with relation to plate 29, that one reason why the upper grooves of British baroque stages were hinged was so that they could be tucked out of the way in order to allow certain scenes to deploy the full height of the proscenium in a portrait-format picture. This practice seems to have died out before the rise of pictorialist theatre in our sense, though the Byron Collection of the Museum of the City of New York includes a set of four photographs for David Belasco's production of *The Girl of the Golden West* (New York, 1905) which show what seems to be either an act drop or a shallow staging with a backdrop in one of the front grooves representing the Californian Sierras; the trunks of two giant trees occupy the foreground, and they are carried right up to the limit of the proscenium opening, on to the curtain running across its top fifth. The four views are differently lit, with the sun in the centre of the drop brighter and darker and higher or lower, so presumably they represent a sunrise or sunset. However, the setting seems incompatible with the only sunrise or sunset in the play, the epilogue as Minny and Ramirez leave California for ever, so we are not sure what the photographs depict.

20. Eisenstein's lecture of 17 Sept. 1930 was reworked as 'The Dynamic Square', published in *Close-up* (Mar. and June 1931), and repr. in *Film Essays and a Lecture*, ed. Jay Leyda (New York: Praeger, 1970), 48–65.

21. Gad, *Filmen*, 83; Colin N. Bennett, *The Guide to Kinematography* (London: E. T. Heron, 1917), 27. See also C. L. Gregory (ed.), *Motion Picture Photography* (New York: New York Photographic Society, 1920), 65, and F. Paul Liesegang, *Handbuch der praktischen Kinematographie*, 5th edn. (Düsseldorf: Ed. Liesegang, 1918), 326.

22. Colin N. Bennett et al., *The Handbook of Kinematog-raphy*, 2nd edn. (London: Kinematograph Weekly, 1913), 18.

23. 'Knotty Points Answered', *Kinematograph and Lantern Weekly*, 14, no. 352 (22 Jan. 1914), 74–5. The argument is spurious, because it ignores the fact that the spectator can (indeed must) move his or her eyes from side to side, and one can take in much more than 16 degrees that way without turning one's head, which the cinema spectator can easily do, too; it also assumes that the screen should occupy no more nor less than the full field visible to the stationary eye, a still-photography prescription that is by no means obviously extendable to the situation in a moving-picture house.

24. David S. Hulfish, *Cyclopedia of Motion-Picture Work* (Chicago: American Technical Society, 1911), 131–2 (section 'Motography', 63–4). The prescription is reprinted unchanged in the 1915 edition of the book, entitled *Motion Picture Work*.

25. 'The Degradation of the Motion Picture', *Photo-Era*, 21, no. 4 (Oct. 1908), 163; cit. Kristin Thompson, in Bordwell, Staiger, and Thompson, *Classical Hollywood Cinema*, 221. (For the problem of depth of field at issue here, see below.) Writing much later, in 1939, but describing standard Edison-film cameras contemporaneous with the wide-film Biograph, i.e. cameras of the 1900s, G. W. Bitzer notes: 'There were other drawbacks in Biograph cameras. The lenses had to be of longer focus to cover the wider film. The optical formula then being that of a two-inch focus to cover a one-

inch field. The sprocket-hole 35 mm film cameras were using that as a standard lens, a 50 mm or two-inch lens' ('The Biograph Camera', *Journal of the Society of Operating Cameramen*, 5, no. 1 (Spring 1995), 8). It should be said that there are indirect contemporary references to the two-inch lens. In *Technique of the Photoplay*, 2nd edn. (New York: Moving Picture World, 1913), 21, Epes Winthrop Sargent says: 'Generally diagrams are made of the sets, either in free hand or to scale. In the latter way paper lightly ruled into squares is used. Each of these squares represents a square foot of space. At one point a line is drawn across six of these squares. This is known as the *front line* and corresponds to the footlights of the dramatic stage. The Editor [i.e. the studio's scenario editor] knows that the lens his cameraman uses will just take in the six foot line if placed twelve and a half feet back of the line.' To the extent that these figures can be trusted (see n. 29 below), this lens is a two-inch one, allowing the actors a small latitude to stray beyond the strict 6 feet.

26. Salt, *Film Style and Technology*, 84.

27. 'It is not usual to go below two and a half inches on the short side, and indeed only a few of the cameras on the market would be able to be fitted with a shorter focal length than this' (*Handbook*, 31). But in *Practical Cinematography and Its Applications* (London: Heinemann, 1913), Frederick A. Talbot takes the Williamson 'Topical' camera, a cheap non-professional model, as his standard example, and says of it that it 'is fitted with a Zeiss-Tessar 2-inch lens' (p. 24).

28. For example, James Slevin, *On Picture-Play Writing: A Hand-Book of Workmanship* (Cedar Grove, NJ: Farmer Smith, 1912), 85: 'In producing a picture-play . . . a certain wedge-shaped space is laid out and marked with lines. The narrow end of this space, about five to eight feet wide, starts about eight or ten feet of the camera.' This implies a slightly shorter lens than two inches, while the most restricted framing he refers to is 'when the principal characters are brought very close to the camera and are cut off at the knees or waist' (p. 86). Eustace Hale Ball, *The Art of the Photoplay*, 2nd edn. (New York: G. W. Dillingham, 1913), 19, gives 'a stage width of six or eight feet, at a distance of ten feet from the lens,' implying a somewhat shorter lens (too short for one to be confident in the accuracy of his figures). In a much later interview, James Morrison, a Vitagraph stock-company member from 1912, recalled: 'We were the first people to bring people up to within nine feet of the camera. . . . The next innovation in the movies was when Griffith did the close-up. We thought of the nine-foot line, but we didn't think of the close-up' (Kevin Brownlow, *The Parade's Gone by* (London: Secker & Warburg, 1968), 18). Note that Morrison is clear that the nine-foot position did not put the actor into close-up. See the extensive discussion of this development in Salt, *Film Style and Technology*, 88–90; Thompson, in Bordwell et al., *Classical Hollywood Cinema*, 190–1; and Bowser, *Transformation of Cinema*, 93–102.

29. Unfortunately, most of the evidence in this question, apart from the look of the films themselves, derives from screen-writing manuals, in the sections where the authors are explaining to their would-be screenwriter readership the peculiarities of filmmaking. The figures they give for the distance of the front line from the camera and the width of that line differ greatly, and are rarely compatible with plausible lens lengths, or even internally consistent. J. Berg Esenwein and Arthur Leeds, in *Writing the Photoplay* (Springfield, Mass.: Home Correspondence School, 1913), 160, present what purports to be a producer's diagram of the film stage

'the same as the one used by at least three Licensed and two Independent producing companies' (p. 161). The camera's angle of view in this diagram is exactly 25 degrees, i.e. the lens assumed is about 2¼ inches. But figures written on the plan say the front line is 14 feet from the camera and 4 feet 1¼ inches wide, which implies a lens of nearly 3½ inches.

30. See Leslie Stroebel, John Compton, Ira Current, and Richard Zakia, *Photographic Materials and Processes* (Boston: Focal Press, 1986), 159.

31. Gregory, *Motion Picture Photography*, 65. What appears to most spectators as a 'natural' view and a view from the centre of vision are not necessarily the same thing, however. See the discussion of movement in depth, below.

32. E. G. Lutz, *The Motion-Picture Cameraman* (New York: C. Scribner's Sons, 1927; repr. New York: Arno Press, 1972), 79, figure 1. Although written outside our period, this set-up is frequently found in American filmmaking within it. Before the frequent use of scenes with less than full figures, Pathé cameramen in France usually used a lower camera, about 3 feet from the ground, and therefore appreciably closer to those figures.

33. Ball, *Art of the photoplay*, 18–19. Similarly, Slevin (*On Picture-Play writing*, 85) remarks of the cinematic stage, 'you see at a glance that this is just contrary to an ordinary stage setting where the widest end of a more or less wedge-shaped space is toward the audience and is usually painted in perspective'.

34. *Le Cinéma* (Paris: La Renaissance du Livre, 1919), 95.

35. Gad, *Filmen*, 76.

36. O. Winter, 'The Cinematograph', *New Review* (May 1896), repr. *Sight and Sound*, 51, no. 4 (Autumn 1982), 295; and A. D. Digmelov, '50 let nazad', typescript in the V. Vishnevsky archive, Gosfilmofond, Moscow, cit. Tsivian, *Early Cinema in Russia*, 145–6.

37. Bennett, *Handbook*, 28. The subject discussed is a waterfall rather than a character, confirming the specialized nature of the field in which Bennett was offering advice.

38. The earliest example usually cited is the 1919 film *Broken Blossoms*, which has a few soft atmospheric establishing shots. Yuri Tsivian (*Early Cinema in Russia*, 107–8) says that in the same year, Aleksandr Sanin's film *Polikushka* was soft throughout, as a result of the use of defective stock, but that the effect was so admired that later films recreated it artificially.

39. Gad, *Filmen*, 77.

40. Modern definitions of focus for 35 mm film demand a circle of confusion less than 0.001 inches, but this is to allow for the greater magnification in projection of anamorphic and wide-screen formats. The circle of confusion implied by figures for depth of field given by Talbot in 1913 (p. 47) and Bennett in 1917 (*Guide to Kinematography*, 28) is about one four-hundredth of an inch, i.e. 0.0025. The only direct statement we have found from our period of the appropriate circle of confusion is by C. L. Gregory (*Motion Picture Photography* 361): 'Usually taken at 0.01 inch but for critical definition 0.005 is necessary.' This seems very large, and may perhaps be a figure taken over carelessly from formulae appropriate to full- and half-plate still photography. However, Lutz in 1927 (*Motion-Picture Cameraman*, 65) gives figures for hyperfocal distance and depth of field with a two-inch lens that imply a circle of confusion of 0.004 inches. Does this reflect the prevalence of the 'soft style' of cinematography in the later 1920s?

41. Gad, *Filmen*, 122.

42. It was possible, with appropriate development, to achieve an exposure index of about 25 ISO with the film stocks of this period; in a note in Karl Brown, *Adventures with D. W. Griffith*, ed. Kevin Brownlow (London: Secker & Warburg, 1973), 18, George J. Mitchell suggests this as the speed of film when Karl Brown started working in 1914, and Colin Bennett's 1913 advice that 'generally speaking . . . a stop of about f8 with the shutter opening of about one third of a circle [i.e. an exposure of 1/48th second at 16 fps] is right for most things' implies about the same speed if he is using a rule of thumb equivalent to the modern one that in bright daylight exposure at f16 should be the reciprocal of the ISO speed of the film in seconds (see Stroebel *et al.*, *Photographic Materials*, 112). At this exposure index, shooting at f16 would require illumination of around 5,000–6,000 foot-candles, well within the range of unassisted daylight. In Northern Europe and the East coast of the USA, the light for studio-shot interiors involving this kind of deep staging was always boosted artificially with arc or mercury-vapour lamps; in California and Italy, for most of the year such light levels could be guaranteed without any addition to daylight.

43. *Handbook*, 29. Cecil Hepworth had deprecated the tendency to film at full aperture for the same reason much earlier, in 1900: 'If a smaller stop be used, all parts of the view, both near and distant, may be kept well in focus, while rapidly moving objects will not be caught with sufficient speed to prevent a slight blurring of their outlines. It is a question whether such objects are better portrayed with absolute crispness of detail when, as projected, they will appear to cross the sheet in a series of very rapid jerks, or whether it is better to have the stiller objects in perfect focus, and those that move rapidly to betray their movement by slight blurring of their vertical lines' (*Animated Photography: The ABC of the Cinematograph* (London: Hazell, Watson, & Viney, 1900), 91).

44. See n. 36. Compare Cecil Hepworth in 1900: 'Again, the use of a wide-angle lens, nearly always reprehensible, is generally most abominable in connection with the production of a living photograph. The mere movement of the objects from place to place in the picture is sufficient to lend to it a heightened perspective effect, which, in a single photograph, would be by no means as marked, and the exaggerated perspective of wide-angularism becomes horribly exaggerated. For instance, what could be much more ridiculous than a representation of a boxing match, intended to inspire the spectators with excitement and dread, when the participants alternately dwindle to Lilliputian pigmies and swell into ungainly giants, as they dance around one another in the ring?' (*Animated Photography*, 97–8).

45. Salten, 'Zu einem Kinodramen, Anmerkungen', 364.

46. Victorin Hyppolite Jasset, 'Étude sur la mise-en-scène en cinématographie', *Ciné-Journal* (21 Oct.–25 Nov. 1911), repr. in Marcel Lapierre (ed.), *Anthologie du cinéma* (Paris: La Nouvelle Édition, 1946), 97. See also Esenwein and Leeds, *Writing the Photoplay*, 194: 'The actors must be constantly on the alert to avoid "getting out of the picture".'

47. See Salt, *Film Style and Technology*, 32–3 and 81–2.

48. 'Théâtre et cinéma', *Esprit* (June and July–Aug. 1951); repr. in *Qu'est-ce-que le cinéma? Édition définitive* (Paris: Éditions du Cerf, 1978), 160.

49. Nevertheless, there were complaints about them, and in 1912, F. H. Richardson reported in the *Moving Picture World* that Vitagraph had decided to abandon the device. See 'Projection Department', *Moving Picture World*, 13, no. 5 (3 Aug. 1912), 449; and 13, no. 7 (17 Aug. 1912), 666.

50. Salt, *Film Style and Technology*, 127.

51. Ibid. 70; John Fullerton, 'The "Golden Age" of Swedish Film: Towards a New Historiography', unpublished paper delivered at Milestones of Cinema, a conference at the University of Wisconsin Madison, Oct. 1995; Yuri Tsivian, 'Portraits, Mirrors, Death: On Some Decadent Clichés in Early Russian Films', paper presented at Le Portrait peint au cinéma/The Painted Portrait in Film, a conference held at the Musée du Louvre, Apr. 1991, published in *iris*, 14–15 (1992), 67–83.

52. Reproduced in the microfiche collection *Theatre Set Designs in the Victoria and Albert Museum* (Haslemere: Emmett Publishing, 1985), fiche 14, frames E11 & 12.

53. Ibid. fiche 12, frame E11.

54. See also Brewster, 'La Mise en scène en profondeur dans les films français'; and David Bordwell, 'La Nouvelle Mission de Feuillade; or, What Was Mise en Scène?', *Velvet Light Trap*, 37 (Spring 1996), 10–29.

55. For Edison, see Musser, *Emergence of Cinema*, 80; and *Before the Nickelodeon*, 160; for Smith, Rachael Low and Roger Manvell, *The History of the British Film*, vol. i: *1896–1906* (London: Allen & Unwin, 1948), plate 4, and compare Williamson's and Paul's studios in plates 3 and 6; for Méliès, Maurice Noverre, 'L'Œuvre de Georges Méliès', *Le Nouvel Art cinématographique*, 2nd ser., no. 3 (July 1929), and for an English translation of the most important passages, John Frazer, *Artificially Arranged Scenes: The Films of Georges Méliès* (Boston: G. K. Hall, 1979), 38–41.

56. See Richard Abel, *The Ciné Goes to Town: French Cinema, 1896–1914* (Berkeley: University of California Press, 1994), 20–1.

57. See Salt, *Film Style and Technology*, 134–5; and Raymond Fielding, 'Norman O. Dawn: Pioneer Worker in Special-Effects Cinematography', *Journal of the Society of Motion Picture Engineers*, 72 (Jan. 1963), repr. in Raymond Fielding (ed.), *A Technological History of Motion Pictures and Television* (Berkeley: University of California Press, 1967), 141–9.

58. The 'theatrical' disposition of live action and model was not entirely abandoned, however. In *Swing Time* (1936), when the hero and heroine visit a country lodge in midwinter, their arrival is filmed with the lodge midground left, its driveway across the front, and a snowy landscape rear right. An automobile is seen to enter from behind the lodge, very small, far off in the snowy landscape. It exits rear right, then re-enters front right, stops, and the passengers descend. The rear right landscape is a model (or part glass part model), as is the car which crosses it.

Chapter 10
Staging and Editing

MOST of the examples discussed here so far have been concerned with space in a scene filmed as a single take, i.e. continuously from either a single position or a continuously moving one. This requires no special justification in many cases, since in the 1910s fiction films largely consist of such scenes linked by relatively elliptical breaks, usually covered by an intertitle; these breaks closely resemble scene changes in a stage play. But in many other cases, devices of a similar kind appear in sequences which consist of shots edited together. Here the theatrical analogy is much less clear-cut. Considerations of the relations between camera and filmed space are not necessarily adequate to deal with questions of cinematic space in a series of shots as opposed to a single one.

The standard modern ways of conceiving this problem derive from one of Kuleshov's experiments. A shot of Aleksandra Khoklova walking down Petrov Street in Moscow was followed in turn by a shot of Leonid Obolensky walking along the embankment of the Moscow River, a shot of them shaking hands on the Boulevard Prechistensk, also in Moscow, and then looking off, and a shot of the White House in Washington.[1] The result is a place which never existed in the real world—a city in which remote Moscow streets are next to one another, and also to a famous building in the United States. Cinematic space thus becomes a matter of the synthesis of a set of views by positing plausible connections between them—connections of action, such as a character walking out of one scene and entering into the next; connections via looks, such as a character looking out of one scene, with the second a view they might plausibly be able to see; and connections via overlapping elements, such as furniture, or body parts seen from different angles and distances in different views, but plausibly posited as identical.

Clearly, theatrical scenes have to be linked in similar ways; the castle has to be the appropriate distance from the forest for characters to move from one to the other in the interval between the scenes implied by the plot. The earliest multiple-shot films related their shots in the same fashion. Most notably, in chase films characters run through succeeding landscapes in a single pursuit, such that the landscapes have to be conceived as more or less, but not necessarily precisely, adjacent to one another. However, the Kuleshovian schema supposes a much closer relationship between the different views than this—a relationship where physical and mental actions in one view have immediate repercussions in the next. The expectation, in this schema, is that each element of the action will be isolated in a shot which is a link in the chain of shots, and that the space will exist solely as an inference from this sequence. The pictorial tradition in the theatre, on the contrary, tries to bring the elements of a causal concatenation together into the single space of a scene, conceived as the simultaneous representation of a situation.

A typical instance of this tendency to unify the space of dramatically important action is provided by the multiple-room set. As we have seen, Percy Fitzgerald criticized such sets in *Jonathan Bradford* because they attempted to occult the real space of the theatre and replace it with an artificial one constituted by the fiction. Hassan El Nouty makes the same point in relation to the first scene of Dumas *père*'s *La Reine Margot* (1847), which shows action simultaneously in two rooms of an inn and the street outside. El Nouty goes on to link this artificial space to the typical space in the Kuleshovian notion of cinema, a space in which the camera is ubiquitous, in so far as it can be placed anywhere, but only in a sequence of shots, not in the simultaneity of a single scene. The multiple-room set in the theatre is thus for El Nouty a false compromise of protocinematic theatre. Rather than showing two spaces simultaneously, the scene should alternate between views of each of these spaces in turn, as it does in the cinema.[2] If El Nouty is correct, multiple-room sets would be expected to

disappear from the cinematic representation of situations in which the nineteenth-century theatre resorted to them.

Multiple-room sets are, in fact, found quite frequently in films made before 1910 for the representation of simultaneous actions in different but adjacent spaces. In the films produced by the Vitagraph Company of America between 1906 and 1908, such a set is probably the commonest way to represent a character in one room overhearing something in the next, e.g. in *Foul Play* (1907), *Father's Quiet Sunday* (1907), and *Circumstantial Evidence* (1908) (Figure 4.36). However, the alternative of a cut from a view of one space to one of another was possible. By 1908, Vitagraph films regularly use room-to-room cutting for more or less simultaneous action in different adjacent spaces, e.g. in *The Boy, the Bust, and the Bath*.

D. W. Griffith at Biograph adopted this method of construction for his interiors. By early 1912, a film like *Three Sisters* has a climactic sequence of 28 shots alternating between three set-ups—long-shot views of three rooms, a kitchen, a hall, and a bedroom, which movements from room to room that coincide with cuts establish as side by side. As Griffith is careful (in interiors) to preserve screen direction—a character who leaves the scene of one shot on the left will enter the scene of the next on the right, and vice versa—and films each space frontally, along a room axis, the total space of the house is like a doll's house, the front wall of the three adjacent rooms being as it were transparent to the camera (Figures 4.37–4.40.). However, unlike the practicable multiple-room sets of *Jonathan Bradford* or *La Reine Margot*, this doll's house only exists by inference. All the scenes on each set would have been shot together in the Biograph Studio, then that set struck and the set for the next mounted, and so on—the whole house never existed, even in the studio.

Thus far, the standard account would seem to be borne out: a theatrical simultaneity is succeeded by a cinematic fragmentation and linearization. Yet handling strictly simultaneous actions remains a problem. In a relatively early use of room-to-room cutting by Griffith, the 1908 film *An Awful Moment*, at the climax of the alternation between set-ups around a crucial door a multiple-room set is introduced. The wife of a jailed Black Hand gangster seeks to revenge herself on the judge in the case. She stupefies the judge's wife

4.36

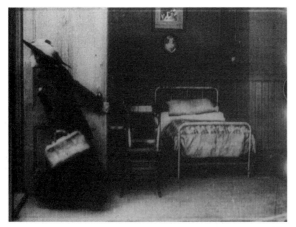

4.37

4.38

4.39

4.40

and ties her to a chair with a shotgun rigged pointing at her, its trigger tied by a cord to the door knob. On his return, the judge, opening the door, will bring about the shooting of his own wife. At the last minute, as the judge is reaching for the door knob, their little daughter unhooks the cord from the knob on the other side of the door. The surviving print of the film (a copyright deposit paper print) is out of order, grouping all scenes on each set together (presumably preserving a shooting order), but the regular appearance and disappearance of coats, hats, and parcels makes it possible to reconstruct the likely sequence of these scenes, including an alternation around the door as the judge goes towards it looking for his wife. But the shot in which he opens the door, and his daughter takes off the cord, shows both rooms at once, with the door at the centre.

In general thereafter Griffith (while by no means abandoning a predilection for suspenseful climaxes produced by infernal machines) avoided situations which demanded such an immediate association of actions in two different rooms; in *A Lonely Villa* (1909) and *The Lonedale Operator* (1911), the final confrontations occur in the rooms in which the heroines have sequestered themselves; in *The Coming of Angelo* and *Fate* (both 1913), the heroes escape the room in which a bomb is planted, and the villain and his son respectively are there when the bomb explodes—the explosion is filmed in the interior in the first case and the exterior in the second. When the simultaneous actions have more duration, as in scenes of eavesdropping or watching others from hiding, Griffith does use alternation between spaces. Thus, in *The Voice of the Child* (1912), when the husband learns his wife is

190

4.41

4.42

4.43

4.44

about to elope, he hides round the corner of their house with a gun, intending to shoot the seducer. The seducer drives up, the wife comes down the steps, but before she can get into the car, her little daughter comes running out of the house; unable to desert her, the wife rejects the lover and returns to the house. The seducer drives off, and the husband rejoins his wife. While the husband is in hiding there are a series of identically framed shots of him looking off front left, while his wife, the seducer, and the daughter are seen in two views (neither point-of-view shots), by the house door and at the garden gate (Figures 4.41–4.44).

The Vitagraph Company devised a different way of handling such situations when they, too, abandoned multiple-room sets around 1909. When Eliza overhears her master selling little Harry and Tom to Haley, in the Vitagraph *Uncle Tom's Cabin*, she is just visible through the double sliding doors at the rear centre of the set representing the Shelbys' dining-room. There is then a 180-degree cut to a closer (medium-long-shot) view of Eliza listening on the other side of the doors (Figures 4.45 and 4.46). All the principal actors involved in the situation are visible in both shots, but the reversal of the viewpoint brings out the contrast between one group and another. In Griffith's alternation, on the contrary, the simultaneity of the theatrical tableau is replaced by the repetition of different framings in the film sequence.

Alternation remains one of the key ways of emphasizing the simultaneity of differently located actions in the cinema. In a sense this extends the plausible space of the stage picture and obviates such distortions of verisimilitudinous action as the return of characters who have exited simply to be part of the

4.45

4.46

act-end tableau. However, the option of alternation did not spell the end of the multiple-room set in the cinema. On the contrary, the early feature seems to have given it a new life. For a now lost film, *The Hand of Peril* (Paragon for World, 1916), Maurice Tourneur's set designer Ben Carré built a nine-room house set, with all the rooms on one side of a house visible simultaneously or separately.[3] Perhaps even more striking, because it adopts an angle of view impossible in the theatre, is the bank set in the opening sequence of Tourneur's *Alias Jimmy Valentine* (1915). The scene in the bank occurs neither in the 1909 play by Paul Armstrong on which the film is based, nor in the short story by O. Henry, 'A Retrieved Reformation', which provided the starting-point for the play. The latter begins in the Warden's office at Sing Sing prison with the hero already a prisoner; the short

story begins even later with the safe-cracker's release from prison. The film starts earlier than either, with the crime for which Lee Randall, alias Jimmy Valentine, is arrested and sent to Sing Sing.

After a credit sequence with a portrait of Lee Randall and a dissolve to Jimmy in convict garb, Randall is seen leaving his office and going to an apartment in a poor quarter, setting his alarm clock and going to sleep. Waking in the small hours, he goes to a rendezvous in waste ground with two accomplices, Red Joclyn and Bill Avery. Outside a bank they meet the fourth member of the gang, Cotton. While Avery stays outside as look-out, the other three men enter the bank by a back-alley basement entrance. So far the film has used a *découpage* with shots of moderate length simply following the principal actors, usually with somewhat elliptical connections between the shots, and only minimal alternation for the scenes of the two rendezvous. As soon as Valentine, Red, and Cotton disappear down the basement trapdoor and Avery settles to wait as look-out, the whole of the bank interior is shown in a single bird's-eye view, not from directly above but obliquely, and at an angle to the prevailing direction of the walls (see the plan, Figure 4.47). As this is the double-height ground floor of a bank, the walls we can see the tops of might plausibly be partitions that do not reach all the way to the ceiling, but even so, it looks impossible for a camera actually in a real bank to have such a comprehensive view of all the interior spaces. Throughout the subsequent robbery, this is the only view of the ground-floor bank interior that we get, apart from one final closer view of the tellers' counter.

1 Very high-angle, very long shot of the bank interior. The

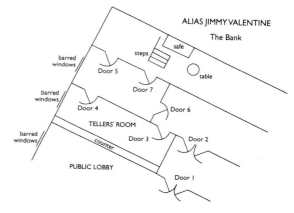

4.47

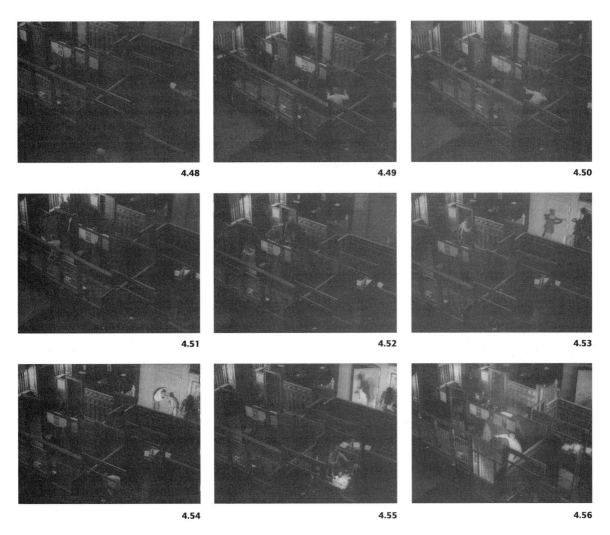

4.48	4.49	4.50
4.51	4.52	4.53
4.54	4.55	4.56

interior is dark, and all the doors through the partitions are closed, except door 1. Valentine, Red, and Cotton enter front centre (Figure 4.48). Red periodically consults a plan he carries in one hand, and then advises Valentine of the route.

Although the action is quite fast (the whole shot is 79 seconds at 16 frames per second), it is choreographed to produce a series of attitudes, with all the actors freezing when each door in the set is opened, as the thieves wait to be sure no one has seen or heard them.

After entering, Valentine, Red and Cotton go cautiously through doors 1, 2, and 3, arriving in the tellers' room, separated from the public lobby front left by a series of counter grills. Pan left as Red goes to the window left and looks out (Figure 4.49). He tells Valentine the route, and

Valentine opens door 4, as Cotton watches the way they came through door 3 (Figure 4.50). Valentine goes through door 4 and looks out of the window rear left, Red follows him through, consulting his plan, while Cotton comes to door 4 (Figure 4.51). Valentine opens door 5 (Figure 4.52). Pan right as Valentine, then Red, go through door 5, round and down the steps to the safe rear right, and Cotton goes to door 5 and waits. Red lights a lamp (Figure 4.53).

A small arc concealed behind the partition wall in front of the safe goes on—presumably a dark lantern in the fiction.

Valentine and Red take off their jackets and start to work on the combination, while Cotton goes back from door 5 through doors 4, 3, and 2, and stands watching at door 1 (Figure 4.54).

2 Avery is standing in medium long shot by the trapdoor to the basement entrance, more or less facing camera. He waits.

This cutaway covers the lengthy business of finding the safe combination and opening the safe.

3 As 1. The safe is open; Jimmy is packing some of its contents into a bag, while Red is walking the path to Cotton near the door they entered, carrying a tray of money or jewellery. When Red hands the tray to Cotton, the latter drops it, and all three freeze. (Figure 4.55)

4 The bars of a cage with a dog behind, jumping and barking furiously.

5 As 2. Avery reacts.

6 A room in the bank basement. The nightwatchman is asleep in his chair rear centre in medium long shot, his timer key hanging on the wall left. He stirs, and looks slowly off left.

7 As 4. The dog barks.

8 As 1. The three burglars are frozen in the positions of the end of shot 1.

9 As 2. Avery looks off front right in alarm.

10 As 6. The nightwatchman rises, picks up a truncheon from the table left, and exits cautiously front left.

11 Another basement room, with cleaning equipment and an electrical cupboard on the whitewashed wall rear centre. The nightwatchman enters right in medium long shot, opens the cupboard and turns a switch. Lights go on off front left. He exits front left with trepidation.

12 As 1, but now lit from above, with the dark lantern out. No one is in sight, and the safe is closed.

The reappearance in shot 12 of the same view of the bank, but with the characters who were frozen to the spot at the end of shot 3 and still in the same positions in shot 8 now nowhere to be seen, obviously creates suspense as to what has become of them, but also draws attention to the highly motivated tableau they constituted during the freeze.

> The nightwatchman enters midground right in the room beyond door 2, goes cautiously through doors 6 and 7 to get to the safe, notices nothing amiss, comes through door 5 and looks out of the window left. Valentine and Red come out from inside the safe and tiptoe to door 5. As the nightwatchman comes forward through door 4 into the tellers' room, Cotton steps from behind the door and attacks him, dragging him back through door 4 into the room behind, where they are joined by Jimmy and Red from door 5. The nightwatchman breaks free and draws a gun. Jimmy and Red flee through door 5, closing it behind them, as Cotton runs through door 4 and towards

door 3, pursued by the nightwatchman, who shoots but misses. Cotton runs through doors 3 and 6, still pursued by the nightwatchman. Valentine and Red grab their bags from in front of the safe. Cotton and the nightwatchman run through door 4 into the tellers' room, as Valentine and Red come through door 7. Cotton runs through door 3, closing it, and off through doors 2 and 1. As the nightwatchman vainly tries to open door 3, Valentine tiptoes to door 4. The nightwatchman turns, sees him, and aims his gun (Figure 4.56), but Valentine closes and locks door 4. Valentine and Red go through door 6 towards doors 2 and 1 as the nightwatchman, now locked in the tellers' room, starts to front left.

13 View through the tellers' grille as the nightwatchman, in medium shot, puts down his gun, and pulls out and blows a whistle.

After a short sequence showing Avery spotted, pursued, and arrested by three policemen, we see the other three re-emerge from the basement trapdoor and run off.

In *An Awful Moment*, the resort to a multiple-room set at the climax might seem almost a matter of desperation, or a lack of confidence in what, to the director, was the relatively novel device of alternation. In *Alias Jimmy Valentine*, however, it is exploited for its spectacular effect, even in a context in which simultaneity via editing is standard. (Compare the cutaways to Avery, the barking dog, and the nightwatchman, followed by the cut back to the frozen burglars.) By showing a complex spatial layout as a whole, the divided set aids the suspense of the tiptoed break-in and the subsequent search by the nightwatchman. It also makes the movements of the characters from space to space comprehensible in a way which would have been extremely difficult if no view exceeded the visible space of a single room. It allows the burglary to be presented as a kind of ballet; this reinforces one of the running themes of the film—crime as a jubilatory exercise of skill. (Indeed, as opposed to the play, which never shows any actual crime, the film's speeches condemning crime never really outweigh its visual celebration of it.) *Alias Jimmy Valentine* here finds a way to represent a situation and a theme in a picture, thus demonstrating an appeal to a theatrical tradition while using a technique, the bird's-eye view, which is virtually unknown in the theatre.[4]

The suspenseful wait while the nightwatchman searches for the criminals is a typical situation, but this does not seem to be the principal motivation for the bird's-eye-view staging. This scene, and everything which follows up to Detective Doyle's discovery of the dropped cufflink that implicates Jimmy in the robbery, is exposition—it can be thought of as an expansion of the opening dissolve between Lee Randall and Jimmy Valentine. As a picture, it has more in common with the beginning of the slave-auction scene in *Uncle Tom's Cabin* than the scene on a rocky pass in these plays and films. It offers a typical view of crime before introducing the particular story of the hero.

While *Alias Jimmy Valentine* harkens back to the theatrical tradition of the multiple-room set in its construction of this pictorial effect, other films of the 1910s utilize the kind of deep space which is specific to the cinematic stage in order to provide all-inclusive framings of the principal actors in key dramatic situations. In many cases, too, this kind of staging is retained even when the films otherwise employ a high degree of editing. An example is the sequence in *L'Enfant de Paris* (Gaumont, 1913) where Captain de Valen attempts to ransom his daughter from her apache kidnappers.

Captain de Valen is reported dead after a Berber attack on his North African fort, and his wife dies of grief soon after, leaving a young orphan, Marie-Laure. Marie-Laure is unhappy in her boarding-school, and runs away. She is found by an apache gang-leader, Le Bachelier, who discovers who she is from a locket she is wearing, and decides to wait to see if he can turn the find to his advantage. He gives her to be looked after by Tiron, a drunken shoe-maker, whose assistant, the young hunchback Le Bosco, befriends her. De Valen turns out to have been captured, not killed; he escapes and returns to Paris, to find his wife dead and his daughter missing. When he advertises for news of Marie-Laure, Le Bachelier sees his chance. He invites the Captain to meet him, advising him to bring his cheque-book. The Captain goes to the rendezvous and is led to the back room of a slum bar.

The situation which develops resembles the deadlock in Puff's play in Sheridan's *The Critic*. De Valen is cautious and reluctant to sign a cheque before securing his daughter's release, while the apaches are determined to maintain control of the girl and secure the money. The deadlock is broken by Le Bachelier violently seizing control of the situation, only to lose

the intitiative thanks to an external intervention by the police.

The back room of the bar is filmed with the largely glassed partition to the bar at the rear, up a short flight of steps, with the door in the centre. Another flight of stairs leads to a door rear right, giving on to the upper floors of the building. The furniture in the room consists of two tables front left and right, with several chairs round the right-hand table, and especially behind it, and two chairs at the table left. The set is lit in a way which emphasizes its depth: the moderately lit bar is visible through the partition in the rear, and the front is brightly lit by a single high front arc, with no front fill from below; the middle ground is almost entirely in darkness (a characteristic of the set design and lighting in Perret's films, as noted above).

Le Bachelier and his apache henchmen occupy the front of the scene at the beginning (Figure 4.57). A look-out enters the bar in the rear from the right, and announces de Valen's arrival through the rear centre partition door. As de Valen enters following the look-out and stands in the doorway to accustom himself to the gloom, the apaches scatter and sit at the tables casually drinking, while Le Bachelier goes to greet de Valen rear left (Figure 4.58). De Valen comes forward and is invited to sit front centre, as Le Bachelier introduces him to the apaches. De Valen does not sit but draws a revolver. The apaches jump, except for Le Bachelier, who laughs and says de Valen will not need it. Finally de Valen agrees to sit down. Le Bachelier asks him to sign a cheque for 50,000 francs (title). As he gets out his cheque-book, Le Bachelier's second-in-command attempts to secure the gun he has laid on the table, but de Valen spots the manœuvre and grabs the gun. Le Bachelier reproves his henchman and apologizes to de Valen. De Valen signs the cheque (insert) and hands it to Le Bachelier (Figure 4.59). Le Bachelier leaves, and de Valen settles down to wait, surrounded by the apaches, whose offer of a drink he refuses.

There follows a 27-shot sequence in which Le Bachelier visits Tiron's apartment, Le Bosco helps get Marie-Laure ready, and Le Bachelier takes her away, followed unseen by Le Bosco, who watches them enter the bar and runs for the police. A closer view through the partition to the bar from the back room (i.e. from the same angle as the earlier scene in the

4.57

4.58

4.59

4.60

back room) shows Le Bachelier, holding Marie-Laure, in discussion with his second-in-command (Figure 4.60). The second-in-command comes forward into the lair, closes the door and exits front left (Figure 4.61). In a return to the original framing, he comes to de Valen and indicates the door behind them. It opens, and Le Bachelier holds up Marie-Laure (Figure 4.62). De Valen runs towards her, and the second-in-command secures de Valen's revolver from the table, and covers him, ordering him to stop. Le Bachelier enters through the door, and demands a further 50,000 francs (title). De Valen agrees, if he can embrace his daughter (Figure 4.63). He sits at the table and writes the cheque. Marie-Laure is brought to him, but held by Le Bachelier, who demands he sign. De Valen hesitates, eager to embrace his daughter yet afraid the apaches will spirit her away, creating a

tableau (Figure 4.64). Le Bachelier allows him to kiss Marie-Laure, and he signs. Le Bachelier immediately hands Marie-Laure to two henchmen who carry her off right, seizes the cheque, and gives a signal for de Valen to be overpowered, and taken from the room.

In the police raid which follows, in which de Valen is rescued, but Le Bachelier escapes with Marie-Laure, followed only by Le Bosco, the same basic framing is used twice more, at the beginning of the raid, as a look-out announces the arrival of the police, and at the end, as Le Bosco sets out in search of Marie-Laure.

In this scene, the characteristic shape of the cinematic stage is used to emphasize the way the gang menacingly regroup themselves around de Valen, who spends most of the scene sitting or standing more or less front centre in a long-shot to medium-long-shot framing, while in the wider shadowy space

4.61

4.62

4.63

4.64

behind, the second-in-command makes first an unsuccessful, then a successful attempt to secure de
Valen's revolver, and Le Bachelier, usually close to de
Valen and to his right, treats him with oily courtesy,
showing complete unconcern at the first appearance
of the gun (in marked contrast to everyone else), and
acting as de Valen's apparent ally until the very moment that he gives the signal to overpower him.
Marie-Laure's appearance gives rise to a true tableau,
although, as usual in the cinema, this is brief and well
motivated by the action. Despite the interpolation of
three sequences outside the apache lair—the trip to
the shoemaker's garret, the carrying of the tied-up de
Valen into an attic, and his subsequent rescue by the
police, the film insistently returns to the same framing of a deep space, with the principals grouped in the
brightly lit area at the front. It is the use of this fram-

ing, as well as the distinct tableaux realized by the actors, that constitutes the pictorial organization of
this scene, contrasting de Valen's cautious movements with the elaborate machinations of his enemies.

The tendency to maintain the high points of situations in a single scene, often in a complex, deeply
staged set, is further illustrated by a climactic sequence in the 1914 Danish film *Det hemmelighedsfulde
X*. The wife of the naval Lieutenant van Houven is
courted by a rich foreigner, Count Spinelli, who has
persuaded her to give him a photograph of herself,
which he promises to return in exchange for a final
meeting (or possibly she sends him a photograph in
exchange for a promise that he will cease to impor-
tune her).[5] War is declared, and van Houven is given
command of a naval squadron, with sealed orders as

197

to its course and actions. Spinelli is, in fact, a spy act-ing for the enemy power. The scene described then follows.

The crucial action here is staged in the film's most complex set, representing the van Houvens' sitting-room and the vestibule leading to the front door of their house. The sitting-room occupies two floors of the house, while the vestibule is a single-storey room opening off it, with van Houven's office above it, access to the office being provided by a gallery over the opening to the vestibule with a balustrade overlooking the sitting-room. This set is always filmed from the same side, although various parts of it are isolated in a series of set-ups with a roughly parallel lens axis. In the most inclusive framing, the front right is occupied by a fireplace in a projecting embrasure with a mantelpiece over it. Further back, there is a

door in the right-hand wall leading to Fru van Hou-ven's boudoir and the sons' bedroom; beyond this door is a second one leading to stairs that go up to the gallery. Beyond this second door are a pair of French doors leading to the garden, angled across the rear corner of the sitting-room. Rear left a few steps lead up to the vestibule, which has a large mirror on its rear wall, tilted forward so that it reflects the vestibule floor. The main house door is off rear left.

At the opening of the sequence, Spinelli is driven to the front gates of the van Houven house, climbs over them and steals up the drive. (Shots are numbered from the beginning of the prints of the film that we have seen.)

106 The van Houvens' sitting-room. Fru van Houven is sitting in an armchair front left in medium long shot. Spinelli enters through the French doors rear right

4.65

4.66

4.67

4.68

(Figure 4.65), comes forward, puts his overcoat on another chair, and touches her shoulder. She rises and leans against the mantelpiece right, and they argue—she seems to be demanding he leave her alone, he imploring her to continue the affair. As Spinelli becomes insistent, Fru van Houven turns on the lights using a switch by the fireplace (Figure 4.66). They hear someone coming, and she pushes Spinelli front right so that he is hidden by the chimney embrasure, but can see and hear what happens in the room, and remains largely visible to the spectator, though reframing movements of the camera nearly cut him off at times. She tucks the overcoat under a chair cushion as her elder son runs in from the midground right door. She asks what is the matter.

107 Title: 'What do you want, child?' 'To pray for papa, who is going off to war.'

108 As 106. She embraces him, they come to front centre and the son kneels and prays with his head in his mother's lap, while she glares at Spinelli front right (Figure 4.67).

109 Closer view, same angle as 106. The son's head in Fru van Houven's lap lower left, Fru van Houven glaring at Spinelli left, Spinelli right, all in medium shot (Figure 4.68).

110 Gates of the house as a car with van Houven and other naval officers enters rear right and stops. Van Houven gets down and opens the gates. One of the officers also gets down, shows van Houven his watch and signals with two fingers (presumably 'you only have two minutes') , and van Houven exits front right up the drive.

111 As 106, but slightly panned to the right. Van Houven enters through the French doors and greets Fru van Houven and his son; he shows her the briefcase.

112 Title: 'We start tonight. Here are the sealed orders.'

113 As 106. He puts the briefcase on the mantelpiece, and exits midground right with his son. Fru van Houven makes sure they are gone, then shows Spinelli out through the French doors, comes back to the door to the bedrooms and exits through it. Spinelli re-enters through the French doors, comes to the fireplace, picks up the briefcase, opens it, takes out the orders and reads.

114 Insert: 'Orders for the 2nd squadron. Up anchor at dawn, course South-South-West.'

115 As 106. Spinelli expresses amazement.

A five-shot sequence follows in the sons' bedroom, where Van Houven finds a paper elephant that the children's nurse had cut from a letter from Spinelli to Fru van Houven, the fragmentary text of which seems to imply that she has been unfaithful (insert). Van

Houven rejects his wife's offered embrace, to her mystification, and exits; she ponders for a moment, then has a dawning suspicion and follows him off.

121 As 106. Spinelli finishes reading the orders, replaces them in the briefcase, and puts it back on the mantelpiece. He starts for the French doors, but retreats to his hiding place front right as van Houven and his wife enter midground right and quarrel. Van Houven collapses into the front left armchair, his head in his hands, and Fru van Houven demands to see the paper. Spinelli tries to tiptoe to the French doors, thus revealing his continued presence to Fru van Houven, but van Houven lifts his head, and Spinelli is forced back into his hiding place. The officer with the watch enters through the French doors; he kisses Fru van Houven's hand and turns to van Houven, who rises. Turning his back to the officer to hide his discomposure (Figure 4.69), he sees Spinelli front right (Figure 4.70). Spinelli

4.69

4.70

starts to come forward to make some explanation, but van Houven thrusts him back and signals him not to say a word. The officer speaks to van Houven.

122 Title: 'Lieutenant, we must leave, we are very late!'

123 As 106. Van Houven nods, and the officer exits through the French doors. Van Houven picks up the briefcase from the mantelpiece and walks to the rear. As he passes his wife, he turns to her and accuses her, pointing to Spinelli front right. He seizes her and pushes her towards Spinelli, then exits through the French doors. Fru van Houven staggers to front left staring vacantly off towards camera. Spinelli comes front right to her and says something.

124 Fru van Houven left, Spinelli right, in medium shot from the same angle. She turns to him, he mumbles an apology, goes rear right and exits through the French doors. She comes forward and gazes towards camera again, expressing grief. She turns away to the right, leans on the mantelpiece, and buries her head in her arms. After a moment she rises and goes towards the rear.

125 Title (text missing in the prints we have seen).

126 As 106. She picks up Spinelli's coat and exits right toward the bedrooms.

In her dark boudoir, we see her put the coat into a closet; then there is a sequence in which Spinelli walks to the old mill on his estate and sends a pigeon with the news.

This sequence thus sets up the most important situation for the film: Van Houven will not exculpate himself from a charge of espionage after the theft of the orders has been discovered by his superiors, even when condemned to death, because he believes to do so will irredeemably tarnish his wife's and hence his own honour. He is powerless to resolve this situation, and his wife is prevented from solving it by his stubborn insistence on undermining every effort she makes to shift the blame to Spinelli, who cannot be found until the last minute; even when her husband is cleared of the charge through her realizing where Spinelli is, finding him in the middle of a battle, and securing a signed confession, this is not enough to persuade her husband of her fidelity. It is in this scene that the family drama of adultery and the patriotic one of war and espionage are fatefully locked together.

Three spaces are represented here: the gates of the van Houven house, the sons' bedroom, and the sitting-room. Whereas in the first two, shots are brief,

with simple action, the bulk of the sequence takes place in the sitting-room, which is shown in two framings, a long shot showing the whole room, and a medium shot isolating the figures in the front centre; ignoring titles and the cutaway shots and sequences, the sitting-room is shown in long shot, in medium shot, in long shot again, in medium shot, and again in long shot. Both long shots and medium shots contain a few reframing pans, but these are slight, and simply ensure that all the significant characters remain in view; they neither isolate some characters from others, nor conceal any character (unlike the reframings in *Das Mädchen ohne Vaterland* and *Die Sumpfblume*). Indeed, the medium shots are used purely as a form of emphasis, since they show exactly the same characters from the same angle as the long shots (unlike the cut-ins to medium shot in the Holbeins' dinner sequence in *Ma l'amore mio non muore!*). Achieving this involves an extreme stretching of verisimilitude. In the long shots and even one of the medium shots, Spinelli has to remain for long periods unseen by one of the other characters in the same shot. In the long shots, when he is hiding front right Spinelli is framed from the knees up, and the front playing space is 6 feet across (i.e. he is less than 12 feet from the lens, assuming a two-inch lens is being used); both the van Houvens' elder son and van Houven himself come to front centre and stay there for long periods, unaware of his existence only 2 feet away from them. The narrative action could have been much more plausibly handled by having him hide in a closet or outside a door front right (or indeed anywhere else adjoining the sitting-room), with cutaways to indicate his seeing and hearing what was necessary for him to secure the sealed orders. Christensen, however, sacrifices verisimilitude in order to bring the elements of the situation, the characters linked together and isolated from one another by partial knowledge and misconceptions, into the same frame.

These examples show that the emergence of much more highly edited scenes in feature films in the 1910s in both Europe and America by no means displaced a situational emphasis on the co-presence in space and time of significantly contrasted characters in the interests of some notion of cinematic ubiquity. Indeed, rapid editing and even alternation, the device which has been taken as typical of that cinematic ubiquity, have another function in the 1910s that we have already remarked on in relation to the World version of *Uncle Tom's Cabin*—the use of flurries of shots, often with contrasting scales and angles, to orchestrate a situation, notably in that film's presentation of the canonical scene on a rocky pass, and the newly invented sequence of the trip up the Red River to Legree's plantation. The same principle can be seen at work even more starkly in *The Whip*.

This Drury Lane Autumn Melodrama, written by Cecil Raleigh and Henry Hamilton and first produced 9 September 1909 at Drury Lane by Arthur Collins with sets by Henry Emden, R. McCleery, and Bruce Smith, and then, with the same sets, at the Manhattan Opera House, New York, on 16 December 1912, has many sensation scenes, but the most sensational was probably the train crash which ends Act 3. In the play, the villains, Captain Greville Sartorys and Mrs D'Aquila, depend on the Marquis of Beverley's horse The Whip losing in the Two Thousand Guineas at Newmarket. Knowing that the horse is to travel in a car attached to the local train at Falconhurst station, then to be unhitched at Manston junction and attached to the express to Newmarket, they plan to slip the horsebox earlier, near the mouth of Falconhurst tunnel, so that it will be destroyed by the oncoming express. Their plans are overheard by the horse's trainer, Tom Lambert, in Madame Tussaud's, but before he can warn Beverley, he is locked into the Chamber of Horrors in the waxworks show for the weekend. By the time he is able to reach a telephone and call Beverley, The Whip is already in the horsebox and Sartorys on the train. Mrs Beamish, a widowed relative of Beverley's who is the companion of his granddaughter Diana (and the object of Lambert's persistent suit), sets off in a car to ride after the train.

A first spectacular staging, using a panoramic backdrop, enables the train's trip from the station to the tunnel to be shown, with Sartorys coming out of his compartment while the train is in the tunnel, inching along the running board and uncoupling the horsebox (Figure 4.71). The local then disappears off stage right, while the horsebox comes to rest in the mouth of the tunnel. As the express is heard approaching through the tunnel from the left, Mrs Beamish arrives in her car, knocks on the box, waking the jockey Harry Anson who is travelling with the horse, and together they manage to get The Whip

out of the box. The express emerges from the tunnel and crashes into the box, smashing it to pieces; the locomotive is derailed, falling back from the tracks in a huge cloud of steam, and injured passengers are strewn all over the forestage. As Mrs Beamish's car arrives, the script indicates, 'when motor horn sounds, train music, sections I, II, & IV when train smashes'. The curtain falls, then rises again to show Vernon Haslam, the drunken curate whom Sartorys had blackmailed into abetting his plans, redeeming himself by heroically attending to injured passengers while himself wounded in the crash (Figure 4.72).

It is sensation scenes such as this that have led commentators like Vardac to argue that nineteenth-century spectacular theatre is essentially anti-theatrical, and that the cinema was a far more appropriate medium for them. An illusionistic representation of an event like a train crash might seem next to impossible on stage, whereas a real train crash could be photographed with a moving-picture camera and projected in a movie house, its illusionistic effect guaranteed by the photographic instrument used to record and reproduce it. When *The Whip* was made into a film by Maurice Tourneur's Paragon company in 1917, the filmmakers did indeed photograph a real train crash for the scene, but before discussing that moment, and how it works in the film as a whole, it is necessary to indicate some significant changes in the story introduced in the adaptation of the play by Charles Everard Whitaker. First, the scene of the action is moved to the United States, with Lord Beverley becoming a Long Island judge, Madame Tussaud's the New York Eden Musée, Newmarket Saratoga Springs, and only the villains remaining a European aristocrat and *demi-mondaine*. More important for the train-crash scene, the adaptation eliminates Tom Lambert and Mrs Beamish, the traditional comic man and comic woman of nineteenth-century melodrama, and assigns most of their action to the romantic hero and heroine, Hubert Brancaster and Diana Beverley. Thus, it is Diana who overhears Sartoris (spelt with an 'i' in the film's intertitles) and Mrs D'Aquila plotting the crash in the Eden Musée and is then locked in for the weekend; and she calls Brancaster rather than her father when she manages to get to a telephone, so he drives to the rescue of The Whip.

The photographic record of the train crash itself

4.71

4.72

4.73

4.74

4.75

4.76

consists of four relatively short shots in a five-shot segment (the fifth is a cutaway reaction shot). All four are in very-long-shot framing, from relatively high positions beside the tracks. The part of those tracks where the horsebox comes to rest after it is slipped from the train is on an embankment in fairly open country, not a tunnel mouth, as in the play. The sequence is as follows:

1   Slight high-angle, very long shot. The tracks cross the field of view from rear right to front left, with the horsebox midground centre. As the shot begins, the train is steaming in from the rear right (Figure 4.73). The locomotive hits the horsebox, pushes it to front left, and begins to fall forward off the embankment to the front right (Figure 4.74).

2   Slight high-angle, very long shot from further to the right (Figure 4.75). Very precise matching of the position

of the locomotive at the end of shot 1. Pan left as the locomotive and its tender fall towards front centre.

3   Medium long shot. Brancaster facing camera, with a telegraph pole behind him, and a background cornfield. He gazes off front right, expresses horror (Figure 4.76), covers his face with his hands, turns, and buries hands and face in the pole.

4   Slight high-angle, very long shot, from the other side of the tracks. Pan right across derailed but upright carriages past a steam-filled gap where the locomotive has fallen off the embankment to the rear to the remains of the horsebox right. The pan reverses as the steam begins to disperse (this shot and the next could not be illustrated because of the quality of the print and the nature of the shot).

5   Slight high-angle, very long shot. The shot, rather short in this print, is so steam-filled that the precise position of the camera is impossible to determine; it shows billowing steam and smoke in front of vaguely visible wreckage. Fade out.

It is clear that the filmmakers crashed a real locomotive and carriages (presumably condemned machines bought as scrap) into a horsebox and filmed the crash simultaneously from at least three positions (though the third shot of the crash might possibly have been filmed with one of the cameras brought over from the other side of the tracks while the wreckage was still steaming). It is possible, given the obviously corrupt state of the surviving print in the Library of Congress American Film Institute collection, that there were once more shots of the crash, but it seems unlikely that they would have been able to do much more than redundantly repeat the content of these. No more action is needed once the crash has occurred (the adaptation has also eliminated Vernon Haslam, so scenes of the succour of the injured would have no narrative function). It therefore seems unlikely that the sequence was much prolonged in time. Closer camera positions would have been visible in the very long shots, and too dangerously close to the train as it tumbled down the embankment to have been risked.[6] The sequence thus reveals the difficulties of making a sensation scene by simply recording a spectacular event with a moving-picture camera. The actual collision of a train with an obstacle on the track takes very little time, and can only be rendered with intelligibility (not to speak of safety) if shot from a distance which turns the locomotive and its surrounding into toys. The moment is a sensational one, none the less, but its sensational character is rendered not by photography but by resort to alternation.

On stage the train crash as a narrative action occupies two (perhaps really three) scenes—Act 3, scene 4, the morning-room at Falconhurst, and scene 5, Falconhurst station, leading (via the panoramic backcloth, after a curtain as the train leaves the station) to Falconhurst tunnel and its mouth (described in the script as separate 'tableaux' within the same scene). Lambert's rescue from the Chamber of Horrors and conveyance of the news of the conspiracy against The Whip is handled at long distance, on the telephone, and Mrs Beamish's drive to the tunnel entrance occurs off, while the audience sees Sartorys's activity on the local train. In fact, there is a temporal overlap, with the scene in the morning-room occupying the same diegetic time as the first part of the scene at the station. Scene 4 ends with a train whistle off, and Lord Beverley proclaiming, 'Hark! The train has started.' The same whistle occurs just before the curtain in scene 5.[7] In the Library of Congress print of the film, the same action occupies more than 100 shots (including intertitles). It is not uncommon for the cutting rate of surviving prints of films from this era to have been raised by increasing alternation—cutting two scenes in half and putting the first half of the second before the second half of the first, thus making four scenes out of two; this print has certainly undergone re-editing by a distributor or collector at some point, and some of the shots in this sequence in it look suspiciously like the same footage reprinted. Nevertheless, there can be no doubt that there were always a relatively large number of shots in the sequence. The play's two sites of action, Falconhurst house and the train, become multiple in the film: Falconhurst station, the Chamber of Horrors and an office at the Eden Musée, Brancaster's home, the hotel where he is staying, Sartoris's compartment on the train, the horse box, the exterior of the moving train as Sartoris slips the box, Brancaster's car as it races with the express to reach the stationary horsebox, the crash site. The Whip is loaded into the box and Sartoris boards the local; then Diana and Myrtle Anson (who is trapped in the Musée with her) succeed in attracting the attention of a watchman, are taken to his office, and call Brancaster's home. His butler answers, telling them that Brancaster is staying at Hollybush Inn. Diana calls the inn, and speaks to Brancaster. This alternation has several brief cutaways to a speeding train (it is never quite clear which train, the local or the express). Brancaster hangs up and goes to his car, as Diana and Myrtle embrace in relief. Sartoris climbs to the roof of the train, crawls to the end of the last carriage, climbs down, and uncouples the box; the sequence has a cutaway to Brancaster driving furiously, before we see the box come to a stop on the embankment, and Sartoris returns to his compartment. There follows a title—'The Saratoga Express'—and an alternation between shots of a train speeding along, and of Brancaster driving furiously, the two finally appearing in the same shot, as Brancaster stops at a level crossing to let the train past. A series of shots shows the car drawing ahead of the train. Then we see Anson asleep in the box and the box on its embankment, then Brancaster arriving by the box. He climbs to it, pounds on the door, Anson wakes, and they get The Whip out. There follow the five shots of the crash already described.

We have no doubt that the simple presentation of the crash on a stage, by virtue of its relative closeness to the audience and its large scale, the continuity of space achieved in the tunnel sequence of the un-hitching of the car, and the mere feat of having an event like a train crash occur on the stage of a theatre, was far more spectacular than the four shots of a real train crash in the film. The climactic sense of the train crash as a situation in the film is assured not primarily by the reality of the photographed crash, but by its orchestration through alternation. And this alternation is not really a filmic method of represent-ing space and time *à la* Kuleshov—in some elements of the alternation, like the first shots of a train, we do not even know which train this is, and in many others the supposed location is quite indeterminate, so the shots provide the spectator with no new spatio-temporal information—but rather a cinematic equivalent of the music that underscored the stage presentation of the crash; such music would, of course, also have been present during screenings of the film, so the editing is not a substitute for it, but rather a supplement to it—an essentially 'non-realistic' means of emotionally underscoring a crucial narrative situation.

The same principle is at work in the film's version of another of the sensation scenes in the play—not one involving a physically hyperbolic event like the train crash, but an extreme dramatic situation. This is the hunt breakfast scene (Act 2, scene 3).

Diana Sartorys, Lord Beverley's granddaughter, nurses back to health a neighbour, Hubert, Earl of Brancaster, after a car crash which has destroyed his short-term memory. Brancaster has hitherto been os-tracized by local society for his dissolute life-style; in particular, because he has been living with a notori-ous divorcée, Mrs D'Aquila. Mrs D'Aquila had nearly succeeded in persuading Brancaster to marry her; he had gone so far as to fill out a marriage licence, but had then refused to go through with the ceremony on learning of one of her divorces. Immediately after the crash, when there seems a good chance Brancaster will die, and the doctor says that if he recovers he will suffer from memory loss, Sartorys, who desperately needs money to cover gambling debts and has

been rejected by the heiress Diana, points out to Mrs D'Aquila that if they can forge an entry in a mar-riage register, no one, including Brancaster, will be able to claim that the marriage has not taken place. He knows of Vernon Haslam's secret past, and offers to use this knowledge to blackmail Haslam into al-lowing the entry to be made in his register. After his recovery, Brancaster falls in love with Diana and re-jects Mrs D'Aquila and his whole former life-style. He is welcomed back into local society, and his recovery is celebrated at a hunt breakfast, during which he is offered the position of Master of the Beverley Hunt, but refuses it on health and other grounds, and in-stead, to great acclaim, suggests the honour go to Diana. Lord Beverley proposes a toast:

MARQUIS. (*Rising*) Gentlemen, the hounds wait! It's time for a stirrup cup. Fill your glasses. I give you a toast.
(*Shouts of 'The Whip! the Whip! Lady Di!'*)
Yes, the Whip and Lady Di—and not only the Whip and my dear Di—for the Whip may soon have a new handle to its name. (*General murmur*) Falconhurst and the Rievers may be bound by a new thong. On a day like this it's a great pleasure to ask you to drink not only to your new Whip, to my grandchild Di, but to the future—
FOOTMAN. (*at door R.*) Lady Brancaster!
(*Sensation. Some rise. All turn to R. Haslam rises and takes a step towards Sartoris. Enter Mrs. D'Aquila, who comes down slowly R.*)
MARQUIS. Madam!
MRS D'AQUILA: Lord Beverley, pray forgive this—er—intru-sion. Certain rumours having reached my ears, I had come to ask for a private interview with a view to obviating a public scandal. But happily—or unhappily—I have just heard the words that have fallen from your lips. There-fore, though I regret the pain that I may cause, it is due to myself that I should speak here, as publicly as you have spoken, and say that—I am Lord Brancaster's wife.

As noted above, the Hall at Falconhurst is a two-wall set, with the breakfast table near the rear left cor-ner (as usual, directions here are given in film terms, i.e. from the viewpoint of the audience or the camera, except in quotations from the script, which uses stage conventions), parallel to the long axis of the room, and at an acute angle with the front of the stage; it is essentially viewed by the audience from its long side. Behind it, rear centre right, a flight of stairs rises to a landing. There is a grand doorway front left. (The New York set is for a smaller stage than Drury Lane's and therefore less elaborate, but the essential

4.77

dispositions are the same.) The footman enters from the doorway front left, followed by Mrs D'Aquila.[8] She pauses as all rise and look at her, then moves to front centre-left (where she is in all the photographs of the scene that we have seen) for the confrontation with Beverley and Brancaster, which ends when Haslam reluctantly perjures himself by confirming the truth of the marriage, Beverley orders Brancaster from the house, Diana collapses in Beverley's arms, and the principals form a line: Mrs D'Aquila–Brancaster–Beverley–Diana–Haslam–Sartoris, with the guests grouped behind them (Figure 4.77, from the London production); the curtain falls (the stage direction reads '*pictures*', implying several curtains with variations on this arrangement for each call).

Mrs D'Aquila's entrance here recalls the example of the dramatic entrance at the top of the stairs adduced by John Emerson and Anita Loos as most appropriately representable in film by a tableau (see p. 33 above). The film version of *The Whip* does fulfil that prescription to some degree, though by no means simply. The dramatic intensity of the situation, however, is marked by suspense rather than, as in the stage version, by surprise.

Although a relatively wide range of camera angles is used, the inclusive ones which really display the space of the hall are along its long axis. The stairs down to the hall are placed on the short rather than the long wall, and the long breakfast table has its short side facing the stairs, which are in the rear of these inclusive shots. The long wall of the hall to the left of the stairs (seen in only one framing and three shots) has large windows in it; the opposite side has two fireplaces (they are never seen in the same shot, so they may possibly be one—but if so, camera angles and directions of glance are considerably cheated to bring characters standing at the fireplace closer to the stairs in some parts of the scene than they are at others). The sequence begins with a very long shot parallel to the axis of the room, but to the right of the table and stairs, which are more or less in that axis (Figure 4.78—compare Figure 4.77). Four shots from this set-up showing preparations for the breakfast, and culminating with Beverley informally telling some of the guests about the impending engagement (intertitle), are intercut with a series of shots of Brancaster dressing for the breakfast and reading a letter from his bankers about a cheque drawn on his account to the bookie Kelly which he evidently cannot remember having signed, and two shots of Mrs D'Aquila getting into a car and being driven through

the countryside in it. A closer (but still long-shot) framing of the table down its axis towards the stairs (Figure 4.79) alternates with a set of detailed views, some from the stairs end of the table, showing speeches made by guests and Beverley, and Brancaster's, then Diana's entrances, the former down the stairs from rear left, the latter from a door at the hall level rear right. Diana is declared Mistress of the Hunt. Then follows the sequence of Mrs D'Aquila's entrance (shots are numbered from the title that begins the Hunt Breakfast sequence):

35 Sartoris in medium long shot leaning against the mantelpiece. He reaches for his fob watch, looking anxiously off left (Figure 4.80).
36 A dark hallway to an outside door with steps leading down to a stationary car rear centre facing right. A servant is holding the car's rear door open (Figure 4.81). Mrs

4.78

4.79

4.80

4.81

207

4.82

4.83

4.85

4.86

4.88

4.89

4.84

4.87

4.90

D'Aquila, in long shot, gets down and comes forward through the door front centre as the car drives off right.

37 As 35. Sartoris looks anxiously at his watch (Figure 4.82).

38 Very long shot parallel to the axis of the hall. The table is front left, the stairs go up rear left, and the doorway through which Diana entered is visible rear right (Figure 4.83). Beverley leads Diana's companions from the rear to front centre down the right side of the table, and proposes a toast to Brancaster and Diana. Brancaster and Diana enter front left. As the toast is drunk, a servant enters rear right on the landing, followed by Mrs D'Aquila.

39 Title, decorated with a drawing of a spider's web with Mrs D'Aquila's face at its centre: 'The uninvited guest.' (Figure 4.84).

40 The landing with the stairs descending off front left. Mrs D'Aquila, in long shot, is entering from the rear right, richly dressed and carrying a parasol. She stands at the top of the stairs and looks down off left with an insolent expression on her face (Figure 4.85).

41 The guests at the table turn and look off front centre in long shot (Figure 4.86).

42 As 40 (Figure 4.87).

43 As 35. Sartoris smiles sardonically (Figure 4.88).

44 As 38. Mrs D'Aquila stands at the top of the stairs, a servant next to her, and everyone else gazes up towards her, their backs to camera (Figure 4.89).

In the framing of shot 40, Mrs D'Aquila starts to come down the stairs. Another reverse angle shows Brancaster and Diana approaching the stairs from the left side of the hall, then follows a closer view of Mrs D'Aquila as she speaks. Title: 'I see I am in time to stop rumors about Mr. Brancaster's future. We are to be married shortly.' A series of shots isolate characters or pairs of characters more or less in medium long shot as Mrs D'Aquila presents Beverley with the licence, Brancaster is helpless to deny its genuineness, Sartoris corroborates it as a witness (replacing Haslam, who has been eliminated from the film version), Diana runs from Brancaster to fall into Beverley's arms, and Beverley points up the stairs and shouts at Brancaster (title): 'Get out of my house!' Brancaster tries to appeal to Diana and then exits up the stairs in a similar shot. The final shot of the sequence is a return to the opening very long-shot framing, as the guests gathered at the foot of the stairs watch Brancaster, followed by Mrs D'Aquila, go up the stairs to the rear centre (Figure 4.90).

There is thus one very long shot (44) on Mrs D'Aquila's entrance, more or less in the middle of the sequence, in which, as in the stage version, all the guests turn and look as she stands and surveys them. This is not, however, the first shot of Mrs D'Aquila in the sequence, or even in the hall itself. The alternation of shots of her trip to Falconhurst and shots of an anxious Sartoris anticipates her arrival, and she is shown arriving at the top of the stairs in the very long-shot framing. Then there is an introductory title and a reverse-angle sequence of her on the stairs and the staring guests, before the overall 'tableau' view is produced (difficulties with the timing of titles and the ways the dialogue in them can be attributed to characters presumably prompted the filmmakers not to attempt the stage version's substitution of the footman's 'Mrs Brancaster' for the same words in Beverley's speech). As in the train-crash scene, cutting is used, here not alternation between significantly remote sites within a complex arena of action, but fragmentation of a single room space into less inclusive framings from a variety of angles, what is usually called 'scene dissection'. The editing does not establish a synthetic space—what could have been truly synthetic in it, such as the two fireplaces that might be one, is unsuccessful in so far as it remains spatially ambiguous—but stands in for, or more precisely, supplements, the frozen moment of the tableau of surprise as Mrs D'Aquila enters to assume the position of Brancaster's rightful wife.

In these examples we see a range of dramatic situations—from the epitomizing view of crime in the opening of *Alias Jimmy Valentine*, to the misunderstandings and emotional impasses produced by the interventions of the villain in *Det hemmelighedsfulde X* and the hunt breakfast scene in *The Whip*, to the deadlock produced by the threat of violence in *L'Enfant de Paris*, to the more purely spectacular train crash of *The Whip*. While a variety of strategies for staging these scenes are also employed, significant and often contrasting elements are brought together in a unified picture, not simply through the use of tableaux by the actors, but more generally through the framing of the scene. In *Alias Jimmy Valentine* this is achieved through the use of the bird's-eye view, while in *L'Enfant de Paris* and *Det hemmelighedsfulde X* deep staging is utilized. These options are 'specific' to the cinematic stage, in the sense that they exploit the distinctive shape of the playing area in the cinema—narrow in front and wide at the back, as opposed to the playing space of the theatre which was narrow at the back and wide at the front—and depend on complex uses of depth made possible by the camera's single viewpoint on the action—as opposed to the theatre in which such blocking options are restricted by the fact that it must accommodate spectators in many viewing positions. But none the less the relation between situation and picture established in the theatrical tradition remains in evidence. This is so even in the case of highly edited scenes like those in *The Whip*, where alternation serves to augment the spectacular effect of the train crash, and scene dissection to elaborate upon the dramatic revelation and tableau of the hunt breakfast scene. This demonstrates the importance of spectacular theatre as a model for the utilization of new cinematic devices. The development of cinematic staging and editing in the 1910s were not attempts to lay the basis for a specifically cinematic approach to narration, but the pursuit of goals well-established in nineteenth-century theatre with new means which imposed a different approach to represented space.

1. Lev Kuleshov, 'Art of the Cinema', in *Kuleshov on Film, Writings of Lev Kuleshov*, trans. Ronald Levaco (Berkeley: University of California Press, 1974), 52.
2. El Nouty, *Théâtre et pré-cinéma*, 87.
3. See Kevin Brownlow, 'Ben Carré', *Sight and Sound*, 49, no. 1 (Winter 1979–80), 46–50, esp. the illustration on 49.
4. Other film directors at this period made somewhat similar use of the bird's-eye view to hold two related but distinct elements of an action in the same frame. In Evgenii Bauer's 1914 film *Nemye svideteli*, the wedding breakfast at which the heroine, the maid in a rich household, has to serve the guests as she watches the man she loves, her young master, about to leave with the bride who she knows is unfaithful to him, is filmed from a similar position, as Nastya takes drinks round to the family and friends, then coats as they dress for the honeymoon trip.
5. Both prints we have seen, a 16 mm copy in the Museum of Modern Art, New York, and a 35 mm one in the Cinémathèque Royale, Brussels, derive from the same copy, one whose titles are missing (their places indicated by a few frames of blank leader or, in a small number of cases, by a flash title in German), whose length is more than 1,600 35 mm feet shorter than the original release length, and which may therefore be missing scenes as well as titles. In this form, the film gives no explanation of the relations between Fru van Houven and Spinelli before the start of the action, so we remain slightly uncertain about the status of the photograph of Fru van Houven which Spinelli is holding the first time

we see him, which seems to be what gives him some hold over her which induces her to make compromising assignations with him, which he eventually relinquishes to her with his dying confession of his espionage activities, which she passes to a soldier to convey to the Admiral of the fleet, her husband's father, which the soldier eventually gives to the van Houven boys' nurse, Jane, which Jane nearly burns, which van Houven eventually finds and which has something written on the reverse that exculpates Fru van Houven in his eyes. According to Ronald Mottram, who has seen a print or prints at the Dansk Filmmuseum, Fru van Houven sends Spinelli a picture of herself with a rejection of his suit written on the reverse (see *The Danish Cinema before Dreyer* (Metuchen, NJ: Scarecrow Press, 1988), 113). Mottram also gives the family name as van Hauen; we have used the form found in the flash titles in the prints we have seen.

6. Long lenses to produce apparently closer shots from a safe distance were certainly available at this time, but we do not know of any examples of their use for scenes such as this.

7. This overlap is of the same type as the notorious one in *Life of an American Fireman* (see Burch, *Life to Those Shadows*, 204–7),

which, as André Gaudreault notes, also if less patently characterizes the relationship between the scene in the mail car and that on the locomotive footplate, and between the robbery scenes and those in the telegrapher's office and the bar-room in *The Great Train Robbery* ('Les Détours du récit filmique: Sur la naissance du montage parallèle', *Cahiers de la cinémathèque*, 29 (Winter 1979), 88–107). By 1917, such marked overlap between sequences was rare in films.

8. The stage directions seem clear about this ('*At door R.*'), and at least one New York stage photograph (in the file for *The Whip* in the theatre collections of the Museum of the City of New York) also suggests it—it shows Mrs D'Aquila centre left holding the licence out to Beverley centre, and a footman stands prominently left in the position one would expect of a servant who has just announced an arrival via a door immediately to the left. An entrance down the staircase rear right would seem more striking, but Diana and her companions have already entered that way, which seems to mark it as leading further into the house, not to the outside doors.

Conclusion

WE have argued that much nineteenth- and early twentieth-century theatre was characterized by a situational and pictorial approach to narrative. That is, rather than considering plot in an Aristotelian way as a matter of a chain of cause and effect (his 'beginning, middle, and end'), playwrights, stage managers, directors, actors, audiences, and even critics (despite the latter's genuflections to classical dramaturgy) treated it as a way of producing and resolving situations, momentary states embodying in extreme form the causal tensions that drive the story. Such situations were the moments that painters and sculptors took as appropriate for the representation of significant action in an atemporal medium. In a temporal medium like drama, conversely, they arrested the forward motion the better to underline its significance. Far from being pictures that assert their sovereign autonomy from the spectator, like Fried's absorptive paintings, they are insistent in their address to a spectator. However, the stage picture's appeal to spectatorial complicity should not be seen simply as an ideological reinforcement, a Barthesian mythological connotation, but rather as a means to structure the performance, to give it a rhythm and to orchestrate its high and low points.

This pictorialism ran through all aspects of theatrical practice in this period. We have considered three of these aspects, two of them broad domains—acting and staging—the third a specific device—the tableau. In acting, the picture affected both the way the actor presented the immediate situation and feelings of his or her character to an audience, and the way the ensemble of actors created a series of group pictures and moved from one to another, directing the audience's attention to the key characters in the scene at each moment, and orchestrating their attitudes with appropriate accompanying attitudes from the subordinate figures. In staging, pictorialism dominated the settings—separate scenes were, in France, called 'tableaux'—but also more transient effects like the relationship between the actors and the sets and scenic transformations. The tableau as a special device most directly transported to the stage certain characteristics of painting—the fixity, and the distribution of contrasting elements across the field of vision that demands the duration of that fixity for the whole to be read.

Although the early cinema took over many features of the live stage quite literally—notably the pictorial idea of the stage setting, actors' attitudes, and occasional tableaux—the brevity of most early films made it neither necessary nor possible to resort to the devices of the developed pictorial stage. The stories remained too simple to involve the peripeteia that give rise to complex situations; actors did not have time to use attitudes in a way to punctuate and modulate the performance of a scene (when they had the expertise and the skill, which they often did not); tableaux could not be held for long enough for any but the most stereotyped situations to be conveyed in them. Moreover, the development of cinematic devices in the first fifteen years of moving pictures—the adoption of a close camera position, creating a playing area quite unlike the theatrical stage, the deployment of deep staging within that area, and the development of devices such as intertitles and assemblage of scenes to tell relatively complex stories without dialogue—moved the cinema away from a simple reproduction of stage practices.

With the rise of the feature film in the 1910s, films became much more like plays in the kind of narratives they related—indeed, many, perhaps most of them were adaptations of stage plays, ancient and modern. In this new, longer form, the pictorial theatre again became a model, but the established practices of filmmaking were not simply abandoned for a photographic record of stage performances. Nevertheless, pictorialism flourished, in modified forms.

Despite claims for a new acting style specific to the new medium, film acting remained reliant on attitudes. While acting and the film star (the diva and her male counterparts) became increasingly important in the 1910s both for the film industry and as a structural component of film narrative, the greater length of the film gave the actor more room for virtuoso display—simply carrying out the necessary actions, as many of the 'actors' of the earliest films had done, was no longer sufficient. The appropriate deployment of attitudes became central to film acting. In Europe, filmmakers held down cutting rates to allow this virtuoso display to unfold in continuity. In America, faster editing did not leave space for lengthy reiteration of poses, and framings that isolated individual characters diminished the need for attitudinal ensemble to direct the spectators' attention to the narratively significant characters and their actions. To that extent, pictorial acting lost

some of its structuring functions, but the expressive means at the actor's disposal remained the traditional attitudes.

Scene- and act-end tableaux, too, lost their structuring function in films, in so far as the principal divisions of films, reels, were increasingly shown continuously, without any break equivalent to a curtain. Even where breaks between reels persisted, and at the ends of movies, audiences were always reluctant to applaud actors who were not present to acknowledge the applause, and films adopted (from literary narratives rather than the theatre) epilogues to handle the ends of sections and whole films. Within scenes, tableaux in the strict sense of arbitrary freezes at significant moments were also rare; with sufficient motivation, most notably by surprise or the threat of violence, they were still seen, but were usually much briefer than they had been in the theatre. The tableau persisted, however, in various transformations: notably, in a tendency even in highly edited sequences to use an inclusive framing at the climax, and in the multiplication of cinematic devices, often devices of editing, to ensure that the high point that had been represented by the tableau in the theatre received an equivalent elaboration in the film, despite the absence of a long-held freezing of all actors in attitudes.

Finally, the idea that a scene was a 'stage', and a stage defined pictorially, was not immediately abandoned for the notion of an analytic montage in which a chain of isolated fragments was synthesized by the audience into a diegetic world never seen as a whole. Rather, the inclusive long shot prevailed as the principal framing of a scene, and most closer shots were axial cut-ins to a detail locatable by reference to the broader framing. As noted above, climaxes tended to return to the broad framing to include all the counterposed elements within a single picture. The visual pyramid carved out by the lens, all of whose parts were equally visible to all members of the audience, gave rise to a new kind of pictorial composition, one in many ways closer to that of flat perspective paintings than was possible for the live theatre, forced to push almost all significant elements to a front plane to ensure their visibility. On the other hand, the cinema screen remained small in comparison with the stage, and the spectacular pictorial elements of both popular and respectable nineteenth-century theatre were replaced, not by simply filming spectacular reality, which tended to produce derisorily miniaturized versions of that reality, but by the use of the other significant kind of editing in use in this period, the alternation, to create a spectacular impression without ever showing a truly spectacular scene.

A brief comparison between these conclusions and other accounts both of the relations between cinema and theatre, and of the early history of cinema in general, is in order here.

First, it should be obvious that we reject the view that the history of the cinema is one of a steady emancipation from theatrical models. Early filmmakers had other models (still photography, lantern slides, cartoons, vaudeville acts, short stories, novels), and gave the theatrical ones short shrift if they proved inconvenient. Film lighting, for example, always owed more to still photography and painting than it did to theatrical lighting. On the other hand, when those models became appropriate, as they did with the development of longer films after 1910, theatrical models came back with a force that overwhelmed all of the others except perhaps the literary ones. Far from being a restriction on the development of the cinema, in the 1910s the theatre became a storehouse of devices for the cinema, and has remained so (though, of course, the traffic is not so one-way as it was in the 1910s).

Second, our differences from those like Vardac who see nineteenth-century popular theatre as 'proto-cinematic', as attempting to be cinematic without the appropriate technology, are more subtle. We share with them a conviction that there are major continuities between the theatre and the cinema, at any rate after 1910. However, rather than seeing the theatre as striving to be cinematic, to be what the cinema was, as it were, automatically, we believe that the cinema strove to be theatrical, or to assimilate a particular theatrical tradition, that of pictorialism, a tradition to which neither medium is obviously more appropriate, although each made specific demands which mean that pictorialism in theatre and in cinema are not the same.

Third, we are reluctant to concede the priority many accounts give to the development of film editing as the 'spine' of film history. This is linked to the first conception listed above, as editing is usually also seen as a feature differentiating cinema from

theatre. An editing-centred approach also tends to privilege the American cinema, as most editing innovations started in the USA and were only slowly adopted in Europe, if at all, in the 1910s. However, the ways the cinema of this decade assimilated features of theatrical pictorialism have complex relations to film editing. In Europe, pictorialism in acting probably delayed the increase in cutting rates, whereas in the USA it found an accommodation with rapid editing; spectacular settings, too, both demanded inclusive shots, and called for editing effects to supply the lack of theatrical scale.

A fourth issue is the persistent attempts (from 1910 to the present) to link the cinema *en bloc* with the modernist movement in the other arts. The high valuation put on the absorptive, anti-theatrical picture is a case in point. In proposing it, Michael Fried is not so much characterizing eighteenth-century French painting or even eighteenth-century French art criticism, as he is offering a prehistory of a certain conception of modernist painting, one where the painting is concerned solely with itself, and does not solicit the spectator. His account of Diderot's views enables him ingeniously to distinguish this conception of modern painting from one based on the notion of non-representationalism as such—both by finding a perfectly representational art that can be located in the tradition, and by finding an argument to damn those kinds of abstract art (most notably certain of the New York minimalist painters and sculptors) that seem palpably to address a spectator, as 'theatrical'. And when Svetlana Alpers champions the 'Northern' tradition of Flemish and Dutch painting against the orthodox attribution of centrality to the Italians, and borrows a title of György Lukács's ('Narrate or Describe?') for an essay which, unlike Lukács, puts the descriptive above the narrative or historical, she, like Fried, is polemically adopting a modernist stance while, again like Fried, freeing it from an exclusive bent towards non-representationalism. Much of the attraction of Fried's and Alpers's positions to film historians lies in the way they make possible an assimilation of film to modernism. A pictorial cinema in our sense, on the contrary, has roots in the kinds of painting and theatre that the modernist movement set itself against.

There is an alternative to Fried's 'high' modernism in the writings of Walter Benjamin. When

Benjamin appealed to the exclamation 'Tableau!', he did so to compare the opportunities for that exclamation with the scenes in Brecht's epic theatre. This use of picture seems much closer to ours, and Benjamin goes on to indicate that what these pictures show is the *Zustand* in which the characters caught in them are suddenly frozen, and *Zustand* can be translated 'situation' (indeed, Benjamin uses the word '*Situation*' in an early draft for the essay in this context). Moreover, Benjamin hints at a kind of popular, anti-classical tradition behind these aspects of Brecht's theatre. This 'low' modernism seems more appropriate to characterize the range of theatrical devices we have described as pictorial. However, we would stress that pictorialism in this sense was not simply a 'low' or vulgar form. While a taste for spectacle and a situation-based dramaturgy could certainly be found in the melodramas which dominated the working-class theatre in London or New York, we have argued that they are also a feature of the respectable theatrical productions of a Belasco or an Irving. Given its broad appeal, and given the tradition of academic painting and of illustration on which spectacular theatre draws, it seems more appropriate to characterize it as 'middlebrow' rather than assimilating it to either Benjamin's 'low' or Fried's 'high' modernism. There is nothing particularly 'modern' about the pictorial tradition, unless the modern can be dated back to the eighteenth century, a definition which would dilute the notion of modernism to mean no more than 'contemporaneous with capitalism'. By the same token, the cinema of the 1910s should not be seen as a 'modern' phenomenon in any but the most banal sense that it was produced in the twentieth century.

Our last point we regard as an unresolved issue. It is generally accepted that, before about 1907, that is, before the rise of specialized venues for the showing of films almost exclusively, and appropriate structures of production and distribution of films for such venues, films were very different from what they became in the cinema with which we are familiar, which, despite important changes, has been held to remain remarkably similar from around 1917 to the present. Currently, the most common way of formulating this is to contrast a 'cinema of attractions' in the early period, with a 'classical narrative cinema' in the later, with the intervening decade one of transition between the two. To some extent, our account cuts across this distinction. We regard the cinema of attractions as essentially an institutional matter of a type of exhibition, appropriate to both narrative and non-narrative films, and would emphasize the brevity of the films appropriate to these types of exhibition as the crucial feature. We link the influence of pictorial theatre to the rise of the feature film, and the problems of handling narrative in a much longer format. We do not see the theatrical picture as in some sense inimical to narrative but rather as one of its modes.

However, most characterizations of the narrative cinema that emerged after 1917 seem remote from pictorialism. For example, David Bordwell, Janet Staiger, and Kristin Thompson's 'classical Hollywood cinema' is founded on an Aristotelian plot with the causes centred on the principal characters—essentially a protagonist sets him- or herself a goal the struggle for which, against external obstacles or the efforts of antagonists, takes the story from its beginning to its end, whether that end is the achievement of the goal or some other resolution, happy or unhappy. As we have pointed out, situations can be established in other ways than by setting obstacles to characters' achievement of their goals, so, although both a situational and a causal account can be given of many narratives, causal consistency is less important in a situational dramaturgy, while effective situations are less important for one that is 'Aristotelian' in this sense. Effective situations certainly remained crucial to 'classical Hollywood cinema'; does the undoubtedly widespread demand for causal consistency and character-centredness found in manuals and the cinematic trade press in the classical period represent a shift away from pictorialism, or is it a further instance of the discrepancy between intellectuals' commentary (obliged to bow to classical dramaturgy) and actual film-making practice? To take another example, Christian Metz argues that in classical narrative cinema the absence of the actors when the spectator views the film abolishes the exhibitionism which constitutes the live stage picture as theatrical rather than absorptive in Fried's sense. Is this argument incorrect, or is there a shift between the films of the 1910s we have been discussing and those of the classical cinema? Finally, Jean-Louis Baudry, Raymond Bellour, and Noël Burch have all made the highly edited style of classical films, and in particular the devices of shot-reverse-shot, and matching of eye-lines and movement, central to their account of those films and the cinematic institution which produced them. If we are right, and editing does not play such a part in the films of the 1910s, are the films of the next decades essentially different? These questions are beyond the scope of this book, but in so far as we have made our case for the 1910s, they need an answer.

Appendix:
Plot Summary of *Uncle Tom's Cabin*

This summary follows the original novel, and the reader should be warned that the play and film versions discussed in Part 2 often more or less deviate from it.

Uncle Tom lives with his wife Chloe and children in Kentucky, where he is one of the most valued field slaves of the planter George Shelby. Shelby is unable to redeem a note that has fallen into the hands of the slave trader Haley, who forces him to sell Tom and little Harry, the son of Eliza Harris, Mrs Shelby's maid. Eliza's husband George has already fled the nearby plantation of a harsher master, and, overhearing the plans for the sale of her son, Eliza decides to take the boy and try to join George in his flight to Canada. She warns Tom, but he decides not to resist his master's decision. Eliza and Harry are pursued by Haley to the Ohio River, which is too iced up for a boat to get over. Cornered by Haley, Eliza crosses the river, leaping from floe to floe with Harry in her arms. She is taken in by Senator Bird and his wife, who help her contact an abolitionist rescue organization, through which she is able to join her husband and a Quaker guide on the trip north through Ohio to Lake Erie. Haley entrusts the search to a professional slave-hunter, Loker, and his associate, the lawyer, Marks, and returns to the Shelby plantation. When Loker catches up with the runaways, George shoots and wounds him, and the Harrises reach Canada safely.

Tom says goodbye to his family and to Shelby's son, who swears to redeem him when he grows up. Haley takes Tom and sets off on a steamer down the Mississippi to New Orleans where he plans to sell him. Tom meets Eva, the little daughter of Augustine St Clare, who is returning home to New Orleans with his daughter and her aunt Ophelia, a Yankee hostile to slavery. Tom rescues Eva when she falls overboard, and, at Eva's request, St Clare buys him. He becomes the family's coachman. St Clare also buys Ophelia a slave child, Topsy, to test her abolitionist sentiments. Topsy is a thief and liar, impervious to Ophelia's moral suasion, and only corrigible by Eva's love. Eva sickens and dies, extracting from her father the promise to free his slaves. Before he can do so, St Clare is killed trying to prevent a duel. Tom is put up for auction with the rest of the slaves, except Topsy, who returns to Vermont with Ophelia, where she is set free.

Tom and a young girl, Emmeline, are bought by a dissolute Red River planter, Simon Legree. On his plantation, Legree tries to install Emmeline as his mistress, but she is protected by her forerunner, Cassy, whom Legree fears as a witch. Legree tries to force Tom to whip a sick slave woman, Lucy, who brings short weight of cotton to the weighing house, and has Tom beaten senseless by his overseers, Sambo and Quimbo, when he refuses. Cassy and Emmeline outwit Legree and flee the plantation. In an attempt to get him to reveal their whereabouts, Legree tortures Tom to death.

Shelby's son arrives too late to save Tom's life, but hears his dying words, and buries him. Cassy and Emmeline reach Canada and encounter the Harrises. It is discovered that Eliza is Cassy's long lost daughter. As the novel ends, the Harrises are setting out for a new life in Liberia.

Bibliography

Unpublished Sources

Billy Rose Theatre Collection, Performing Arts Research Center of the New York Public Library

AIKEN, GEORGE, *Uncle Tom's Cabin*, three promptscripts (annotated copies of published edition, New York: Samuel French, n.d.): one unsigned; one signed J. S. MacNeill without date; and one signed J. B. Wright and dated 1866.

ARMSTRONG, PAUL, *Alias Jimmy Valentine*, four annotated typescripts: a quarto one in a Rosenfeld Stenography agency binding; a quarto one in a Liebler & Co. binding; an unbound folio one; and a quarto one in a Rialto Service Bureau binding.

BRADLEY, ALICE, *The Governor's Lady*, New York City, 10 Sept. 1912, stage photographs.

HERMANN, CHARLES, *Uncle Tom's Cabin; A Drama of Real Life*, promptscript (annotated copy of an unidentified printed edition).

LEMON, MARK, and TAYLOR, TOM, *Slave Life; or, Uncle Tom's Cabin*, promptscript (annotated copy of published edition, London: Webster & Co., n.d.).

MORTON, CHARLES, *Uncle Tom's Cabin*, typescript prepared for copyright deposit in 1912.

RALEIGH, CECIL, and HAMILTON, HENRY, *The Whip*, Drury Lane Theatre, London, 9 Sept. 1909, stage photographs.

Byron Collection, Museum of the City of New York

BELASCO, DAVID, *Girl of the Golden West*, Belasco Theatre, New York City, 14 Nov. 1905, stage photographs.

Uncle Tom's Cabin, William A. Brady production, Academy of Music, New York City, 4 Mar. 1901, stage photographs.

Daniel Blum Collection of the Wisconsin Center for Film and Theater Research, Madison, Wisconsin

Scrapbooks, vol. 28, 1909–10, microfilm reel 4, frames 814–953.

Pettingell Collection, Special Collections, University Library, University of Kent at Canterbury

(Since the research for this book was completed, parts of the Pettingell Collection have been published in a microform edition as *The Popular Stage: Drama in Nineteenth Century England* (Brighton: Harvester Microform).)

FITZBALL, EDWARD, *Uncle Tom's Cabin; or, Negro Life in America*, promptscript (annotated copy of published edition, London: John Dunscombe, n.d.).

HAZLEWOOD, COLIN, *The Christian Slave; or, The Life and Death of Uncle Tom*, fairhand copy.

HERMANN, CHARLES, *Uncle Tom's Cabin: A Drama of Real Life*, fairhand copy and promptscript (annotated copy of published edition, London: Samuel French, n.d.).

JERROLD, DOUGLAS, *The Rent Day*, promptscript (annotated copy of 3rd published edition, London: John Miller, 1834).

LEMON, MARK, and TAYLOR, TOM, *Slave Life; or, Uncle Tom's Cabin*, promptscript (annotated copy of published edition, London: Webster & Co., n.d.).

Playbill advertising a benefit for Frank Towers, Royal Victoria Theatre, 15 Mar. 1860.

Playbill for the Theatre Royal, Bristol, advertising 'The Second Part of *Uncle Tom's Cabin*'.

The Tams-Witmark/Wisconsin Collection of Music Theatre Production Materials, Mills Music Library, Memorial Library, University of Wisconsin-Madison

BENEDICT, JULIUS, *The Lily of Killarney* (opera), stage manager's annotated score.

DONIZETTI, GAETANO, *Lucia di Lammermoor* (opera), stage manager's annotated score.

Theatre Files, Museum of the City of New York

ARMSTRONG, PAUL, *Alias Jimmy Valentine*, clippings.

BRADLEY, ALICE, *The Governor's Lady*, souvenir programme: *The Story of the Governor's Lady Told in Pictures*.

RALEIGH, CECIL, and HAMILTON, HENRY, *The Whip*, Manhattan Opera House, New York City, 16 Dec. 1912, stage photographs.

Uncle Tom's Cabin, playbill for a production at the Grand Opera House, New York City, 27 Oct. 1877.

Uncle Tom's Cabin, clean typescript for the William A. Brady production, Academy of Music, New York City, 4 Mar. 1901.

Theatre Museum, Covent Garden, London

Uncle Tom's Cabin, playbills for various productions.

RALEIGH, CECIL, and HAMILTON, HENRY, *The Whip*, Drury Lane Theatre, London, 9 Sept. 1909, stage photographs.

Published Sources

ABEL, RICHARD, *The Ciné Goes to Town: French Cinema 1896–1914* (Berkeley: University of California Press, 1994).

ADLER, DANKMAR, 'The Chicago Auditorium', *Architectural Record*, 1, no. 4 (Apr.–June 1892), 415–34; repr. in William C. Young (ed.), *Famous American Playhouses 1716–1899: Documents of American Theatre History*, vol. i (Chicago: American Library Association, 1973), 292–302.

AIKEN, GEORGE, *Uncle Tom's Cabin; or, Life among the Lowly*, French's Standard Drama, the Acting Edition, no. 217 (New York, n.d.); repr. in Daniel C. Gerould (ed.), *American Melodrama* (New York: Performing Arts Journal Publications, 1983), 75–133.

ALB., 'A Rehearsal at the Française', *Time* (June 1879), 350.

ALFIERI, VITTORIO, 'Oreste', in *Tragedie*, ed. Nicola Bruscoli (Bari: Laterza, 1946), i. 327–82.

ALGAROTTI, FRANCESCO, *Saggio sopra l'opera in musica* (Livorno: Marco Coltellini, 1763; repr., ed. Annalisa Bini, Lucca: Libreria Musicale Italiana Editrice, 1989).

ALHOY, PHILADELPHE MAURICE, HAREL, FRANÇOIS ANTOINE, and JAL, AUGUSTE, *Dictionnaire théâtral, ou douze cent trente trois vérités sur les directeurs, régisseurs, acteurs, actrices et employés des divers théâtres; confidences sur les procédés de l'illusion, examen du vocabulaire dramatique; coup d'œil sur le matériel et le moral des spectacles* (Paris: J.-N. Barba, 1824).

ALLEN, ROBERT C., *Horrible Prettiness: Burlesque and American Culture* (Chapel Hill, NC: University of Carolina Press, 1991).

ALLEVY, MARIE-ANTOINETTE (Akakia Viala), *Édition critique d'une mise en scène romantique, indications générales pour la mise en scène de 'Henri III et sa cour' (drame historique en cinq actes, en prose, de M. A. Dumas) par Albertin, directeur de la scène près le Théâtre Français (1829)* (Paris: Droz, 1938; repr. Geneva: Slatkine Reprints, 1976).

—— *La Mise en scène en France dans la première moitié du dix-neuvième siècle* (Paris: Droz, 1938; repr. Geneva: Slatkine Reprints, 1976).

ALPERS, SVETLANA, 'Describe or Narrate? A Problem in Realistic Representation', *New Literary History*, 8 (1976–7), 15–41.

—— *The Art of Describing: Dutch Painting in the Seventeenth Century* (Chicago: University of Chicago Press, 1983).

ALTICK, RICHARD D., *The Shows of London* (Cambridge, Mass.: The Belknap Press of Harvard University Press, 1978).

ALTMAN, RICK, 'Dickens, Griffith, and Film Theory Today', *South Atlantic Quarterly*, 88, no. 2 (Spring 1989), 321–59.

American Film Institute Catalog of Motion Pictures Produced in the United States, vol. F2: *Feature Films 1921–1930*, ed. Kenneth W. Munden (New York: R. R. Bowker Co., 1971).

ARCHER, FRANK, *How to Write a Good Play* (London: Sampson Low, Marston & Co., 1892).

ARCHER, WILLIAM, *About the Theatre: Essays and Studies* (London: Fisher Unwin, 1886).

—— *Play-Making: A Manual of Craftsmanship* (London: Chapman & Hall, 1913).

ARISTOTLE, *The Poetics*, Longinus, *On the Sublime* and Demetrius, *On Style*, trans. W. Hamilton Fyfe and W. Rhys Roberts, Loeb Classical Library (Cambridge, Mass.: Harvard University Press, 1927).

ARMSTRONG, WILLIAM A., 'Peter Nicholson and the Scenographic Art', *Theatre Notebook*, 8 (Oct. 1953 to July 1954), 91–6.

'Art, Music and the Drama', *Illustrated London News*, 136, no. 3703 (9 Apr. 1910), 536.

AUBERT, CHARLES, *L'Art mimique suivi d'un traité de la pantomime et du ballet* (Paris: E. Meuriot, 1901).

BABLET, DENIS, *Esthétique générale du décor de théâtre de 1870 à 1914* (Paris: Éditions du Centre National de la Recherche Scientifique, 1965).

BALDWIN, JAMES, 'Everybody's Protest Novel', *Partisan Review* (June 1949); repr. in *Notes of a Native Son* (Boston: Beacon Press, 1955), 13–23.

BALL, EUSTACE HALE, *The Art of the Photoplay*, 2nd edn. (New York: G. W. Dillingham, 1913).

BARISH, JONAS, *The Anti-theatrical Prejudice* (Berkeley: University of California Press, 1981).

BARNETT, DENE, 'The Performance Practice of Acting: The Eighteenth Century, Part I: Ensemble Acting', *Theatre Research International*, 2, no. 3 (1977), 157–86.

—— 'The Performance Practice of Acting: The Eighteenth Century, Part II: The Hands', *Theatre Research International*, 3, no. 1 (1977), 1–19.

—— 'The Performance Practice of Acting: The Eighteenth Century, Part III: The Arms', *Theatre Research International*, 3, no. 2 (1978), 79–93.

—— 'The Performance Practice of Acting: The Eighteenth Century, Part IV: The Eyes, the Face and the Head', *Theatre Research International*, 5, no. 1 (1980), 1–36.

—— 'La Vitesse de la déclamation au théâtre (XVIIe–XVIIIe siècles)', *XVIIe Siècle*, 128, no. 3 (July–Sept. 1980), 319–26.

—— 'The Performance Practice of Acting: The Eighteenth Century, Part V: Posture and Attitudes', *Theatre Research International*, 6, no. 1 (1981), 1–32.

—— *The Art of Gesture: The Practices and Principles of 18th Century Acting* (Heidelberg: Carl Winter, 1987).

BARTHES, ROLAND, *S/Z* (Paris: Éditions du Seuil, 1970).

BAUGH, CHRISTOPHER, *Garrick and Loutherbourg*, set of slides with commentary (Cambridge: Chadwick-Healey in association with the Consortium for Drama and Media in Higher Education, 1990).

BAZIN, ANDRÉ, 'Théâtre et cinéma', *Esprit* (June and July–Aug.

1951); repr. in *Qu'est-ce-que le cinéma? Édition définitive* (Paris: Éditions du Cerf, 1978), 129–78.

BEDDING, THOMAS, 'The Modern Way in Moving Picture Making', *Moving Picture World*, 4, no. 11 (13 Mar. 1909), 294–5.

BELASCO, DAVID, 'Why I Stayed out and Why I Went into the Movies', *New York Times* (31 May 1914), section VII: 8, col. 3.

BENJAMIN, WALTER, 'What is Epic Theatre? [First Version]', in *Understanding Brecht*, trans. Anna Bostock (London: New Left Books, 1973), 1–13.

—— 'Was ist das epische Theater?', in *Gesammelte Schriften* (Frankfurt am Main: Suhrkamp Verlag, 1977), ii. 519–31; and the commentary and notes, ii. 1379–87.

BENNETT, COLIN N., 'Knotty Points Answered', *Kinematograph and Lantern Weekly*, 14, no. 352 (22 Jan. 1914), 74–5.

—— 'Knotty Points Answered', *Kinematograph and Lantern Weekly*, 20, no. 447 (18 Nov. 1915), 71.

—— *The Guide to Kinematography* (London: E. T. Heron, 1917).

—— et al., *The Handbook of Kinematography*, 2nd edn. (London: Kinematograph Weekly, 1913).

BIRDOFF, HARRY, *The World's Greatest Hit: Uncle Tom's Cabin* (New York: S. F. Vanni, 1947).

BITZER, GOTTFRIED WILHELM (BILLY), 'The Biograph Camera', *Journal of the Society of Operating Cameramen*, 5, no. 1 (Spring 1995), 6–9.

BLANEY, CHARLES E., 'Good and Bad Melodrama', *New York Dramatic Mirror*, 19, no. 1533 (9 May 1908), 2.

BLUNT, WILFRID, and STEARN, WILLIAM T., *The Art of Botanical Illustration*, rev. edn. (Kew: Royal Botanical Gardens, 1994).

BOOTH, MICHAEL, *Victorian Spectacular Theatre 1850–1910* (London: Routledge, 1981).

BORDWELL, DAVID, 'La Nouvelle Mission de Feuillade; or, What Was Mise en Scène?', *Velvet Light Trap*, 37 (Spring 1996), 10–29.

—— STAIGER, JANET, and THOMPSON, KRISTIN, *The Classical Hollywood Cinema: Film Style and Mode of Production to 1960* (London: Routledge, 1985).

BOUCICAULT, DION, with an introduction by Otis Skinner, *Papers on Acting I: The Art of Acting*, Publications of the Dramatic Museum of Columbia University, in the City of New York, 5th ser. (New York: Columbia University Press, 1926).

—— 'Coquelin-Irving', in *Papers on Acting II: The Art of Acting, a Discussion by Constant Coquelin, Henry Irving and Dion Boucicault*, Publications of the Dramatic Museum of Columbia University, in the City of New York, 5th ser. (New York: Columbia University Press, 1926), 54–62.

—— 'The Poor of New York', in Daniel C. Gerould (ed.), *American Melodrama* (New York: Performing Arts Journal Publications, 1983), 31–74.

BOUSQUET, HENRI, *Catalogue Pathé des années 1896 à 1914* [part 2] *1907–1908–1909* (Paris: published by the author, 1993); [part 3] *1910–1911* (Paris: published by the author, 1994);

[part 4] *1912–1913–1914* (Paris: published by the author, 1995).

—— and REDI, RICCARDO, *Pathé Frères: Les Films de la production Pathé (1896–1914)*, part 1: [1896–1906], *Quaderni di cinema*, 8, no. 37 (Jan.–Mar. 1988).

BOWSER, EILEEN, *The Transformation of Cinema 1907–1915*, vol. ii of *A History of American Cinema*, ed. Charles Harpole (New York: Scribner's, 1990).

BRAHM, OTTO, 'Die Freie Bühne in Berlin', *Berliner Tageblatt* (16, 18 Oct. 1909); repr. in *Kritiken und Essays*, sel., introd., and ed. Fritz Martini (Zurich: Artemis Verlag, 1964), 513–28.

BREWSTER, BEN, 'La Mise en scène en profondeur dans les films français de 1900 à 1914', in Pierre Guibbert (ed.), *Les Premiers ans du cinéma français* (Perpignan: Institut Jean Vigo, 1985), 204–17; English trans. as 'Deep Staging in French Films 1900–1914', in Thomas Elsaesser and Adam Barker (eds.), *Early Cinema: Space, Frame, Narrative* (London: British Film Institute, 1990), 45–55.

—— 'Film', in Michael Irwin and Daniel Cohn-Sherbok (eds.), *Exploring Reality* (London: Allen & Unwin, 1987), 145–67.

—— '*Traffic in Souls*: An Experiment in Feature-Length Narrative Construction', *Cinema Journal*, 31, no. 1 (Fall 1991), 37–56.

BROOKS, PETER, *The Melodramatic Imagination* (New Haven: Yale University Press, 1976).

BROWN, KARL, *Adventures with D. W. Griffith*, ed. Kevin Brownlow (London: Secker & Warburg, 1973).

BROWNLOW, KEVIN, *The Parade's Gone by* (London: Secker & Warburg, 1968).

—— 'Ben Carré', *Sight and Sound*, 49, no. 1 (Winter 1979–80), 46–50.

BURCH, NOËL, *Life to Those Shadows*, trans. Ben Brewster (London: British Film Institute, 1990).

BUTLER, JAMES H., 'Early Nineteenth-Century Stage Settings in the British Theatre', *Theatre Survey*, 6, no. 1 (May 1965), 54–64.

BYRNE, M. ST. CLARE, 'Early Multiple Settings in England', *Theatre Notebook*, 8 (1954), 81–6.

CAHN, JULIUS, *Official Theatrical Guide*, vol. i (New York: Publication Office, Empire Theatre, 1896–7).

CAHUSAC, LOUIS DE, *La Danse ancienne et moderne; ou Traité historique de la danse* (The Hague [in fact Paris]: Jean Neaulme, 1754); repr. in *Épître sur les dangers de la poésie suivie de La Danse ancienne et moderne; ou Traité historique de la danse* (Geneva: Slatkine Reprints, 1971), 23–182.

CALVERT, LOUIS, *Problems of the Actor* (New York: Henry Holt, 1918).

CARLSON, MARVIN, 'French Stage Composition from Hugo to Zola', *Educational Theatre Journal*, 23, no. 4 (Dec. 1971), 363–78.

—— '*Hernani*'s Revolt from the Tradition of French Stage

Composition', *Theatre Survey*, 13, no. 1 (May 1972), 1–27.

—— *The German Stage in the Nineteenth Century* (Metuchen, NJ: Scarecrow Press, 1972).

CASTLE, DENNIS, *Sensation Smith of Drury Lane* (London: Charles Skilton, 1984).

CAVELL, STANLEY, *The World Viewed: Reflections on the Ontology of Film* (New York: Viking Press, 1971).

CAYLUS, ANNE-CLAUDE-PHILIPPE DE TURBIÈRES, comte de, *Tableaux tirés de l'Iliade, de l'Odyssée d'Homère et de l'Énéide de Virgile, avec des observations générales sur le costume* (Paris: Tilliard, 1757).

[CHALMERS, J. P., and BEDDING, THOMAS], 'The Factor of Uniformity', *Moving Picture World*, 5, no. 4 (24 July 1909), 115–16.

CHERCHI USAI, PAOLO, '*Cabiria*, an Incomplete Masterpiece: The Quest for the Original 1914 Version', *Film History*, 2, no. 2 (June–July 1988), 155–65.

CHINOY, HELEN KRICH, 'The Emergence of the Director', in Toby Cole and Helen Krich Chinoy (eds.), *Directors on Directing: A Sourcebook of the Modern Theatre* (Indianapolis: Bobbs-Merrill, 1963), 1–77.

CHION, MICHEL, 'Quiet Revolution . . . and Rigid Stagnation', *October*, 58 (Fall 1991), 69–80.

'Le Cinématographe: Une merveille photographique', *Le Radical* (30 Sept. 1895); repr. in Georges Sadoul, *Louis Lumière*, Cinéma d'aujourd'hui no. 29 (Paris: Seghers, 1964), 117–18.

CLARKE, CHARLES G., 'Practical Filming Techniques for Three-Dimension and Wide-Screen Motion Pictures', *American Cinematographer*, 34, no. 3 (Mar. 1953), 107, 124–9, 138.

CLAUDY, C. H., 'The Degradation of the Motion Picture', *Photo-Era*, 21, no. 4 (Oct. 1908), 161–5.

—— 'Too Much Acting', *Moving Picture World*, 8, no. 6 (11 Feb. 1911), 288–9.

COLBURN, OTIS, 'Chicago Stage Gossip', *New York Dramatic Mirror*, 62, no. 1620 (8 Jan. 1910), 12.

'Comments on the Films, . . . *A Girl's Stratagem*', *Moving Picture World*, 15, no. 12 (22 Mar. 1913), 1219.

'Comments on the Films, . . . *The Hero of Little Italy*', *Moving Picture World*, 16, no. 3 (19 Apr. 1913), 279.

CONTANT, CLÉMENT, and FILIPPI, JOSEPH DE, *Parallèle des principaux théâtres modernes de l'Europe et des machines théâtrales françaises, allemandes et anglaises*, expanded version (Paris: Lévy, 1860 [1st edn. 1842]; repr. New York: Benjamin Blom, 1968).

COQUELIN, CONSTANT, 'Actors and Acting', in *Papers on Acting II: The Art of Acting, a Discussion by Constant Coquelin, Henry Irving and Dion Boucicault*, Publications of the Dramatic Museum of Columbia University, in the City of New York, 5th ser. (New York: Columbia University Press, 1926), 5–42.

DAVIS, JIM (ed.), *The Britannia Diaries 1863–1875: Selections from the Diaries of Frederick C. Wilton* (London: Society for Theatre Research, 1992).

DAVIS, TRACY C., 'Acting in Ibsen', *Theatre Notebook*, 39, no. 3 (1985), 113–23.

DELSARTE, FRANÇOIS, *Delsarte System of Oratory* (New York: Edgar S. Werner, 1893).

DE MILLE, HENRY C., and BELASCO, DAVID, *Men and Women*, repr. in Barrett H. Clark *et al.* (eds.), *America's Lost Plays*, vol. xvii (Princeton, NJ: Princeton University Press, 1940; repr. Indiana: Indiana University Press, 1963), 269–342.

DESLANDES, JACQUES, and RICHARD, JACQUES, *Histoire comparée du cinéma*, vol. ii: *Du cinématographe au cinéma, 1896–1906* (Paris: Casterman, 1968).

DETMERS, FRED H. (ed.), *American Cinematographer Manual*, 6th edn. (Hollywood, Calif.: ASC Press, 1986).

DIAMANT-BERGER, HENRI, *Le Cinéma* (Paris: La Renaissance du Livre, 1919).

DICKENS, CHARLES, *Nicholas Nickleby* (London: Chapman & Hall, 1839; repr. London: Penguin, 1978).

DIDEROT, DENIS, *Le Fils naturel*, in *Œuvres complètes de Diderot*, vol. x: *Le Drame bourgeois*, ed. Jacques Chouillet and Anne-Marie Chouillet (Paris: Hermann, 1980), 13–81.

—— *Entretiens sur Le Fils naturel*, in *Œuvres complètes de Diderot*, vol. x: *Le Drame bourgeois*, ed. Jacques Chouillet and Anne-Marie Chouillet (Paris: Hermann, 1980), 83–162.

—— and ALEMBERT, JEAN LE ROND D' (ed.), *Theatre Architecture and Stage Machines: Engravings from the Encyclopédie, ou dictionnaire raisonné des sciences, des arts et des métiers* (New York: Benjamin Blom, 1969).

'Dramatic Machinery', article in *Cyclopaedia, or Universal Dictionary of Arts, Sciences and Literature, Illustrated with Numerous Engravings*, ed. Abraham Rees, vol. xii (London: Longman, Hurst, Orne, & Brown, 1819).

DUMAS, ALEXANDRE, *fils*, *Histoire du supplice d'une femme: Réponse à M. Émile de Girardin* (Paris: Michel Lévy Frères, 1865).

DUMONT, GABRIEL PIERRE MARTIN, *Parallèle de plans des plus belles salles de spectacles d'Italie et de France* (Paris: published by the author, n.d. [c.1774]; repr. New York: Benjamin Blom, 1968).

DUPONT-VERNON, H., *Diseurs et comédiens* (Paris: Paul Ollendorf, 1891).

Early Rare British Film-Makers' Catalogues 1896–1913 (London: World Microfilm Publications, 1983, eight reels).

EISENSTEIN, SERGEI M., 'The Dynamic Square', *Close-Up* (Mar. and June 1931); repr. in *Film Essays and a Lecture*, ed. Jay Leyda (New York: Praeger, 1970), 48–65.

EL NOUTY, HASSAN, *Théâtre et pré-cinéma: Essai sur la problématique du spectacle au XIXe siècle* (Paris: A.-G. Nizet, 1978).

EMANAUD, MAURICE, *Géométrie perspective* (Paris: Doin, 1921).

EMERSON, JOHN, and LOOS, ANITA, *How to Write Photoplays* (New York: James A. McCann Co., 1920).

ESENWEIN, J. BERG, and LEEDS, ARTHUR, *Writing the Photoplay*

(Springfield, Mass.: Home Correspondence School, 1913).

FELL, JOHN, *Film and the Narrative Tradition* (Norman, Okla.: University of Oklahoma Press, 1975).

FIELDING, RAYMOND, 'Norman O. Dawn: Pioneer Worker in Special-Effects Cinematography', *Journal of the Society of Motion Picture Engineers*, 72 (Jan. 1963); repr. in Raymond Fielding (ed.), *A Technological History of Motion Pictures and Television* (Berkeley: University of California Press, 1967), 141–9.

FITZGERALD, PERCY, *Principles of Comedy and Dramatic Effect* (London: Tinsley Brothers, 1870).

—— *The World behind the Scenes* (London: Chatto & Windus, 1881; repr. New York: Benjamin Blom, 1972).

FRAMÉRY, NICOLAS ÉTIENNE, and GINGUENÉ, PIERRE LOUIS (eds.), *Encyclopédie méthodique, musique* (Paris: Panckoucke, 1791).

FRAZER, JOHN, *Artificially Arranged Scenes: The Films of Georges Méliès* (Boston: G. K. Hall, 1979).

FREEBURG, VICTOR OSCAR, *The Art of Photoplay Making* (New York: Macmillan, 1918).

FREYTAG, GUSTAV, *Technique of the Drama: An Exposition of Dramatic Composition and Art*, trans. Elias J. MacEwan (Chicago: Scott, Foresman & Co, 1894).

FRIED, MICHAEL, *Absorption and Theatricality, Painting and the Beholder in the Age of Diderot* (Berkeley: University of California Press, 1980).

FULLERTON, JOHN, 'The "Golden Age" of Swedish Film: Towards a New Historiography', paper presented at Milestones of Cinema, a conference at the University of Wisconsin Madison, Oct. 1995.

GAD, URBAN, *Filmen, dens midler og maal* (Copenhagen: Gyldendalske Boghandel/Nordisk Forlag, 1919).

GAREAU, MICHEL, *Charles Le Brun: First Painter to King Louis XIV* (New York: Harry N. Abrams, 1992).

GARNIER, CHARLES, *Le Théâtre* (Paris: Hachette, 1871).

GAUDREAULT, ANDRÉ, 'Les Détours du récit filmique: Sur la naissance du montage parallèle', *Cahiers de la cinémathèque*, 29 (Winter 1979), 88–107.

GENETTE, GÉRARD, 'Vraisemblance et motivation', in *Figures II* (Paris: Éditions du Seuil, 1969), 71–99.

GOETHE, JOHANN WOLFGANG, *Gedenkausgabe der Werke: Briefe und Gespräche*, ed. Ernst Beutler (Zurich: Artemis Verlag, 1949).

—— *Goethes Gespräche*, 5 vols. (Zurich: Artemis Verlag, 1969–84).

GOLDIE, ALBERT, 'Subtlety in Acting', *New York Dramatic Mirror*, 68, no. 1769 (13 Nov. 1912), 4.

GOMBRICH, ERNST, *Art and Illusion: A Study in the Psychology of Pictorial Representation*, rev. edn. (New York: Bollingen Foundation/Pantheon Books, 1961).

—— *Means and Ends: Reflections on the History of Fresco Painting* (London: Thames & Hudson, 1976).

GOSSETT, THOMAS F., *Uncle Tom's Cabin and American Culture* (Dallas: Southern Methodist University Press, 1985).

GOURNERIE, JULES DE LA, *Traité de perspective linéaire, contenant les tracés pour les bas-reliefs et les décorations théâtrales, avec une théorie des effets de perspective*, 2nd edn. (Paris: Gauthier-Villars, 1884).

Grand Larousse de la langue française, ed. Louis Guilbert, René Lagane, and Georges Niobey (Paris: Librairie Larousse, 1971–8).

GRAU, ROBERT, *The Theatre of Science: A Volume of Progress and Achievement in the Motion Picture Industry* (New York: Broadway Publishing Co., 1914; repr. New York: Benjamin Blom, 1969).

GREGORY, C. L. (ed.), *Motion Picture Photography* (New York: New York Photographic Society, 1920).

GREEN, ROGER LANCELYN, *Fifty Years of 'Peter Pan'* (London: Peter Davies, 1954).

GUNNING, TOM, 'The Cinema of Attractions: Early Film, its Spectators, and the Avant-Garde', *Wide Angle*, 8, no. 3/4 (Fall 1986), 63–70; rev. repr. in Thomas Elsaesser and Adam Barker (eds.), *Early Cinema: Space, Frame, Narrative* (London: British Film Institute, 1990), 56–62.

—— *D. W. Griffith and the Origins of American Narrative Film: The Early Years at Biograph* (Urbana, Ill.: University of Illinois Press, 1991).

'Hah! to Mr. Sheridan', *St James's Chronicle* (11–13 Nov. 1779).

HAMMOND, ANTHONY, 'Introduction', in William Shakespeare, *King Richard III*, the Arden Edition of the Works of William Shakespeare (London: Methuen, 1981; repr. Routledge, 1994), 1–119.

HARRISON, LOUIS REEVES, 'Alas, Poor Yorick!', *Moving Picture World* 19, no. 13 (28 Mar. 1914), 1653.

HARTOG, WILLIE G., *Guilbert de Pixérécourt: Sa vie, son mélodrame, sa technique et son influence* (Paris: Honoré Champion, 1913).

HASSEL, FRIEDRICH WILHELM VON, *Briefe aus England* (Hanover: Ch. Ritscher, 1792).

HENNEQUIN, ALFRED, *The Art of Playwriting: Being a Practical Treatise on the Elements of Dramatic Construction Intended for the Playwright, the Student and the Dramatic Critic* (Boston: Houghton, Mifflin & Co., 1897).

HEPWORTH, CECIL M., *Animated Photography: The ABC of the Cinematograph* (London: Hazell, Watson & Viney, 1900).

HERZBERG, CHARLOTTE, 'The Motion Picture Theater and Film Exhibition 1896–1932', Ph.D. thesis (Northwestern University, Evanston, Ill, 1980).

HILL, WYCLIFF A., *Ten Million Photoplay Plots* (Los Angeles: Feature Photodrama Company, 1919; repr. New York: Garland Publishing, 1978).

HOFFMAN, H. F., 'Cutting off the Feet', *Moving Picture World*, 12, no. 1 (6 Apr. 1912), 53.

HOLLAND, ROBERT STEPHEN (ed.), 'Introduction to the Play by

Colin Hazlewood, *The Christian Slave; or, The Life and Death of Uncle Tom, A Drama in Two Acts*, A parallel diplomatic text based on unpublished manuscripts in the Lord Chamberlain's Collection in the British Library (BL Add 52958X) and the Frank Pettingell Collection in the University of Kent at Canterbury Library', MA thesis (University of Kent at Canterbury, 1983).

HOLLANDER, ANNE, *Moving Pictures* (Cambridge, Mass.: Harvard University Press, 1991).

HOLMSTRÖM, KIRSTEN GRAM, *Monodrama, Attitudes, Tableaux Vivants: Studies on some Trends of Theatrical Fashion 1770–1815* (Uppsala: Almqvist & Wiksells Boktryckeri, 1967).

HOPFEN, HANS, 'Die Meininger in Berlin', in *Streitfragen und Erinnerungen* (Stuttgart: J. G. Cotta, 1876), 237–51.

[HUGO, ABEL, MALITOURNE, ARMAND, and ADER, JEAN-JOSEPH], *Traité du mélodrame par mm. A! A! A!* (Paris: Delaunay, 1817).

HULFISH, DAVID S., *Cyclopedia of Motion-Picture Work* (Chicago: American Technical Society, 1911).

—— *Motion Picture Work: A General Treatise on Picture Taking, Picture Making, Photo-Plays, and Theater Management and Operation* (Chicago: American Technical Society, 1915).

HUMBOLDT, WILHELM VON, 'Ueber die gegenwärtige Französische tragische Bühne: Aus Briefen', *Propyläen*, 3, no. 1 (1800); repr. in *Wilhelm von Humboldts Gesammelte Schriften*, ed. Königlich Preussischen Akademie der Wissenschaften, *Werke* (ed. Albert Leitzmann), vol. ii, part 1, section 2: *1796–1799* (Berlin: B. Behr's Verlag, 1904), 377–400.

JACKSON, RUSSELL, *Victorian Theatre* (London: A. & C. Black, 1989).

JACOBS, LEA, 'Belasco, DeMille and the Development of Lasky Lighting', *Film History*, 5, no. 4 (1993), 405–18.

JAMES, LOUIS, 'Was Jerrold's Black Ey'd Susan More Popular than Wordsworth's Lucy?', in David Bradby, Louis James, and Bernard Sharratt (eds.), *Performance and Politics in Popular Drama: Aspects of Popular Entertainment in Theatre, Film and Television, 1800–1976* (Cambridge: Cambridge University Press, 1980), 3–16.

JASSET, VICTORIN HYPPOLITE, 'Étude sur la mise-en-scène en cinématographie', *Ciné-Journal*, 165 (21 Oct. 1911), 51; 166 (28 Oct. 1911), 33, 35–7; 167 (4 Nov. 1911), 31, 33, 35; 168 (11 Nov. 1911), 38–9; 170 (25 Nov. 1911), 25–7; repr. in Marcel Lapierre (ed.), *Anthologie du cinéma* (Paris: La Nouvelle Édition, 1946), 82–98.

JELGERHUIS, JOHANNES, *Theoretische Lessen over de Gesticulatie en Mimiek: Gegeven aan de Kweekelingen van het Fonds ter Opleiding en Onderrigting van Tooneel-Kunstenaars aan den Stads Schouwburg te Amsterdam* (Amsterdam: P. M. Warnars, 1827; repr. Uitgeverij Adolf M. Hakkert, 1970).

JENN, PIERRE, and NAGARD, MICHEL, 'L'Assassinat du Duc de Guise' [shot breakdown], *L'Avant-Scène Cinéma*, 334 (Nov. 1984), 57–72.

JOHNSON, STEPHEN, 'Evaluating Early Film as a Document of Theatre History: The 1896 Footage of Joseph Jefferson's *Rip Van Winkle*', *Nineteenth Century Theatre*, 20, no. 2 (Winter 1992), 101–22.

—— 'Translating the Tom Show: A Comparison of Edwin S. Porter's 1903 film and William Brady's 1901 Stage Production of *Uncle Tom's Cabin*', paper presented at Celebrating 1895, a conference held in Bradford, July 1995.

JUDSON, HANFORD C., 'What Gets Over', *Moving Picture World*, 8, no. 15 (15 Apr. 1911), 816.

KAPLAN, JOEL H., 'Henry Arthur Jones and the Lime-Lit Imagination', *Nineteenth Century Theatre*, 15, no. 2 (Winter 1987), 115–41.

KELLY, JOHN ALEXANDER, *German Visitors to English Theaters in the Eighteenth Century* (Princeton: Princeton University Press, 1936).

KESSLER, FRANK, and LENK, SABINE, ' " . . . levant les bras au ciel, se tapant sur les cuisses": Réflexions sur l'universalité du geste dans le cinéma des premiers temps', in Roland Cosandey and François Albéra (eds.), *Cinéma sans frontières / Images across Borders, 1895–1918* (Lausanne: Payot-Lausanne, 1995), 133–45.

KINSILA, EDWARD, *Modern Theatre Construction* (New York: Chalmers, 1917).

KLABER, JOHN, 'Planning the Moving Picture Theatre', *Architectural Record*, 38, no. 5 (Nov. 1915), 540–54.

KNAPP, BETTINA, *The Reign of the Theatrical Director: French Theatre, 1887–1924* (New York: Whitston, 1988).

KNILLI, FRIEDRICH, and MÜNCHOW, URSULA (eds.), *Frühes deutsches Arbeitertheater 1847–1918* (Munich: Carl Hanser Verlag, 1970).

KOSZARSKI, RICHARD, *An Evening's Entertainment: The Age of the Silent Feature Picture 1915–1928*, vol. iii of Charles Harpole (ed.), *History of the American Cinema* (New York: Scribner's, 1990).

KRANICH, FRIEDRICH, *Bühnentechnik der Gegenwart*, vol. i (Munich: R. Oldenbourg, 1929).

KULESHOV, LEV, 'Art of the Cinema', in *Kuleshov on Film: Writings of Lev Kuleshov*, trans. Ronald Levaco (Berkeley: University of Calfornia Press, 1974), 39–123.

LANG, FRANCISCUS, *Dissertatio de actione scenica cum figuris eandem explicantibus et observationibus quibusdam de arte comica* (Munich: Typis Mariae Magdalenae Riedlin, 1727).

LAWRENCE, FLORENCE, in collaboration with KATTERJOHN, MONTE M., 'Growing up with the Movies', *Photoplay*, 7, no. 2 (Jan. 1915), 95–107.

LEACROFT, RICHARD, *The Development of the English Playhouse* (London: Eyre Methuen, 1973).

LE BRUN, CHARLES, *A Method to Learn to Design the Passions Proposed in a Conference on their General and Particular Expression*, trans. John Williams (London: John Fielding, 1734; repr. Los Angeles: Augustan Reprint Society, Publication number 200–1, William Andrews Clark Memorial Library,

University of California, Los Angeles, 1980).

LESSING, GOTTHOLD EPHRAIM, *The Hamburg Dramaturgy*, trans. Helen Zimmern (New York: Dover, 1962).

—— *Laocoön: An Essay on the Limits of Painting and Poetry*, trans. Edward Allen McCormick (Baltimore: Johns Hopkins University Press, 1962).

LEWES, GEORGE HENRY, *On Actors and the Art of Acting* (London: Smith, Elder & Co., 1875; repr. New York: Grove Press, 1957).

LEWIS, LEOPOLD, *Henry Irving and 'The Bells': Irving's Personal Script of the Play by Leopold Lewis*, ed. and introd. David Mayer (Manchester: Manchester University Press, 1980).

LIESEGANG, F. PAUL, *Handbuch der praktischen Kinematographie*, 5th edn. (Düsseldorf: Ed. Liesegang, 1918).

LITTRÉ, ÉMILE, *Dictionnaire de la langue française* (Paris: Hachette, 1875).

LLOYDS, FREDERICK, *Practical Guide to Scene Painting and Painting in Distemper* (London: G. Romney & Co., n.d. [1875]).

LOW, RACHAEL, and MANVELL, ROGER, *The History of the British Film*, vol. i: *1896–1906* (London: Allen & Unwin, 1948).

LUND, RALPH EUGENE, 'Trouping with Uncle Tom', *Century*, 115 (1928), 329–37.

LUTZ, EDWIN GEORGE, *The Motion-Picture Cameraman* (New York: C. Scribner's Sons, 1927; repr. New York: Arno Press, 1972).

MCDOWELL, JOHN H., 'Scenery and Staging of *Uncle Tom's Cabin*: Selected Scenes', *Ohio State University Theatre Collection Bulletin*, 10 (1963), 19–31.

MACHT, STEPHEN R., 'The Origin of the London Academy of Music and Dramatic Art', *Theatre Notebook*, 26, no. 1 (Autumn 1971), 19–30.

MACPHERSON, JEANIE, *Preparation and Motivation*, one of a series of lectures especially prepared for student members of the Palmer Course and Service (Hollywood: Palmer Photoplay Corporation, 1923).

MARKER, FREDERICK J., *Hans Christian Andersen and the Romantic Theatre* (Toronto: University of Toronto Press, 1971).

—— and MARKER, LISE-LONE, 'Fru Heiberg: A Study of the Art of the Romantic Actor', *Theatre Research*, 13, no. 1 (1973), 22–37.

—— —— *Ibsen's Lively Art: A Performance Study of the Major Plays* (Cambridge: Cambridge University Press, 1989).

MARKER, LISE-LONE, *David Belasco: Naturalism in the American Theatre* (Princeton: Princeton University Press, 1975).

MAYER, DAVID, 'Nineteenth Century Theatre Music', *Theatre Notebook*, 30, nos. 22 and 23 (1976), 115–22.

—— 'The Music of Melodrama', in David Bradby, Louis James, and Bernard Sharratt (eds.), *Performance and Politics in Popular Drama: Aspects of Popular Entertainment in Theatre, Film and Television, 1800–1976* (Cambridge: Cambridge University Press, 1980), 49–63.

—— 'The Victorian Stage on Film: A Description and a Selective List of Holdings in the Library of Congress Paper Print Collection', *Nineteenth Century Theatre*, 16, no. 2 (Winter 1988), 111–22.

—— (ed.), *Playing out the Empire: Ben-Hur and Other Toga Plays and Films, 1883–1908: A Critical Anthology* (Oxford: Clarendon Press, 1994).

MAYHEW, EDWARD, *Stage Effect; or, The Principles which Command Dramatic Success in the Theatre* (London: Mitchell, 1840).

MEISEL, MARTIN, *Realizations: Narrative, Pictorial and Theatrical Arts in Nineteenth-Century England* (Princeton: Princeton University Press, 1983).

MERRITT, RUSSELL, 'Mr. Griffith, *The Painted Lady* and the Distractive Frame', *Image*, 19, no. 4 (Dec. 1976); repr. in Marshall Deutelbaum (ed.), *'Image': On the Art and Evolution of the Film* (New York: Dover Publications and International Museum of Photography, 1979), 147–56.

METZ, CHRISTIAN, 'The Imaginary Signifier', in *Psychoanalysis and Cinema: The Imaginary Signifier*, trans. Celia Britton, Annwyl Williams, Ben Brewster, and Alfred Guzzetti (London: Macmillan, 1982), 1–87.

—— 'Story/Discourse (A Note on Two Kinds of Voyeurism)', in *Psychoanalysis and Cinema: The Imaginary Signifier*, trans. Celia Britton, Annwyl Williams, Ben Brewster, and Alfred Guzzetti (London: Macmillan, 1982), 89–98.

MITRY, JEAN, *Histoire du cinéma: Art et industrie* (Paris: Éditions Universitaires, 1967), vol. i: *1895–1914*.

MOORE, DUNCAN, 'Size or Realism?', *Optical Magic Lantern Journal and Photographic Enlarger*, 5, no. 58 (1 Mar. 1894), 56.

MORGAN, HENRY, *Perspective Drawing for the Theatre* (New York: Drama Book Specialists, 1979).

MORROCCHESI, ANTONIO, *Lezioni di declamazione e d'arte teatrale* (Florence: Tipografia all'insegna di Dante, 1832).

MORROW, JOHN C., 'The Harmount Company: Aspects of an *Uncle Tom's Cabin* Company', *Ohio State University Theatre Collection Bulletin*, no. 10 (1963), 10–18.

Motion Picture Catalogs by American Producers and Distributors 1894–1908, ed. Charles Musser (Ann Arbor: University Microfilms, 1984–5).

MOTTRAM, RONALD, *The Danish Cinema before Dreyer* (Metuchen, NJ: Scarecrow Press, 1988).

MOYNET, GEORGES, *La Machinerie théâtrale: Trucs et décors* (Paris: Librairie Illustrée, n.d. [1893]).

MOYNET, J., *L'Envers du théâtre: Machines et décorations* (Paris: Hachette, 1873).

'Mr. Benedict's "Lily of Killarney" ', *Dwight's Journal of Music* (29 Mar. 1862), 413.

MÜLLER, CORINNA, 'Filmografie', in Helga Belach, *Henny Porten, der erste deutsche Filmstar 1890–1960* (Berlin: Haude & Spener, 1986), 171–232.

MUSSER, CHARLES, 'The Changing Status of the Film Actor', in

Before Hollywood: Turn-of-the-Century American Film (New York: Hudson Hills Press, 1987), 57–62.

—— *Before the Nickelodeon: Edwin S. Porter and the Edison Manufacturing Company* (Berkeley: University of California Press, 1990).

—— *The Emergence of Cinema: The American Screen to 1907*, vol. i of Charles Harpole (ed.), *A History of the American Cinema* (New York: Scribner's, 1990).

NAPIER, FRANK, *Curtains for Stage Settings: A Practical Guide to their Use with the Necessary Adjuncts* (London: F. Muller, 1937).

NAREMORE, JAMES, *Acting in the Cinema* (Berkeley: University of California Press, 1988).

NEVILLE, HENRY GARSIDE, 'Gesture', in Hugh Campbell, R. F. Brewer, and Henry Neville, *Voice, Speech and Gesture: A Practical Handbook to the Elocutionary Art* (New York: G. P. Putnam's, 1895; repr. in Granger Index Reprint Series, New York: Books for Libraries Press, 1972), 101–69.

[NICHOLSON, PETER], article 'Scenography', in *Cyclopaedia, or Universal Dictionary of Arts, Sciences and Literature, Illustrated with Numerous Engravings*, ed. Abraham Rees, vol. xxxi (London: Longman, Hurst, Orne, & Brown, 1819).

NICOLL, ALLARDYCE, *The Development of the Theatre: A Study of Theatrical Art from the Beginnings to the Present Day*, 5th rev. edn. (New York: Harcourt Brace Jovanovich, 1966).

NOVERRE, MAURICE, 'L'Œuvre de Georges Méliès', *Le Nouvel Art cinématographique*, 2nd ser., no. 3 (July 1929).

—— 'Le Gala Méliès', *Le Nouvel Art cinématographique*, 2nd ser., no. 5 (Jan. 1930), 71–90.

OHNET, GEORGES, *Roi de Paris*, from the series *Les Batailles de la vie*, 8th edn. (Paris: Paul Ollendorff, 1898).

The Oxford English Dictionary, 2nd edn., prepared by J. A. Simpson and E. S. C. Weiner (Oxford: Clarendon Press, 1989).

PALMER, FREDERICK, *Photoplay Plot Encyclopedia*, 2nd edn. (Los Angeles: Palmer Photoplay Corporation, 1922).

—— *Palmer Handbook of Scenario Construction* (Hollywood: Palmer Photoplay Corporation, n.d. [1922?]).

PASTRONE, GIOVANNI, *Cabiria, visione storica del III secolo a.C.*, titles by Gabriele D'Annunzio, introd. Maria Adriana Prolo, continuity described from an original tinted and toned print by Roberto Radicali and Ruggero Rossi (Turin: Museo Nazionale del Cinema, 1977).

PEARSON, ROBERTA, *Eloquent Gestures: The Transformation of Performance Style in the Griffith Biograph Films* (Berkeley: University of California Press, 1992).

PHILLIPS, HENRY ALBERT, *The Photodrama* (New York: Stanhope-Dodge Publishing Co., 1914; repr. New York: Arno Press, 1970).

' "Photodrama is a Distinct Art," Declares Tourneur', *Motion Picture News*, 13, no. 4 (Jan. 1916), 516.

PILES, ROGER DE, *Cours de peinture par principes* (Paris: J. Estienne, 1708; repr. Geneva: Slatkine Reprints, 1969).

'Plays and Players', *Hampton's Magazine*, 24, no. 5 (May 1910), 697–703.

'The Plays of the Week', *New York Dramatic Mirror*, 63, no. 1623 (29 Jan. 1910), 6.

Playwriting: A Handbook for Would-be Dramatic Authors by 'A Dramatist' (London: Macrae, Curtice & Co., 1888).

PLUTARCH, *Table-Talk*, part 5, trans. Herbert B. Hoffleit, *Plutarch's Moralia*, Loeb's Classical Library (London: Heinemann, 1969), vol. viii.

POLTI, GEORGES, *Les Trente-six situations dramatiques* (Paris: Mercure de France, 1895).

—— *The Thirty-Six Dramatic Situations*, trans. Lucile Ray (Franklin, Oh.: James Knapp Reeve, 1924).

PORTE, JOSEPH DE LA, and CHAMFORT, SÉBASTIEN-ROCH-NICHOLAS, *Dictionnaire dramatique* (Paris: Lacombe, 1776).

POUGIN, ARTHUR, *Dictionnaire historique et pittoresque du théâtre* (Paris: Librarie de Firmin-Didot et Cie., 1885).

POWELL, A. VAN BUREN, *The Photoplay Synopsis* (Springfield, Mass.: The Home Correspondence School, 1919).

POZZO, ANDREA (Puteus), *Rules and Examples of Perspective Proper for Painters and Architects, & c.*, in English and Latin, English translation, from the edition in Latin and Italian published in Rome in 1693 by John James (London: printed for J. Senex and R. Gosling in Fleetstreet; W. Innys in St Pauls Church Yard; J. Osborn and T. Longman in Paternoster Row, n.d. [1709?]).

PRATT, GEORGE, *Spellbound in Darkness: A History of the Silent Film* (Greenwich, Conn.: New York Graphic Society, 1966).

PUDOVKIN, VSEVOLOD I., *Film Technique and Film Acting: The Cinematic Writings of V. I. Pudovkin*, trans. Ivor Montagu, introd. Lewis Jacobs (New York: Lear Publishers, 1949).

PUJOULX, JEAN BAPTISTE, *Paris à la fin du XVIIIe siècle, ou esquisse historique et morale des monumens et des ruines de cette capitale; de l'état des sciences, des arts et de l'industrie à cette époque, ainsi que des mœurs et des ridicules de ses habitans* (Paris: Brigite Mathé, 1801).

QUARNSTROM, I. BLAINE, 'Early Twentieth Century Staging of *Uncle Tom's Cabin*: Harmount's Tom Show—Selected Scenes', *Ohio State University Theatre Collection Bulletin*, 15 (1968), 32–42.

[QUESNAY, FRANÇOIS], *Tableau économique, avec ses explications*, separately paginated part 8 of Victor Riqueti, marquis de Mirabeau, *L'Ami des hommes; ou Traité de la population*, rev. edn. (Avignon, 1758–61).

RANGER, PAUL, 'I Was Present at the Representation . . .', *Theatre Notebook*, 39, no. 1 (1985), 18–25.

REDE, LEMAN THOMAS TERTIUS, *The Road to the Stage; or, The Performer's Preceptor, Containing Clear and Complete Instructions for Obtaining Theatrical Engagements, with a List of All the Provincial Theatres, the Names of the Managers, All Particulars as to their Circuits, Salaries, etc., with a Complete Exploration of All the Technicalities of the Histrionic Art* (London: J. Smith, 1827).

REES, TERENCE, *Theatre Lighting in the Age of Gas* (London: Society for Theatre Research, 1978).

RÉMOND DE SAINTE-ALBINE, PIERRE, *Le Comédien*, rev. edn. (Paris: Vincent fils, 1749; repr. Geneva: Slatkine Reprints, 1971).

Review of *The Critic*, by Richard Brinsley Sheridan, *Public Advertiser* (1 Nov. 1779).

Review of *Love Potion no. 9, New York Times* (13 Nov. 1992), B9.

REYNAUD, CHARLES, *Musée rétrospectif de la classe 18, Théâtre, à l'-Exposition Universelle Internationale de 1900 à Paris*, report of the committee of installation (Saint-Cloud: Belin Frères, 1903).

RICCOBONI, FRANÇOIS, *L'Art du théâtre, suivi d'une lettre de M. Riccoboni fils à M*** au sujet de l'art du théâtre* (Paris: Simon et Giffart, 1750; repr. Geneva: Slatkine Reprints, 1971).

RICHARDSON, F. H., 'Operator's Column', *Moving Picture World*, 7, no. 9 (27 Aug. 1910), 470.

—— 'Projection Department', *Moving Picture World*, 13, no. 5 (3 Aug. 1912), 449.

—— 'Projection Department', *Moving Picture World*, 13, no. 7 (17 Aug. 1912), 666.

RICHTER, HANS, *The Struggle for the Film*, trans. Ben Brewster (Aldershot: Scolar Press, 1986).

ROACH, JOSEPH R., *The Player's Passion: Studies in the Science of Acting* (Newark, Del.: University of Delaware Press, 1985).

ROSENFELD, SYBIL, *A Short History of Scene Design in Great Britain* (Oxford: Blackwell, 1973).

SACHS, EDWIN O., and WOODROW, ERNEST A., *Modern Opera Houses and Theatres*, 3 vols. (London: Batsford, 1896, 1897, and 1898; repr. New York: Benjamin Blom, 1968).

SADOUL, GEORGES, *Histoire générale du cinéma* (Paris: Denoël, 1948; repr. 1973), vol. ii: *Les Pionniers du cinéma (de Méliès à Pathé), 1897–1909*.

SALT, BARRY, paper on Lubitsch and operetta presented at the conference Silent Cinema 1916–26: Space, Frame, Narrative, held at the University of East Anglia, Norwich, in 1983.

—— 'From German Stage to German Screen', in Paolo Cherchi Usai and Lorenzo Codelli (eds.), *Prima di Caligari: Cinema tedesco 1895–1920* (Pordenone: Edizioni Biblioteca dell'Immagine, 1990), 402–22.

—— *Film Style and Technology: History and Analysis*, 2nd edn. (London: Starword, 1992).

SALTEN, FELIX, 'Zu einem Kinodramen, Anmerkungen', *Dresdner neueste Nachrichten*, 112 (27 Apr. 1913, 1st edn.), 1; repr. in Jörg Schweinitz (ed.), *Prolog vor dem Film: Nachdenken über ein neues Medium, 1909–1914* (Leipzig: Reclam, 1992), 359–65.

SARGENT, EPES WINTHROP, 'The Photoplaywright: Scenes and Leaders', *Moving Picture World*, 13, no. 6 (10 Aug. 1912), 542.

—— *Technique of the Photoplay*, 2nd edn. (New York: Moving Picture World, 1913).

SCHÖNE, GÜNTER, *Die Entwicklung der Perspektivbühne von Serlio bis Galli-Bibiena nach der Perspektivbüchern*, *Theatergeschichtliche Forschungen* founded by Berthold Litzmann, ed. Julius Petersen, no. 43 (Leipzig, Leopold Voss, 1933; repr. Neudeln: Kraus Reprints, 1977).

SENELICK, LAURENCE, 'Rachel in Russia: The Shchepkin–Annenkov Correspondence', *Theatre Research International*, 3, no. 2 (1978), 93–114.

SHERIDAN, RICHARD BRINSLEY, *The Critic*, in *The Dramatic Works of Richard Brinsley Sheridan*, ed. Cecil Price (Oxford: Oxford University Press, 1973), ii. 463–555.

SIDDONS, HENRY, *Practical Illustrations of Rhetorical Gesture and Action; Adapted to the English Drama: From a Work on the Same Subject by M. Engel* (London: Richard Phillips, 1807).

SLEVIN, JAMES, *On Picture-Play Writing: A Hand-Book of Workmanship* (Cedar Grove, NJ: Farmer Smith, 1912).

SLIDE, ANTHONY (ed.), *Selected Film Criticism 1896–1911* (Metuchen, NJ: Scarecrow Press, 1982).

—— *The Big V: A History of the Vitagraph Company*, rev. edn. (Metuchen, NJ: Scarecrow Press, 1987).

SLOUT, WILLIAM L., '*Uncle Tom's Cabin* in American Film History', *Journal of Popular Film*, 2 (1973), 137–51.

SMITH, HARRY JAMES, 'The Melodrama', *Atlantic Monthly*, 99 (Mar. 1907), 320–8.

SMITH, JAMES, *Melodrama* (London: Methuen, 1973).

SONREL, PIERRE, *Traité de scénographie, évolution du matériel scénique, inventaire et mise en œuvre du matériel scénique actuel, technique de l'établissement des décors, perspective théâtrale, autres scènes en usage* (Paris: O. Lieutier, 1943).

SOURIAU, ÉTIENNE, *Les Deux cent mille situations dramatiques* (Paris: Flammarion, 1950).

SOUTHERN, RICHARD, *Proscenium and Sight-Lines: A Complete System of Scenery Planning and a Guide to the Laying out of Stages* (London: Faber, 1939).

—— 'The Picture Frame Proscenium of 1880', *Theatre Notebook*, 5 (Apr. 1951), 59–61.

—— *Changeable Scenery: Its Origin and Development in the British Theatre* (London: Faber & Faber, 1952).

SPRENGEL, CHRISTIAN CONRAD, *Das entdeckte Geheimniss der Natur im Bau und in der Befruchtung der Blumen* (Berlin: Friedrich Vieweg, Sr., 1793).

STAIGER, JANET, 'The Eyes Are Really the Focus: Photoplay Acting and Film Form and Style', *Wide Angle*, 6, no. 4 (1985), 14–23.

—— *Interpreting Films: Studies in the Historical Reception of American Cinema* (Princeton, NJ: Princeton University Press, 1992).

STANISLAVSKY, KONSTANTIN, *An Actor Prepares*, trans. Elizabeth Reynolds Hapgood (New York: Theatre Arts, 1936).

—— *Stanislavsky on the Art of the Stage*, trans. David Magarshack (London: Faber & Faber, 1950).

STARK, E., 'S nogami na stole', *Teatr i iskusstvo*, 39 (1913), 770.

STEBBINS, GENEVIEVE, *Delsarte System of Dramatic Expression* (New York: Edgar S. Werner, 1886).

STEVENS, ASHTON, review of 'Judith of Bethulia', *San Francisco Examiner* (7 Jan. 1906).

STOKES, JOHN, BOOTH, MICHAEL R., and BASSNETT, SUSAN, *Bernhardt, Terry, Duse: The Actress in her Time* (Cambridge: Cambridge University Press, 1988).

'Stories of the Films . . . Uncle Tom's Cabin', *Moving Picture World*, 7, no. 6 (6 Aug. 1910), 314.

STOWE, HARRIET BEECHER, *Uncle Tom's Cabin; or, Life among the Lowly* (Boston: John P. Jewett, 1852; repr., ed., and introd. by Ann Douglas, London: Penguin Classics, 1986).

STROEBEL, LESLIE, COMPTON, JOHN, CURRENT, IRA, and ZAKIA, RICHARD, *Photographic Materials and Processes* (Boston: Focal Press, 1986).

SYMONS, ARTHUR, *Eleonora Duse* (New York: Duffield & Co., 1927).

TALBOT, FREDERICK A., *Practical Cinematography and its Applications* (London: Heinemann, 1913).

'*Temptations of a Great City [Ved fængslets Port]*, A Special Release that has been Successful in Europe', *Moving Picture World*, 8, no. 24 (17 June 1911), 1367.

Theatre Set Designs in the Victoria and Albert Museum, microfiche collection (Haslemere: Emmett Publishing, 1985).

THOMPSON, KRISTIN, 'The International Exploration of Cinematic Expressivity', in Karel Dibbets and Bert Hogenkamp (eds.), *Film in the First World War* (Amsterdam: Amsterdam University Press, 1995), 65–85.

'Too Near the Camera', *Moving Picture World*, 8, no. 12 (25 Mar. 1911), 634.

TRAPIDO, JOEL (ed.), *An International Dictionary of Theatre Language* (Westport, Conn.: Greenwood Press, 1985).

TSIVIAN, YURI, 'Some Preparatory Remarks on Russian Cinema', in Paolo Cherchi Usai, Lorenzo Codelli, Carlo Montanaro, and David Robinson (eds.), *Testimoni Silenziosi: Film russi, 1908–1919 / Silent Witnesses: Russian Films, 1908–1919* (Pordenone/London: Edizioni Biblioteca dell'Immagine/ British Film Institute, 1989), 24–43.

—— 'Portraits, Mirrors, Death: On Some Decadent Clichés in Early Russian Films', *iris*, 14–15 (1992), 67–83.

—— *Early Cinema in Russia and its Cultural Reception*, trans. Alan Bodger (London: Routledge, 1994).

VARDAC, A. NICHOLAS, *Stage to Screen: Theatrical Origins of Early Film. From Garrick to Griffith* (Cambridge, Mass.: Harvard University Press, 1949).

VICTOR, PIERRE, *Mémoire contre le Baron Taylor* (Paris: Ponthieu, 1827).

VOLTAIRE (François Marie Arouet), *Appel à toutes les nations de l'Europe, des jugemens d'un écrivain anglais; ou, manifeste au sujet des honneurs du pavillon entre les théâtres de Londres et de Paris*, in *Œuvres complètes de Voltaire*, xxiv: *Mélanges*, part 3 (Paris: Garnier Frères, 1879), 191–221.

—— '[Remarques sur] *Ariane*, tragédie [de Thomas Corneille]' in *Les Œuvres complètes de Voltaire / The Complete Works of Voltaire*, lv: *Commentaires sur Corneille*, critical edn. by David Williams, part III (Banbury: The Voltaire Foundation, 1975), 980–1001.

WALLER, GREGORY A., *Main Street Amusements: Movies and Commercial Entertainment in a Southern City, 1896–1930* (Washington: Smithsonian Institution Press, 1995).

WALLS, HOWARD LAMARR, *Motion Pictures 1894–1912 Identified from the Records of the United States Copyright Office* (Washington: Copyright Office, Library of Congress, 1953).

WEICHBERGER, ALEXANDER, *Goethe und das Komödienhaus in Weimar 1779–1825: Ein Beitrag zur Theaterbaugeschichte, Theatergeschichtliche Forschungen*, established by Berthold Litzman, ed. Julius Petersen, no. 39 (Leipzig: Leopold Voss, 1928).

WELSH, ROBERT, 'D. W. Griffith Speaks', *New York Dramatic Mirror*, 71, no. 1830 (14 Jan. 1914), 49, 54.

WEST, EDWARD J., 'Histrionic Methods and Acting Traditions on the London Stage from 1870 to 1890', dissertation (Yale University, June 1940).

WILKES, THOMAS, *A General View of the Stage* (London: J. Coote, 1759).

WINN, PETER, 'Multiple Settings on the Early Nineteenth-Century London Stage', *Theatre Notebook*, 35 (1981), 17–24.

WINTER, O., 'The Cinematograph', *New Review* (May 1896); repr. *Sight and Sound*, 51, no. 4 (Autumn 1982), 294–6.

[WOODS, FRANK], ' "Spectator's" Comments', *New York Dramatic Mirror*, 62, no. 1612 (13 Nov. 1909), 15.

—— 'Reviews of Licensed Films, . . . All on Account of the Milk', *New York Dramatic Mirror*, 63, no. 1622 (22 Jan. 1910), 17.

—— 'Reviews of Licensed Films . . . Gold Is Not All', *New York Dramatic Mirror*, 63, no. 1633 (9 Apr. 1910), 17.

—— ' "Spectator's" Comments', *New York Dramatic Mirror*, 63, no. 1641 (4 June 1910), 16.

—— 'Reviews of Licensed Films . . . Uncle Tom's Cabin', *New York Dramatic Mirror*, 64, no. 1650 (6 Aug. 1910), 26.

—— 'Reviews of Licensed Films . . . The Merry Wives of Windsor (Selig, 1910)', *New York Dramatic Mirror*, 64, no. 5177 (30 Nov. 1910), 30.

—— ' "Spectator's" Comments', *New York Dramatic Mirror*, 67, no. 1736 (27 Mar. 1912), 24.

WOOLLCOTT, ALEXANDER, *Mrs. Fiske: Her Views on the Stage* (New York: The Century Company, 1917).

ZOLA, ÉMILE 'From *Naturalism in the Theatre*', trans. Albert Bermel, in Eric Bentley (ed.), *The Theory of the Modern Stage* (Harmondsworth: Penguin Books, 1968), 349–72.

Filmography

This filmography lists all the films mentioned in this book by their title in their country of origin, together with an indication of that country, the producing company that made them (p.c.), the year of release (with a parenthetic date of shooting if there was an exceptionally long gap between shooting and release), the length as originally advertised or as recorded by censors, and the name of the director (d.). For those films for which it seemed important to specify the print or prints we have seen, there is an indication of the source(s) and length(s) of the print(s). It should perhaps be pointed out that the source cited, usually an archive, was not always responsible for the preservation of the film in question, but acquired it from another archive which was. For silent films, lengths are given in metres or feet for 35 mm prints except where otherwise stated; lengths of sound films are given in minutes.

After Many Years, USA, p.c. American Mutoscope and Biograph Co., 1908, 1,033 feet, d. D. W. Griffith, print: Library of Congress, Washington, Paper Print Collection, 390 feet (16 mm).

Aladin ou la lampe merveilleuse, France, p.c. Pathé Frères, 1906, 250 metres, d. Albert Capellani, print: National Film and Television Archive, London, 788 feet.

Alias Jimmy Valentine, USA, p.c. World Film Corp., 1915, 5 reels, d. Maurice Tourneur, print: Library of Congress, Washington, 4,612 feet.

All on Account of the Milk, USA, p.c. Biograph Co., 1910, 999 feet, d. Frank Powell.

Die arme Jenny, Germany, p.c. Deutsche Bioscop, 1912, 858 metres, d. Urban Gad, print: George Eastman House, Rochester, NY, 2,025 feet.

L'Assassinat du duc de Guise, France, p.c. Le Film d'Art, 1908, 340 metres, d. Charles Le Bargy and André Calmettes, prints: National Film and Television Archive, London, 1,025 feet; Museum of Modern Art, New York, Circulating Library (16 mm).

Au bagne, France, p.c. Pathé Frères, 1905, 215 metres, d. Ferdinand Zecca, print: Museum of Modern Art, New York, 678 feet.

Au pays noir, France, p.c. Pathé Frères, 1905, 250 metres, d. Ferdinand Zecca, print: National Film and Television Archive, London, 789 feet.

The Avenging Conscience; Thou Shalt Not Kill, USA, p.c. Majestic Motion Picture Co., 1914, 7–8 reels, d. D. W. Griffith.

An Awful Moment, USA, p.c. American Mutoscope and Biograph Co., 1908, 737 feet, d. D. W. Griffith, print: Library of Congress, Washington, Paper Print Collection, 302 feet (16 mm).

Barbe bleue, France, p.c. Star Film, 1901, 210 metres, d. Georges Méliès, print: National Film and Television Archive, London, 651 feet.

Ben Hur, USA, p.c. Kalem Co., 1907, 1,000 feet, print: EmGee Film Library, Reseda, Calif., 362 feet (16 mm).

Ben-Hur, USA, p.c. Metro-Goldwyn-Mayer Pictures, 1925, 11,693 feet, d. Fred Niblo.

Bold Bank Robbery, USA, p.c. Siegmund Lubin, 1904, 600 feet, print: EmGee Film Library, Reseda, Calif., 218 feet (16 mm).

The Boy, the Bust, and the Bath, USA, p.c. Vitagraph Company of America, 1907, 425 feet, print: National Film and Television Archive, London, 407 feet.

Broken Blossoms, USA, p.c. D. W. Griffith, 1919, 6 reels, d. D. W. Griffith.

Cabiria, Italy, p.c. Itala Film, 1914, 4,000 metres, d. Giovanni Pastrone, prints: National Film and Television Archive, London, 8,345 feet; Museum of Modern Art, New York, Circulating Library, 3,132 feet (16 mm).

Cendrillon, France, p.c. Star Film, 1899, 120 metres, d. Georges Méliès, print: National Film and Television Archive, London, 356 feet.

Le Chat botté, France, p.c. Pathé Frères, 1903, 180 metres, d. Lucien Nonguet, print: National Film and Television Archive, London, 529 feet.

Circumstantial Evidence; or, The Innocent Victim, USA, p.c. Vitagraph Company of America, 1908, 460 feet, print: Library of Congress, Washington, Paper Print Collection, fragments.

The Coming of Angelo, USA, p.c. Biograph Co., 1913, 1,000 feet, d. D. W. Griffith, print: National Film and Television Archive, London, 967 feet.

A Corner in Wheat, USA, p.c. Biograph Co., 1909, 953 feet, d. D. W. Griffith, print: Library of Congress, Washington, Paper Print Collection, 396 feet (16 mm).

Coronets and Hearts, USA, p.c. Vitagraph Company of America, 1912, 1,000 feet, print: National Film and Television Archive, London, 898 feet.

The Country Doctor, USA, p.c. Biograph Co., 1909, 942 feet, d. D. W. Griffith, print: Museum of Modern Art, New York, 943 feet.

Cowboys and Indians Fording River in a Wagon, USA, p.c. Edison Manufacturing Co., 1904, d. A. C. Abadie, print: National Film and Television Archive, London, Library of Congress Paper Print, 30 feet (16 mm).

The Curtain Pole, USA, p.c. American Mutoscope and Biograph Co., 1909, 765 feet, d. D. W. Griffith, print: National Film and Television Archive, London, 713 feet.

Daisies, USA, p.c. Vitagraph Company of America, 1910, 995 feet, print: National Film and Television Archive, London, 722 feet.

Les Débuts d'un patineur, France, p.c. Pathé Frères, 1907, 125 metres, d. Louis Gasnier, print: National Film and Television Archive, London, 393 feet.

Deti Veka, Russia, p.c. A. Khanzhonkov and Co., 1915, 1,337 metres, d. Evgenii Bauer, print: Cinémathèque Royale, Brussels, 3,675 feet.

Dial M for Murder, USA, p.c. Warner Bros., 1954, 105 minutes, d. Alfred Hitchcock.

Dimples, USA, p.c. Twentieth Century-Fox, 1936, 78 minutes, d. William A. Seiter.

[*Dreyfus at Rennes*], France, p.c. Mutoscope and Biograph Co., 1899, print: Nederlands Filmmuseum, Amsterdam.

The Drive for a Life, USA, p.c. American Mutoscope and Biograph Co., 1909, 940 feet, d. D. W. Griffith, print: National Film and Television Archive, London, 887 feet.

A Drunkard's Reformation, USA, p.c. American Mutoscope and Biograph Co., 1909, 983 feet, d. D. W. Griffith, print: National Film and Television Archive, London, 501 feet.

En avant la musique!, France, p.c. Pathé Frères, 1907, 75 metres, d. Segundo de Chomón, print: National Film and Television Archive, London, 191 feet.

L'Enfant de Paris, France, p.c. Gaumont Co., 1913, 2,346 metres, d. Léonce Perret, print: Gaumont Archive, Paris, 7,450 feet.

Engelein, Germany, p.c. PAGU, 1913, 1,617 metres, d. Urban Gad, print: Cinémathèque Royale, Brussels, 3,427 feet.

Enoch Arden, USA, p.c. Biograph Co., 1911, part 1: 1 reel, part 2: 1 reel, d. D. W. Griffith, print: Museum of Modern Art, New York, Circulating Library, 777 feet (16 mm).

Fate, USA, p.c. Biograph Company, 1913, 1,038 feet, d. D. W. Griffith, print: National Film and Television Archive, London, 1,012 feet.

Father's Quiet Sunday, USA, p.c. Vitagraph Company of America, 1907, 625 feet, print: Library of Congress, Washington, Paper Prints Collection, fragments.

La Fin d'une royauté, France, p.c. Le Film d'Art, 1910, d. André Calmettes, print: Cinémathèque Royale, Brussels, 818 feet.

A Fool There Was, USA, p.c. William Fox Vaudeville Co., 1915,

6 reels, d. Frank Powell, print: Museum of Modern Art, New York, Circulating Library (16 mm).

Foul Play, USA, p.c. Vitagraph Company of America, 1907, 875 feet, print: George Eastman House, Rochester, NY, 802 feet.

A Girl's Stratagem, USA, p.c. Biograph Co., 1913, 998 feet, d. D. W. Griffith(?).

Gold Is Not All, USA, p.c. Biograph Co., 1910, 988 feet, d. D. W. Griffith, print: National Film and Television Archive, London, 971 feet.

Grandma's Reading Glass, UK, p.c. GAS Films, 1900, 100 feet, print: National Film and Television Archive, London, 88 feet.

The Great Train Robbery, USA, p.c. Edison Manufacturing Co., 1903, 740 feet, d. Edwin S. Porter, print: National Film and Television Archive, London, 668 feet.

Hamlet, UK, p.c. Hepworth Manufacturing Co., 1913, 5,800 feet, d. E. Hay Plumb, print: National Film and Television Archive, London, 4,846 feet.

The Hand of Peril, USA, p.c. Paragon Films, 1916, 5 reels, d. Maurice Tourneur.

Havsgamar, Sweden, p.c. Svenska Biografteatern, 1916, 982 metres, d. Victor Sjöström, print: National Film and Television Archive, London, 2,787 feet.

Hell Bent, USA, p.c. Universal Film Manufacturing Co., 1918, 5,540 feet, d. Jack Ford, print: Narodny Filmowy Archiv, Prague.

Det hemmelighedsfulde X, Denmark, p.c. Dansk Biografkompagni, 1914, 1,977 metres, d. Benjamin Christensen, prints: Cinémathèque Royale, Brussels, 5,028 feet; Museum of Modern Art, New York, 1,925 feet (16 mm).

The Hero of Little Italy, USA, p.c. Biograph Co., 1913, 1 reel, d. D. W. Griffith(?).

Himmelsskibet, Denmark, p.c. Nordisk Films Kompagni, 1918, 1,993 metres, d. Holger-Madsen, print: Cinémathèque Royale, Brussels, 5,306 feet.

His Lost Love, USA, p.c. Biograph Co., 1909, 968 feet, d. D. W. Griffith, print: Library of Congress, Washington, Paper Print Collection, 380 feet (16 mm).

Le Homard, France, p.c. Gaumont Co., 1912, 310 metres, d. Léonce Perret, print: Gaumont Archive, Paris, 1,083 feet.

L'Homme à la tête en caoutchouc, France, p.c. Star Film, 1902, 50 metres, d. Georges Méliès, print: National Film and Television Archive, London, 125 feet.

Ingeborg Holm, Sweden, p.c. Svenska Biografteatern, 1913, 1,975 metres, d. Victor Sjöström, print: Svenska Filminstitutet, Stockholm, 4,347 feet.

Ingmarssönerna, Sweden, p.c. Svenska Biografteatern, 1919, 4,203 metres, d. Victor Sjöström, print: Cinémathèque Royale, Brussels, 8,555 feet.

The Inherited Taint, USA, p.c. Vitagraph Company of America, 1911, 998 feet, print: National Film and Television

Archive, London, 905 feet.

Intolerance, USA, p.c. Wark Producing Corp., 1916, 13–14 reels, d. D. W. Griffith, print: Museum of Modern Art, New York.

Jack and the Beanstalk, USA, p.c. Edison Manufacturing Co., 1902, 625 feet, d. Edwin S. Porter, print: National Film and Television Archive, London, Library of Congress Paper Print, 245 feet (16 mm).

Judex, France, p.c. Gaumont Co., 1917, serial in 12 episodes with a prologue and epilogue, 8,168 metres, d. Louis Feuillade, print: Gaumont Archive, Paris, 24,226 feet.

Kärleken segrar, Sweden, p.c. Hasselbladfilm, 1916, 1,278 metres, d. Georg af Klercker, print: Svenska Filminstitutet, Stockholm, 4,153 feet.

The Kindling, USA, p.c. Jesse J. Lasky Feature Play Co., 1915, 4–5 reels, d. Cecil B. DeMille, print: George Eastman House, Rochester, NY, 4,484 feet.

The King and I, USA, p.c. Twentieth Century-Fox, 1956, 133 minutes, d. Walter Lang.

The Kleptomaniac, USA, p.c. Thomas A. Edison, 1905, 670 feet, d. Edwin S. Porter, print: National Film and Television Archive, London, Library of Congress Paper Print, 302 feet (16 mm).

Klovnen, Denmark, p.c. Nordisk Films Kompagni, 1917, 1,375 metres, d. Anders Wilhelm Sandberg, print: Cinémathèque Royale, Brussels, 4,583 feet.

Korol' Parizha, Russia, p.c. A. Khanzhonkov and Co., 1917, 5 reels, d. Evgenii Bauer, print: Cinémathèque Royale, Brussels.

The Lady and the Mouse, USA, p.c. Biograph Co., 1913, 999 feet, d. D. W. Griffith, print: Museum of Modern Art, New York, Circulating Library, 384 feet (16 mm).

Die Landstrasse, Germany, p.c. Deutsche Mutoscop und Biograph, 1913, 1,008 metres, d. Paul von Woringen, print: Bundesarchiv, Koblenz.

La Légende de Polichinelle, France, p.c. Pathé Frères, 1907, 410 metres, d. Albert Capellani, print: National Film and Television Archive, London, 1,102 feet.

Life of an American Fireman, USA, p.c. Thomas A. Edison, 1903, 425 feet, d. Edwin S. Porter, print: National Film and Television Archive, London, Library of Congress Paper Print, 165 feet (16 mm).

The Little Doctor and the Sick Kitten, UK, p.c. GAS Films, 1901, 100 feet, d. George Albert Smith, print: National Film and Television Archive, London, 54 feet.

The Lonedale Operator, USA, p.c. Biograph Company, 1911, 998 feet, d. D. W. Griffith, print: National Film and Television Archive, London, 962 feet.

A Lonely Villa, USA, p.c. Biograph Co., 1909, 750 feet, d. D. W. Griffith, print: Museum of Modern Art, New York.

Love Potion No. 9, USA, p.c. Anarchy Productions, 1992, 104 minutes, d. Dale Launer.

Ma l'amor mio non muore!, Italy, p.c. Film Artistica 'Gloria', 1913, 2,600 metres, d. Mario Caserini, prints: Museum of Modern Art, New York, Circulating Library, 1,856 feet (16 mm); Cineteca Italiana, Milan, 4,757 feet.

Das Mädchen ohne Vaterland, Germany, p.c. Deutsche Bioscop, 1912, 1,010 metres, d. Urban Gad, print: George Eastman House, Rochester, NY, 2,094 feet.

Le Manoir de la peur, France, p.c. Films Alfred Machin, 1927 (shot in 1924), 1,615 metres, d. Alfred Machin, print: Cinémathèque Royale, Brussels.

The Merry Wives of Windsor, USA, p.c. Selig Polyscope Co., 1910, 1,000 feet.

Les Misérables, France, p.c. SCAGL, 1913, 3,480 metres, d. Albert Capellani, print: Cinémathèque Française, Paris, 9,585 feet.

The Mothering Heart, USA, p.c. Biograph Co., 1913, 1,525 feet, d. D. W. Griffith, print: Museum of Modern Art, New York, Circulating Library (16 mm).

Mysteriet Natten till den 25:e, Sweden, p.c. Hasselbladfilm, 1917, 971 metres, d. Georg af Klercker, print: Svenska Filminstitutet, Stockholm, 3,093 feet.

Nemye Svideteli, Russia, p.c. A. Khanzhonkov & Co., 1,245 metres, 1914, d. Evgenii Bauer, print: Cinémathèque Royale, Brussels, 3,806 feet.

Notre Dame de Paris, France, p.c. SAPF, 1911, 810 metres, d. Albert Capellani, print: National Film and Television Archive, London, 2,087 feet.

An Official Appointment, USA, p.c. Vitagraph Company of America, 1912, 1,000 feet, d. Charles Kent, print: Library of Congress, Washington, 766 feet (as *His Official Appointment*).

The Painted Lady, USA, p.c. Biograph Co., 1912, 1 reel, d. D. W. Griffith, print: Museum of Modern Art, New York, Circulating Library (16 mm).

Le Petit Poucet, France, p.c. Pathé Frères, 1909, 310 metres, d. Segundo de Chomón, print: National Film and Television Archive, London, 719 feet.

Polikushka, USSR, p.c. Rus', 1922 (shot in 1919), 1,366 metres, d. Aleksandr Sanin.

The Politician, USA, p.c. Edison Manufacturing Co. (Edison Kinetophone), 1913, print: Library of Congress, Washington, 377 feet.

Quatre-vingt-treize, p.c. SCAGL, 1921, d. Albert Capellani (in 1914, completed by André Antoine after the war), print: Cinémathèque Française, Paris, 11,475 feet.

Quo Vadis?, Italy, p.c. Cinès, 1913, 2,250 metres, d. Enrico Guazzoni, prints: National Film and Television Archive, London, 5,613 feet; Museum of Modern Art, New York, Circulating Library, 2,961 feet (16 mm).

Red and White Roses, USA, p.c. Vitagraph Company of America, 1913, 2,000 feet, print: Library of Congress, Washington, 1,974 feet.

Rescued by Rover, UK, p.c. Hepworth Film Manufacturing Co., 1905, 425 feet, d. Lewin Fitzhamon, print: National Film and Television Archive, London, 413 feet.

Rescued from an Eagle's Nest, USA, p.c. Edison Manufacturing Co., 1908, 515 feet, d. J. Searle Dawley, print: National Film and Television Archive, London, 497 feet.

Le Roman d'un mousse, France, p.c. Gaumont Co., 1914, *c*.2,000 metres, d. Léonce Perret, print: National Film and Television Archive, London, 6,246 feet.

The Sealed Room, USA, p.c. Biograph Co., 1909, 779 feet, d. D. W. Griffith.

Shylock, France, p.c. Eclipse, 1913, d. Henri Desfontaines, print: National Film and Television Archive, London, 1,979 feet.

The Social Secretary, USA, p.c. Fine Arts Film Co., 1916, 5 reels, d. John Emerson, print: Emgee Film Library, Reseda, Calif., 1,540 feet (16 mm).

A Summer Idyl, USA, p.c. Biograph Co., 1910, 991 feet, d. D. W. Griffith.

Die Sumpfblume, Germany, p.c. Treumann-Larsen-Film GmbH, 1913, 4 reels, d. Viggø Larsen, print: Stiftung Deutsche Kinemathek, Berlin, 3,601 feet.

Swing Time, USA, p.c. RKO Radio Pictures, 1936, 103 minutes, d. George Stevens.

La Terre, France, p.c. SCAGL, 1921, 2,300 metres, d. André Antoine, print: Cinémathèque Française, 6,933 feet.

Thou Shalt Not, USA, p.c. Biograph Co., 1910, 987 feet, d. D. W. Griffith.

Three Sisters, USA, p.c. Biograph Company, 1911, 997 feet, d. D. W. Griffith, print: National Film and Television Archive, London, 943 feet.

Topsy and Eva, USA, p.c. Feature Productions, 1927, 7,456 feet, d. Del Lord.

La Tosca, France, p.c. Le Film d'Art, 1909, 380 metres, d. Charles Le Bargy, print: National Film and Television Archive, London, 1,143 feet.

Uncle Josh at the Moving Picture Show, USA, p.c. Thomas A. Edison, 1902, 125 feet, d. Edwin S. Porter, print: National Film and Television Archive, London, Library of Congress Paper Print, 48 feet (16 mm).

Uncle Tom without the Cabin, USA, p.c. Paramount, 1919, 2 reels.

Uncle Tom's Cabin, USA, p.c. Lubin Film Manufacturing Co., 1903, 1 reel, print: Library of Congress, Washington, Paper Print Collection.

Uncle Tom's Cabin, USA, p.c. Thanhouser, 1910, 1,000 feet.

Uncle Tom's Cabin, USA, p.c. Vitagraph Company of America, 1910, 3 reels, prints: National Film and Television Archive, London, 2,107 feet; Emgee Film Library, Reseda, Calif., 1,143 feet (16 mm).

Uncle Tom's Cabin, USA, p.c. Imp, 1913, 3 reels, d. Otis Turner.

Uncle Tom's Cabin, USA, p.c. Kalem, 1913, 2 reels, d. Sidney Olcott.

Uncle Tom's Cabin, USA, p.c. World Producing Corp., 1914, 5 reels, d. William Robert Daly, prints: Cinémathèque Française, Paris, 1,516 feet (16 mm); Library of Congress, Washington, (i) 3,795 feet, (ii) 3,385 feet; National Film and Television Archive, London, 2,820 feet.

Uncle Tom's Cabin, USA, p.c. Famous Players-Lasky Corp., 1918, 5 reels, d. J. Searle Dawley, print: National Film and Television Archive, London, 406 feet (fragment).

Uncle Tom's Cabin, USA, p.c. Universal Pictures, 1927, 13,000 feet, d. Harry Pollard.

Uncle Tom's Cabin; or, Slavery Days, USA, p.c. Thomas A. Edison, 1903, 1,100 feet, d. Edwin S. Porter, print: National Film and Television Archive, London, 1,055 feet.

An 'Uncle Tom's Cabin' Troupe, USA, p.c. Biograph Co., 1913, 679 feet, d. Dell Henderson.

Uncle Tom's Caboose, USA, p.c. Century, 1920, 2 reels, d. Jim Davis.

Ved fængslets Port, Denmark, p.c. Nordisk Films Kompagni, 1911, 820 metres, d. August Blom.

La Vie et la Passion de Jésus-Christ, France, p.c. Pathé Frères, 1902, 580 metres, print: National Film and Television Archive, London (as *Vita e passione di Cristo*), 661 feet.

La Vie et Passion de N.S. Jésus-Christ, France, p.c. Pathé Frères, 1907, 950 metres, d. Ferdinand Zecca, print: National Film and Television Archive, London (as *The Life of Jesus Christ*), 2,354 feet.

The Voice of the Child, USA, p.c. Biograph Company, 1912, 998 feet, d. D. W. Griffith, print: National Film and Television Archive, London, 836 feet.

The Voice of the Violin, USA, p.c. American Mutoscope and Biograph Co., 1909, 978 feet, d. D. W. Griffith.

The Warrens of Virginia, USA, p.c. Jesse J. Lasky Feature Play Co., 1915, 5 reels, d. Cecil B. DeMille, print: George Eastman House, Rochester, NY.

Die weisse Rosen, Germany, p.c. PAGU, 1917 (made in 1915), d. Urban Gad, prints: George Eastman House, Rochester, NY; Cinémathèque Royale, Brussels, 3,085 feet.

The Whip, USA, p.c. Paragon Films, 1917, 8 reels, d. Maurice Tourneur, print: Library of Congress, Washington, 4,356 feet.

Wig Wag, USA, p.c. Vitagraph Company of America, 1911, 1,000 feet, d. Larry Trimble, print: National Film and Television Archive, London, 591 feet.

Index